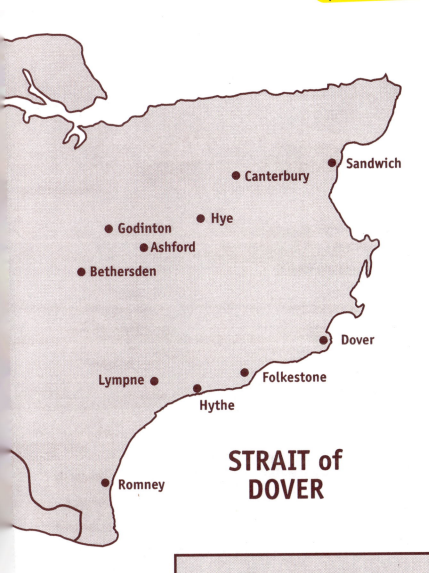

Sandwich

● Canterbury

● Hye

● Godinton
● Ashford

● Bethersden

Dover

Lympne ●
Folkestone

Hythe

Romney

STRAIT of DOVER

South-Eastern England
The Winder Ancestral
Homeland

Ferral Cay Swink

8491 So. 1430 E,   COMPLETED
SANDY, UTAH   READING 10-26-05
      84093 -

801-566-5848

John R. Winder

• Member of the First Presidency •
• Pioneer • Temple Builder • Dairyman •

John Rex Winder
1821-1910

John R. Winder

• Member of the First Presidency •
• Pioneer • Temple Builder • Dairyman •

Michael Kent Winder

First Printing: November 1999

International Standard Book Number:
0-88290-676-3

Horizon Publishers' Catalog and Order Number:
1259

Printed and distributed
in the United States of America by

Horizon
Publishers
& Distributors, Incorporated
50 South 500 West
P.O. Box 490
Bountiful, Utah 84011-0490

Store and library orders should be placed with Horizon Publishers.
Individual books can be ordered from the author:
4400 West 4100 South
West Valley City, Utah 84120
(801) 955-0603

Back cover photo: LDS First Presidency, 1902
John R. Winder, Joseph F. Smith, Anthon H. Lund
(Photograph by H. H. Thomas.
Courtesy of Wheeler Historic Farm.)

Contents

To my dear wife Karyn,
For her patience and support;
And to my children—
May their heritage provide them strength.

Acknowledgments

The idea to write a biography on John R. Winder arose when I first realized as a young boy that there wasn't one. I thought a lot about doing it while serving as a missionary, and finally saw a chance to fulfill the dream while an undergraduate in history at the University of Utah. This project began as my honors thesis, and the first four chapters were submitted under the title: "The Early Years of John R. Winder: A Case Study in Mormon British Immigrants' Native Heritage." Dr. Dean L. May, one of Utah's foremost historians, served as my advisor. I am grateful to him for his assistance early on in finding enlightening sources and for his guidance and encouragement throughout the project.

Many good people assisted me in conducting my research, and I would like to thank Stan Larson at the U's Marriott Library's Special Collections Department, as well as Ron Watt and Bill Slaughter at the LDS Church Historical Department. The staff of the LDS Family History Library, the Utah State Archives, the Utah Historical Society, and the Lee Library's Special Collections Department at Brigham Young University all were very helpful.

The members of the Winder Family Organization provided important encouragement and advice, as well. Gloria, Harlan, and Adrian Bangerter helped read various chapters, as did Jeanne Jensen and Joyce Parsons. Phillip Winder was another great supporter, and provided many of the photographs used. Doug and Jim Colby at Forms Plus gave valuable assistance by helping prepare the maps used in the inside covers of the book.

Geoff and Brenda Copus of Royal Tunbridge Wells, England deserve a special acknowledgment, for they graciously hosted me for a week in their lovely Victorian home. During that time they took me all throughout Kent, to Biddenden, Tenterden, Rolvenden, Canterbury, and the archives at Maidstone. This in-depth look into my ancestral heartland produced invaluable insights and increased my resolve to do this project.

I am greatly indebted to my Grandpa and Grandma Winder for their examples and support. Grandpa was gracious enough to pen the Foreword, and Grandma helped me tremendously with genealogy work, especially in preparing for this publication. A special tribute is owed to my parents, Kent and Sherri Winder, for a solid upbringing and teaching me to cherish my heritage and seek after my dreams.

My greatest love and appreciation goes out to my supportive wife, Karyn. I was greatly assisted by her readings of the manuscript, assistance with the index, her ideas and suggestions, and for her encouragement throughout. Allowing me to work many nights and weekends on this book is a testament to me of her undying love and support.

I also wish to thank the people at Horizon Publishers for helping me turn a rough manuscript into a beautiful hard-bound book. Duane Crowther, Horizon Publishers' President and Senior Editor, edited the book and supervised its production. Sam Richardson and Karyl Dowling worked to design and typeset it, and Val Schultz led the bindery crew.

I take responsibility for any errors in this work. Anything good which is within these pages I attribute to God, whose inspiration was felt often. Much encouragement and guidance on this project by parties on both sides of the veil has made this work one of the most rewarding experiences of my life.

Foreword

It is an honor for me to write a foreword in this history of John Rex Winder, who is my great-grandfather. It is amazing to me that no one has ever published a book on this great man. It is true that histories have been written on all presidents of the Church, their counselors, members of the Twelve, and the other General Authorities, but none on President John R. Winder.

I never knew this good man, as he died twelve years before I was born. However, I recall his name from my earliest memories. I especially grew up hearing about him from my father, grandfather, and other older members of his family. His virtues of resourcefulness, thrift, spirituality and a keen intellect were frequently mentioned. I also remember my dad recalling that he had a certain sternness about him that caused some "fear and trembling" in them being in his presence. That, he admitted, came more out of respect for his high Church callings and the prominence he had in many businesses and in the community.

I also recall my teen years, and when I was on my mission, of the many people who would upon learning my last name ask of my relationship to President John R. Winder. I would with "righteous pride" tell them he was my great-grandfather. Most often they would say that he sealed their parents or grandparents in the Salt Lake Temple. It was evident to me that he sealed many hundreds of people in the temple. Even today as a sealer myself in that same temple, I will hear people say that he sealed their grandparents, or even their great-grandparents. All of these things have given me a great appreciation of John R. Winder and has motivated me to honor the wonderful heritage I have been given.

I am pleased to see that it is my next-door neighbor and grandson, Michael Kent Winder, who has written this history. His parents are Kent Layton Winder and Sherri Jepson Winder. Kent is the executive vice president of Winder Dairy, and Mike is the marketing director there. They represent the fifth and sixth generation of this 120-year-old family business.

From a very early age, like 5 or 6, Mike has been extremely interested in his family's history. Even as a pre-teen he had a remarkable knowledge of his Winder ancestry. He became a valuable committee member of our very active Winder Family Organization and became especially interested in John R. Winder.

Mike is a very bright, friendly and resourceful young man. He was student-body president at Taylorsville High School, and in 1994 was selected as the outstanding student in social science for the Deseret News Sterling Scholar program for the state. He served in the LDS Taiwan, Taipei Mission and was an outstanding leader during that two-year service. He graduated with an Honors Bachelors Degree from the University of Utah in history, and in May 2000 will have completed his Masters degree at that same school.

One of the smartest things he ever did was to marry Karyn Hermansen, a pretty and talented returned missionary. They have one child, so far!

It has been Mike's goal for many years to write the biography of John R. Winder. He has not just dreamed of this goal, but in those same years has worked tirelessly in studying, interviewing, researching, and compiling everything he could to make this book interesting and accurate. The family praises his great labor and integrity.

—Edwin Cannon "Ned" Winder

Introduction

The story of John Rex Winder has been largely forgotten by the people and region he fought so hard to build up. Men of his nature do not have statues gracing the halls of public buildings, or even take up much space in the history books, when mentioned at all. Winder was a quiet, humble, unassuming man who did most of his work behind the scenes. Yet, his story is worth telling because of the many hats he wore in his long life and the ability with which he was able to perform every task assigned to him. His influence is noteworthy because of the men he counseled, the events he witnessed, and the testimony that he bore. Nonetheless, John R. Winder has heretofore been an historic anomaly in the annals of Church and Utah history. Despite his lack of publicity, however, this builder of the kingdom has a saga as interesting as other more famous LDS General Authorities.

John R. Winder is perhaps best known for having served as First Counselor to Joseph F. Smith from 1901 to 1910. He is a rarity in Church history as one of the very few to be called to the First Presidency without having ever been an apostle, he having previously served in the Presiding Bishopric (1886-1901). He oversaw the completion of the Salt Lake Temple, was a principle editor of the Manifesto on polygamy, and helped formulate such doctrinal expositions as *The Origin of Man* (1909). He contributed his financial acumen as a general authority, acting as the receiver of all Church property during the intense anti-polygamy persecutions, and helping to steer the Church out of debt.

The life story of John R. Winder is also an instructive lesson in Utah history. Revealing glimpses into the daily activities and relationships of a polygamous family in nineteenth century Utah are displayed, as are details of the early leather tannery industry in the state. Winder was an officer in the territorial militia, the Nauvoo Legion, and figured prominently in the Utah War and the Black Hawk Indian War. He also was a key figure in the development of political parties in Utah, the city government of Salt Lake City, and he was the "Father of the Utah State Fair." In the business community he was an influential industrialist, perhaps remembered as the founder of Winder Dairy, who six generations and 120 years later is still Utah's milkman, delivering their famous dairy products to 20,000 households. John R. Winder, through four wives and twenty children, is also the patriarch of an enormous posterity numbering in the thousands.

Perhaps one reason why the story of his noteworthy life has never before been published is because, unlike many of the pioneer General Authorities, Winder never kept a diary. If he did keep a journal, it has yet to be found. The closest work he produced of an autobiographical nature was a four-page life sketch that was published as a Christmas greeting to the members of the Church in their magazine, *The Improvement Era*. Consequently, the following work is not a simple rewriting of a good pioneer diary; rather, it is a complex mosaic of details gathered together to reveal a great life. This biography has been a laborious jig-saw puzzle, comprised of a newspaper clipping here and a contemporary's quotation there. A smattering of remembrances by grandchildren produced some more pieces, as did some excerpts from President Winder's own conference addresses. All in all, the pieces come together, and a clearer portrait of President Winder shines through. The forgotten General Authority rises from the mists of the past, standing as a faithful servant to the God he worshiped. His human frailties are also made manifest, but the virtues of this spiritual giant easily surpass them.

John R. Winder lived to the remarkable age of eighty-eight, passing away on March 27, 1910. Consequently, his long life is an epic that saw an ever-changing world through the eyes of one with never-changing faith. He lived a life that spanned the entire Victorian Age. As a boy he had been able to glimpse the sun setting on an old English gentry society, as a young man he encountered the heart of the Industrial Revolution, as an immigrant he arrived to the world of the Wild West, later he was a "Captain of Industry" in America's Gilded Age, and at the turn-of-the-century he was an LDS General Authority. He saw many different worlds in his long life and achieved tremendous success through his faith in God. Indeed, there is much to be learned by exploring the world of John Rex Winder.

1
Roots: The Rise of the Winder Family in England, 1066-1820

"Continued from generation to generation . . ."

The roots of one's character reach from deep in his ancestral past, and a thorough biography requires some understanding of his genealogical "stock." John Rex Winder broke away from the small geographic realm that had contained his family for perhaps a millennium or more, but he nonetheless retained a strong sense of identity and the values that had been a part of his clan for centuries in England and which he would pass on to his American posterity. In 1858 an LDS patriarch remarked about this legacy in a blessing given to him. In the blessing the patriarch noted the "birthright" and "blessings" of Winder's heritage and prayed that "the promises of the Fathers" which have "continued from generation to generation" in Winder's lineage "be extended upon [his] Posterity."[1] A look into the origin of this family, then, is in order.

The Origin of the Family Name

The surname Winder has often been held to be occupational in origin, being an appellation for "a winder of wool,"[2] for instance, or "one who winds (things like yarn or thread)."[3] Although "it is possible that this may be the origin in some areas," writes an English expert on surname derivation, "no conclusive evidence has been produced for this."[4] Winder is the name of several places in northern England, a local word meaning 'wind shelter,'[5] and in some instances, the surname may be derived from such locales. This is often the case in Lancashire, Westmorland, Cumberland, and Cumbria, home to picturesque Lake Windermere (literally "Lake of the Winder's"). These northern Winders at one point established a coat of arms, which seems to have originated in Cumberland. This shield, with a bull's head on top holding a rose in its mouth, can be found in most exhaustive dictionaries of British heraldry.

These northern Winders had some of their clan emigrate to Maryland in the seventeenth century, from which sprang several American branches of the Winder family, including Maryland's eighteenth governor Levin Winder, and a prominent Civil War officer for the Confederacy, General John H. Winder.[6]

Several black families in the South also acquired the surname Winder at that time, presumably adopting it from their white masters, as was often the custom. Descendants of these Winders live in the United States today, and include former professional football player Sammy Winder, who played for the Denver Broncos.

However, available evidence suggests that the Winder clan of northern England arose distinctly separate from other Winder families south of London. One difference between the two lies in the pronunciation of the name. Traditionally, "in the north of England it is pronounced as in 'win.' In the south it is 'wine.'"[7] It is the Winders of southeastern England that John Rex Winder and his descendants hail from, even though they pronounced the name like "win" once they were situated in the United States. Consequently, this chapter will solely treat the origin of the Winder family of southeastern England.

The family name first appears in an early form in the county of Sussex during the 1200's, near Hastings. Just two short centuries prior, in that very locale, William, Duke of Normandy, made his infamous invasion of Britain, defeating King Harold and his Anglo-Saxon forces in the most famous English battle of all times, the Battle of Hastings. The early Winders appeared to possess some sort of prominence and authority in their villages, suggesting that they may have been descendants of those who came over with the Conqueror. The Domesday Book of 1086 reveals that there was indeed a definite shift when the Normans arrived as the conquerors appropriated the property of the Anglo-Saxons.[8]

However, the Hastings area of Sussex had been occupied for centuries prior by the pastoral Saxons, and if the Winder ancestors were not accompanying the Duke of Normandy, their roots would lie there. Nevertheless, be they among the victors or the vanquished, the Battle of Hastings certainly had an effect on those early Winder progenitors who lived so close to the epicenter of this event that rocked England forever. In an understatement by one scholar regarding Hastings, "the change was dramatic."[9]

Here in this historic county of Sussex the family name Winder developed from "atte Wynde." A unique Sussexian system of surnaming, it was quite common during the 1200's in the county to have "atte" as a prefix to a last name, which would be dropped centuries later as "er" was added as a suffix. For instance, atte Welle would evolve into Weller, atte Wode into Atwood, atte Whitch into Whitcher, atte Boure into Bourer, and so on. The name atte Wynde (probably meaning 'at the winding path or street') occurs in East Sussex from the late thirteenth century on.[10] It would have been derived from the Old English word wende, meaning "bend."[11]

The early examples of atte Wynde all occur in Wilting in Crowhurst (a small locality near Hastings) or its neighborhood, and it seems very probable that all the persons involved belonged to one family.[12] During the fifteenth century the name appears at places not far from Wilting, such as the villages of Rye and Udimore. However, by this late date the "atte" prefix was fading out of usage in Sussex, as most of the families had "modernized," along with many of their neighbors, by changing over to the "er" suffix.[13]

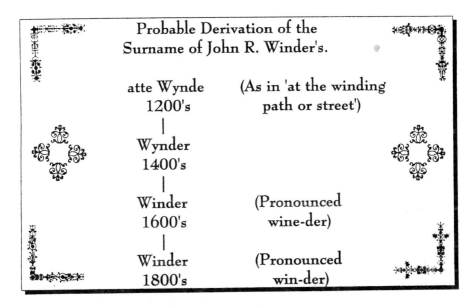

Probable Derivation of the
Surname of John R. Winder's.

atte Wynde   (As in 'at the winding
1200's   path or street')

Wynder
1400's

Winder   (Pronounced
1600's   wine-der)

Winder   (Pronounced
1800's   win-der)

Wynder, as a family name, first appears in Sussex during the fourteenth century, at Whatlington and Winchelsea, both not far from Wilting. In Whatlington in the Middle Ages there was a Winder's Wood that has been assumed to be associated with the family of a John Wyndere, who was living in 1340.[14] During the late fourteenth century and into the fifteenth, the surname appears at Hastings, and at other places in the same part of Sussex, but it has not been found elsewhere in the county. One example mentions a Thomas Wynder of Hastings, who had at least one servant, indicating some status possessed by these early Wynders.[15] Another example in nearby Peasmarsh mentions a William Wyndere who was alive in 1417 and thought to be associated with the parish's Winder Farm.[16]

Wynder Leadership Among the Cinque Ports

Several generations of Wynders were heavily involved in community affairs, a family obligation that would become characteristic of many of John Rex Winder's ancestors, John R. himself, and even much of his American posterity down to the present day. Periodically, mayors, jurat, and members of the gentry from the Cinque Ports (Hastings and the four neighboring coastal towns of Romney, Hythe, Dover and Sandwich) met together as a guild of sorts to resolve common municipal concerns. These meetings were held at Romney, and over time became known as the General Brotherhood or Brodhull. The function of the

Brotherhood as a legislative body was an innovative experiment in local government for the Middle Ages, indeed a "confederation which was without parallel amongst English constitutional institutions."[17] It also helped to provide the five towns with a common front in Parliament, and in the early days of the confederation "they provided the King's Navy, in so far as one could be said then to exist."[18] Individual port towns were autonomous, and at no time did they specifically hand over powers to any other body, yet these assemblies of the Cinque Ports "ordered many local affairs in a most autocratic fashion, both expecting and receiving obedience."[19]

As fishermen, the portsmen were concerned with the movement of the herring and securing fishing rights, even as far as the Norfolk coast and Yarmouth on the North Sea. During the time of the great Herring Fair each fall, the ports sent their bailiff to Yarmouth to administer justice, in cooperation with the bailiffs of Yarmouth. Usually "the government of the town was carried out by the bailiff, assisted by twelve jurat." He was also the Coroner and had to serve writs, make arrests, and "was responsible for the maintenance of law and order in the town."[20] The election of these bailiffs and hearing their reports formed a great part of the Brotherhood's routine business. It is therefore not surprising to learn that those elected to be bailiffs "were men of no mean stature."[21]

Under the politics of General Brodhull several Wynders rose to prominent positions in the local government. On 27 July 1439 at the General Brodhull in Romney, a Thomas Wynder of Hastings was elected to the important post of bailiff, and would go to Yarmouth. Two years later in 1441, the Brotherhood chose William Wynder to serve as their ambassador to Yarmouth with the title of bailiff. Thirty-six years later in 1477 a William Wynder, possibly the former bailiff but certainly a relative, was chosen as one of the four deputies in Hastings. Again in 1479, William Wynder was selected for this post.

It was often a dangerous job to represent the Cinque Ports at Yarmouth, "a privilege which the men of Yarmouth came to resent more and more as a derogation from their own natural rights." On one occasion at least, a Cinque Ports bailiff was killed by a rival Yarmouth bailiff.[22] Nonetheless, these early Wynders must have had a deep sense of duty and loyalty to their sovereign to continue serving, values that they certainly would have wanted to instill in their posterity. Upon being elected bailiff, these Wynders would have taken the bailiff's oath:

> I will bear faith to our sovereign the King of England and the commonalty and the franchise and the usages of the same rightfully will maintain and the common profit will keep, and to rich and poor will do right so far as I can, so help me God and the Saints.[23]

At the General Brodhull on 7 April 1467, a Richard Wynde was chosen to serve as one of three deputies to Mayor Babylon Gramforde of Rye. Richard

Wynde repeatedly served as one of the town of Rye's deputies for several decades, his last election being in 1483.[24]

A mention of a John Wynder is noted in Robertsbridge, ten miles north of Hastings, as one of the fifteen jurors in the March 1472 murder trial of a William Woller.[25] One had to be of some prominence in the community to sit on a jury in fifteenth-century England, hence this reveals something of the social standing of the family in the late 1400's.

The honorable witness of a Wynder was again required in July of 1527. This time the mayor of Rye was taking evidence from a Thomas Wynder and two others regarding "evyll and obprobryus" words spoken by Richard Ingram against the Brotherhood.[26]

By the late fifteenth century, several of the family in the county began using the current spelling of the last name: Winder. The earliest mention of such a spelling is with a Richard and Agnes Winder who were noted in the town of Lewes in 1493.[27] This spelling would often serve interchangeably with Wynder, and different generations would prefer one way or another alternately until the dawn of the seventeenth century when the modern spelling settled as the standard, at least for the branch of the family with which we are concerned.

The Wynders of Burwash, Sussex

In light of the fact that the surname Wynder was confined to a limited district of Sussex County, it seems probable that this name belonged to a single family. And although the names mentioned thus far have yet to be connected genealogically, based on geography and frequently reoccurring given names, it is evident that the atte Wyndes and Wynders mentioned hitherto are of the same family as the line of Wynders and Winders that hail from a Richard Wynder, who was born around the beginning of King Henry VIII's reign in Burwash, Sussex.[28]

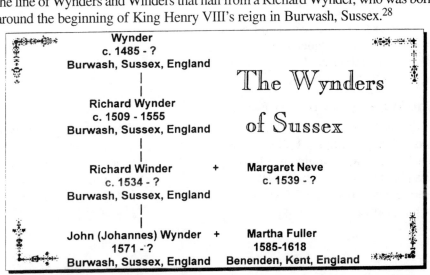

Wynder		
c. 1485 - ?		
Burwash, Sussex, England		**The Wynders**
Richard Wynder		
c. 1509 - 1555		**of Sussex**
Burwash, Sussex, England		
Richard Winder	+	Margaret Neve
c. 1534 - ?		c. 1539 - ?
Burwash, Sussex, England		
John (Johannes) Wynder	+	Martha Fuller
1571 - ?		1585-1618
Burwash, Sussex, England		Benenden, Kent, England

Not much is known about Richard Wynder except that he is the eldest son of a man surnamed Wynder who was born about 1485 in Burwash, a small town located half way between Royal Tunbridge Wells and Hastings. Burwash was named for a former warden of the Cinque Ports, Baron Bartholomew Burgwash[29] and is a village "well situated on the high wooded ground" between two rivers, "the Rother and its affluent the Dudwell."[30] The village Burwash is in a picturesque area, "where the Kentish oast-houses are beginning to creep into the Sussex scene."[31] Richard is thought to have been born there about 1509 and married about 1533. He died in July of 1555 in Burwash.

His oldest son, also named Richard, preferred the Winder spelling, was born about 1534 in Burwash, and had a first marriage with a lady named Johanna, and later a second marriage with a Margaret Neve. That ceremony took place on 27 November 1559 in Ticehurst, a town five miles north of Burwash, also in Sussex County. Apparently Richard and Margaret returned to Burwash, for Margaret gave birth to seven children there between the years of 1560 and 1573. On 2 September 1571 their sixth child and third son John was christened there.

John, or Johannes, returned to the Wynder spelling of his grandfather, but left the traditional county of the family by migrating ten miles or so into Kent county. Who knows how many generations of Winders, Wynders, and atte Wyndes had dwelt in beautiful Sussex County? Perhaps for five hundred years or more Winder progenitors had resided in fair Sussex, a land Rudyard Kipling, who lived in Burwash at the height of his fame,[32] would later revere:

> God gives all men all earth to love,
> But, since man's heart is small,
> Ordains for each one spot shall prove
> Beloved over all.
> Each to his choice, and I rejoice
> The lot has fallen to me
> In a fair ground—in a fair ground—
> Yea, Sussex by the sea![33]

The Winders Come to Kent

It was in the village of Benenden, Kent County, where John Wynder married a local girl, Martha Fuller, in a ceremony on New Year's Day 1602. Their son Thomas, who would switch the spelling back to Winder for the last time, was christened there on 23 October 1609. He was the fourth of six children. Martha died when the boy was nine, but John remarried two years later to an Agnes Kadwell.

The Winders

Come to Kent

John (Johannes) Wynder	+	Martha Fuller
1571 - ?		1585-1618
Burwash, Sussex, England		Benenden, Kent, England

Thomas Winder	+	Suzan Relph
1609 - 1641		1614-1677
Benenden, Kent, England		Tenterden, Kent, England

John Winder	+	Elizabeth Younge
1637 - 1701		1637 - 1675
Tenterden, Kent, England		Tenterden, Kent, England

John Winder	+	Ann Sawkins
1675 - 1733		1679 - 1721
Tenterden, Kent, England		Lyminge, Kent, England

Sir William Winder	+	Susanna Henden
1708 - 1765		1705 - 1778
Tenterden, Kent, England		Biddenden, Kent, England

Thomas Winder was mobile like his father, and in June of 1636 married a Suzan Relph in Rolvenden, a village about three miles east of his birthplace, Benenden. Suzan, a daughter of prominent Kent physician Dr. Richard Relphe, apparently convinced her new husband to return with her to her native Tenterden, another three miles up the road, east of Rolvenden.

It is said that "the villages along these heights are the most picturesque in the county . . . a necklace of pearls!" and that "proudest of all these sister villages, perhaps, is Tenterden, with its magnificent broad High Street" and its stately church tower.[34] Tenterden is not only a "very attractive old town,"[35] but is surrounded by miles and miles of "gentle undulations of woodland."[36]

It was here in Tenterden that a son, John Winder, was born about Christmas Day, 1637 to Thomas and Suzan. They would have three more children in Tenterden over the next three years. John stayed in that town all of his days, and married local Elizabeth Younge on 6 September 1655.

After giving birth to six daughters, John and Elizabeth finally were blessed with a son, who of course was named for his father. Born in January of 1675 in Tenterden, the younger John married Ann Sawkins just six months before his father died in October of 1701 after having been a widower for twenty-five years. The younger John died in Tenterden in August of 1733. He too endured his final years as a widower, a common fate in a time when many women died in childbearing.

John and Ann's third child, William Winder, had been born in the summer of 1708 and christened on 25 July in Tenterden. William was not unlike his great-grandfather Thomas or great-great grandfather John, in that he left his hometown as a young man to marry and settle in a neighboring village.

These generations of Winders maintained something of the class distinction that had rested with their apparent ancestors and were likely prosperous yeomen or gentlemen farmers. In fact, the Winder family at this point was probably not unlike a number of yeomen in Kent, who "bordered on gentleman status . . . 'half farmer and half gentleman.'"[37]

By the time William was twenty, the John and Ann Winder family would have become concerned about whom their second son would marry. This was extremely important in eighteenth-century England, for marriage was regarded as "a social duty . . . it obliged the family and helped to widen social contacts."[38] In fact, "normally, the son's marriage brought a handsome dowry into the family"[39] and therefore was an important financial decision as well. One scholar on the English gentry noted that these marriages were "a matter of great import, for clearly a groom or bride of inferior standing reflected on the family's status; a marriage connection with families of superior rank enhanced it."[40]

Therefore, "to protect and possibly increase the family standing, fathers were primarily interested in ensuring that their sons . . . married within a socially acceptable field."[41] It would be safe, then, to assume that John Winder would have encouraged his children, including William, to attend fancy dinner parties and dances where "potential brides and grooms moved in circles where they were more than likely to meet partners of the same rank."[42] After all, "marriage partners were generally sought within a narrow social elite"[43] and such social gatherings were commonplace.

The family could not have been more thrilled than when twenty-year old William announced his betrothal to Susanna Henden. Miss Henden, who was three years older than William, was a catch that would make any yeoman father proud. She was the fourteenth child of Sir William Henden and Lady Katherine Toke (they had two more children after Susanna!). The Henden family had for generations been prominent titled nobility in the village of Biddenden, a small hamlet but three miles north of Tenterden. Two of the principal manors in the village, Biddenden Place and Henden Hall, had been seats of the family for generations. Sir William Henden had inherited Biddenden Place through his father, Sir John Henden, who had received it from his uncle Sir Edward Henden, a Baron of the Exchequer in the reign of Charles I.[44]

Susanna's mother, Lady Katherine Toke, hailed from an even more aristocratic lineage. Katherine's father, Sir Nicholas Toke of Godinton, had been one of the most prominent gentlemen in the county and had served faithfully for a generation as captain of the Kentish militia.[45] The Tokes had long been one of the leading families of Kent, and Katherine's mother's side, the Dyke family, had served for generations as knights in neighboring Sussex.

Through the Toke ancestry young Susanna Henden could claim a noble heritage that included William the Conqueror and his son King Henry I, King Alfred the Great, kings of Scotland, Bavaria, and Sweden, Grand Dukes of Russia, and even the great medieval ruler Charlemagne, Holy Roman Emperor.[46] It has been said that "it was because antiquity mattered that so many gentry interested themselves in their family tree, even if enthusiasm for an extensive lineage occasionally led them into claims that were doubtful or spurious."[47] However, although Susanna and William apparently taught their posterity of their noble heritage,[48] it was indeed a legitimate tale, as it has been confirmed by modern genealogical research.

When Susanna Henden was in her twenties, her parents, like the Winders, would also have been anxious to secure for her a suitable mate, for in Georgian England "anxious fathers looked to marry their daughters as advantageously as possible."[49] Apparently William Winder proved acceptable, or else Sir William and his Lady would definitely have rejected such a proposal. After all, "the social standing of the family was endangered by marriage outside the group."[50]

Geoffrey Copus, a professional researcher in Kent who has assisted the Winder Family Organization in recent decades, once remarked that the Winder-Henden marriage probably occurred at a time when the Winders were gradually moving upward socially, and the Henden-Toke clans were beginning to decline in status. Thus, the union of William and Susanna would have fit with the social norms of the day.[51] It is also not surprising that Susanna would marry a young man from a neighboring village, for "among the minor gentry" in Kent County, "more than four-fifths married locally."[52]

The Biddenden Winders

Certainly such a commitment was worthy of young William leaving familiar Tenterden and moving three miles north to Biddenden, the area where the Henden family wielded their greatest influence. The ceremony took place on 9 January 1729 in All Saints Church in Biddenden, and the union would greatly impact succeeding generations of Winders, who apparently remained close to their Henden cousins. William Winder was eventually knighted, bringing great distinction to the family.

Sir William and Susanna reared a large family of nine children in Biddenden, and would certainly have instilled in them the proper manners of a genteel family. Sir William Winder would have been considered a member of the gentry, the elite group that "always made up but a tiny proportion of the total population, even in the countryside."[53] Certain values distinguished gentlemen like William and their families from the masses.

The gentry were, especially in Kent, "conservative, and Anglican," with a deep deference toward tradition, their duties, and their God.[54] These virtues were still strong in the Winder family ethos nearly a century later when John Rex Winder was growing up, as were the following "means to discern a gentleman" as offered by Sir William Vaughan:

> First he must be affable and courteous in speech and behaviour. Secondly, he must have an adventurous heart to fight and that but for very just quarrels. Thirdly, he must be endowed with mercy to forgive the trespasses of his friends

and servants. Fourthly, he must stretch his purse to give liberally unto soldiers and unto them that have need; for a niggard is not worthy to be called a gentleman. These be the properties of a gentleman, which whosoever lacketh deserveth but the title of a clown or a country boor.[55]

Other noble values of a good English gentleman included "good stewardship, simplicity, right use, frugality." Of these, frugality[56] was especially emphasized in genteel families like the Winders. The aristocracy of the day described frugality as: "the willingness to forego having more than one needs, to live by the standards of the natural economy although in the midst of the artificial."[57] These, too, all became an important part of what was taught in the Winder households throughout the eighteenth and nineteenth centuries.

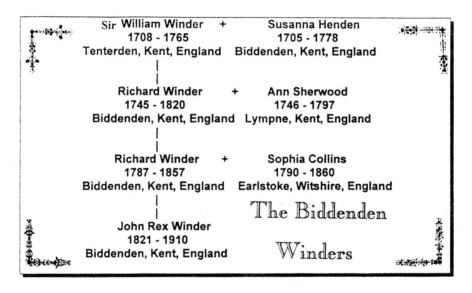

Sir **William Winder**   +   **Susanna Henden**
1708 - 1765   1705 - 1778
Tenterden, Kent, England   Biddenden, Kent, England

Richard Winder   +   **Ann Sherwood**
1745 - 1820   1746 - 1797
Biddenden, Kent, England   Lympne, Kent, England

Richard Winder   +   **Sophia Collins**
1787 - 1857   1790 - 1860
Biddenden, Kent, England   Earlstoke, Witshire, England

John Rex Winder
1821 - 1910
Biddenden, Kent, England

The Biddenden Winders

William and Susanna's seventh child, Richard Winder, was born in March of 1745 and married Ann Sherwood of Lympne, a town near the southeast Kentish coast. However, the couple decided to reside in Biddenden, where the Winder and Henden families still maintained some prominence. They were wed there on Christmas Day, 1783. After two girls, a boy was born to the couple on 14 September 1787, just three days before the leaders of the fledgling United States signed their new constitution. As had been the custom in the family since the Middle Ages, the oldest son was named for his father. Young Richard Winder would marry a young lady from distant Wiltshire county named Sophia Collins, and from this union would come the family of John Rex Winder.

The Winder family at the beginning of the nineteenth century was one blessed with a long foundation of values that had been passed from generation to generation by both word and example. They included a centuries-old respect for family tradition, for community involvement, loyalty to King, and deep devotion to God and the Church. Because of their connection to the aristocracy, a tradition of fine manners and etiquette, proper speech and writing, frugality, and a rigid work ethic were all incorporated into the family ethos. An appreciation for the niceties of gentry society would also have been cultivated: appreciations for fine country estates, architecture and gardens, good food and entertainment, dancing and the arts, and the land itself, as well as livestock.

These formed a rich tapestry that constituted the backdrop of John R. Winder's heritage. As will be seen, he carried each of these attributes with him throughout his long life—attributes that he did not acquire in a school house but rather must have been taught to him by his family. With such a noble core of genteel virtues, it is no surprise that Winder was called a "perfect gentleman," or that the first governor of the State of Utah would declare at his funeral: "I know no better man—no man of greater virtue, integrity and all the Christian graces that go to make a gentle, loving, noble, manly man, than was John R. Winder."[58] Let us now explore the place where these deep-rooted virtues began to take root with that man—his boyhood in Biddenden.

2
Boyhood in Biddenden: President Winder's Youth, 1821-1840

"The beginning of my success in life"

The Setting of His Birth

It was the spring of 1809 in "one of the loveliest villages in the Weald of Kent."[1] Twenty-one-year-old Richard Winder, son of Richard and Ann Sherwood Winder, had come of age to find a wife, and had proposed to an 18-year-old young woman named Sophia Collins. Although Richard's family had been in Biddenden ever since his grandfather William Winder married his grandmother Susanna Henden 80 years before, Sophia was fairly new to the small village nestled in the thick forests of Kent. She was born and raised about 150 miles west of Biddenden in the small chapelry of Earlstoke, located in the inland county of Wiltshire. Earlstoke, claiming a population then of just 375 souls, was located on a rich tract of relatively flat land on the Salisbury Plain.[2]

Sophia's family had resided there for generations, but for some reason she left the traditional hamlet of her ancestors and traveled across southern England to Biddenden. It remains a puzzle today as to why this young lady, while still in her teens, made the trek there. One family historian notes that "Sophia may have gone to Kent County to work in the home of royalty."[3] This was a common practice for young girls in early nineteenth-century England, and Kent would have been a realistic destination, for "so many of royal descent occupy the county"[4] and "the number of gentry in Kent," when compared to other English counties, "was exceptionally large."[5] One register of the period listed Sophia as a spinster, although it does not specify her employer.[6]

If Sophia was in the small hamlet of Biddenden as hired help to a family of some influence, possibly even one of the Winder or Henden families, she would certainly have been around to catch the eye of young Richard Winder. More surprising, perhaps, is how one hailing from a respected family, like Richard, ended up proposing to a servant girl like Sophia. After all, Sophia's pedigree reveals no traces of nobility or wealth, and not only was her father an illegitimate child, but Sophia herself was born just 46 days after her parents' wedding. However, "the further one went down the social scale the more individual feelings of the young people were respected," and in fact, "lesser landowners could accept more easily a match which did little for the family's wealth or position."[7] Although Richard's grandfather, Sir William Winder, was wealthy enough to bequeath to his "loving Wife" a considerable sum in his will, as well as guarantee her "the best bed with all its furniture and the best pair of sheets,"[8] it is important to realize that the family fortune was divided equally by William and Susanna's eight living children, and that any prestige or wealth from that generation would have been considerably diluted by the time Richard had proposed to Sophia.

It therefore seems likely that Richard simply was smitten with young Sophia's charm and good looks, and the two became romantically attached. The couple was married in All Saints Church, Biddenden on the 5th of June 1809, just 19 days before the bride's 19th birthday. They would be man and wife for 48 years.

Although his mother had been dead nearly 12 years, Richard's 64-year-old father would certainly have attended the Anglican ceremony in All Saints, as would have his uncles William and John Winder, lifelong Biddendenites who were now 79 and 71, respectively. (They would each live to be 84.) Richard's six living siblings, who all resided in the vicinity, would probably also have attended the festivities, as would have many Winder and Henden cousins.

The young Winder couple obtained a comfortable two-story home and established a farm which took care of most of their needs.[9] One account claims that Richard and Sophia *"bought"* the "lovely two-story home and *inherited* farm land from which to earn their living," and it was "because he was of royal descent" that "Richard had the privilege of owning land."[10] If this was the case, the young couple was indeed fortunate to own their land and home, as land ownership in England was still reserved to the elite of society.

Family photos of the old Winder home, including those possessed by John R. Winder, show that the stately two-story home of Richard and Sophia's was the manor known as Biddenden Place.[11] Biddenden Place has been called "one of the most historically interesting homes in the country."[12] It was built in the fourteenth century by Flemish weavers on the site of a much-earlier house which was built by Sir Edward de Mayney, a companion of William the Conqueror.

A Sir John de Mayney lived in it during the reign of Edward III, and 200 years later John de Mayney founded the village school. It has a bedroom known as the Jacobean room where, it is claimed, James I spent a night. John's grandson, Sir Anthony de Mayney, sold the estate to Sir Edward Henden, who was one of the Barons of the Exchequer in the reign of Charles I. Sir Edward had the house faced with brick and set his coat of arms in the brickwork on the front of the house, and had a sundial built with his initials, E.H., and the date, 1626, in the brickwork on the south wall. Both markings remain today, and John R. Winder had in his possession a picture of the sundial.[13]

The historic manor called "Biddenden Place" was the home to several genera-tions of Winder and Henden families. It became the home of Richard and Sophia Winder, and was consequently the boyhood abode of young John Rex Winder. Today the manor is a bed-and-breakfast.

"The Place," as it was called, passed to Edward's nephew, Sir John Henden, who was "Sherif of the County" in 1662, and then to his son, Sir William Hen-den. Sir William, Richard Winder's great-grandfather, "dissipated his patrimony, pulled down the greatest part of this seat, and left the poor remains of it, con-sisting of only three or four rooms, and a very few acres of the old garden and park, to his son William."[14] However, a twentieth-century realtor noted that "by modern standards these 'poor remains' constitute a sizeable house."[15] William, who was born in 1703, sold it later in that century to the trustees of Sir Horace Mann.[16]

At the time Richard and Sophia brought the historic home back into the fam-ily, presumably by purchasing it from the Mann trustees, Biddenden Place had, "like many other large houses in the area," just recently been "used during the Napoleonic war as a camp for French prisoners of war."[17] Although Napoleon would not face his final defeat at Waterloo until 1815, six years later, apparent-ly the French prisoners of war had been removed from "The Place" by the time the newlywed couple moved into the historic manor in the summer of 1809.

It is significant that Richard and Sophia obtained this particular house, which was one of the premier mansions in the village. "Long residence in a particular spot enhanced a family's standing," it was said, and "a centuries-long association with a house gave a family a strong sense of identity and feeling of permanence"[18] which the young Winder couple would have enjoyed. After all, "the power of inherited land to span the generations and to transcend individual mortality gave it a special virtue as the foundation of society,"[19] and with only a brief interruption, "The Place" had now been in the Winder-Henden family since 1626.

Some may argue that because Biddenden Place was not directly inherited by the Winders, that it may have lacked some of the prestige of a regularly inherited estate. However, "in reality, statistics show the brevity of most ennobled lines," and so "cadet branches of the family," like the Winders were to the Hendens, "might take over the estate and ensure an overall sense of continuity."[20]

Apparently one of the reasons Richard married the young servant girl Sophia was that she was already three months pregnant with their first child. Little Richard was born six months and three days after the wedding, on 8 December 1809. Five months after the boy named for his father had turned two, the couple gave birth to a little girl, who was named for her mother. Sophia had also been the name of Richard's younger sister who died just three months after her birth.

Another two-and-one-half years later, Richard and Sophia's third child was born. A son, born on 29 September 1814, he was named John, the popular name of saints and apostles, and a family name for literally centuries. This descendent of royalty was given the middle name of Rex, the Latin word for king. John Rex Winder had a younger sister, Matilda, who was born in April of 1817. However, tragedy struck the Winder household in 1819 when they suffered the loss of four-year-old John Rex Winder. The child was buried on March 30.

Another daughter, Elizabeth, was born that August, but the family faced another loss in November 1820 when Richard's father passed away at the age of 75. The senior Richard Winder had left his namesake "all those sheep and lambs that are my property," as well as furniture, blankets, linen, his watch, and all of his "wearing Apparel,"[21] assets which must have helped the young and growing family.

Birth of John Rex Winder

The next year at the historic Biddenden home, on December 11, 1821, Richard and Sophia's sixth child "first saw the light of this world."[22] It was decided that, following a common practice, he should be named for his recently deceased brother, and so he was christened in the Church of England the following May as John Rex Winder.[23] He later remarked that at that time he had been "baptized (sprinkled) as an infant into the Church of England, of which my father and mother were both members."[24]

At his funeral 88 years later, President Richard W. Young noted some interesting facts regarding Winder's birth date on that winter day in 1821:

> At that time George IV was king of England; Louis XVIII was king of France; the emperor Napoleon had been buried scarcely seven months; James Monroe was president of the United States; Jefferson, who wrote the Declaration of Independence, John Adams, the second president of the United States, James Madison, the chief instrument in producing the Constitution of the United States, were then alive. Only two expeditions had found their perilous way across the great wilderness that intervenes between the Mississippi and the Pacific ocean, so far as we know. No civilized man had ever gazed upon the waters of the Great Salt Lake, the chief geographical feature of the region President Winder was so long identified. The electric telegraph had not been conceived. No railroad train ran in America.[25]

When little John Rex was three and a half, a little brother, William Henden Winder, was born in June 1824. His name indicates the affinity that the family still felt with their Henden ancestry, even though it was approaching 100 years since the marriage of Susanna Henden to William Winder. A younger sister, Ann, was born when little John was just five, in 1827.

Early Religious Awakenings

"The nineteenth century was a very religious century," it has been said regarding Britain, "and if we are ever to attempt to understand nineteenth-century men and women and their doings, we must consider carefully" their religious and spiritual activities and development.[26] Being born into a devout Anglican family, John Rex would have had a thorough religious upbringing, including being

Researcher Geoffrey Copus and the author examine old Winder tombstones in the churchyard of All Saints' Church, Biddenden. It was here that the Winder and Henden families married and worshiped for over one-hundred years.

taught the scriptures by his parents and older siblings, as well as having frequent church attendance. The Winder home at Biddenden Place was just across the street from their relative's stately, but smaller, Henden Hall. Both residences were on Biddenden's Tenterden Road, near the Village Hall, and just a short walk to the north would have led to the Village Green, where the village's High Street intersected. Just a few dozen yards up High Street was the old All Saints Church, largely built of Tunbridge Wells sandstone, with an impressive tower constructed in 1400 with Bethersden Marble.

With such a close proximity to the church and the heart of the village, the Winder family would likely have been heavily involved in church and civic activities. "The central act of worship is the Holy Communion and there is always one celebration of that service each Sunday," reported one Rector of Biddenden. The Reverend Canon Peter Naylor also remarked that "the church is very much part of the village community and we do our best to play our part."[27] It seems it has been so for centuries in Biddenden. Therefore, having been reared in such a religious environment, it is not surprising to learn that, even as a young boy, little John had an understanding of prayer.

"Of almost all Kentish families the land afforded the principal livelihood," as it did for the Winder family in Biddenden. Even "the more prosperous farmed much of the land themselves rather than let it out," especially in Kent, where "few had a patrimony so large that they could afford to cast upon it the casual eye of a Georgian duke."[28]

This aerial photograph of Biddenden Place, boyhood home of John Rex Winder, was taken in the 1950's. It is easy to imagine a lonely spot in the surrounding fields where a young boy became frightened and first prayed to God.

Young lads, like John Rex, could therefore hardly be excused from helping out on the family farm. In fact, "apart from the constraints of skill and physical strength, there was little that a boy could not undertake or assist with: 'At eight years old', says a farmer in East Kent, 'a boy is fit to help his father in the barn a little at threshing.'"[29] For six-year-old John R. Winder, contributing to the family farm meant keeping the birds away from the grain in the fields. It was while in this capacity that he had his first experience with prayer.

One day the boy had been sent out into the fields to keep the birds off the grain. The field was in a beautiful clearing surrounded by the thick woods of the Kentish Weald. "It was a very lonely spot," Winder later recalled. The child looked around him at the thickly wooded area that hid the house from sight and became frightened. "Being entirely alone," he later explained, "I was somewhat fearful, and I remember," as though someone spoke to him, "that I was impressed to kneel down in the brush and pray to the Lord that His angels might watch over and protect me from harm." He arose from his knees and the fear was gone. As he later told a group in the Salt Lake Temple, "I remember now just as well as I see your faces, that that was the end of my fear. I also think that that was the beginning of my success in life." A granddaughter would later declare that "Never again did he feel frightened."[30]

This event, minor as it may seem, greatly affected John R.'s outlook on life and was a catalyst for a lifelong faith that God would indeed protect him. Even at the time of his eighty-second birthday, that incident in the fields remained vivid in his memory. Winder reported that it was "as far back in my life as I could well remember." Nonetheless, at that time he told a party in Salt Lake City that "although that spot is many thousand miles distant, and it is more than seventy years ago, I could walk straight to that very spot where I knelt down, and where I received that blessing." Regarding the prayer in the fields of Biddenden Place, he said that throughout his life, "I have often thought of that incident, particularly when I first heard the Gospel."[31] One biographer explained that this "little incident in this his early life . . . shows his trust in the watchcare of God."[32]

John was seven when his sister Eliza was born in 1829, and 11 years old when the family's youngest child, Frederick, was born in May of 1833. However, as a two-month-old child, Frederick tragically died. The boy's death occurred the very day after his christening in August of 1833, suggesting that he may have fallen suddenly ill and that the family desired to give him a name quickly before he passed on.

The infant mortality rate for rural England at this time was 87.8 deaths per 1000 infants, meaning that in a family who had ten children, as the Winders had, it was common to have one die in infancy.[33] Nonetheless, such a loss would have been painful, and feelings of grief would have run deep.

Eleven-year-old John Rex would have been old enough to have been deeply saddened by the loss of his baby brother, and even old enough to wonder where baby Frederick had gone, why God had allowed such a tragedy to happen, and other questions that inquisitive children always ask when faced with such trying circumstances. Death again struck the family two years later, in October of 1835, when 13-year-old John R. Winder's older sister Sophia died at the age of 23. These losses were probably formative experiences for a young boy already beginning to identify his spirituality and develop his relationship with God.

Another religious experience in his youth occurred in conjunction with the Church of England in 1836. "At the age of fourteen I was confirmed a member of that church by the Archbishop of Canterbury," Winder reports.[34]

The Archbishop of Canterbury was one of the most prominent figures in all of Great Britain. Since 1353 he had held the title of "Primate of All England," denoting his rank as the primary ecclesiastical leader of the country. Great and legendary men had served in that office over the centuries: "Some were saints, some men of learning, many were great leaders of men, skilled in the practice of civil government. And with few exceptions they were men who rose to the high ideal of that great office, and whose hearts were set on the things of God."[35]

William Howley had been the Archbishop of Canterbury since John R. Winder was six years old. Howley, while previously serving as Bishop of London, had baptized Princess Victoria and served in the House of Lords. The Archbishop was "humble, modest, and benevolent" and was described as "gentle among the gentle," by Prime Minister Gladstone, "and mild among the mild." Usually a popular archbishop, Howley was severely jeered five years before in 1831 when he opposed a Reform Bill: "He was mobbed in the streets of Canterbury, and the chaplain in attendance complained that a dead cat had hit him in the face, the archbishop replied that he should be thankful it was not a live one."[36]

The archbishop had an itinerary "to make an almost complete visitation of his diocese" when his busy schedule would permit. One day in 1836 he must have made a rare stop in the small hamlet of Biddenden, or at least a neighboring village. Howley always "drove abroad in a coach and four," and it would have been quite an event for the little village when the 70-year-old Primate of All England stepped out of his fancy coach with his famous "gold shoe buckles" glittering in the sun.[37]

In the Church of England at the time, the Sacrament of Confirmation limited "the laying on of hands to the bishop," which is one reason why the rite was not performed while Winder was younger. It was also important that the person being confirmed had "attained an age capable of deliberate choice."[38] Archbishop Howley probably would have anointed the heads and pronounced a blessing of Confirmation on several young people that day he confirmed John R. Winder. He was known for his "tremulous voice."[39]

Anglicans believe that this "laying on of hands" is "the sign of the bestowal of some spiritual gift." The Church of England professes that "by the laying on of hands and anointing with oil the Holy Spirit is bestowed upon us in a special way and for a special purpose, to help and strengthen us to fulfill the work of the order conferred upon us." They also believe that "by the laying on of hands of the Bishop and anointing with holy oil in Confirmation we are made, by him who acts as an agent of God through His Church, a royal priesthood, an holy people of God."[40]

John R. Winder said "I continued to worship in that Church until I was caught in the Gospel net," meaning his conversion to Mormonism twelve years later.[41] During those years in the Church of England, however, "he was an active member of that sect."[42] As for Archbishop William Howley, he would be at the death bed of William IV one year later, and, together with the Lord Chamberlain, would announce to the young princess at Kensington Palace her accession to the throne. On the 28th of June 1838 Archbishop Howley would crown Victoria queen in Westminster Abbey, officially ushering in the Victorian Age. Howley would die in 1848 at the venerable age of 82.[43]

Life in the Village of Biddenden

It has been written of Winder that "his early life was spent in his native town,"[44] a village where everybody would have known everybody else. Biddenden was famous for many beautiful timbered houses and the Biddenden Maids, Eliza and Mary Chulkhurst. Born there in the twelfth century, the sisters were notable both as Siamese twins, joined at the shoulders and hips, and as benefactresses who began the generous Chulkhurst Charity.

The Winder family, like other large families inhabiting the village's prominent estates, would have been part of "the dominating influence in the neighbourhood, whose views and conduct shaped the social life of the village, and whose affairs provided unbounded scope for speculation and discussion."[45] "The Place," where they lived, was not only equipped to house Richard and Sophia and their seven living children, but had space to provide for the various needs of a socially prominent and active family. "This lovely old house has a reception hall with an inglenook and a polished brick floor, three reception rooms (drawing room, dining room and paneled sitting room), a sun room, an oak fitted kitchen, six principal bedrooms, three bathrooms and two attic bedrooms."[46]

However, regarding the income of John R. Winder's parents, one biographer has remarked on "the limited means of his parents,"[47] and even Winder himself referred to his childhood as a time when he "was a poor little boy."[48] And when compared to wealthier members of the aristocracy in England at the time, or even John R. Winder's status later in life, the Richard and Sophia Winder family was of relatively "limited means." This does not remove the fact, however, that they were still one of the most fortunate families in Biddenden, and that throughout Britain there were literally millions who were less fortunate than they. The old Winder home sold for the equivalent of nearly one million U.S. dollars in 1992.[49]

On a family farm there was a need to enlist help from all in the family, and as has been mentioned, young John R. had assisted since his early childhood. "From the day he was old enough," writes Edward Anderson, "he had been compelled to toil for his own living."[50] It was important that he help earn his own keep, and therefore, Winder writes, "I was forced by circumstances to depend upon my own exertions."[51] He later said, "I commenced to labor and rustle for myself from the time I was about ten years of age. . . My life has been a busy one, it has been work, work, work from my childhood until the present time."[52] This was not unusual, though, even among the propertied classes. Winder's third great-grandfather, Sir Nicholas Toke of Godinton, who was a distinguished captain in the Kentish Militia and a large property owner, "supervised the work of his estate very largely himself."[53] However, such involvement with the family farm did have a negative effect on John R.'s formal education. "There was a feeling that school education, book-learning, did little to mold a potential agricultural labourer. School might be a budding agriculturalist's 'general education', but labour was his 'special education'. . . . This skill was acquired at a father's side and not in a school room."[54]

John R. Winder consequently received but little formal schooling.[55] This would not have been obtained at Oxford or Cambridge, either, but rather, probably consisted of just a grade or two at the John Mayne School across the street from All Saints Church. This simple academy for boys had been established in Biddenden in 1566.[56] Any other educational experiences he might have had were "derived through his own efforts."[57]

Throughout his life Winder was known for his fine mastery of the English language and for being well read, attributes that he must have begun to cultivate on his own in his youth. "With a pen he was swift and accurate,"[58] it was said of John R., and "he used language not as the French statesman said 'to conceal the meaning,' but to express what he meant."[59] In addition, "he was a great reader, especially of the daily newspapers, and having a very retentive memory, he came to be regarded as a walking encyclopedia of information on current history."[60] His grandson, George Winder, mentioned that "speaking proper English, using appropriate grammar, and developing adequate writing skills were important elements in the upbringing of Winder families for generations." George remarked that "John R. certainly would have been taught proper English by his parents in England."[61] Again, this shows the station of the Winder family in Britain, for between 1750 and 1850, only about half of the adult males in the United Kingdom could even sign their own names. "The gentry," however, "were 100 per cent literate," even if they labored on their own land, like the Winders.[62]

However, despite "an education far from complete," John R. Winder was nonetheless "amply supplemented with good sense and practical judgement."[63] He was regarded, like his son William C. Winder, who was also pulled out of school after just a few grades to help on the family farm, as "a self-educated intelligent man," who "read constantly and kept himself up on current events," and whose "English and grammar were perfect."[64]

In his boyhood in Biddenden, John Rex Winder had learned faith, as well as loyalty to God and the Church. He had acquired the basics of the English language, which he would continue to add to and refine throughout his life, and he had developed the work ethic of one who had grown up on a farm. Winder would later comment that "my success has been due to a determination, formed early in life, to do my duty faithfully and conscientiously in whatever position I might be placed. I have always believed that a thing worth doing at all is worth doing well, and I have done my best to reduce that principle to practice."[65]

Armed with such a "can do" attitude, the boy from Biddenden, "when just out of his teens," left the village and travelled thirty miles north, where "he made his way to the commercial centre of the universe—London."[66] There in Europe's largest metropolis, the young farm boy embarked on the adventure of making a living in industrial England.

3
Setting Out on His Own: Career and Family in Victorian London, 1841-1847

"An honest desire to labor"

"[In the mid-nineteenth century] with locomotion constantly diminishing the distance between the village and the city, with the spread of science and machinery even in the processes of agriculture, in a small island with a dense urban population that had now lost all tradition of country life, it was only a question of time before urban ways of thought and action would penetrate and absorb the old rural world, obliterating its distinctive features and local variations."[1]

Although a third of England's work force was still employed in agriculture in 1811, that percentage diminished significantly over subsequent decades, for "as industrialisation produced its vast urban conglomerations so the consequence of the land declined."[2] In nineteenth century Britain, the old pre-eminence of the landed interest was "eroded by the rise of the industrial state, and its parallel, the coming of democracy." Indeed, the entire balance of the economy shifted from "agriculture to industry and trade."[3]

The Winder Family's Urban Shift

This would greatly affect the lifestyle of landed families, like the Winders, who had for generations depended upon agriculture to supply their livelihood. As farming became decreasingly profitable, the country gentleman was forced to diversify his assets in order to survive the challenge of the industrial age. Unfortunately, "many of the lesser squires," like the Winders, "had little means or opportunity for diversifying. Their surplus income was small or non-existent, and their estates too small or too encumbered for them to contemplate parting with land."[4] Therefore, many, like the Winders, were forced to part without their land. Richard Winder had tried his hand at shoemaking, possibly out of this need to bring more income to the family farm. He apparently began this line of work about the time Matilda was born in 1817, and in John R.'s christening record he is listed as a cordwainer, or a shoemaker specializing in cordovan leather.[5]

However, be it for economic or other reasons, in the early 1840's Richard and Sophia left the rural village of Biddenden, which had been the home of Winder-Henden families for generations. They moved north to the much larger town of Lambeth, in Surrey County, not far from London.[6] As for the family estate, Biddenden Place eventually came into the hands of the Raymond family, who in the 1950's, would set out to restore much of the old house and replant its beautiful gardens.[7] Towards the end of the twentieth century the house would serve as the "Biddenden Place Carvery & Hotel," a popular bed and breakfast.[8]

The Winders may have gone to Lambeth because of other relatives who were living there. John R.'s first cousin, Frederick, son of Jeremiah and Louisa Driver Winder, lived in Lambeth and later joined the LDS Church.

Richard Winder died in Lambeth in 1857, a mere sixteen days after his seventieth birthday. Three years later, Sophia died in Rolvenden, Kent, where she was then living with her oldest child, Richard. John R.'s oldest brother Richard had married Louisa Poolley, and that couple stayed in Kent County when the rest of the family migrated to Lambeth. Richard died at age eighty, like his father, in 1890, in the town of Rolvenden, Kent.

It is not certain what happened to the two youngest Winder children, Ann and Eliza, who would have been but in their teens when their parents moved to Lambeth. Perhaps they went with them, or maybe they stayed behind with their elder brother Richard or other relatives. However, we do know that Eliza did return to (or remained in) Biddenden, for it was there that she died in 1863 at the age of 34. Elizabeth Winder, who was twenty-two when her parents moved from Biddenden, married Stephen Ward in Faversham, Kent, six years later in 1847.

Richard Winder (1787-1857), the father of John Rex Winder, died in Lambeth, Surrey, England at the age of 70. John R. Winder was his only child to join the LDS Church and emigrate to America.

As for the three other Winder children, they were apparently sent off to make their own way in the world when Richard and Sophia moved to Lambeth. Twenty-four year old Matilda took her 17-year-old brother, William Henden Winder, and traveled to the town of St. George Hanover in Middlesex County, north-west of London. There in St. George Hanover, William married Caroline Smith in 1847, and Matilda married William Betsworth in 1850. William Henden Winder, loyal to his name, returned to Biddenden, where he died in 1855 at the young age of 31. Matilda would live to be 85 and would be the only one of Richard and Sophia's children, besides John Rex, to glimpse the twentieth century. She died in England on the 24th of July, 1902, one year after Queen Victoria.

Learning the Leather Trade in London

As for John R. Winder, "when he became twenty years of age, he left his family for London in hopes of finding profitable employment."[9] His story is typical of the traditional Englishman of the time. A great many like him were leaving the countryside for the great cities of Industrial England, especially the imperial capital, the thriving metropolis of London. By the time John R. entered the fast-paced world of cosmopolitan London it could be said that, like Winder himself, "the typical Englishman was no longer a countryman but a town-dweller."[10]

Victorian Britain was like no other period in its history. "It was an age of apparently inexhaustible vigour and self-confidence," recorded Stephen Neill. "It was also an age of outstanding men and women in every department of national, intellectual, and religious life. . . In the application of power to production, in invention and the application of science to industry, Britain led the world."[11] Britain was not only the leader of the worldwide Industrial Revolution, but also operated a worldwide empire on which the sun never set, and London was the heart of it all. "Victorian London was the center of the largest empire the world had ever seen."[12]

The Industrial Revolution, and the wealth it generated for the country, had altered traditional British society. "A new middle class came into being, merging partly with" families like the Winders, who had been part of "the old landowning aristocracy."[13] Young John R. Winder was part of this new middle class, and "was able to secure a position in a fashionable shoe store in London's West End."[14]

"The posh West End," where John R. established himself, was once known as the City of Westminster, and still today "boasts royal palaces and parks, theaters, smart shops and residential areas."[15] Some of London's best-known streets provide the major thoroughfares of the district, including Oxford Street, Regent Street, and Piccadilly, culminating in the boisterous Piccadilly Circus. Piccadilly Street "set out in life centuries ago as a country lane, growing up into a highly fashionable thoroughfare and still anxious to keep up with the old times."[16] This was the part of the great city where Winder lived and worked as a young shoe clerk. The classy West End was dramatically different from the East End, where working class London and the Cockneys resided and labored.

All throughout Victorian London, however, the sound of industry rang in the air, as industrial progress changed the face of the city. Rail lines, steam engines, underground trains, sewage systems, and new building techniques were transforming the ancient city into a modern metropolis.[17]

The shop where John R. Winder worked was called the West End Shoe and Grocery Store.[18] It was at this "boot and shoe establishment,"[19] that Winder developed his vocation as "a leather and shoe man."[20] His father, Richard, had also been a shoemaker during part of the time the family was in Biddenden.[21] Much of the work would have been concentrated on the manufacturing of boots, for "the predominant footwear, as the British set out to conquer the world, was naturally boots."[22] And in a fashionable shoe store like the West End Shoe and Grocery Store, stylish boots would have been the demand—boots like the hessian and the top boot. "The hessian is a boot only worn with tight pantaloons," dictated the fashion of the day, and it was said that "the top boot is almost entirely a sporting fashion."[23] As for shoes, since 1830 the shallow square toe was predominant for men, and for shoes "to be anything like the fashion, they should have the toes at least an inch and a half square."[24]

In his new job, "John R. made a good impression with his energy and outgoing personality."[25] He later noted that "I found that an honest desire to labor and a persevering effort to obtain employment would not go long unrequired, and I kept steadily at work at any and every honorable task that came my way."[26]

Ellen Walters Becomes His Wife

The West End Shoe and Grocery Store proved to be a good place for young John Winder, for not only did he acquire an occupational skill that would serve him well for decades, but "it was here that he met Ellen Walters," his wife to be.[27] Ellen Walters had been born to William and Susan Chave Walters on April 8, 1822 in Tiverton, Devonshire (a county on England's most south-westerly peninsula). "Had you known her you would have been persuaded by instinct, that she came with the Spring," her granddaughter would later reminisce, "her nature was so life-inspiring, her heart was so full of warm love that promotes growth and develops beauty." Young Ellen "grew in spirit and body," and "in her young womanhood, she felt the urge to seek greater opportunities than the town of Tiverton afforded."[29] She became employed as a shop girl at a store in London, where she met the young shoemaker John Rex Winder.

Winder, finding Miss Walters "an attractive and compassionate girl,"[30] desired to see her socially. So "neatly dressed and derby-hatted John R. went calling on" Ellen Walters, "to whom he had become attracted."[31] Not long after both "were attracted to each other," they "decided to travel life's journey together."[32] The wedding took place in St. Clements Church, London on November

24, 1845, about three years after John R. Winder had begun his employment in the West End shoe store.

The Joys and Sorrows of Parenthood

The newlywed couple "obtained a flat in the bustling city,"[33] and although "their first home was small," it was "filled with love and happiness."[34] Several months into their marriage, the young couple was thrilled to learn that the new Mrs. Winder was expecting. "The wonderful thrill of motherhood filled her soul," granddaughter Adelaide Eldredge Hardy wrote of her Grandmother Winder:

> Oh, the joys of those days of preparation! Experience had provided no intruding memories to intimidate her soaring hopes, anticipations and visionings of her first-born. This new world, coming nearer, and nearer, seemed bathed in perpetual sunshine. While she sewed the little garments, the imagined picture of her little loved one, made her clasp them close to her. Those were sacred plans Ellen was making those days. New responsibilities were being visualized, new joys anticipated, new ambitions were begun for this greater life.
>
> The days of expectation were fulfilled, January 31, 1847, and the little treasure of warm, living flesh breathed at her side. It is difficult to describe the supreme joy of a mother's soul as she presses her newborn babe close to her.[35]

The Winders were "overjoyed" with their new daughter, Ellen Sophia Winder, who was named for both her mother and grandmother.[36] "Baby Ellen was an immense source of joy for both of her parents and she grew into a beautiful child."[37] At this time "John R. was still employed at the shoe store and the family was contented and happy."[38]

As part of the growing middle class of Victorian London, the young Winder family would have been influenced by the conservative values that swept the city at that time. "Victorian London," it is said, "was shaped by the growing power of the bourgeoisie, the queen's personal moral stance, and the perceived moral responsibilities of managing an empire."[39] The young couple espoused the Victorian values of morality, integrity, and frugality, which were easily incorporated with the gentleman manners with which Winder was brought up. "The racy London of the preceding three centuries moved underground," as Victorian values set in on the capital, especially in classy neighborhoods like the West End.[40]

After a brief fourteen months with their new daughter, the Winders were crushed when baby Ellen died "most unexpectedly" on March 14, 1848.[41] "It was a great disappointment to mother Ellen. However, she trusted, and bore her trial as became her noble soul, in meekness and humility."[42]

Soon after the tragic death of baby Ellen in the spring of 1848, a "wealthy boot and shoe manufacturer"[43] arrived in London from Liverpool. Mr. Collinson "came to the store in search of a man to take charge of his establishment in Liverpool."[44] Apparently impressed with Winder, Collinson gave "a flattering offer to John to take over the management of a boot and shoe store in Liverpool."[45] Although a "similar business"[46] to the West End Shoe and Grocery Store, Collinson's establishment up north was a much larger one,[47] and the offer for a "respectable position with [this] leather firm,"[48] was "an enticing one and John R. was quick to accept it."[49]

Such a big decision required consultation with his still-grieving wife, however. "There was a spot in a London cemetery that Ellen was loathe to leave, but an apparent opportunity of advancement was before them and the inherent urge within Ellen to live more to do more and to be more, impelled her to accept."[50] So in the summer of 1848, John Rex and Ellen Walters Winder, who was again with child, moved northward to that great port city of the Irish Sea—Liverpool. Winder had spent about seven years in the metropolis of London, years that had given him a practical vocation and a dedicated companion; but when he "filled his engagement"[51] in "that rumbustious, cosmopolitan city"[52] on the banks of the Mersey, he could scarcely have imagined how his life's path would quickly change. He would soon be encountering the Mormons in Liverpool.

4

Caught in the Gospel Net: Encountering the Mormons in Liverpool, 1848-1852

"Convinced of the truth"

"Liverpool is by English standards a modern city—which is to say Victorian—her sprawl ungoverned by the medieval focal points of church, castle, ford, or market. It just happened. And it happened all at once."[1]

Liverpool really began to "happen" in the 1840's when hundreds of thousands of Irish refugees fleeing the potato famine arrived. The year before John R. Winder and his wife arrived, 300,000 Irish had landed in the port city—more than the city's native population.[2] The cosmopolitan port spreads along the Mersey's north shore with her seven miles of noble docks and warehouses, which helped the city serve as the great traffic center of Queen Victoria's global empire. Liverpudlians, as they are called, were consequently at the crossroads of a myriad of cultures, manufactured goods, agricultural products, and new ideas.

The Latter-day Saints Come to Liverpool

One of the new ideas to flow into Liverpool in the mid-nineteenth century was the teachings of an American named Joseph Smith. Just seven years after Smith organized The Church of Jesus Christ of Latter-day Saints in Fayette, New York, the first missionaries of the new faith had arrived in Great Britain, via the great port city of Liverpool. Joseph Smith claimed to be a prophet called to restore the ancient gospel of Jesus Christ on the earth. His bold message of a loving, anthropomorphic Father in Heaven who again communicated with mankind proved popular to thousands in the British Isles.

Elders Heber C. Kimball and Orson Hyde first arrived in Liverpool in July of 1839, but soon moved on to neighboring locales to preach, such as Preston, where the first baptisms took place. In January, 1840 Liverpudlians heard their first sermons by the Latter-day Saints when Elder John Taylor began to preach there. Elder Brigham Young and other LDS apostles soon joined Taylor in Liverpool.

The Church continued to gain converts in the 1840's, and in January of 1841 the Latter-day Saints' "other testament" of scripture, the Book of Mormon, was published for the first time abroad in Liverpool.[3] In 1842 (the year after most of the Twelve left for home) the mission office moved from Manchester to Liverpool. "In the 1840s conditions had been ripe for the introduction of the restored gospel into England,"[4] and Liverpool was at the heart of this unprecedented movement. By 1848, when the Winders arrived in Liverpool, there were 18,000 Latter-day Saints in the British Isles.[5]

Although "new religions, such as the Latter-day Saints, typically took root first among the working classes in the cities,"[6] the Mormons, as they were commonly called, also had "some wealthy gentlemen newly converted to the faith," including Mr. Collinson, the owner of the boot and shoe establishment where John R. Winder had just taken up his position as manager.[7] It should therefore come as no surprise that Winder first encountered the Church while being employed by one of their members.

The Conversion Miracle of John R. Winder

It has been written of John R. Winder that when he first arrived in Liverpool that "so far, his life had followed the usual line of the majority of Englishmen." However, soon after arriving, "the whole trend of his character and his life was changed."[8] One morning "shortly after their arrival,"[9] a most thrilling event came into the Winders' lives, one John R. recognized as very "singular" and as "a manifestation of the overruling providence of God."[10] It was his chance encounter with the Latter-day Saints, "and the manner in which it came to his notice was not only unique," reports Orson F. Whitney, "but serves to illustrate how an important result may spring from a seemingly insignificant cause. His whole career hinged on what most men would call an accident, but which he himself recognized as an instance of the over-ruling providence of God."[11]

Winder, himself, related the incident: "The occasion of my conversion to the new faith was somewhat peculiar. One day in July, 1848, while in the store, I chanced to stoop and pick from the floor a small bit of paper, a fragment of a torn-up letter, on which were the words 'Latter-day Saints.'"[12] His granddaughter, Helen Midgley Ross, would later note that the letter had been "an announcement of a meeting of The Church of Jesus Christ of Latter-day Saints."[13] Winder later added the detail that someone had "torn up" the letter "into very small fragments and thrown it on the floor." He was "impressed to pick up a small piece of it, and on that piece of paper were the words, 'Latter-day Saint.'" He "looked at it and wondered what it meant." "I never had heard of Latter-day Saints," Winder recalled, "or Mormons, or Joseph Smith, or anything of the kind."[14]

"I inquired of one of the clerks what it meant," Winder continues, "as I had never seen or heard the name before."[15] He noted that "the man who was in the desk . . . happened to be a Latter-day Saint," like their employer, Collinson.[16]

The Mormons in Liverpool at the time were "very active in the proselyting program," and for over a year even lay members, like the clerk in the store, were taught Orson Spencer's "system for gaining converts." As president of the European Mission, Elder Spencer had developed "an invitation system which was geared to interest people initially and [then] invited them to a meeting where they learned more of the LDS Church. The invitation listed several specific doctrines of the Church and was geared to arrest the curiosity of an individual."[17]

The clerk, apparently well instructed in Elder Spencer's invitation system, "replied that there was a religious sect in America whose members called themselves Latter-day Saints, though they were commonly known as 'Mormons'; that they had a prophet named Joseph Smith, and that some of them held regular meetings in the Music Hall, Bold Street, Liverpool."[18] Granddaughter Adalaide Eldredge Hardy reported that Winder "felt an urge to learn about the message of the Latter Day Saints."[19] The curiosity designed to attract investigators to their meetings now gnawed at John R. Winder, and "he was prompted to attend the meeting."[20]

"I was so impressed with what I heard, and so anxious to learn more concerning these people," Winder reports, "that I went to their meeting, creeping up a back stairs and peeping through the banisters to get a glimpse of the inside."[21] So, "the young shoe clerk crept up the creaky back stairs of the Music Hall on Bold Street," and "peered through the balustrude as he neared the top and saw a crowd seated in the hall listening

This illustration was featured in the Church News section of the Deseret News on March 10, 1962. It accompanied an article in their "LDS Leaders of Prominence" series entitled "From Shoe Clerk to Presidency—John R. Winder." It was while peering through the banister during Orson Spencer's sermon that John R. Winder first heard the Gospel message.

to a speaker."[22] During the meeting he sat on the top step of the flight of stairs and heard the missionaries bear their testimonies and sing hymns.[23]

Winder recalled that the "congregation was addressed by a speaker whom I afterwards learned to be Elder Orson Spencer of Salt Lake City."[24] Since late January, 1847 when he arrived in Liverpool, Orson Spencer had served ably in his position as President of the European Mission. En route to his assignment in England a letter had reached the British Isles reporting that he had died, and the January 1, 1847 issue of the *Millennial Star* erroneously declared that "ELDER ORSON SPENCER IS NUMBERED WITH THE DEAD!!!" However, the February 1 issue carried the news that the new mission president was not only "very much alive," but also humorously noted that "he was one of a select few who were able to read their own obituary and death notice while still alive." As mission president, Spencer "was the chief representative of the Church and he kept busy traveling to different areas of the British Isles," often speaking to the Saints, missionaries, and investigators of the Church, as he was this summer night in the Music Hall.[25]

John R. reported that Elder Spencer "was speaking on the first principles of the Gospel—faith, repentance, baptism by immersion and the laying on of hands for the gift of the Holy Ghost."[26] Spencer's teachings were "full of reason and logic involving the Mormon gospel," and was not only a defense for the faith, but his teachings "were also an offense for Mormonism." His biographer noted that "Mr. Spencer was an intellect who appealed to intellectuals. His approach was aimed at those of his own caliber. He sought the educated and the learned for he knew these would help to build the LDS Church."[27] It is therefore not surprising that a logical and thoughtful presentation of the basic tenets of the restored gospel made a powerful impression on young John R. Winder. "I thought he must know that I was there," John declared, "for every word fitted my case and seemed meant especially for me."[28] At that meeting, "his mind and heart were touched by the Spirit and he knew he had heard the truth."[29]

The impact of that first meeting made an indelible impression on the heart of the young shoe clerk. "There he heard principles that entered his soul," principles which remained and were "brought forth to the glory of God."[30] Indeed it was amazing, for "the speaker hardly could have known John was there, yet he seemed to be speaking directly to John."[31] It would change him for the rest of his life.

At the opening of the Church's General Conference in October of 1909, then-President Winder reflected on the meeting in the Music Hall that was half a century and half a world away:

> As I looked over this congregation this morning, I thought of the time when I first heard the Gospel in a far off land, from an elder of the Church of Jesus Christ of Latter-day Saints. I was convinced of the truth when I heard it, and I knew that Joseph Smith was a prophet of God. I am thankful to say, this morning, that faith has grown and increased with me as the years have passed along;

and every day I live I see new evidences of the truth of this work. I testify to you, my brethren and sisters, that I know that Joseph Smith is a prophet of God. I am thankful that this testimony has never left me since I first heard the Gospel more than sixty years ago.[32]

One granddaughter wrote that because he "liked what he heard," after the momentous meeting on Bold Street, John R. Winder "took the message home to his wife."[33] Helen Midgley Ross said he "went home and told Grandmother about the meeting and although she was not eager to go, they went back time and again and Grandmother was convinced of the truth of the gospel."[34]

He commenced to study[35] and "at once began to investigate the principles."[36] Besides the Book of Mormon, Winder probably also studied some of the many doctrinal tracts being published at the time by the mission president. "The most famous of the religious tracts published by Spencer was published in Liverpool under the title *Spencer's Letters*. The series of 14 letters appeared in 1848."[37] Winder consequently "went from one stage of conviction to another."[38] And "as the wonderful light burst upon him, he recalled the day when as a small boy he had received the great manifestation of God's love. He felt the same sweet Spirit now." It was a testimony that would remain "with him for the rest of his life."[39] As for the pregnant Mrs. Winder, "Ellen was equally enthusiastic and the couple desired to be baptized."[40]

After having thoroughly investigated the principles taught, and acquiring conviction of their truth, twenty-six-year-old John R. Winder was baptized into the Church, September 20, 1848, by Elder Thomas D. Brown.[41] "By that time," Winder later remarked, "I was a husband and father."[42] In fact, the ordinance took place the day after the birth of their second child and oldest son, John Rex Winder Jr. "For nearly seventy-five years he bore this name with unusual pride," reported Junior's niece. He would not pass on until 1923.[43] After the new mother recovered from the trauma of giving birth, Ellen Walters Winder was baptized on October 15, 1848, by Elder Orson Pratt, of the Quorum of the Twelve Apostles.[44] A new chapter in their lives had begun, and later as a member of the First Presidency of his new-found faith, Winder would declare: "Every day of my life I see new evidences of the truth of the everlasting Gospel, and of the mission of the Prophet Joseph Smith."[45] Nearing his eightieth birthday, President Winder said in reflection of those many productive years, "All that I am I owe to 'Mormonism.' The blessings of the Lord have followed me all the days of my life, and to Him I give the glory for what may have been accomplished through my humble endeavors."[46]

Actively Embracing His New Faith

It was said that "John R. grasped the new found religion with great zeal and determination."[47] This energy and devotion was greatly needed in the rapidly growing branch in Liverpool. In fact, membership had exploded all throughout

England, and by 1850, three-fifths of the English saints had been baptized, like the Winders, within the past three years. In the decades of the 1840's in Britain alone, 42,316 souls embraced Mormonism, showing a 748% increase in membership there in just ten years. This created "a situation much like the one the Church faces in South America today."[48] A plethora of new converts had to learn the basic doctrines and procedures of their new-found faith, and leaders to help in this effort were zealously sought after. Soon after his baptism, John R. was chosen to be the branch clerk in the burgeoning Liverpool Branch and later served as a counselor in the branch presidency.[49]

On January 9, 1850, an Elder Harvey baptized John R.'s cousin Frederick Winder, who had lived in Lambeth with John R.'s parents, Richard and Sophia. It is not known whether John R. had informed his family in Lambeth of his new faith and Frederick sought out the Mormons, if John R. sent missionaries to visit them, or if it is merely a coincidence that this cousin joined the Church just a year and a half after John R. Winder and his wife. When 65-year-old Frederick Winder died in 1876 the *Millennial Star* reported that "Elder Winder was for many years President of the Lambeth Branch, and very faithful in that position. The Lambeth Saints will miss a true friend in Brother Winder."[50] However, evidently none of his seven children ever joined the Church.

In 1850 John R. and Ellen Winder were expecting again, and on June 27 of that year their second son was born. He was named Alma Winder, after the great prophet whose history and words are recorded in the Book of Mormon. "Alma remained with them one brief year," his niece later reported. "Another treasure was taken from them, heaven-ward, to lure their souls upward and onward,"[51] she wrote. But despite little Alma's tragic death on July 6, 1851, it "was a trifle easier for his parents to bear, armed with the truths of the Gospel in its promise of eternal family relationships."[52]

While on a mission to France in 1849-50, Elder John Taylor was urged in a letter by President Brigham Young "to get ideas and machinery if necessary to send to 'Deseret' to further and build up her industries." In France, Elder Taylor became convinced that the sugar beet industry could bring some manufacturing and growth to the Great Basin. The Deseret Manufacturing Company was formed and would be the organization to bring sugar production to Utah, later establishing its plants in what became known as the Sugar House district of Salt Lake City. However, to get this organization off and running, John Taylor, then age 41, was required to assemble a large amount of capital. He consequently went on a special mission to England to procure the equivalent of $60,000 among some wealthy gentlemen newly converted to the faith.[53]

In England in 1850, Elder Taylor was successful in finding enthusiastic supporters. Captain Russell, a wealthy ship builder and recent convert of Scotland and Mr. John W. Coward, a salt dealer in Liverpool and also a recent convert, both helped with the investment. The third contributor was "Mr. Collinson, a wealthy boot and shoe manufacturer in Liverpool, and for whom John R. Winder, later to become so prominent in the church—no less a member of its presiding bishopric, and later a member of its first presidency—was then at work."[54]

John Taylor, who would later succeed Brigham Young to become the third president of the LDS Church, first became acquainted with John R. Winder that year in Liverpool. They would become life-long friends, and later as president of the Church John Taylor would call Winder to the ranks of the general authorities with a call to the Presiding Bishopric. In a letter to the family of the late President John Taylor, written on Halloween 1902, Winder recalled that "from the time President Taylor visited my home in Liverpool in the year 1850 until the day of his death, he was a friend to me, and I always took pleasure in doing him honor."[55]

Later in 1850, Brother Winder was called to serve in a post in the Liverpool Conference. A dozen or so "conferences" were organized throughout Britain, and were important units of organization that oversaw the progress of the Church in the handful of branches that it presided over. In February of 1853, the presidency of the Liverpool Conference commended then Elder Winder for his "faithfulness and integrity in the discharge of [his] duties as Secretary of the Liverpool Conference for the space of near three years, in addition to your other important responsibilities in connection with the Church."[56] In addition to serving as secretary of the Liverpool Conference, Winder also "served as a local missionary visiting several branches including Hemel Hempstead."[57]

It was an important time to assist in one of England's most dynamic conferences, Liverpool. Its membership was continuously changing as new converts joined their ranks, or as saints from around Great Britain came to the area in preparation for embarking on their voyage to America. It was consequently a very important conference, with apparently some very spirit-filled meetings. One Elder Fullmer attended a Wednesday night meeting in the Liverpool Branch in the early 1850's, where he reported: "We had a fine time. Speaking in tongues and interpretations."[58]

In 1850, the LDS Church claimed a membership of 30,747. This year was an impressive milestone, for at that point there were more members of the Church in Britain than in all of North America![59] In that year, Elder Franklin D. Richards of the Quorum of the Twelve began his tenure as president of the European Mission, with headquarters still in Liverpool. His predecessor, President Orson Pratt, recognized that the English saints were "scattered from one end of the land to the other, and unless there is a united exertion on the part of the officers of the Church, there cannot be maintained that union necessary to the enjoyment of the blessings of the Kingdom of God."

It therefore became a priority of President Richards for the Saints to be provided with adequate literature in which to learn their new religion, "the order of the Church, and the duties of the several offices thereof." Regarding the Book of Mormon and the book of Doctrine and Covenants, President Richards felt that it was "quite inexcusable for the Saints to remain ignorant of their precious contents."[60] Consequently, during the 1850's Liverpool emerged as the leading book supply depot for LDS literature in the world.

In 1851, President Richards published in the Liverpool office a pamphlet that eventually became one of the four standard works of the Church—the Pearl of Great Price. "The members of the Church immediately recognized President Richard's work as a major contribution to their literature."[61] John R. and Ellen Winder would have been among those privileged Saints to be the first in the world to pour over that sacred collection of inspired writings.

The young Winder family was progressing both spiritually and socially in the Liverpool Branch. John R. had experienced his first church leadership roles and began to gain a greater understanding of how the Church operated. The things learned in these humble experiences and by being "active in Church work"[62] in Liverpool would serve him well in a lifetime full of service in church government. Here he also enlarged his role as a father. On July 7, 1852, Ellen gave birth to twin girls, who were named Mary and Martha after John R. Winder's grandmother Collins and her twin sister.

The years as a new convert were indeed a pivotal time in John R. Winder's ambitious life, for he found that his new found faith was not only a way to religious fulfillment, but he began to visualize a fresh start in America, where he could develop a life of lasting contributions. "The Church in the British Isles had little sense of permanence," wrote Richard Jensen, "for hearts were set on a home across the ocean."[63] Upon visiting the Saints in England, George Halliday must have encountered many who were like the Winders, for he said that "they feel that this is not their home, and their eyes and expectations are westward."[64] Soon enough it was time for the young Winder family to prepare to leave the United Kingdom and embark on their journey to a new kingdom, a Kingdom of God in the mountains and deserts of the American West.

5

Journey to a New Kingdom: The Winder Family Comes to America, 1853

"Moving to the gathering place"

The concept of the gathering shaped the course of Church history in Britain for more than a century. For decades missionaries declared it in the same breath that announced the dispensation of the fullness of times. It aroused enthusiasm and controversy, swelled congregations, and then depleted them. The emigration of approximately 65,000 saints from the British Isles provided great strength to

John R. and Ellen Walters Winder as sketched by Frederick Hawkins Piercy in 1853. Piercy traveled with the Saints from Liverpool to Salt Lake that year and made many historic illustrations along his route. Winder was 31 years old when he brought his young family to America.

the establishment of the Church in Nauvoo, and later in Salt Lake City and the American West.[1]

Bidding Farewell to Mother England

Emigration to the United States to help build the main body of the Church was the recommended pattern for members during the first century of the Church in the British Isles. From 1847 to 1869, more than 32,000 British converts to the Church left their homelands for a new life in pioneer America.[2] It has been said that "the very forces that had paved the way for the Church's growth in England now opened the door to its decline." Many of the new converts were "attracted to the gospel at least partly by the vision of a better life in 'The Valley', and these people responded by the thousand to the invitation to 'gather to Zion'. . . . Hence during the first half-century of its existence in Great Britain, the Church served partly as an agency for recruiting builders for the Zion in America. As converts came in one door, a similar number of emigrants went out another."[3] Latter-day Saint converts sought to "flee the impending woes of a sinful world by gathering 'home to Zion,'" and did so with "millennial fervor."[4]

As the converts were encouraged to emigrate, the leaders often spoke of "helping to build temples and of the blessings to be received therein."[5] In the case of Elder John Rex Winder the leaders of the Liverpool Conference specifically told him that he was to go to Zion to help "build up Cities and Temples to the name of the Most High God."[6] Therefore, not only did "a great desire to live with the Saints in Zion possess all early converts to the Church," but for the Winder family, "the spirit of gathering seemed a very compelling force," and "John and Ellen did not escape it." Very shortly after their baptisms it could be said that preparing to emigrate "was now the paramount purpose in their lives."[7]

Although they realized it would take a small fortune to travel half-way around the globe, "John and Ellen were determined to leave England and join the body of Church members in far off Salt Lake City as soon as they had enough money to make the journey."[8] Winder later recalled, "I obeyed the Gospel, and I began to prepare for moving to the gathering place."[9]

Adalaide Hardy also reported that "In God's appointed way, success follows righteousness and sincere desire," and that "shortly after the birth of their twins, Martha and Mary, Ellen's father passed on. His estate was distributed and Ellen appropriated her portion to the fulfilling their desire to emigrate to America."[10] The couple apparently wasted no time in booking their passage to America. "As soon as I could conveniently I came here,"[11] John R. later remarked.

Despite their desire to start a new life in America, "it was with mixed emotions" that the Winders left their Mother England, with four-year-old John R. Winder Jr., the four-month-old twins, and a 16-year-old Irish girl by the name of Mary Shanks (who the Winders had reared and cared for as if she were their own).[12] Realizing what a task it would be for such a young family to cross an ocean and a vast continent, granddaughter Helen Midgley Ross mentioned that "Grandmother was not eager to leave."[13] In fact, in many ways the Winders were naturally a bit reluctant to leave their beautiful homeland. It was the beginning of the Victorian era and their lifestyle had been civilized and sedate. Nonetheless, their faith was strong and they were anxious to fulfill the counsel of the brethren to "head for Church headquarters to be strengthened and fortified with the larger group of saints."[14]

John and Ellen Winder planned to board their ship and sail out of Liverpool harbor in February of 1853. However, before the couple could slip away to begin their new life in America, many grateful souls in the Liverpool Conference put together a heartfelt "Testimonial" and honored the family with its presentation. The grand document, penned in superb handwriting on a magnificent sheet of parchment, reads as follows:

> Testimonial presented to ELDER JOHN REX WINDER
> Secretary of the Liverpool Conference of the
>   Church of Jesus Christ of Latter-day Saints
> by the Saints of the said Conference
> on his departure for Great Salt Lake City N.A.
>
> Beloved Brother John R. Winder,
> As you with your esteemed Lady and intaisting (?) little ones, are about to bid farewell to your friends, acquaintances, and native land, in obedience to the great command of this last Dispensation to gather to the land of Joseph, that you may assist to build up Cities and Temples to the name of the Most High God, that His Saints may learn His ways more perfectly and be united in still more sacred and enduring covenants to Him and to each other, we, the Saints of the Liverpool Conference feel that we cannot bid you adieu without presenting you with a heavy though humble Testimonial of our love and esteem towards you.
>   Your faithfulness and integrity in the discharge of your duties as Secretary of the Liverpool Conference for the space of near three years, in addition to your other important responsibilities in connection with the Church, your unwavering adherence to the counsels of those who were set over you in the Lord, and your unwavering diligence in assisting by way means in your power to advance the interests of the Kingdom of God and to promote the welfare of your Brethren and Sisters; are well worthy of all emulation, and entitle you to the highest confidence and esteem. And if your faithfulness in the discharge of your public duties have secured our confidence and esteem, your constant humility, unwavering kindness, and uniform cheerfulness of deportment in your private and social capacity, have won the Tribute of our love and affection.

With sentiments of love and high consideration we now say Farewell! Dear Brother Winder . . May the God of Israel protect you in your journey yea the rolling billows of the mighty deep, and the flowing waters and vast prairies of the land of Zion to the home of the Saints—the valleys of the mountains of Ephraim: may you become a pillar in the Temple of the Lord, to go no more out for ever, and may the blessings of Abraham, Isaac, and Jacob, be sealed upon your head in the name of Jesus Christ, Amen.

As is a heart that kindly serves another,
So even our gratitude is sweet, we deem,
Then from a people who hail thee as Brother,
Receive a parting tribute of esteem,

Thou hast been with us, and hast done thy part
To prosper Zion's cause, and all have known
That thou hast wrought this blessing to impart,
Thy Brethren's need while careless of thine own.

We say farewell! and saintisbly we pray
That God will speed thy cause over seas and plains,
And when we meet thee in a happier day,
We hope to greet thee in more worthy strains.

Signed in behalf of the Liverpool Conference,
C. H. Wallace (?) Pastor of the Manchester, Liverpool,
    and Preston Conferences
A. F. McDonald President of the Liverpool Conference
 Traveling Elder in duty
John Jacques Elder
Liverpool February 1853[15]

It seems that even as a young man and newer member of the Church, John R. Winder had already begun to develop some of his talents and the attributes that would mark his entire life. These virtues would include his faithfulness, integrity, obedience, humility, and diligence in carrying out assignments. Such enthusiasm for the work and faith and trust in God would be essential characteristics for him to survive the "hard trip on shipboard."[16] Little did he or Ellen know that their trip across the ocean, would be "one filled with hardship and horror."[17]

The Voyage Across the Atlantic

By the time the Winders set sail aboard the sailing packet *Elvira Owen* in 1853 the Church had more than a decade of experience in organizing emigrant groups and in dealing with shipping firms and provision merchants. Mission leaders were thus able to offer "relatively healthy and efficient arrangements for transporting the greatest possible number of people across the Atlantic at low cost."[18] They would be emigrating during the peak period of Mormon British immigration. Between 1851 and the end of the decade, nearly 13,000 members of the Church would emigrate to the United States.[19]

The *Elvira Owen* was specifically chartered to carry LDS immigrants from the Liverpool area to New Orleans.[20] Elder Joseph W. Young, who had presided over the Preston Conference of the Church in England, was placed in charge of the 345 Saints on board. Among the passengers was Elder Jonathan Midgley, who had presided over the Manchester Conference.[21] Well in advance of the departure date, Church leaders had collected deposits to reserve places on this particular vessel. Church agents had also negotiated relatively inexpensive group fares for passage. Where necessary, mission personnel made arrangements for provisions and for cookware and eating utensils. In hectic last-minute efforts they helped hundreds of passengers board the ship and get under way. Mormon emigrants were noted for their heavy luggage, having been encouraged to take tools and equipment with them, and some captains were heard to complain that their ships were an inch lower in the water than usual.[22]

The Mormon ships were always more orderly than most other immigrant vessels, and many who observed Mormon emigration parties made positive observations. When the novelist Charles Dickens visited a ship similar to the *Elvira Owen*, he noted:

> I . . . had come aboard this Emigrant Ship to see what eight hundred Latter-day Saints were like. . . Nobody is in an ill-temper, nobody is the worse for drink, nobody swears an oath or uses a coarse word, nobody appears depressed, nobody is weeping, and down upon the deck in every corner where it is possible to find a few square feet to kneel, crouch or lie in, people, in every suitable attitude for writing, are writing letters. Now I have seen emigrants ships before this day in June. And these people are strikingly different from all other people in like circumstances whom I have ever said, and I wonder aloud, 'What would a stranger suppose these emigrants to be!'. . . I should have said they were in their degree, the pick and flower of England.[23]

The *Elvira Owen* that the Winders sailed on weighed 874 tons, and was 168 feet long, 34 feet wide, and 17 feet deep. The ship was relatively new when she set sail from the Mersey Docks in Liverpool on February 15, 1853. She was just built the year prior by R. Morse & Sons at Bath, Maine, on the other side of the Atlantic. *Elvira Owen* was "full-rigged with a square stern, no galleries, two decks, and a billet head."[24]

Ships leaving Liverpool "were quickly towed down the Mersey, past the Rock Lighthouse and the Fort at the mouth." When the right wind hit, the great white sails would unfurl until filled and the ship would set out to sea. As one passenger leaving Liverpool for Zion in February 1853 later wrote, watching Mother England fade from sight was quite an emotional moment. One can imagine the Winders having similar feelings as they bid farewell to Island Britannia:

> Thoughts crowded my brain; of course I thought of old England. It is impossible to leave the land of one's birth without regret, or to leave one's kindred and friends, even for a few months, without a sigh. I wondered whether I should ever see them again, or if my ears would ever again be greeted with gentle words of affection in fond tones from their loving lips. I thought of the perils of the sea—tempest, fire, and disease; the dangers in strange cities, and risks among treacherous Indians; but again reflected and comforted myself with the assurance that it was childish and useless to fear, and that men died not by accident, that none fell without God's notice! I felt it was a worthy enterprise, and that the greater the difficulties the greater would be the honour if they were surmounted. Others had safely traveled over the same road, then why should not I?[25]

Crossing the Atlantic was particularly miserable during winter time, for not only is the North Atlantic by far the most dangerous of oceans, but given to violent mood swings of weather, a winter crossing is a particularly miserable experience. One family historian would later remark that the crossing of the *Elvira Owen* in February of 1853 "bore absolutely no resemblance to a pleasure cruise."[26] Soon after the ship left port, one woman reported that "the vessel pitched and tossed on the stormy sea."[27]

To add to the misery of the seasickness that must have been felt by all in the storm, John R. Winder contracted smallpox ten days into the voyage and fell critically ill. He described the experience in these words:

> It was discovered that smallpox was on board, a child infected with the malady being among the ship's passengers and in the apartment next to mine. I was the first to discover it, and one of the first among five who came down with the disease, and had to be quarantined in a little house built on deck for that purpose. This was a trying time both to me and my wife, who was left without my assistance to care for her twin babies, which was no small task on shipboard. To add to our anxiety, one of the patients, lying next to me, a young brother named William Jones, died a few days later, about nine o'clock in the evening, and soon the sailors came and took the body out and cast it into the sea. I heard them say, 'We will have him next,' meaning me, but I had faith that I would recover and get to Zion, and in due time my faith was confirmed. There was but one death during the voyage.[28]

John R. "prayed earnestly that his life would be spared and that he would be able to raise his family in the light of the Gospel in the Valley of the Mountains."[29] This abiding faith carried him through many dangers, for decades later in Salt Lake City, Winder declared, "Several times I have been snatched, as it were, from death by the hand of the Lord. I know this as well as I stand here."[30]

On a crowded ship in the middle of the stormy North Atlantic in the dead of winter, it would have been quite a task for Ellen to help keep the family happy and totally care for feisty four-year-old John R. Jr., the four-month-old infant twins, and the "frail Mary Shanks who was unable to render much assistance." [31] The little Irish girl whom the Winders had informally adopted would unfortunately remain ill throughout the journey.[32] However, "undaunted, Ellen met her trials in fearless faith and won."

Most of those on the ship expected that John would die, but he recovered and lived many active and useful years. "John was to experience a miraculous recovery,"[33] and it is said that he "gradually regained his health by the time the ship reached New Orleans,"[34] landing in America "sound and well."[35] Nonetheless, he was "left in a weakened condition for several months."[36]

Men traveling with the group, usually returning missionaries, were appointed as presidencies for the ship and were responsible for the conduct and morale of the passengers and for holding religious services. Generally, the daily routine involved prayer, washing the decks, cooperative cooking arrangements, and special meetings to discuss problems that arose.[37] According to the British Parliament's Passengers' Act of 1842, all ships leaving the United Kingdom were required to carry three quarts of fresh water per passenger per day and seven pounds of bread, biscuits, flour, oatmeal, or rice for each passenger each week.[38] Church agents worked hard so that, meager as they still were, "Mormon arrangements exceeded those mandated by the Passenger's Act."[39]

Because the Saints traveled as a Church family under priesthood leadership—and with the assistance of an experienced and well-organized system— LDS emigration impressed nonmember observers as orderly and civilized compared with the tumult generally surrounding emigrant ships. As Charles Dickens observed, the whole process seemed divinely inspired: "Some remarkable influence had produced a remarkable result," he wrote.[40] The organization by the Church was important because officers and crew were preoccupied with their work of sailing the ship, and could concern themselves little with the emigrants' welfare.[41]

One LDS passenger, Sarah Birch Waters of Kent County, reported some details of the voyage: "There were three deaths, one marriage, and one or two births during the voyage. . . . The name of the captain was Owen. His wife's name was Elvira, so the ship was called the Elvira Owen."[42] Captain Owen, a quarter-owner of the ship, was especially kind to the passengers—particularly the sick. In appreciation for his "fatherly conduct to all," the Saints presented him with a memorial at the end of their voyage.[43]

The voyage was not entirely gloomy, as there certainly were good days as well as bad. "We left winter behind us," it was said, "as we went south we were greeted by the most delicious warmth and sunshine." Sometimes on Mormon immigrant ships, even in February and March, "merry groups assembled on the deck, and, sitting in the sunshine, told stories, sang songs, and cracked jokes by the hour together, and generally with the propriety most unexceptionable."[44] Passengers also enjoyed games such as chess, as well as beautiful sunsets. "The most unimpressible must have been affected by the glorious rising and setting of the sun, by the beauty and vastness of the ocean, and by the power of the winds."[45]

After just a few weeks out from Liverpool, the ship cruised through the turquoise waters of the Gulf of Mexico where it was reported that "the weather was pleasant." The day that the emigrants first saw land was "an exciting time." The deep green coast of Haiti was the first to greet them, and later they would sail by Cuba, the largest of all Caribbean islands, and in 1853 the principal colony of Spain.[46]

The ship made good time, especially through the Gulf of Mexico. In fact, the crossing of the *Elvira Owen* that winter was "the quickest trip," the captain said, "on record for a ship of that kind."[47] In the words of LDS passenger John V. Adams of North Hamptonshire, the *Elvira Owen* "safely arrived in New Orleans after a pleasant voyage of six weeks and three days."[48] They had traveled nearly 5000 miles since leaving Liverpool. Upon arriving, Captain Charles Owen brought his square-rigger to the bar at the mouth of the Mississippi. For those Saints who reached the mouth of the Mississippi, their first American experience was probably that of being dragged by a steamboat over the sandbar and then towed a hundred miles to New Orleans.[49] Being towed up to New Orleans usually took four days, and the passengers would have been treated to a curious scene of muddy swamps and rushes, and upon the low banks both plantations and the planters' large houses with their broad verandas.[50] After a delay of several days off New Orleans the emigrants landed on 31 March. Before the Mormon immigrants disembarked, they would receive instructions about the next leg of their journey and about exchanging their British pounds for American dollars.[51]

Landing in New Orleans

It must have been exhilarating for John and Ellen and the four children traveling with them to walk down the creaky gang plank and, for the first time in over six weeks, to set their boots on solid ground. Amidst the excitement of sailors, immigrants, street vendors and money changers on the bustling docks of the largest port in the South, a few American flags might have been waving in the salty sea air. "I am not a native of this land of liberty," Winder later declared, "though I have always been a lover of freedom and an ardent admirer of American institutions. For the sake of these, and above all for the Gospel of Jesus Christ—'the perfect law of liberty'—I left my native land and came to this country."[52] They had now finally made it to the land of the stars and stripes. The Winders had come to America!

The America the Winders entered in 1853 was a land teaming with adventure and opportunity. The early 1850's, however, were a "deceptively peaceful eye of a great national hurricane" in regards to the great slavery debate that would pit brother against brother in civil war less than a decade later. Henry Clay and the Congress had recently passed the Compromise of 1850—a "band-aid" solution that merely postponed a final resolution to the issue of slavery, but one that created "a time of apparent tranquillity," nonetheless. However, the year before the Winders arrived, 1852, Harriet Beecher Stowe shook the conscience of millions with *Uncle Tom's Cabin*, demonstrating that the nation's mind was never too far away from the divisive slavery issue.

Franklin Pierce had been sworn in just weeks prior as America's fourteenth president. In his inauguration, the Democrat from New Hampshire "proclaimed an era of peace and prosperity."[53] The country had just defeated Mexico and acquired vast new territories in the west, and thousands were following trails toward the setting sun in search of fertile soil in Oregon and gold in the nation's newest state—California. Antebellum America was alive with industry, commerce, and adventure, and nowhere did it bustle like it did along the great highway of the nation—the mighty Mississippi.

As for the vessel that brought them there, the fate of the *Elvira Owen* remains unknown. Its last registration in 1886 stated "sold foreign years ago."[54]

Since 1842, British Mormon migration had crossed to New Orleans because it was cheaper and easier to travel up the Mississippi River by boat to reach trail heads heading west. When John R. Winder and his family arrived in the United States in 1853 there was no federal restriction on immigration. Consequently, the only restriction upon entrance into the country was a head tax of $2 enacted by the Louisiana legislature upon passengers coming from foreign ports. The proceeds supported the charity hospital of the City of New Orleans. Nonetheless, for the Winders and their fellow Mormon migrants, entrance into the United States was relatively inexpensive and quite simple.[55]

"The Metropolis of the South" is what Mark Twain called the great city that served as the port of entry for the Winders. New Orleans was also known as the Crescent City for the great bend in the Mississippi that had cradled the town since the French built an outpost there in 1718. With its colorful and boisterous history, this "welcome mat" to America greeted immigrants like no other. It had elements of a Caribbean city, a French outpost, a Spanish colony, a Yankee frontier town, and a Dixieland cotton center. This city of Creoles and Cajuns was a wild contrast to the Victorian Liverpool the Winders had left behind! Of the 100,000-plus denizens of this cosmopolis in 1853, about half were black, both slave and free.

John R. and Ellen Winder arrived in New Orleans at the height of its golden age. The 1840's and 1850's created a burgeoning port, choked with seagoing ships and riverboats laden with not only passengers, but also sugar, molasses, cotton, raw materials from upriver, and refined goods from Europe and the eastern states.[56]

Since 1848, much to the advantage of the Saints, a Church emigration agent was stationed at New Orleans to help them along this portion of their journey. In 1853 the agent was Elder James Brown, who was known to give further advice to the immigrants regarding the danger from swindlers. He would also warn them to be careful of rich food and strong drink, which seemed to cause problems among those who were used to hard shipboard fare. Some Mormon immigrants wanted to find work in New Orleans to earn money for the journey to Utah, and a branch of the Church was organized four years before to keep such people together. However, these were the exceptions and not the rule, and James Brown made strenuous efforts to send everyone forward at once.[57] Nonetheless, the Mormon immigrants, "elated with the successful termination of their voyage," did find time to stop at a street restaurant in the "quaint, old-fashioned city" and enjoy some French cooking for five cents a meal. It was said by a traveler that "French is so commonly spoken that one may visit several cafes or restaurants without being able to converse in English."[58]

Steamboating the Mississippi

Part of Brown's job as the Church's agent in New Orleans was to find cheap passage on steamboats. In 1853 Brown could secure passage to St. Louis for the Saints at the rate of $2.25 for each adult, half fare for children three to fourteen, with younger children free.[59] In the case of the passengers of the *Elvira Owen*, they were transferred that spring to a steamer named the *James Rob* and began their 1,100 mile journey up the Mississippi.[60] Passage to St. Louis would have cost the Winders about $7.50 for the two adults, their two children, and young Mary Shanks.

Steamboat travel on the mighty river was at its height in the 1850's, and the *James Rob* was a handsome craft like the other riverboats of that heyday. The steamboats were floating palaces, open to all who could pay. Many had fine salons and parlors, baths, a barber's shop, a library, and a band. A dinner menu might have fifty dishes. To travel on the great maids of the Mississippi was a source of interest and pride to all. Mark Twain described the "handsome sight" of an approaching steamboat as follows:

> She is long and sharp and trim and pretty; she has two tall, fancy-topped chimneys, with a gilded device of some kind swung between them; a fanciful pilot-house, all glass and 'gingerbread,' perched on top of the 'texas' deck behind them; the paddle-boxes are gorgeous with a picture or with gilded rays above the boat's name; the boiler deck, the hurricane deck, and the texas deck

are fenced and ornamented with clean white railings; there is a flag gallantly flying over the jackstaff; the furnace doors are open and the fires glaring bravely; the upper decks are black with passengers; the captain stands by the big bell, calm, imposing, the envy of all; great volumes of the blackest smoke are rolling and tumbling out of the chimneys.[61]

"New Orleans" was a steel engraving done by Frederick Hawkins Piercy. Piercy traveled up the Mississippi River via steamboat in 1853, the same year as the Winders. Both groups followed the river from New Orleans upstream to St. Louis, and then on to Keokuk, Iowa, where the wagon trains outfitted that year.

However, despite the splendor above deck, immigrants could usually afford only to stay on the lower deck, between cargo and machinery. Here the Mormons spent their time preparing their own food, drawing water perhaps from the muddy river, sleeping at best on planks, slung from the deck above on ropes. Samuel Claridge, who would later become a close friend of John R. Winder's while crossing the plains, reported that "Ordinary passengers are obliged to be content with lying on the boards; sometimes a berth may be obtained, but not often."[62] They were in some danger if the boat struck a snag or developed engine trouble. In return for their cheap passage, they would be expected to help, under the direction of a loud-voiced and heavy-handed mate, in loading wood from the piles maintained at frequent intervals along the banks.[63] Nonetheless, the ride up the river was not nearly as long as the voyage across the Atlantic, the quarters were probably less cramped, and the "quality and variety of the food was much improved over that of the ocean voyage."[64]

Despite John R.'s miraculous recovery from small pox at sea, he "was left in a weakened condition for several months,"[65] and because of this he had "none too good an experience at any stage of his journeyings."[66] Nonetheless, the determined Englishman toughed it out on the trip up the mighty river, and after eight days and nights they approached where the Missouri emptied into the Mississippi; they arrived at the "Meeting of the Waters." St. Louis.[67]

St. Louis was a success almost from the day that Pierre Laclede picked the site for his fur-trading post. In the spring of 1853 when the Winders arrived, it was a bustling frontier city coming of age and known affectionately as "America's Gateway to the West." Just the year before, the first railroad track in the state of Missouri was laid between St. Louis and the neighboring town of Cheltenham, and later that year the state's first public high school would open in "Saint Looey." Just a few years prior, in 1847, St. Louis became illuminated by gaslight and was connected to the East by telegraph. When John R. Winder and his family stepped off the steamer *James Rob* they would have seen the famous old levees lined with cobblestones that protected St. Louis from spring floods. They would also have seen a town still rebuilding from the Great St. Louis Fire of 1849 that had burned up the heart of the city just four years prior.[68]

It was April 9, 1853, when the Winders and those traveling with them arrived in St. Louis.[69] As in New Orleans, the Saints were met by a Church agent who would help them find a place to stay for a couple of days until they could be sent on to the trail-head for the journey west. The agent in St. Louis in the mid-1850's was William Empey, who would find houses at reasonable rents for those who wished to stay in town and earn some more money before heading to Zion. However, for most of the Saints, the Church authorities would try "to trans-ship them as quickly as possible."[70]

Here in St. Louis the Winders learned that "instead of going up the Missouri River to Kanesville, as emigrants had in previous years, the emigrants of 1853 would fitout at Keokuk on the Mississippi, in southeastern Iowa, and cross Iowa by wagon." So after just a few days in St. Louis, they were placed, as a fellow passenger described, "on an old boat with scarcely any accommodations" for Keokuk, about 200 miles above St. Louis.[71] The group left St. Louis on April 11 and arrived upriver at Keokuk, Iowa, "the evening of the 12th."[72]

Outfitting in Keokuk, Iowa

Situated at the foot of the Lower Rapids of the Mississippi River, the flourishing town of Keokuk was "at the head of navigation for the large class of steamers and the natural outlet of the fertile valley of the Des Moines, the most populous part of the State."[73] Iowa became the twenty-ninth state in 1846 and was experiencing a boom in population as America continued to move west— her population would triple in the 1850's. The town named for Chief Keokuk was a frequent residence of Mark Twain, who would hand set the type for the town's first directory in 1856.[74] The Church agents had made excellent arrangements at Keokuk for camping and organizing the emigrants, and city officials and citizens seemed altogether pleased to assist the Saints with a temporary residence.[75]

With the outfitting place near Keokuk, this year's emigration would very nearly retrace the trail of the Mormon exodus from Nauvoo, although under greatly improved circumstances. Seven years before, in February 1846, the first of the exiles crossed the Mississippi River and camped at nearby Sugar Creek to wait until the first of March to begin the long and arduous trek across Iowa and on to the West.[76]

One of the Winder's fellow emigrants described the outfitting camp at Keokuk as follows:

> About half a mile from the river . . . on top of a hill, surrounded by wood, and commanding a view of the country for miles around, the Camp of Israel burst to my view. Here were hundreds of tents and wagons with hundreds and thousands of Saints all preparing for a 1,300-mile journey across the plains. . . . The emigrants from each nation had wisely been placed together, and those who had crossed the sea together were still associated as neighbors in Camp . . . The arrangement of the wagons and tents, with their white covers, looked quite picturesque amidst the spring foliage of the country.[77]

At the frontier the emigrants remained encamped until all arrangements could be completed for the arduous overland trek.[78] Those emigrants wealthy enough to buy the wagons, oxen, provisions and equipment necessary for the trek to the Salt Lake Valley were called "independent" emigrants. During the 1850's Church agents helped these families by selling them everything required for their outfit for crossing the plains.[79] The John and Ellen Winder family were one among several in their company that "traveled as an independent detachment, using their own means."[80]

At Keokuk, the pioneers camped and waited for five weeks for teams and wagons to be put together. Some of the party "secured work in the town" so that they "could earn enough to purchase a few things (they) needed, before starting upon that long and tedious journey."[81] Those who could not work at their trades took advantage of the opportunity to participate in working on the roads.[82] Many of the brethren worked to obtain enough cattle for the pioneer company. They needed to purchase "thousands of cattle all over the country which was quite an undertaking." The search for stock was complicated in 1853 by "California speculators" who "have their agents out through all the Western States, buying up all cattle, horses, and sheep that they can lay hold of, and sending them off by tens of thousands to the markets on the Pacific coast, where it is said they command an incredible price." All this added to the cost of Mormon emigration that year.

It was said that "Joseph W. Young was one of the principal buyers," and was assisted by several others returning to the west from missions.[83]

John R. Winder displayed a passionate interest in cattle throughout his entire life, and was certainly fascinated by this process of gathering them at Keokuk. The Mormon pioneers were highly dependent upon oxen to pull their wagons and on cows for a source of milk and butter in the trek across the plains. In many cases "the animals served the dual purpose of power and food." The Joseph W. Young company, like all pioneer companies from the very first, were instructed to acquire good quality animals. The cattle that they ended up bringing to Utah were "rather varied but good specimens of the early Shorthorn, Devon and, to lesser extent, Hereford types. This early Shorthorn type was that from which the English Milking Shorthorn was derived."[84] Years later John R. would become one of the first to bring Jersey and Holstein cows to Utah, but as an emigrant he would have had to settle for specimens of the above type of cattle. The Winder party was fortunate to be able to obtain one wagon, three oxen, and two cows to take with them on the long journey to the Valley of the Great Salt Lake.[85]

While waiting to head west from Keokuk, many of the pioneers of 1853 took advantage of the close proximity of historic Nauvoo and, sometime in their five-week wait, many ventured the twelve miles upstream to visit the "City Beautiful." Considering most of his traveling companions made an excursion to visit Nauvoo, and considering it was a place spoken of since his first introduction to Mormonism, it is highly improbable that John R. Winder did not take advantage of visiting the nearby historical site. Frederick Piercy, who was in Keokuk at the same time as the Winders, remarked after a day trip to Nauvoo, "It is the finest possible site for a city, and its present neglected state shows how little a really good thing is sometimes appreciated." Ruins of the great Temple were still to be seen in 1853 and Lucy Mack Smith, the Prophet Joseph's mother, and Emma Smith, his widow, along with her children, still resided in the Nauvoo Mansion and frequently entertained guests who came up from Keokuk that spring.[86]

The Overland Trek

There were twelve or more companies that made the overland trek the summer of 1853, all moving out between mid-May and June 20. On the morning of May 20, it was the Joseph W. Young Company's turn to leave Keokuk. The company consisted at the outset of 420 souls, 56 wagons, and 224 oxen; and they moved out onto the prairie northward toward New Boston. John R.'s friend, Samuel Claridge, remarked:

> Our first starting out was rather comical. Here were Welsh, English, German, Scandinavians and none of us had ever had experience in driving cattle and the cattle had to learn all languages . . . there was a great deal of awkward driving. But we got started.[87]

Ten miles northward brought them to New Boston, on the Mormon Trail of 1846, just five miles west of Nauvoo. About this time they "went to Montrose, a nice camp among the trees, stayed there 2 or 3 days." The company remained at Montrose May 20-31 "waiting for the delivery of cows, for the 'Ten Pound' Company and otherwise preparing for the long overland journey."[88] On Friday, May 27, the company held a meeting to organize their ranks.

Six years before when the first group of Mormon pioneers began their arduous trek, Brigham Young announced how their companies would be formed, a pattern which was followed religiously by each company thereafter:

> Let all the people . . . be organized into companies, with a covenant and promise to keep all the commandments and statutes of the Lord our God. Let the companies be organized with captains of hundreds, captains of fifties, and captains of tens, with a president and his two counselors at their head . . . Let each company provide themselves with all the teams, wagons, provisions, clothing, and other necessaries for the journey, that they can.[89]

In addition to the above organization, each company had an appointed clerk to keep a historical record and log of the journey. A chaplain was made responsible for regular church services, to see that the Lord's Supper was attended to on the Sabbath day, and to visit the sick. Commissaries were also chosen to help distribute rations.

At that Friday meeting, Joseph W. Young was sustained as president. He had been with the Winders and others since the *Elvira Owen* left Liverpool, but for many, this was their first opportunity to meet their company captain. Young, only 24 years-old, was the son of Lorenzo Dow Young and nephew of President Brigham Young. "He was a man of medium height, medium complexion, manner grave and unassuming. He had a beautiful wife with him, but she was an invalid, which perhaps accounted for his grave demeanor."[90] William Parry was sustained as captain of the first Fifty, which consisted mainly of Welsh Saints, and Richard Rostron as captain of the second Fifty. Henry Pugh, Captain Young's father-in-law, was chosen clerk of the company.[91]

In Montrose, Captain Young issued some advice that he wanted his company to hear before they started on their way: "Contend with no one, pray for those who are set over you and they will prove a blessing to you." He also stressed the importance of everyone working together for the good of the whole. "A man who talks about doing 'his share of the work'," he warned, "should be fed with a tea spoon and sleep with his mother!" They were advised to have one wagon and one tent for every ten persons, and that their ration of provisions consist of "one pound of flour and a portion of bacon each day, but we were at liberty to provide any extras we could afford."[92]

On Wednesday, June 1, part of the company moved out towards Sugar Creek, when at 5 o'clock in the afternoon, within three miles of campground at Sugar Creek, "rain began to fall in torrents and continued until midnight." "The roads were so mirey" that they had to stop. One fellow traveler wrote,

> Being no place to pitch our tents we all had to crawl in the wagons and keep out of the rain with our boxes and bedding piled up to the brim. You can imagine how 12 of us slept the first night. This was our first start and all were good natured and we sang.

The next day the company reached Sugar Creek where they waited a week for more cows. On June 7, Captain Young made a modification in the company leadership. Richard Rostron, who had been called as the captain of the second Fifty, was now asked to serve as chaplain, and John R. Winder, age 32, was called to take his place. A close friendship formed between these men. Captain Winder, Captain Young, and Samuel Claridge, one of John R.'s captains of ten, became especially good friends.[93] This position of responsibility for John R. Winder would be his first leadership opportunity in America, but it was far from his last. Despite the challenges of caring for his wife, for 16-year-old Mary Shanks, for little four-year-old John Jr., and for the one-year-old twins Mary and Martha, John R. now had the additional challenge of assisting his Fifty in the great westward trek. One woman in John R.'s Fifty remarked: "A great deal of patience was required by both captains and people to perform a trip of one thousand miles across the plains."[94] Here at muddy Montrose they were forty-four miles from Keokuk.

The trek across Iowa for this 1853 company gave them little trouble except for occasional muddy roads resulting from the spring rains. The road and trail passed "through beautiful woodland scenery, and prairies with grass varying from 1 to 7 ft. in height, affording good feed for cattle." Samuel Claridge wrote, "Our journey through Iowa was quite pleasant . . . I enjoyed myself very much." The trail across Iowa was well known and well defined. The company followed the Des Moines River upstream until Bonaparte, where they would ferry across. From there they went westward to Bloomfield and on to Mount Pisgah, thence in a winding fashion to Council Bluffs. The clerk reckoned that the first leg of the trip, across Iowa, was about 327 miles.[95]

The bugle was sounded early each morning, sometimes as early as three or four, but usually five o'clock in the morning. The first two hours of each day was spent attending to prayers, caring for the stock, getting breakfast, striking tents, packing gear, and preparing to be on the road. By seven or eight a.m. the wagons were rolling westward.

The Saints walked most of the way. Mary Morris, a woman in John R. Winder's Fifty, noted "The wagons were for our baggage and we walked alongside, or ahead of the teams, perhaps riding once or twice a day, for half an hour or so. One day I walked twenty miles, the whole day's journey, without riding at all."[96] They rarely made their goal of twenty miles per day, and across muddy Iowa they averaged only thirteen miles per day. The average for the entire trip was fourteen miles per day. With the oxen only able to go two miles an hour or less, there was plenty of time to walk, to rest, to talk, to hunt, and for the young people to play. Scouts would be sent ahead to look over the trail, and if necessary repair the bridges over streams.

The company would stop for the evening between six and eight, sometimes as early as four. The wagons were arranged in their circles, and often the stock was put to graze within. Fires were made, supper was cooked, various camp duties were taken care of, guards were posted, and the camp went to bed. This rigorous schedule was kept day in and day out on this trip, with few rest days, and only four Sundays during which there was no travel at all. Usually travel on Sunday was reduced by half, allowing for worship services, some catching up, and resting.

The company reached the staging area for crossing the Missouri River on Saturday, July 2, four miles east of Kanesville. There they celebrated the Fourth of July, a first-time experience for the Winders, and repaired several wagons. The actual ferrying of the fifty-six wagons in the Joseph W. Young Company was no small task, and it took several days, July 12 through 15, to row each wagon across the wide Missouri.

Here the Mormon Trail followed the north banks of the Platte and North Platte rivers to Fort Laramie. The Young Company walked much along the sandy banks of the Platte, and it was said "the whole regions of this river seemed sandy." Mary Morris commented, "I remember in walking I was so anxious to save the soles of my shoes that I walked in the grass wherever possible, so the uppers wore out first."[97] The level, hard sandy areas along the river bank made for good traveling, in fact some of their best travel time was made here in what became Nebraska. However, much of the time the river banks were wet and soft with pockets of quicksand in which animals and wagons could quickly become lost. "Horses could not pull against it, and oxen moved too slowly to make any progress and sank. The only solution was to get aid quickly and double or triple the teams and pull."[98] The plains were indeed a continuous struggle against the elements. Too little rain meant dry, dusty roads and unquenchable thirst for both man and beast. When the fierce prairie wind was combined with the dry dust of the sandy trails it "created havoc, covering everything and making breathing difficult."[99] However, too much rain meant flooding streams, muddy roads, and wet campsites. When the rivers were too deep to cross in wagons, John R. and the other men would carry the women and children across.[100]

On the Great Plains obtaining good food was often a challenge. Joseph W. Young succeeded in killing a buffalo once, but most of the fresh meat on this journey was obtained by the men shooting an occasional rabbit or prairie chicken. Some families had the problem of their "milch cows" drying up to the point where you could barely obtain "but a teacup full of milk a day." As they advanced on the plains timber grew scarcer and most meals were cooked using buffalo chips. "We came into camp, tired and hungry and would have to hunt buffalo chips in the dark and could not get a mouthful to eat until bread had been baked using this slow process."[101]

"We now launched forth into the great Indian country where we had to be on our guard night and day."[102] For those coming from England, like the Winders, there had been much talk and anticipation of seeing these "savage" Indians in America. The Mormon immigrants were both fearful and curious of any Indians, for they believed that the Book of Mormon recorded a history of their ancestors, the Lamanites. Mary L. Morris recounts one exciting incident that happened to the Young Company while in Indian territory:

> One afternoon when we were traveling in the vicinity of the Platte River, we saw at a distance, two objects coming toward us. As they approached, we saw that they were Indians, Pawnees, a very savage tribe who were at war at the time with the Sioux, another savage tribe. At sight of these Indians, the teamsters stopped their wagons and reached for their guns, while the women came to the wagons for protection. As the Indians came to a standstill they said 'Pawnees shoot, Pawnees shoot.' Then more Indians came dressed in their trappings and war-paint, their numbers increasing every moment. I was not afraid, for something seemed to bear witness to me that they would not hurt us. One of them came and talked to me and wanted the blue jacket I was wearing. There was no more traveling that night. After the fires had been lighted the Pawnee Chief came and patrolled our camp all night to protect us from his own band. I sat and looked at him with pride and pleasure, he seemed so noble and grand. I could feel his protecting power over us. It seems to me I can never forget the spirit of calm and serenity that surrounded us as I sat on the ox yoke alone, near the dying embers of our camp fire. And so the night passed and the morning dawned, and we were permitted to continue our journey unmolested and unharmed and filled with gratitude to our Heavenly Father for his merciful protection.[103]

As one of the two captains of Fifty, John R. Winder would have been greatly concerned for his flock as he saw the Indians approaching. He would have been alongside Captain Young as they greeted the great Pawnee Chief and discussed the situation. This would be Winder's first experience with Indians, but he would later have many more in Utah during the Black Hawk Indian War and other military encounters. Ellen Winder was apparently quite frightened and developed a life-long fear of Indians.[104] Imagining her frantically trying to gather her baby twins, four year-old John Jr., and young Mary Shanks to the wagons for safety as Pawnee braves approached, one can see why the lady from England might have been so deeply concerned. After the incident with the Pawnees, "extra guards were set and each man was required to watch his wagon." Captain Winder and the other captains also instructed their groups to now travel "four wagons abreast to keep close together, every man packing his gun."[105]

On August 26 the train of immigrants reached Fort Laramie, which they regarded as "about half way." At the fort there was a small company of soldiers and "Those that had got money bought a few supplies." It was also noted at Laramie, in what became Wyoming, "Our cattle did very well up to this time, but our loads being heavy we did not make such good time. Our cattle began to give out and all our luggage that could be dispensed with were thrown out, such as feather beds &c &c."[106] It remains unknown what comforts or precious things hauled all the way from England the Winders chose to leave behind at Fort Laramie.

The Mormon Trail crossed the North Platte River at Fort Laramie and then followed the Oregon Trail to Fort Bridger. "We now began to climb the Black Hills of the Rocky Mountains where it was cooler and the bunch grass very good. We made very good time, had very little sickness."[107] On September 17 they were hit with an early snowstorm near South Pass. The following day they pressed onward through South Pass, over the Continental Divide. Samuel Claridge pointed out: "Our loads were heavy and by the time we got to the Sweetwater our cattle commenced dying."[108] Indeed, by this point many oxen had been lost, and others were trail-worn and weary. Captain Young's wife's health continued to deteriorate, and he worried that she might not achieve her dream of seeing the Great Salt Lake Valley. Fresh teams would have to be brought from the valley to assist the company for the remainder of the journey. Therefore, on Sunday, September 18, Captain Joseph W. Young, his wife, Charles Decker, and a few others left the company and departed for the valley. Mary Ann Pugh Young would die in her wagon two days later, and her husband would bury her at the Green River.

The remaining company was left in the charge of Captain William Perry, with Captain Winder now as second in command. These men led the company on to Fort Bridger. From this point the route followed the Mormon Trail of 1847 (based on the Hastings Cutoff of 1846) and made the difficult, slow passage through canyons into the Salt Lake Valley. The company reached Fort Bridger on September 28, and the next day Captain Joseph W. Young rejoined his company. He remained with them four days, then went back to the Salt Lake Valley to obtain teams to assist his company through the remainder of the journey.

The company then moved into the head of Echo Canyon and in the days that followed proceeded slowly down the canyon until October 7, while wending toward East Creek Canyon, they were met by their captain with "quite a number of oxen which helpt us out in going down the Big Mountain."[109] The following day, Saturday, October 8, the ascent of Big Mountain was made, reaching the summit at 6:00 pm. Mary Morris described the ascent as follows:

> We dreaded the ascent. It was a fine morning . . . and we reached it. We had previously arranged our attire, as best we could, after such a long journey, in expectation of meeting with our friends, as many of the Saints came to greet the companies as they arrived. There was a great variety of trees growing on the side of the mountain. The road was hard, level and well trodden and as we descended into the canyon below the scenery was grand indeed. I remember, while ascending the Big Mountain and stopping to take a breath, I looked around, above and below, and came to the conclusion, that:—Never again, in this life, do I want to cross this mountain. . . We had still one more mountain to cross, called Little Mountain, but upon descending began to feel more cheerful as we began to meet persons, coming to fetch their friends or relatives. . . I was most forcibly struck with the neat, clean and fair appearance of the people as they came up to us and did not realize that in proportion as they looked fair and clean to us we look correspondingly brown and grimy to them.[110]

On Monday, October 10, the Winders and those they were traveling with left their last campsite. They made their way down Emigration Canyon, making repairs on the road as they went, and arrived at the mouth of the canyon at three o'clock. Here the Winder family and their comrades were met by Elders Isaac C. and Hector C. Haight. "We ascended the hill on our right and to the joy of all we came in sight of the city, where we arrived at 5 o'clock p.m. and encamped on Union Square in peace and security."[111]

The following morning, Tuesday, they met for a final meeting:

> The company was aroused by trumpet sound at 6 o'clock to prepare for dismissing. At 9 o'clock a.m. a meeting was called when Pres. Joseph W. Young spoke well to the Saints, enjoining upon them faithfulness, diligence, etc. The Saints were also addressed by Pres. Brigham Young who spoke with power and a manifestation of the Holy Ghost, teaching the Saints that which was essential to their future destiny, also bidding them welcome to this delightful vale. By request of the companies, Pres. Brigham Young then broke up the organization, blessed the people in the name of the Lord Jesus and retired. Good counsel was then given by Elders Isaac C. Haight, (Elder) Wallace and Lorenzo D. Young; the latter pronounced the final benediction and the meeting broke up about 11 o'clock.[112]

How exciting it must have been for the exhausted Winder family to be in the Valley of the Great Salt Lake at last—eight months after leaving their home in Liverpool! The company they traveled with had "experienced its share of hardships in crossing the plains, but on the whole fared quite well."[113] They were fortunate to have safely made this journey half-way around the world. They had arrived! They were now in Zion!

It was there on Union Square in Salt Lake City, on that Tuesday morning, that John Rex Winder first shook the hand of a prophet of the Lord and looked into the blue eyes of the Great Colonizer, Brigham Young. President Young congratulated Captain Winder and the other captains in the company on a job well done. He also welcomed these immigrants from the United Kingdom to a new kingdom—a Kingdom of God just beginning to blossom in the desert.

6
Ascending in
a Bootstrap Economy:
Early Years in Utah,
1853-1856

"Luckily my vocation was in demand"

Getting His Bearings

The semi-annual conference of the Church had concluded in Salt Lake City the day before the Joseph W. Young Company entered the valley (Thursday to Sunday, October 6 to 9). In the months prior there were increasing problems with the Indians throughout central Utah. People had been killed, stock stolen, buildings burned, and the outlying colonies of Deseret sorely needed strengthening. John R. Winder recalled the situation: "Men had been called at the general conference, which had just closed, to go with their families and strengthen the outlying places. In Iron, Tooele, Sanpete and other parts, an Indian war was in progress, and grasshopper visitations were imminent."[1] Box Elder and Juab counties also needed more support. Samuel Claridge, whose family had traveled with the Winders since Keokuk, remembered that first meeting in Salt Lake City, the morning after their arrival in the valley:

> When we arrived in the public square President Young and other brethren met us, spoke highly of our president and company, gave us some good advice. Joseph L. Heywood was president of a new settlement called Nephi, nearly 100 miles south of Salt Lake City, and invited all that could to go and strengthen the settlement. A good many of our number went that fall.[2]

It was not uncommon for the immigrant companies to camp in Union Square for a time while waiting for their assignments. Bishops or their representatives then escorted them to the various settlements to which quotas had been assigned.[3] However, while most of the Joseph Young Company followed Heywood south to Nephi, the Winders did not. John R.'s granddaughter Helen Midgley Ross remarked that "Grandmother was a very timid person and was afraid of the Indians and Grandfather promised her he would never ask her to leave the city and the center of population."[4] John R. Winder was not afraid of Indians or the frontier, as his later adventures with the territorial militia would attest. However, his willingness to respect his wife's wishes on this matter demonstrates the deep and overriding love he held for her. Nonetheless, "Grandfather was eager to get ahead in the business world and in the church," and remaining in the City would provide him with more opportunities to do so.[5]

After about three weeks of living out of their wagons on the emigrant square, President Young gave instructions to "clear the square and get places for the people to go." During those three weeks, Salt Lake Valley experienced typical autumn weather—mostly clear and pleasant, though on October 25 there came up a strong wind bringing with it rain and snow. The ground was covered with snow for the first time that season. Quite likely the snow did not last long, for while the valley experienced freezing nights thereafter, during the daytime it enjoyed clear crisp days, with occasional rains in the valley and snow in the mountains.[6] During such a season, the pioneering Winder family set out to make their way in this new city, in this new world.

"Great Salt Lake City in 1853, looking south" was another steel engraving done by Frederick Piercy. The valley was essentially still a wilderness when the Winder family arrived, the first pioneers having only been there for six years.

Salt Lake City in 1853 was a strange place to these newcomers, and "as was the case with practically all of the pioneers who arrived in those primitive days, the Winders suffered the inevitable case of cultural shock."[7] Many of the conveniences of Victorian England were not to be found in the dry, dusty town that was now their home. John and Ellen "were accustomed to the green rolling hills and large prosperous cities of England. Although acres and acres of the Salt Lake Valley had been cleared and planted, it was still rugged country, so different from their beautiful homeland."[8] It is therefore not surprising to learn that "they were more than a little bewildered as they faced the actual process of realigning their lives and getting established in a home and profession."[9]

Nonetheless, John R. Winder did not hesitate to get things going, and it was later said of him: "His active nature and quick intelligence soon enabled him to get his bearings,"[10] and it was not long before he and Ellen "set up housekeeping."[11] The Winders "obtained a small home in the heart of the City,"[12] on a piece of land purchased from Samuel Mulliner.[13] Like everyone in that era, they "were subjected to many of the hardships of pioneer life."[14] These hardships, however, gave them a common bond with all of their neighbors. Every immigrant had undergone a conversion experience that led them to turn their life about, leave behind old beliefs, old friends, occupation, country, home, and family. All had experienced the long journey from old home to new. Whatever the former life's occupations and situations, all became pioneers in the valleys of the mountains, and who could tell when these pioneering experiences would end? "These shared experiences gave the nineteenth-century Mormon community a particular unity."[15]

One of John R. Winder's first new friends in the city was George Romney, who lived just opposite of the new Winder home on what was called the White House corner. Romney became a lifelong friend of John R.'s and in 1903 remarked "I have known President Winder for the last fifty years. It is fifty years this fall since he first came into the valley, and we were close neighbors. From that time to this I have been personally acquainted with him." Even in those early years as neighbors, Romney developed a great respect for John R. and admired his humility. "One great reason for the love that exists between the brethren and sisters and President Winder is, in my judgement, that he is the same today as he was fifty years ago. In the progress that has been made, in the positions he has occupied, the humility he has manifested is what has produced the great love that now exists and makes him tower high above many of his brethren."[16]

Another man who was quick to befriend John R. Winder when he first arrived was Jedediah M. Grant, a Seventy who was ordained an apostle a few months after Winder arrived, and later served as a counselor to President Brigham Young. His sons Heber J. Grant and Benjamin F. Grant would later become close friends of Winder's, as well. B. F. Grant spoke of his father's friendship with Winder at the latter's funeral. "When John R. Winder arrived in Utah, in early days, my father, Jedediah M. Grant, befriended him. Many people in this life forget those things: they forget the kindnesses that are shown unto them; but President Winder never forgot the help my father extended to him in the early days. He remembered it even to the day of his death."[17] Another early friend of John R.'s was Samuel Mulliner, who, as was mentioned, sold Winder his first lot, and, as will be expounded upon later, became Winder's first business partner in Utah.

With good new friends and neighbors, Winder would have been greatly assisted in learning the "ins and outs" of his new home. As John R. Winder set out to explore Salt Lake City for the first time he would have noticed the peculiar, yet efficient layout of the streets. The city had been laid out in August 1847 according to the plat of the City of Zion given by the Prophet Joseph Smith. The streets ran to the cardinal points of the compass, crossing at right angles, each block containing usually ten acres, and each block subdivided into eight lots of 1.25 acres each. No two houses faced each other, and houses were set twenty feet back from the front line of the lot. Irrigation waters in clean ditches flowed on each side of the street. How different such precision would have seemed to Winder from the wandering, haphazard lanes of London and Liverpool!

Inside the city three blocks had been set aside for the use of the public, the central block being the Temple Block, the site of the future temple. On 14 February 1853, the Temple Block was consecrated and ground broken for the foundation of the temple. The boweries built there in 1847 had been replaced in 1852 by a tabernacle building, often referred to as the Old Tabernacle. The Endowment House was not built until 1854 and the temple had barely progressed past the cornerstones. The Temple Block looked more like an industrial center than a religious center, with its large foundry, blacksmith shop, stone cutting shop, paint shop, modeling shop, and machine shop. Years later, Winder still remembered his first visit to the Temple Block:

> In April of that year the cornerstones of the Salt Lake Temple had been laid. Little did I dream as I gazed upon those humble though massive beginnings, that I would have charge, forty years later, of the work of completing the sacred edifice, and that I would be an assistant to its presiding authority during the happy years that followed.[18]

Outside the Temple Block one saw a few imposing buildings. On the southwest corner of Main and Brigham (South Temple) streets was the Council House, the center of many church and political activities. East along the same street was the Deseret Store, the General Tithing Office, and the Bishop's Storehouse, built between 1850 and 1852. Next stood a little building, the Mint, dating from 1849, its purpose being to turn California gold dust into Deseret gold coins. Next, one came to the Beehive House and associated Office of Brigham Young, built in 1852. (Eagle Gate was not built until 1859.) South a half block from that corner was the Social Hall, on the east side of what became State Street, the social center of the community.

John R. Winder reported that when he first arrived, "Utah was still in the early colonizing period. There were but eight settlements in Salt Lake county. . . . The population of the territory was about twenty thousand souls."[19] Salt

Lake City's population was a mere 5,979, while the rest of the valley's seven set-tlements contained only 2,273. Settlements throughout the territory stretched from Box Elder on the north to Cedar City, 300 miles south. Many villages bare-ly had one hundred souls, while Provo had 1,649 that fall, and Ogden had 1,332. Utah was indeed still in the early colonizing period.

For the territory to survive, the pioneers had to "pull themselves up by their own bootstraps," so to speak, and rely on the resources of their closed-in king-dom in the Great Basin. Prominent Utah historian Leonard J. Arrington described the economic development of the territory at this time:

> The remoteness of early Deseret from the remainder of the nation, the dif-ficulty of transportation, and the separatist inclinations of the settlers forced Utah in the years before the coming of the railroad to go through an almost miraculously successful stage of self-sufficiency that was more complete and long lasting than that of any other section of the United States. Any scientific investigation at the time would have concluded that the settlement of substan-tial numbers of people at even marginal levels was impossible. The land was too barren and the resources were too sparse to support more than a few scat-tered groups of people.
>
> And yet growth and development did occur through hard work and severe sacrifice. The settlers' formula for success was a puritanical attitude toward consumption and saving and an ecclesiastically organized cooperation. With religion as an essential tool of survival, development was based on coopera-tive, rather than individualistic, principles. Under Church direction, there developed group colonization; cooperatively built forts; the construction of cooperative canals, roads, fences, and mills; cooperative livestock herds; and even some cooperative farming of fields. However arid and barren the territo-ry seemed to be, the settlers had faith that God had endowed their promised land with all the resources necessary for their use. Unlike other American states and territories that started by developing extractive export industries, Utah's growth began with a local self-sufficient subsistence agricultural economy mobilized to support an ever-increasing number of people.[20]

Salt Lake City did not originally have a business or commercial district, as much of the business in the early years was conducted out of homes. Howev-er, it was not long before such a district did emerge along Main Street, south of the Temple Block. The city was not lacking in business, though, for the sound of industry rang in the air as the pioneers set about building their Zion. There were flour mills and saw mills, as well as many tradesmen performing their skills in shoemaking, tailoring, blacksmithing, and in the building trades. There were several tanneries, and there were brush, comb, woolen, and hat and cap manufacturers. One also found cooperages, cabinet and wood turner's shops, chair makers, watch makers, jewelers, and whipmakers. There was a paper factory, a carriage and wagon factory, a pottery, and a saddlery.

Although a variety of industry was going on, the "bootstrap economy" was such that one could only make a living with a trade that was in demand. "In those times men had not much choice of employment in this mountain region," John R. Winder later wrote. "They had to do whatever they could get to do, and take their pay largely in articles produced by the farmer and the artisan." In fact, he said, "it was no uncommon sight to see artists, musicians and men of education hauling wood from the canyon, building fences, or cultivating the soil."[21]

Resuming the Leather Trade

John R. Winder and his family were typical of the families in Salt Lake City in the early 1850's. The typical Utah family at the time was made up of five members, two parents in their twenties or early thirties, with three children probably under fifteen. Fully half of the work force was engaged in farming, the other half was engaged in trades. John R. Winder fell into the latter group.

"Luckily my vocation was in demand," said Winder. "Being an experienced shoe and leather man, I engaged, soon after my arrival in Salt Lake Valley (which has ever since been my home) in the manufacture of saddles, boots and shoes, and in the conduct of a tannery. My partner in this venture was Samuel Mulliner."[22] Mulliner was the first of "several prominent men"[23] that Winder would work with in the tannery business while in Utah, and he asked John R. to be the manager of the tannery.[24] In addition to being the manager of the tannery, he also served as a "drawer," a craft that he had developed in the shoe business in England, which was to make "the patterns for the shoes." His wife, Ellen, also helped and "made the eyelets for the shoes."[25] It soon became known throughout the city that in this vocation Winder "was quite successful."[26] Those who worked hard and knew their trade, like Winder, did succeed:

> At Salt Lake City and elsewhere throughout the country manufacturers began to thrive. Isolated, poor, having brought little or nothing with them, these settlers were peculiarly dependent for necessaries and comforts upon themselves, and what they could do with their hands. And it would be difficult to find anywhere in the history of the colonization of settlers who could do more. Among them were many of the best of Europe's artisans, workers in wood, iron, wool, and cotton, besides farmers, miners, and all kinds of laborers.[27]

It is not surprising to learn that John R. Winder began to succeed shortly after his arrival in the valley. "He was a very industrious man, extremely thrifty, and a smart investor," declared grandson George Winder. Once he had some resources, he put them to good use:

> In 1853, a mere six years after the first arrival of the pioneers, there was much land still available in the Salt Lake Valley. John R. Winder, being quite

the opportunist, quickly acquired vast amounts of real estate which would eventually pay great dividends. He had lands near the mouth of Big Cottonwood Canyon and along the east bench.[28]

Although there was later some business success, there were some tough times early on while in that first "small cottage downtown."[29] Granddaughter Helen Midgley Ross wrote, "There were many lean years and Grandmother took in boarders and rented out rooms in her home to complement their income. Among those who lived there was Karl Maeser who later was a professor at Brigham Young University."[30]

Winter when it came, was severe. The next ground snow did not come until December 21, but throughout January and February there were at least seven different snowstorms. Most evenings saw the thermometer drop to the mid-teens, but sometimes the cold was even more severe, such as the night of January 21, when the mercury registered 19 degrees below zero.[31] In this weather, John R. Winder worked to support his young family and keep them warm as best he could. "John R., along with hundreds of other men went to the mountains and brought out a large supply of wood. There was no other fuel to burn."[32]

However, in this cold his wife was still a stalwart and faithful pioneer:

> Ellen was to prove invaluable to the community in her selfless caring for the sick. With a heart full of love and tenderness, she was to make a career of administering solace, love and relief to those in need.[33]

> Immediately, the mother heart of Ellen radiated its warmth to the community. Wherever there was sickness or trouble, Ellen was quickly sought and she always had a heart full of tenderness from which she administered solace, encouragement and true sympathy. By nature she was a wonderful relief worker. Little wonder then that she was soon called by the great organization of the Church, the Relief Society, to be one of their workers. She labored untiringly in this organization as long as she lived.[34]

In addition to Ellen Winder being called as a Relief Society worker, John R. was also busy in the Church. "Winder held important ecclesiastical positions. In 1854 he was ordained a Seventy, and in 1855 became one of the presidents of the 12th Quorum of Seventy."[35] On August 31, 1855, he received his endowment in the Endowment House, an important ordinance administered to worthy adults in the Church. Winder also volunteered his service with the territorial militia, joining the Nauvoo Legion in 1855.[36] The family remained busy, and on August 20, 1854, Ellen gave birth to a girl they named Emily. Unfortunately, the child, John and Ellen's first to be born in America, passed away five days before her first birthday.

After a couple of years in the valley, Winder had firmly planted his feet and was well on his way to a prosperous business career. "In 1855 he enlarged his business interests and entered into a partnership."[37] Things had gone well with Samuel Mulliner, and so, as Winder put it, "Subsequently I formed a similar partnership with William Jennings, and we together built a tannery and kept a meat shop, besides making harness, saddles, boots and shoes."[38] William Jennings had come to Utah from England in 1852 and shared an ambition and drive similar to his new partner's. Jennings would eventually become "one of the great money kings of the intermountain region,"[39] and later served as mayor of Salt Lake City from 1882 to 1885.[40] He would be a lifelong friend of John R. Winder's, and their drive and determination would have kept each other motivated during rough times at the tannery. "Even at that early day [Jennings] manifested the keenness, sagacity and business promptitude that made him in time one of the leading merchants and financiers of the West."[41]

The two English businessmen called their new partnership "Jennings & Winder, Manufacturers, Boots, Shoes, Harness and Saddles," and they were "very successful in all departments." As in his last endeavor, John R. Winder was the manager.[42] Their initial meat market was adjoining William Jennings' residence, "then situated immediately north of the Walker House." In addition to the butcher business, they built a tannery "on the premises in the rear of the market."[43] Here Jennings and Winder were busy "manufacturing leather from the hides of [their] slaughtered beeves, then working up the leather into saddles, harness, boots, and shoes."[44]

In 1856 Jennings took his wife and went on a mission to Carson City, Nevada, to establish that colony. "During his absence Mr. Winder carried on the business and moved the meat market to a location just north of the old Elephant corner (in 1902 the Smith Drug Company), but continued the tannery, etc. at the old stand." Jennings returned in 1857 and they erected another shop on what became known as the Emporium Corner. Later the Utah National Bank was built on that corner.[45] Jennings and Winder became two of the most prominent tanners in the territory. The *Journal History* of September 1855 also lists Philip Pugsley and William Howard.

In 1856 and 1857 Brigham Young asked "Wealthier Mormons" to donate goods to help with the Brigham Young Express & Carrying Company. This company, known by contemporaries as the Y.X. Company, was the largest single venture yet tackled by the Mormons in the Great Basin. If Johnston's Army did not intervene, this bold and well-conceived enterprise "would undoubtedly have changed the whole structure of Mormon, and perhaps Western, economic development." The Y.X. Company was designed to provide way stations for handcart companies and other immigration, to carry the United States mail between the Missouri Valley and Salt Lake City, and to facilitate the movement of passengers and freight between Utah and the East, similar to what the Pony Express and Ben Holladay stagecoach lines did later. Jennings and Winder were asked to help fill the large order of boots and shoes, harness leather, saddles, and cushions. This they did, a demonstration of the sacrifice often required in Brigham Young's Deseret.[46]

John R. Winder stayed extremely busy while working with Jennings. His wife lamented, "He was in partners with Brother Jennings in the Butcher business, and he always went on the range to hunt beef cattle."[47] However, this partnership also helped the family in many aspects. "We lived well as we had a fresh joint of meat from the butcher-shop (which was close by) every second day, then fragments were used the next day."[48]

Hannah Thompson—His First Plural Marriage

One of the most noticeable features about the Mormon community in the 1850s was plural marriage, "And those men who were ambitious to be among the leaders felt a compulsion to accept and practice this principle. Prominent men were counseled by the Church leaders to enter this practice as a qualification for leadership."[49] As president of the 12th Quorum of Seventy, John Rex Winder would have been no exception, especially since he was, as has already been mentioned, "eager to get ahead in the business world and in the church."[50] Furthermore, it was taught at that time that the second wife "opened the door of salvation in the Celestial Kingdom not only for herself, but for her husband and his first wife."[51]

Annie Clark Tanner, a contemporary of Winder's, stated that despite the encouragement to take multiple wives, "polygamy was not practiced by all men in the Church. I have heard the percentage placed at from three to five percent. As stated, it was promoted and practiced almost exclusively by the Church leaders." She reasoned that "this was in part due, perhaps, to the fact that only the more prosperous could afford to assume these added obligations."[52]

Since he had first arrived in Salt Lake City, John R. Winder had been interested in the concept of plural marriage and felt compelled to fulfill the commandment. Finally in 1854, John R. approached Ellen with the supreme test of faith for a first wife to bear, when he asked her to grant permission in allowing him to enter into polygamy. "This came as an immeasurable blow," and Ellen was less than enthusiastic at the prospect of sharing her husband and home with another woman or women and the inevitable children. But Ellen rallied with a "noble, stoic spirit" and faithfully declared her intent on making any sacrifice for the advancement of the Kingdom. She gave her consent to her husband and the couple began the awkward task of shopping around for a young woman sufficiently suitable to share their lives with.[53]

By that time the holiday season of 1854-55 was upon them and the Winders were invited to various social events in the city. It was at one Christmas social that the duo met an eighteen year-old Scottish girl named Hannah Thompson. Hannah later recorded the events of that meeting and the subsequent courtship:

In the winter of 1854, the social times were started, as at previous times, and I was permitted to attend some of them. One night Aunt Anna Ballantyne Taylor, wife of President John Taylor, invited me to accompany her to a party, and during the evening she came to me all smiles and told me there was a smart looking Englishman just anxious to be intriduced [sic] to me, so I said all right. It was John Rex Winder, who afterwards became the councilor to President Joseph F. Smith of the First Presidency of the Church. However, he at the time was only a small man, regarding official standing, but he was then looking for a second wife. So she brought him and introduced him. He was very pleasant and social and we had a dance.

Hannah sensed that John R. was thinking of marriage, "but I did not think that way," she said. When he offered to escort her home, Hannah insisted that he "did not need to see or escort me home," after all, "Aunt Anna was my escort for the evening," and "he was the father of three children."[54] John R. would have been somewhat disappointed at not being able to take her home, as was the gentlemanly custom in those days; however, he must have been quite attracted to this Scottish lass, for he did not give up so easily.

Hannah Ballantyne Thompson had been born in Edinburgh, Scotland on October 25, 1835. She was the youngest daughter of John and Margaret Ballantyne Thompson. Her mother was very religious and when the Mormon Elders were traveling in Scotland preaching the Gospel, she recognized the truth of their message and was baptized. Her children were later baptized as they reached the age of accountability.

Hannah's mother died in December 1843 of an affliction in her lungs. Eight year-old Hannah had been close to her mother and the adjustment to the loss was difficult. Her father was a butler in the household of noblemen and was seldom home, and despite his wife's conversion, he was not interested in the Gospel. When Hannah reached the age of sixteen she was placed, as her sisters had been prior, in the homes of the wealthy to work as a servant. In 1851 her uncle, Richard Ballantyne, sent for her and her sisters to go to America. They went via Liverpool, New Orleans and St. Louis, crossed the plains with the Abraham O. Smoot company, and arrived in the Salt Lake Valley September 3, 1852. Uncle Richard Ballantyne and his young family welcomed them, but Richard left shortly thereafter for a mission to India. "When Uncle left for his mission he wished me to remain with Aunt Maria until his return, which I managed to do, although I had many offers of marriage."[55]

Hannah had been in Salt Lake just over two years when she first met John R. Winder and they began to date. What an awkward challenge it must have been for him to begin courting again, especially while having three children and a loving, caring wife. The courtship situation gives a whole new meaning to the phrase "double date!" Hannah continues her narrative of their courtship:

However as the Hollow Days [holidays] came and went, he often called to invite me to go with him to his home and have tea with himself and wife, and then accompany them to the dance. They had brought an Irish lass, with them, when they emigrated, to help them with the twin babies. Their boy was 3 years old. They came in 1853, and had not as yet had time to collect enough comforts around them to make the one family comfortable; but the men, who were faithful in the Priesthood soon got to see the principle of plural marriage, but it seemed that I could not see it that way yet.

The [Jennings & Winder butcher] shop was close by, where he had secured a building spot on Main Street and Emigration Street [Third South], so he thought to build a pretty home there to accommodate two wives, and he continued to make love to me. I began to think it might be possible for a man to love two wives, if he kept the Spirit of God, but spring was commencing and lots of work to do and I was anxious to earn so as to pay for my emigration, as well as getting food, clothing, shelter and friends.

His wife, Ellen, said she had never seen any one until she met me, that she was willing for him to have, so of course that had great weight with me.

This Englishman began to preach marriage to me. I told him emphatically no. Not at present. My Bible told me this [Honor thy father], and that he had to be willing to await. My Father must be willing. I had letters of him from recent date, stating that he was thinking to emigrate, and that he had to be willing to await his arrival.[56]

Indeed, Hannah's father had been considering emigrating to Utah, especially after his son Alexander's death. Hannah wrote: "He was left without any family in Scotland and became very restless. We continued to write him, reminding him of the blessings in store by obedience to the glorious Gospel."[57] Finally, John Thompson decided to go after his daughters in America. Meanwhile, back in Salt Lake:

The spring opened very hopefully, for news came that Uncle would soon be released to return home to his loved ones, and the assurance that Father was coming, naturally kept up an interest between me and my friends, and when the time of arrival of the company of emigrants was definitely known, preparations were made to meet them in the Canyon, by friends and relatives to escort and welcome them into the Valley and City.[58]

A strange coincidence occurred while on his journey. He had arranged to meet a company of Saints at Atchinson, Kansas. He was to travel with them across the plains. It was a great surprise to find that his own brother-in-law, Richard Ballyntine was in charge of the emigrants with whom he was to travel. Elder Ballyntine was returning from his mission to India. It was a glorious time in their lives to meet under such circumstances. Father was very humble then and Uncle Richard, being enthused with the Spirit of the Gospel, taught him the importance of obedience to baptism and of becoming a member of the Church of Jesus Christ of Latter Day Saints and he was baptized before they left Atchison.[59]

Early in September the company arrived, and Brother Winder took me to meet Father, which was a never to be forgotten day and occasion. It was a joyous time, even more pleasant and thrilling than when we two girls arrived and had been met by our kindred two years previous, and welcomed to their homes. Brother and Sister Winder had prepared picnic, and he took melons and cantaloupes, and good things. His wife had gone on a visit to Salt Creek for a change. She had buried a baby girl not long since, and left the children with the girl [Mary Shanks].

Father was delighted with the reception and warm welcome, by which they had been received, and he couldn't help being pleased with Brother Winder. So we came down the Canyon together.

There had been another fellow out to meet the company the night before, and talked with Father, so when in conversation he said: 'What about Brother Merick?' I said: He was no account. So while we were all happy and the band played lively strains, we soon reached Aunt Maria's and found everything in readiness for a cheerful homecoming. My sister Margaret and baby were there and Father was delighted to meet them and fold them in his arms. His first grandchild.

The trip to the canyon was both enjoyable and profitable to Brother Winder, for he lost no time in making application to President Brigham Young for consent to take to himself a second wife. He had waited now about a year since he had sought my company, so before Father left Salt Lake to go with Sister to her Grantsville home, he had him accompany us to the Council House.

I think it was the second Sunday in September. Brother and Sister Winder, his wife, walked together as she had to be there to show her willingness for the marriage.

Father and I walked together arm in arm. It was the 20 September, 1855, and it was a little over a month before I would be 20 years old.[60]

There, at twelve noon in President Brigham Young's office in the Council House, the prophet married John Rex Winder to his second wife. Hannah's father John Thompson and a Brother D. Mackintosh were the witnesses.[61] After the wedding at the Council House, the newly enlarged Winder family went to their home down the street. The new bride later recalled her thoughts on that night:

It was with peculiar feelings that I went to my new home that Sabbath evening. I was very quiet; his wife furnished me a small bedroom, bed and bedding. I thought after my three years labor, that my Aunt Maria would have furnished my bed and bedding. I had only two faded calico dresses that I soon cut into blocks, and made an extra quilt, as winter was coming on.[62]

Earlier in May of that year, as was mentioned, John R. Winder had obtained some property on Third South Street, just west of Main Street where he began constructing a lovely two-story home. He had purchased the property from William Kay of Davis County, the founder of the town of Kaysville.[63] The new home would be large enough to house himself and his two wives and was completed shortly after John R. and Hannah's wedding. Hannah recorded the experiences of that time, as well:

The Winder home in Salt Lake City on 300 South and just west of Main Street. In May of 1855, John R. Winder purchased the property from William Kay of Davis County, who became the founder of Kaysville. The new home was large enough to house himself and his two wives, and was completed shortly after John R.'s marriage to Hannah.

The New House that was being built would soon be ready for cleaning. In that I had a nice square bed room. He could not afford to have the floors plained, so Hannah (for that was still my name) (His wife was Mrs. Winder) had extra work to do in keeping the house clean. I took, as my duty, the cleaning and washing in the home. Mrs. Winder generally tended to the cooking. There was the Irish Lass [Mary Shanks] to tend the children, so I had nothing to do in that way.

I done all the scrubbing of the new house. There were four bed rooms upstairs, a hall, parlor, kitchen and buttery down, but I liked to work when I could pleases, and it seemed to be so that I could.

I was up early and late helping on the new house. . . Mrs. Winder was a neat careful house keeper. I had nothing to do with the managing, but I was well pleased to be the girl, as I had been well trained on the subject.

There were no fashions, only as we planned them ourselves. I was the dress maker. I had practiced sewing when I kept house for my brother, when 14 years old.

Our close neighbors were dress makers and they would cut and baste the waist for me for nothing, and I could do the rest. The skirts were then made plain. There were no sewing machines that I remember of in the 50 or 60ties. I think it was near 1870 before sewing machines came. We were happy sitting quietly at our sewing, and then we had the spinning wheel for a change. We braided and sewed the children's hats, and knit our winter hoods.[64]

John R. Winder's household ran well, and he must have been pleased with how well his two wives worked together. The two women were held up as an example to ward members as the way the ideal plural marriage family should live. Both wives dressed alike and shared equal responsibilities.[65] Again, Hannah provides some insight into what her feelings were as a polygamous wife:

> Our home got in good running order that winter. Every thing went on in order. There was always good meetings, and no excuse for not living like Latter Day Saints ought to. Our family, for order and union was pointed out as a pattern, both wives after a time were dressed the same.
>
> I took delight in pleasing my husband, and his wife, and by reading and searching I got to feel it was the will of the Lord.
>
> I can bear my testimony of Celestial marriage, it is all right when we keep the law of God, otherwise, it is all wrong. It can be done, for I have lived it, and kept the law for a length of time, and was willing to continue, as I had covenanted to love and obey.[66]

Shortly before the marriage of Hannah and John R., he was sealed to his first wife Ellen "for time and all eternity." This ordinance, which Mormons believe seals a marriage for not only this life, but forever, was performed in the Endowment House on Temple Square on August 31, 1855.[67] The following spring, John R. took Hannah to the Endowment House where, on April 22, 1856, they too were sealed.[68] Later that year, on July 2, Ellen gave birth to a beautiful daughter named Lizzie Walters Winder. Lizzie was Ellen's seventh child, but only her fourth to live until maturity.

Founding the Deseret Agriculture and Manufacturing Society

John R. Winder, probably because of his agricultural background from his boyhood in Biddenden, was very interested in stock raising and farming in the territory from almost immediately after his arrival. He later wrote: "My interest in farming, stock raising and industrial pursuits led to my connection with the Deseret Agricultural and Manufacturing society of which I was president and a director for a period of forty-four years."[69] The Society was first chartered on January 17, 1856 by an act of the territorial legislature. Its purpose was "to promote the arts of domestic industry and to encourage the production of articles from the native elements, primarily through the establishment of an annual exhibition of products."[70] John R. Winder was a charter member of their first board in 1856 and would serve until 1901 both as a director, and as he has mentioned, at times as president. The Deseret Agricultural and Manufacturing Society became the Utah State Fair Board in 1907, and for years thereafter John R. Winder "was always called the father of the state fair."[71]

In this capacity, Winder became acquainted with many of the leading men in the territory that would become his lifelong friends. Some of the other early officials that served with Winder were W. C. Sataines, C. H. Oliphant, S. M. Blair, L. D. Young, R. L. Campbell, James Brown, E. F. Sheets, F. A. Mitchell, A. P. Rockwood, and Bishop Edward Hunter. Edward Hunter had been called to serve as the LDS Church's Presiding Bishop in 1851 and would serve in that important capacity until his death in 1883. Jesse C. Little was also one of the first directors along with John R., and he would be called to serve as Bishop Hunter's second counselor in October of 1856, serving in that capacity until 1874. Elder Wilford Woodruff was also one of the Society's founding directors.[72] He had served as a member of the Church's Quorum of the Twelve Apostles since 1839 and would eventually serve as the Church's fourth president. Wilford Woodruff developed a close friendship with John R. Winder through numerous activities of the D. A. & M. Society. They often worked together on special projects and were sometimes on the same sub-committees.[73] Woodruff and Winder shared a love of agriculture and livestock throughout their lives and, in their later years, worked very closely in both business ventures and completing the Salt Lake Temple.

The Deseret Agricultural and Manufacturing Society served an educational role in the territory. The members formed various branches throughout Utah and helped to instruct farmers in better farming techniques.[74] One of the more notable projects of the Society was the establishment of Deseret Gardens near the mouth of Emigration Canyon. John R. Winder and his colleagues sent to other states and occasionally overseas for new varieties of seeds, trees and breeds of cattle to test in the new territory. These items were then experimentally raised in Deseret Gardens and, if found to be satisfactory, were produced and distributed to settlements throughout Utah Territory for public use. For this particular project, and the society's participation in various reclamation projects, the society became widely known in circles of agriculture and received recognition from as far away as Washington D.C.. John R. Winder and the Board all served without pay, although they allotted money for a gardener at Deseret Gardens.[75]

Winder and his associates worked very hard that first year with the Society to prepare for the territory's first fair, which was held that fall in the Deseret Store (which stood where the Hotel Utah, later re-named the Joseph Smith Memorial Building, was built). On October 8, 1856, the *Deseret News* published the following account of it:

> *The First Deseret State Fair* was held in this city on the 2nd, 3rd, and 4th, and was highly creditable to the skill and industry of our infant settlements.

The articles on exhibition filled most of the spacious rooms in the building known as the Deseret Store. In the basement were large squashes, beets and carrots; various samples of wheat, corn, flour, garden seeds, garden implements, large hens from Land's End, England, etc.

On the first floor was a beautiful carding machine, made at the Public Works for Gov. Young; a very handsome bridle, saddle and buckskin suit . . . cutlery, combs, blankets, cloth, quilts, straw hats and bonnets, nails, leather, etc.

On the second floor a table loaded with grapes, peaches and apples attracted much attention; though it was rather late in the season for a fair show of grapes and peaches. In this room were also exhibited carpets, furniture, specimens of wood-graining, a small steam engine, egg plants . . . and numerous other home products. Various articles from India, interesting relics, beautiful paintings and needlework specimens . . . added much to the interest connected with this department.

On the 2nd, a spirited plowing match came off, in one of the Governor's fields adjacent to the City.

On the 3d, there was a highly creditable exhibition of stock.

This Fair will operate as a great incentive to the development of home resources, by showing the people how much has already been done, and how they can readily do far more and better.[76]

Awards were given at the fair for such things as the best fenced and cultivated farm, the best specimen of raw silk, the best bushel of cocoons and the best ten pounds of native sugar. "Monetary prizes were meager, the primary motivation of exhibits being the pride in excellence of the exhibitor." Early participation in exhibits was sparse, most exhibits being brought out of a sense of public duty, yet "this early attitude soon gave way to greater public participation and competition in later expositions."[77]

John R. Winder's wives often competed in the early fairs. "Our Fairs in those days were furnished with home made materials," wrote Hannah, "and we took first prize on sheeps grey flannels." Winder, himself, was of course involved in exhibiting as well. "Brother Winder was an active worker in the Fair ever since it commenced. Another ambition he had was to have first peas, cucumbers and other vegetables of the season."[78] John R. Winder and William Jennings also exhibited some of their finest cuts from their butcher shop. At the 1857 Deseret State Fair it was noted that "A side of dressed beef from Jennings and Winder's stall would throw the most fastidious epicure into ecstasies." It was also noted that "The show of home made leather was certainly superior, and shows at once that in course of time our market in that line will make us independent of any foreign supplies. Mr. Brewer's saddle and machias were good work, made from Jennings and Winder's leather."[79]

The Deseret Agriculture and Manufacturing Society proved to be an important outlet for John R. Winder. Contacts were made, skills were enhanced, and talents were displayed. Winder was often employed in writing correspondence to the bishops of the territory and others, for example, and he was also used to oversee some of the billing related to the organization.[80]

Elizabeth Parker Becomes His Third Wife

Despite the important work that the Winder family was doing with the fairs, "There was still another crop in which we were becoming very anxious" noted Hannah. "The main object of our union was to live up to the measure of our creation, and obey the law of our first parents, to increase and multiply," she later wrote. Whether or not they would have any children together was a great concern for both John R. and his second wife Hannah. "We had promised, or had been promised through our Patriarchal blessings, by Father Marley, that we would have posterity, and now the year had gone and no prospects."[81] Indeed, when John R. Winder had received his patriarchal blessing from Patriarch Isaac Marley on New Year's Eve, 1856, he was deeply concerned about having a sizeable posterity, and possibly if he would have any more sons to carry on the family name. At that point, he and Ellen were still grieving the loss of their one year-old Emily who had passed away the previous August. Within the last decade, he and Ellen had lost baby Ellen Sophia in London, little Alma in Liverpool, and now Emily in Salt Lake. But Patriarch Marley pronounced the following words while blessing John R.: "Be comforted my son thou art holding keys of Priesthood that places thee at the head of thy family, placed as a Father at the head of a numerous posterity which will be given thee."[82] Apparently his new wife Hannah received a similar promise, but still no children had come from their union.

"He was some disappointed," Hannah wrote of her husband, "and on the 11 January, [1857], he married Elizabeth Parker, his Third Wife."[83] Elizabeth was a nineteen year-old girl who attended church with the Winder family and had been friendly with them. "November 30, 1856, I received an offer of marriage from Brother John Rex Winder, he having first obtained my father's consent" she later wrote. "I afterwards received and accepted an invitation to his home to receive my Patriarchal blessing. I had been acquainted with the Winder family for several years and was partial to them."[84]

Like John R., Ellen, and Hannah, Elizabeth Parker was a native of the British Isles. She was born March 15, 1837 in Chaigley, Lancashire, England to John Parker Jr. and Alice Whittaker. The following year, her parents and grandparents were baptized members of The Church of Jesus Christ of Latter-day Saints. Her grandparents, the John Parker Srs., immediately emigrated to join the Saints in Nauvoo, Illinois. Alice died and left John Parker Jr. a widower with three small children. In 1844 he left England with his little family.

On the voyage across the Atlantic, John Parker Jr. fell ill and was unable to adequately care for his children. Elizabeth Parker had long beautiful hair that became snarled and matted without a parent to care for it. John solved the problem by chopping the poor nine-year-old girl's hair with a large pair of scissors. Little Elizabeth was mortified, and her ruined hair caused a great furor all over the ship. The ship's captain even became so upset as to administer a severe tongue lashing to her father for his extreme lack of consideration in mutilating his child so.

The Parkers, Junior and Senior, were reunited in Nauvoo, and were able to enjoy several happy months. Grandmother Parker died in 1845, and her husband fell ill and died several years later after enduring as a helpless invalid for the final few. After a few years, John Parker Jr. married Ellen Briggs Douglas, a widow with several children. They had three children of their own and established a loving and unified home for their mixed family.

In the late 1840's, mob violence in Nauvoo became severe and the Parkers were forced to escape down river to St. Louis. While there, John Parker Jr. founded a soft drink company which boomed beyond his wildest expectations. At one point he was employing over one hundred men in the making of root beer during a very thirsty and profitable summer. In a short while he was able to amass a great deal of money. However, while he could have stayed in St. Louis to build his soft drink company even larger, he gave it all up to move on west to Zion.

However, with their new-found wealth, the Parker family could travel across the plains in style. Parker was able to completely outfit a private company comprised of relatives to travel to Utah in an enviable fashion. He had even purchased a state-of-the-art threshing machine to be used once they had established themselves in Salt Lake. While most of his Mormon contemporaries bumped across the plains in primitive covered wagons or walked with handcarts, John Parker Jr. provided his family with a large spring mounted carriage, complete with a white canvas top. The independent Parker company traveled in first class swiftly and without incident, and arrived in Salt Lake City in August of 1852. The Parkers built a large home on Second South west of Main Street, where they were in the same ward as the Winders. It was in this association that Elizabeth began to get to know the Winder family and her eventual husband.[85]

After the marriage, Elizabeth moved in with the other two wives at the city home at Third South west of Main Street. Several months after John R. and Elizabeth's January wedding in the Council House, they were sealed "for time and all eternity" in the Endowment House on Temple Square. This ordinance took place on August 7, 1857.[86]

Hannah Thompson Winder and Elizabeth Parker Winder became fast friends, developing a close and lasting bond of sisterhood. They felt comfortable with each other on an equal basis, a relationship that was never quite achieved with Ellen Walters Winder, whom they both referred to respectfully as "Mrs. Winder."[87] Hannah and Elizabeth's bond of great love and respect certainly would have helped them both adjust to life in a plural marriage, and they became closer than sisters.[88]

About the time of John R. Winder's marriage to Elizabeth Parker, her brother, William Parker, married Mary Shanks, the Irish girl who had helped the Winder family with the young children since they had left Liverpool.[89] Mary and William probably became acquainted by being in the same ward, similar to the way John R. and Elizabeth first met. Although the Winder household would have missed the help of Mary Shanks, they now had three women in the house to help share the many household tasks.

In his first few years in his new environment, John R. Winder did a remarkable job of assimilating and getting established economically, socially, and ecclesiastically in the unique culture of Brigham Young's Deseret. While "LDS immigrants, particularly those from northern Europe, were usually assimilated into communities and congregations quickly," this Englishman did exceptionally well.[90] The contributions of John R. Winder and his fellow British immigrants to the early stages of Utah's development were significant. Richard L. Jensen has noted:

Elizabeth Parker (1837-1883), was the third wife of John R. Winder. It was after she began to sell her homemade butter to the neighbors that the Winder family began the business of delivering dairy products.

Although the days of mass emigration to Zion are past, the contributions of the British LDS emigrants in Church history can hardly be overstated. The strength of the early Church was largely due to great numbers of dedicated British immigrants in Nauvoo and the Salt Lake Valley. With much of the British emigration coming relatively early, these saints were in a position to exert a particularly significant influence upon the Church in its most formative years.[91]

Over the next few decades, John R. Winder and his British counterparts would take active roles in building the Church in the Great Basin. They would fill more than their proportional share of local leadership positions in the LDS Church. For example, of 605 bishops and presiding elders in Mormon congregations in the United States between 1848 and 1890, twenty-nine percent were born in the British Isles. Twenty-three percent of stake presidents during the same period were born in the British Isles.[92]

The world John R. Winder entered in October 1853 had been new in many ways. Permanent settlement by the Mormons had begun only six years before, and there was still much work to do to help the "desert blossom as the rose." Winder partook of it fully, with enthusiasm and determination to do his part in building a future for his family in the Kingdom of God in Utah. It was said of Winder in those first few years in Utah: "He made some good business contacts and prospered financially and was a faithful member of the church."[93] He has been hailed as "prominent among the pioneer workers who have so successfully reared a State out of the great American wilderness and developed the natural resources that are hidden in the mountains and valleys."[94]

In the years 1853 to 1857, John Rex Winder endured a daughter's death, cold winters, suffering, and struggles; but he also enjoyed weddings, new friendships, the fairs, and business success. "Thus he became familiar with all of the phases, the hardships and the privations of pioneer life and also enjoyed its privileges and opportunities."[95]

Captain John R. Winder of the Nauvoo Legion, as he appeared during the "Utah War." He courageously guarded Echo Canyon throughout the winter to keep Johnston's Army out.

7
A Knight for the Kingdom of God: Captain Winder in the "Utah War," 1857-1858

"Connection with Utah military affairs"

In the early years of the Utah Territory, the Mormon pioneers realized that despite being half a continent away from the mobs that drove them from their homes time and again in the east, they were not without their troubles. Richard W. Young described their situation:

> They were no longer surrounded by mobs but by savages. On the north were the Snakes or Shoshones, the Bannock Indians. On the northeast were the Crows: on the east, the Utes; on the southeast, the Navajos and the Piutes. There were various tribes of Indians which, despite the kindness with which the people treated them, rose up occasionally and made warfare upon the early settlers. It was in these days that President Winder came to the front as a military man who was identified with the military organization which, in remembrance of the honorable part that had been played by the Legion in Nauvoo, was called by statute the Nauvoo Legion.[1]

John R. Winder, after being in the valley not quite two years, did step up to volunteer with protecting the Saints from the Indians. "My long connection with Utah military affairs began in 1855," Winder later wrote, "when I joined the Nauvoo Legion, as the local militia was then styled."[2] Soon he became prominent in the Territory as a military man.[3] He worked hard with the Legion and on Monday, the 20th of April, 1857, the Nauvoo Legion held a parade in Salt Lake City. Afterwards, the election of new officers took place.[4] John R. Winder was promoted to the rank of captain.[5] As will be shown, "He held the position of captain with signal honor."[6]

Storm Clouds Gather

Not long after Winder joined the Nauvoo Legion, a threat loomed which promised to be a greater problem than Indians. The State of Deseret had been denied statehood in 1849 and was, instead, organized as the Utah Territory in 1850. With this organization came federally appointed officials who were not always friendly with the Saints. With each attempt to extend federal influence into the territory, the Mormons' stubborn adherence to sovereignty sent government appointees back to the East carrying tales about "the debauchery of polygamists" and "the unpatriotic climate."[7]

The exaggerated reports that the Mormons were in a state of rebellion eventually reached the White House, where President James Buchanan and the Democrats had recently been accused by their Republican opponents in the campaign of 1856 of favoring the "twin relics of barbarism"—polygamy and slavery. Seeing a political opportunity to show he opposed polygamy, Buchanan hastily ordered 2,500 federal troops to secretly march to Utah, under the command of Albert Sidney Johnston. Acting without the benefit of an investigation, Buchanan relieved Brigham Young as governor, a position to which Young had been reappointed even after the practice of polygamy had become public knowledge, and sent Alfred Cumming of Georgia to replace him. Unfortunately, Buchanan did everything in secrecy, even stopping the mail to Utah to give the troops the advantage of surprise. This attempted "surprise attack" by the U.S. government led to hostilities known in history as the "Utah War." It would be the largest military operation in the United States between the times of the Mexican War and the Civil War, and one that would deeply involve John Rex Winder.[8]

The 24th of July was met with great celebration in 1857. It had now been an even ten years since Brigham Young and the vanguard company of pioneers had entered the Salt Lake Valley. To celebrate, the Winders and over 2,500 other Saints went up to Silver Lake in Big Cottonwood Canyon for the festivities. However, during the celebrations, Salt Lake Mayor A. O. Smoot, Judson Stoddard and Porter Rockwell, the wily frontiersman who had gained fame as Joseph Smith's bodyguard, rode hastily into the campground to tell Brigham Young that a United States army was advancing toward the Valley. Ironically, the stars-and-stripes flew proudly from tall peaks in the canyon even as the Saints received word that they were being accused of being unpatriotic. Governor Young allowed the Saints to enjoy the day, but at its close announced to his people that an army of the United States was marching toward them. Rumors picked up by Mormon scouts and wagon masters were that the intent of the nation's leaders was to force the Mormons to submit or be destroyed.[9]

It was a shocking announcement that John R. Winder would have seared in his memory for the rest of his life. He recalled that infamous day nearly half a century later while speaking in general conference: "I remember also how, just ten years from the day when the pioneers arrived in this valley, as we were celebrating that event at the head of Big Cottonwood, the word came that a great army of the United States was forming to come up and attack the people in these valleys of the mountains."[10]

Not long after, when the army was almost at their borders, Captain Stewart Van Vliet was sent to Salt Lake City to officially inform Brigham Young that the army was coming and would be stationed in Utah. Young sent word back with him that they would welcome an investigation by a civil commission, but they had retreated for the last time and would make a stand against any invader.[11] Conflict now seemed inevitable.

On August 1, 1857 Daniel H. Wells, Lieutenant-General, and James Ferguson, Adjutant General, sent out a notice to Captain Winder and the other officers of the Nauvoo Legion throughout the state to hold their commands in readiness to meet the invading army:

> Sir: Reports, tolerably well authenticated have reached this office that an army from the Eastern States is now en route to invade this Territory. . . You are instructed to hold your command in readiness to march at the shortest possible notice to any part of the Territory. See that the law is strictly enforced in regards to arms and ammunition, and as far as practicable that each Ten be provided with a good wagon and four horses or mules, as well as the necessary clothing, etc. for the winter.

Meanwhile, every family in Utah was alerted to be ready to give their all for the protection of Zion. "War became the universal theme. Fire-arms were manufactured or repaired; scythes were turned into bayonets; long-unused sabers were burnished and sharpened, and from all parts of the earth the saints were summoned to the defense of Zion."[12] They were advised to store their grain, to avoid waste of any kind, and to receive with open arms those who were being called home from mission fields and from Mormon settlements in other states.[13] "I remember what occurred during the remainder of that summer and the following winter" John R. Winder later recalled, "We were very busy during the winter manufacturing boxes in which to store flour and secure what provisions we could, because the word was that we would have to leave this beautiful city and sacrifice our homes."[14]

Brigham Young ordered out the poorly equipped militia to prepare for the worst. The Nauvoo Legion consisted at this time of all able bodied men between the ages of eighteen and forty-five. At the governor's command, reinforcements from all over Utah hurried to the scene of the impending struggle—old men, young men, and boys—until the force confronting the United States Army was nearly 2,500 strong, or about equal in number to the regular troops. In the Autumn of 1857 the Legion gathered together to prepare to wage a defensive warfare to protect their Zion. The militia was organized into military districts, and it would be a challenge for Captain John R. Winder and the other young officers to help organize and train this mass of volunteers. "The troops began to arrive early this morning. . . . From 2,000 to 3,000 of the Saints of God armed themselves and went into the mountains, according to the counsel of President

Young, and they were led by the noble and valiant General Daniel H. Wells, to hedge up the way of the enemy, should they attempt to come in."[15] The energetic Nauvoo Legion viewed themselves as "do-or-die guardians of Zion's portals," and viewed the conflict as a "holy war." It is as a result of this sentiment that John Rex Winder and the other officers were "prayed over, and individually 'set apart' to holy duty by Mormon 'laying on of hands.'"[16]

The Nauvoo Legion under General Wells adopted defensive measures against their enemy. Captain Winder had worked with the General in planning the strategy to delay the advance of Johnston's army, and they prayed it would work.[17] "Companies commanded by Colonel Robert T. Burton, Lot Smith, Joseph Taylor, John R. Winder, Ephraim Hanks, Porter Rockwell and others sped to block its avenue of approach."[18] They destroyed forage along the army's route, stampeded its livestock, and burned its supply wagons. Grass was burned to inconvenience them, as was Fort Bridger, which the Mormons had previously purchased. There on the high plains of Wyoming, Captain Winder courageously waged the defensive war. "Among the troops that were sent out to the front was a company under the command of John R. Winder," it was later recorded, "and his company found its way clear to the front. They became part of the troops that were in immediate observation of the approaching expedition."[19]

"The report was that it was the flower of the United States army that was coming out here to exterminate the 'Mormons'" John R. reported. "Not only did this army threaten us," he continued, "but the Indians around us were excited, and were robbing the people of horses and cattle. In this condition we remained during the winter and until the next April."[20] Nonetheless, without firing a shot the militia ground the army of the United States to a stop near the charred remains of Fort Bridger in Green River County, Wyoming where snow blizzards pinned it down for the winter. The citizen soldiers had achieved their resolve of preventing the army from passing the Wasatch Mountains without shedding a drop of the enemy's blood. As for John R. Winder, it was later said that he "had been an influential figure in thwarting the advancement of Johnston's Army on their march to Salt Lake City."[21]

Guarding Echo Canyon

One of the main passages that stood between the Salt Lake area and the U.S. army was Echo Canyon. About the 1st of December the militia began returning to their homes, leaving but a small out-post in that canyon to watch the enemy during the winter and report their movements to headquarters at Salt Lake City. General Wells left Echo Canyon on the 4th of December and Colonel Burton followed the next day, both returning to Salt Lake City. They left Captain Winder in charge of the defense.[22] "I was captain of a company of lancers in the Echo Canyon campaign," Winder later recalled, "and during the winter of 1857-8, after most of the militia had returned home and Johnston's army had gone into winter quarters at Fort Bridger, I was left with fifty men to guard the canyon and its approaches and give notice to Gen. Wells and the authorities at Salt Lake City of any further movements of the invading host."[23] The general had given Captain Winder explicit instructions, and declared to him, "Remember that to you is entrusted for the time being the duty of standing between Israel and her foes." His full letter of instruction to Captain Winder reads as follows:

> Headquarters Eastern Expedition,
> Camp Weber, December 4th, 1857
> Capt. John R. Winder.
>
> Dear Brother: You are appointed to take charge of the guard detailed to remain and watch the movements of the invaders. You will keep ten men at the lookout station on the heights of Yellow Creek. Keep a constant watch from the highest point during daylight, and a camp guard at night, also a horse guard out with the horses which should be kept on good grass all day, and grained with two quarts of feed per day. This advance will occasionally trail out towards Fort Bridger, and look at our enemies from the high butte near the place. You will relieve this guard once a week. Keep open and travel down to the head of Echo, instead of the road. Teamsters or deserters must not be permitted to come to your lookout station. Let them pass with merely knowing who and what they are, to your station on the Weber and into the city. If officers or others undertake to come in, keep them prisoners until you receive further advices from the city. Especially and in no case let any would-be civil officers pass. These are, as far as I know, as follows: A. Cumming (governor), Eckels (chief justice), Dotson (marshal), Forney (superintendent of Indian affairs), Hockaday (district attorney). At your station on the Weber you will also keep a lookout, and guard the road at night, also keep a camp and a horse guard. Keep the men employed making improvements, when not on other duty. Build a good horse corral, and prepare stables. Remove the houses into a fort line and then picket in the remainder. Keep a trail open down the Weber to the citizens' road.
>
> Be strict in the issue of rations and feed. Practice economy both in your supplies and time, and see that there is no waste of either.
>
> If your lookout party discover any movement of the enemy in this direction, let them send two men to your camp on the Weber, and the remainder continue to watch their movements, and not all leave their station, unless it should prove a large party, but keep you timely advised so that you can meet them at the defenses in Echo, or if necessary render them assistance. Where you can do so at an advantage, take all such parties prisoners, if you can, without shooting, but if you cannot, you are at liberty to attack them, as no such party must be permitted to come into the city. Should the party be too strong and you are compelled to retreat, do so after safely caching all supplies; in all cases giving

us prompt information by express, that we may be able to meet them between here and the city. Send into the city every week all the information you can obtain, and send whether you have any news from the enemy or not, that we may know of your welfare, kind of weather, depth of snow, etc.

The boys at the lookout station should not make any trail down to the road, nor expose themselves to view, but keep concealed as much as possible, as it is for that purpose that that position has been chosen. No person without a permit must be allowed to pass from this way to the enemy's camp. Be careful about this. Be vigilant, active and energetic and observe good order, discipline and wisdom in all your works, that good may be the result. Remember that to you is entrusted for the time being the duty of standing between Israel and their foes, and as you would like to repose in peace and safety while others are on the watchtower, so now while in the performance of this duty do you observe the same care, vigilance and activity which you would desire of others when they come to take your place. Do not let any inaction on the part of the enemy lull you into a false security and cause any neglect on your part.

Praying the Lord to bless and preserve you in life, health and strength, and wisdom and power to accomplish every duty incumbent upon you and bring peace to Israel to the utter confusion and overthrow of our enemies,

I remain, your brother in the gospel of Christ,
[Signed,] Daniel H. Wells,
Lieutenant-General Commanding.

P. S. Be careful to prevent fire being kindled in or near the commissary storehouse.[24]

This new responsibility was one that John R. Winder took seriously. While they kept watch, Captain Winder kept the fifty under his command very busy. They formed large entrenchments, ditches, and piled up large masses of rock in narrow passes, so as to roll them down upon the enemy and destroy them should they attempt to move any closer to the Great Salt Lake Valley. Each week Captain Winder would rotate the ten mounted lookouts on Yellow Creek, above the head of Echo Canyon. This relay was occasionally to venture out towards Fort Bridger to spy on the American army from "the high butte near that place." Southwest of Fort Bridger, a singular butte with a level top rose eight hundred feet above the valley of Black's Fork. From here, Winder's lookouts could watch the "Expedition's" encampment.[25] The headquarters of Captain Winder and his fifty was called Camp Weber, and was situated on the Weber River at the mouth of Echo Canyon.

Captain Winder sent a report of the situation to General Wells, dated December 9, 1857. He said that the snow between Weber and Yellow Creek was five inches to two and a half feet and that the weather was very cold. He reported that "a little before sunset Sunday evening the boys saw about 6 men, as they supposed, coming west." He said Brother Follet immediately took three men, thinking to head them off, but could not locate them. They finally found tracks which seemed to come from the direction of Fort Bridger. Captain Winder expressed regret that they were unable to ascertain who they were and what they were doing. He said he was inclined to think they had "traveled up 'Lost Creek' to avoid this station" and that they were "messengers to our enemies to let them know, probably, that the armies of Israel have returned to their homes." Winder said he was carrying out the instructions to the best of his ability; that they had built a corral for the horses; had removed four houses into the fort square and built a large room 35 by 16 feet, designed for a meeting house. He said they needed more tools and a grindstone to sharpen the tools. He mentioned that one man was making soap.[26]

Two days later, on his birthday, December 11, Captain Winder wrote another report to Daniel H. Wells. Among other things, he reported that "Col. Johnston" had sent 1000 mules and 400 cattle south to Henry's Fork to winter that were "quite used up." The army was in such a great need for food, however, that the Federal army was also killing and drying 1000 head of cattle, he said. Captain Winder reported to his superior that the men at Camp Weber were not satisfied with their rations and asked "May I increase the amount?"[27] In another letter, Captain Winder had ordered a new spy glass, which was delivered to him on Saturday, December 12. The *Journal History* records a Brother Nelson Merkley taking three letters, a padlock, and the spy glass to him that day.

At this point in time, the Mormons were still not certain whether the U.S. Army would wait near Fort Bridger until spring, or whether they would attempt to surprise the Mormons and force their way into Salt Lake City that winter. Congress that winter authorized two new volunteer regiments. President Buchanan, Secretary of War John B. Floyd, and Army Chief of Staff Winfield Scott assigned 3,000 additional regular troops to reinforce the Utah Expedition.[28] Predictions of hostilities were rampant, and Captain Winder and his troops had to take great care to assure the safety of the Territory.

As has been mentioned, Winder and his lookouts would occasionally see spies from the federal company. Captain Winder seemed especially fearful that the enemy would realize how few men actually guarded the canyon. One night, when he perhaps sensed that they were being watched from a distance, Winder ordered the small detachment to march around and around huge bonfires. With their shadows cast upon the steep canyon walls and a seemingly continuous stream of soldiers appearing, an illusion was made that there were many more soldiers in the canyon than there actually were. "Army scouts reported to their leaders that thousands of soldiers guarded the narrow passageway."[29] The scouts' report to their commanding officers helped them decide to stay put for the winter. Deep snows that fell soon after quickly solidified their decision. This story of John R. Winder's creativity and resourcefulness was one which his grandchildren would hear many times while growing up. George Winder, one grandson, recalled Church President Heber J. Grant delighting in relating the incident at a Winder reunion years after John R. Winder's death.[30]

The young captain was greatly beloved by the young soldiers who served under him. His demeanor as a military man was so impressive that one soldier serving under him mistakenly remembers Winder as a major.[31] "I was a fellow soldier with him in the troubles through which we passed in 1857," said Winder's long-time friend William W. Riter. "I was then but a boy, along with other boys; and his attitude towards us then, in the rougher aspects of life, was kind and gentle and considerate."[32] Seymour B. Young echoed the complement:

> In the work of the militia of the Territory of Utah I have often been associated with President Winder. He was my superior officer always, and I have often heard him speak to the brethren under his care as soldiers, and he always addressed us in that gentle, loving way—"My brethren, this will be best for us to do," or "My brethren, come, let us do this." Never any harsh statements—always "My brethren." I considered this a token of his loving heart, evidencing that he was in fellowship with his brethren, although their superior officer, and that he had no pride lifting him above them.[33]

Two weeks after Captain Winder took command of the picket guard at Echo, he reported to Governor Young that a deep snow had fallen in the mountains. The Governor sent word back to the young Captain that the guard was to be reduced to ten men. The remainder of the militia returned to their homes for the winter.[34] Winder's tiny band gained some international notoriety when the *London Punch* afterward so graphically pictured in cartoon the "flower of the American army" half buried in the snow herded by ten Mormons.[35] *The Millennial Star*, published by the British Saints in Liverpool, later noted that "Brother Winder took an active part in the defense of the Saints during the so-called Echo Canyon war, when United States troops were sent against the people of Utah."[36]

All through the winter, deserters and army teamsters from the Expedition were constantly arriving at Echo Canyon, in many instances in a starving and destitute condition. John R. Winder and the Mormon guard treated them kindly, provided them with food, and passed them on to Salt Lake City. Through this channel, Governor Young and General Wells were kept well informed of the condition and contemplated movements of Johnston's army.[37] Captain Winder and the guards who manned the frostbitten outposts in Echo Canyon, however, spent the cold winter in much the same condition as the U.S. Army. One soldier said that a man couldn't tell if he had his hat on without feeling for it.[38] Nonetheless, these knights for the Kingdom of God dutifully stood their ground.

Replacements were sent from time to time to relieve the men, but John R. Winder remained in charge throughout most of December.[39] "The tenseness of the situation having relaxed, Captain Winder was relieved of vidette duty about Christmas by Major H. S. Beatie, who took command of Camp Weber."[40] Major Beatie in turn was later relieved by Captain Brigham Young, Jr.[41]

Holiday Break and Pursuing Indians in Tooele

John R. Winder would have been overjoyed to return to his beloved family and the warmth of his home. The holiday season that year was one where "mirth and festivity reigned supreme." Orson F. Whitney remarked:

> Balls, theaters, sociables and other amusements served to dispel every thought of gloom, every feeling of nervous apprehension as to what might follow. Though all knew that the advent of spring would witness a renewal of operations in the mountains, no lip quivered, no cheek blanched, no heart faltered at the prospect. Mingling with the song of joy, the paen of praise, welling up from the hearts of a people who felt as sensibly as did Israel of old after passing the Red Sea, that Jehovah had delivered His people and engulfed their foes.[42]

Later that winter, Ellen Winder gave birth to her and John R.'s eighth child. Eliza Ann Winder was born on February 13, 1858. She would be their fifth child to live to maturity and proved to be a joyous ray of sunshine during the stormy years of the "Utah War." Captain Winder, however, was not allowed to enjoy his new daughter for long, for his talents were soon needed again and he was promptly back in the saddle. "His company was called out. . . . to take part in seeking to overtake a band of savages that had ravaged our settlements upon the west."[43] General George D. Grant had called John R. Winder to round up a regiment to pursue a band of Indians who had stolen a large number of horses from settlers in Tooele. By March 8, 1858 he had raised eighty-five mounted men, probably many from among acquaintances made at Echo Canyon.[44] Winder later recalled, "In March, 1858, I was with Gen. George D. Grant and about eighty other mounted men who went in pursuit of a marauding band of Indians in Tooele county, and was caught with my comrades in a terrible storm on the desert."[45] Because of the blizzard they lost the trail of the Indians they had been pursuing and had no choice but to ride home to Salt Lake City.[46] On March 28, Captain Winder sent a report to Adjutant General James Ferguson stating that his party was turning back and heading home through Tooele and Lone Rock Valley.[47]

Captain Winder was much beloved by his "Rough Riders" that accompanied him out to chase Indians in the salt flats. "My first association with Brother Winder was in a military capacity," according to friend W. W. Riter. "I was a common soldier, or a common militiaman, under his direction in the spring of 1858 in an Indian expedition. . . . I remember him well as our commander in the military expedition to which I referred. He was only a boy, and his command were mostly boys. I was less than twenty years of age, and I was about the average age. I can well remember the kindness and the consideration with which he treated us."[48] Francis M. Lyman, who later served as a member of the Church's Quorum of the Twelve Apostles, also gained a close friendship with Captain Winder as a young man. "He was a very dear friend of mine. I knew him in 1858 and have known him ever since. I was then eighteen; he was thirty-six."[49]

In the fall of 1857, when Captain Van Vleit informed Brigham Young of the U.S. troops that would be marching through Salt Lake, the Lion of the Lord responded: "When those troops arrive they will find Utah a desert. Every house will be burned to the ground, every tree cut down, and every field lay waste. We have three years' provisions on hand, which we will 'cache,' and then take to the mountains and bid defiance to all the powers of the government." This was the plan the Church leaders intended to pursue if war became inevitable, a plan which they hoped would turn public opinion to favorably support the Mormon cause. Governor Young wanted the conflict to appeal to the sympathies of people throughout the nation, so that they would view this invasion of Utah as a "holy war" of a people being persecuted for standing up for their constitutional privileges—the freedom of religion. What could be more tragic than to see forty thousand people forced to flee their farms and cities, burn their homes, abandon the civilization they had erected in the desert wasteland rather than forsake their religious tenets?

On March 18, 1858, while John R. Winder was still with his posse in Tooele, the Church leaders and militia officers held a council of war to formulate plans, "to go into the desert and not war with the people [of the United States], but let them destroy themselves." The following Sunday a special conference was held in the tabernacle where "the Move" was announced to the people. President Young said, "I would rather see this city in ashes than have one good Elder killed." Within the days and weeks following, the families of the Salt Lake Valley began their migration to Provo, a city approximately fifty miles to the south.[50]

"The Move"

When Captain Winder returned from his excursion in Tooele, the entire Valley was in a flurry of activity, as everyone was preparing to follow the Prophet and flee the city. He later recalled the situation at that time:

> The people were told that it was necessary to leave this city, and not an objection was raised. We were of one heart and one mind. The move seemed inevitable. Men could be seen gathering up a yoke of cattle or two or three horses and hitching them to an old wagon as best they could, they would put into each wagon a family and all of this world's goods that they could collect, and then march away.[51]

Although many members of the Nauvoo Legion were released to return to their families, John R. was required to return to the defenses at Echo Canyon when the Saints were called upon to evacuate the city. Consequently, he was not there to help his young family flee their home. "Our husband was called out with a bunch of young men as scouts to guard the canyons, and on other duties," explained Hannah of the time.[52] Nonetheless, ten year-old John R., Jr. and the three Winder wives piled straw in their beloved new home for burning and joined the move south with the rest of the valley residents. Ellen not only had ten year -old John, Jr. to care for, but also the five-year-old twins, Mary and Martha, eighteen-month-old Lizzie, and baby Eliza, who was but a newborn. Hannah and Elizabeth would have helped with the children all that they could have, but they were each expecting their first babies at the time of the trek to Utah County.[53] "We were passing through trying times while in our anxious condition," Hannah later wrote, "for it was in the time of the Johnston Army trouble."[54] Nonetheless, the brave Winder women followed the Prophet and fled south.

"The road from here to Utah county was lined with teams passing from this city," John R. later reported, "the people not knowing whether they would be permitted to return again." The situation weighed heavily upon his mind and all others in the Territory. "I remember that it was a serious condition with us at that time," he later said. "It should be remembered that all this was brought about by misrepresentations that were made to the President of the United States."[55] The general populace of Salt Lake City was fearing a devastating confrontation; for although Johnston's army had been foiled for the winter, the Mormons feared that the angry troops would be as volatile as a powder keg with the coming of spring.

The business that John R. was involved with, the Jennings and Winder Tannery, was also disturbed by the "Utah War." "The perturbed state of things precipitated by the coming of Johnston's army put a quietus on the business for the time being, but it was taken up again under improved circumstances later on."[56] On the approach of the army, in 1858, the firm moved south to Provo, along with the vast majority of the Saints, "taking up and moving its tannery vats, intending to start a tannery in Provo." A lot was even purchased for the purpose.[57]

Practically the whole "territory was on wheels," on the move. Those without wagons carried their few belongings on their backs or tied them to the few animals they might own. This site of suffering and poverty began to stir the emotions of the rest of the country, as the Church leaders had hoped. "So extraordinary a migration is hardly paralleled in history," wrote the *New York Tribune*, "The driving of the Mormons from their homes, by military terror, will hardly contribute much to the honor of Mr. Buchanan's presidency." The *New York Times* said of the affair:

Whatever our opinions may be of Mormon morals or Mormon manners, there can be no question that this voluntary abandonment by 40,000 people. . . . is something from which no one who has a particle of sympathy with pluck, fortitude and constancy can withhold his admiration. . . . True or false, a faith to which so many men and women prove their loyalty at such sacrifices, is a force in the world. . . . When people abandon their home to plunge with women and children into a wilderness, they give a higher proof of courage than if they fought for them.

Even across the ocean, the *London Times* seemed moved by the Mormons' condition:

This strange people are again in motion for a new home. . . . There is much that is noble in their devotion to their delusions. They step into the waves of the great basin with as much reliance in their leader as the decendants of Jacob felt when they stepped between the walls of water in the Red Sea. . . . These western peasants seem to be a nation of heroes, ready to sacrifice everything rather than surrender one of their wives, or a letter from Joe Smith's golden plates.[58]

As has been mentioned, Captain Winder was not allowed to join his family in "the Move," for not long after the cavalry returned from Tooele, he was called up again. "Subsequently, he was again sent to the front, the eastern frontier, and remained there until the difficulty was adjusted."[59] In Winder's own words, "I had charge of the defenses at Echo canyon, and remained there until peace was declared."[60]

One young man whom Captain Winder began a life-long friendship with while back in Echo Canyon was Joseph F. Smith. "I have known President Winder since my boyhood," Smith later stated. "I have been intimate with him in the military affairs with which he was associated. I had the honor of serving with him in what was called the Echo War, after my return from my first mission, and became very intimate with him as a youth might know his elder."[61] Joseph F. Smith, son of Hyrum the Patriarch and nephew of the Prophet Joseph, was only a boy of 19 at the time, and had just returned from the Hawaiian Islands where he had served a mission. He returned to Salt Lake City on February 24, 1858 and was sent the next day by Brigham Young to join the Nauvoo Legion in Echo Canyon. The young Joseph F. Smith first served under Colonel Thomas Callister, and then under Captain Winder when he resumed the command at Echo.[62]

Joseph F. Smith quickly developed a kinship with John R. Winder and soon looked to him as a mentor. "I was one of the soldiers of the memorable Echo Canyon war, in the winter of 1857-58," Smith proudly mentioned on another occasion, "in which, of course, Colonel Winder figured very prominently as an officer of the Nauvoo Legion."[63] Young Joseph F. Smith would seek guidance from Winder throughout his life and would serve with him in a variety of civic and ecclesiastical responsibilities. When Joseph F. Smith was later called to serve as the President of the LDS Church, it was his old mentor from Echo Canyon, John Rex Winder, whom he would call to serve as his right-hand advisor and First Counselor.

Earlier in 1858, the Mormon's old friend, Colonel Thomas L. Kane, arrived from Washington D.C. to help in resolving the standoff. While not acting in any official capacity, Kane had offered to act as a mediator between the government and Utah and President Buchanan wished him well on his mission. Brigham Young was pleased to see his old friend when he arrived in Salt Lake City on February 25. After discussing the situation, Young sent him to inform the Federal entourage at Fort Bridger that the inhabitants of the Territory would welcome Governor Cumming and the other federal officials as officers of the central government, but they must come into the Valley without the troops.

After spending a month with the U.S. army, during which time messages had been exchanged with the Mormon leaders in Salt Lake, Colonel Kane finally arranged for Governor Cumming to visit Salt Lake City to learn first hand of conditions there. On April 5th, Governor Cumming accompanied by Colonel Kane began his trip towards Salt Lake. Soon after leaving the federal lines, they were joined by Captain John R. Winder and some of the militiamen who were stationed in Echo Canyon. Crafty Captain Winder, however, was determined that the new governor be fooled into thinking that Echo Canyon was guarded by many more soldiers than there actually were, so that when he returned to the camp of Johnston's army, he would report to them that a formidable barrier of Mormon military might blocked their path to the Valley. Winder's ploy is related as follows:

> Mormon militia met the party at the head of Echo Canyon, presented arms, and bade the new governor a welcome to Utah. By night, and by light of huge bonfires, he was escorted through the canyon. Repeatedly he was challenged by sentries and troops; repeatedly he delivered his firelight speech responsive to the welcome. Actually the whole performance was something of an imposition on Cumming's good nature. After each ritual the same party of Mormons would slip ahead through the darkness, challenge the governor, and repeat the ceremony. Cumming was amazed at the number of Utah troops, and their alertness in guarding Zion's portals.[64]

Governor Alfred Cumming met with Brigham Young and the other Church officials upon reaching Salt Lake. President Young surrendered his political title and soon formed an amiable working relationship with his successor. Cumming found the Mormons to be a good, patriotic people, and learned that the rumors that had instigated the entire fiasco were false. He returned back to Fort Bridger to bring his wife into the valley and to confer with now-General Johnston.

Meanwhile, President Buchanan responded to rising criticism by appointing Lazarus Powell and Ben McCulloch to carry an amnesty proclamation to Utah. Arriving early in June, they found the Church leaders willing to accept Cumming as Governor and a permanent army garrison in exchange for peace and amnesty. Towards the end of June, Johnston's army left their winter quarters and began to march towards the Salt Lake Valley.

Captain Winder and his men had been recalled from Echo Canyon on May 29, 1858, leaving the canyon defenses unmanned and going to help prepare the city for the imminent arrival of the federal troops.[65] As the army approached the city, the Saints resolved to not allow their homes to fall into enemy hands. Men, including John R. Winder, were left in all communities to touch torches to the straw piled in houses and gardens. Their instructions were to burn all flammable property rather than have it fall into the hands of the soldiery. Winder recalled the events as follows:

> The army, which had wintered at Fort Bridger, was permitted to come through the city and pass over the Jordan river. But when that army passed through the city, every house was closed, and not a person was to be seen; houses were shut, windows boarded up, and everything apparently deserted. As the soldiers marched through, the line was more like a funeral procession than a conquering army. A few of us were left to take care of the city, but all the rest had departed. Peace was afterward brought about, and the people were permitted to return to their homes.[66]

Johnston's army maintained splendid discipline by not harming anything. They surely would have had some deep animosity from the tortuous winter they had just endured. However, they continued marching forty miles to the southwest until they reached the western shores of Utah Lake where they established what became known as Camp Floyd. Once the ultimate location of the army camp was learned, the "word" came from Brigham Young, "that all those who desired to return to their homes were at liberty to do so."[67]

The Winder family made the long trek back to their homes in July of 1858.[68] On the entire journey back the Saints would have been anxious to see what condition their beloved homes would be found in after months of neglect. The Winder wives, however, seemed greatly pleased with what they came home to. "The city was like an Eden, when we came home," wrote Hannah. "No foot had tracked around our home. The native currants hung in rich profusion, black and yellow, and that was busy work for me to sit and prepare them for cooking." They seemed to have deeply missed their home and their beloved Great Salt Lake City. "The clear water was running down on both sides of the streets," gushed Hannah, "and green grass was growing on the side-walks."[69]

The Winder family seemed overjoyed to be home at last and back together as a family. "After returning from the move, we were happy to have our husband home with us," declared Hannah. "We had returned in time for the Pioneer Day celebration, July 24, 1858," she added. "It was a joyous day."[70] Indeed, that Pioneer Day would have been a great cause for celebration considering the storm that the Winder family and the rest of Utah had weathered during the year since the last Pioneer Day. It had been a year that the Winder family would never forget.

Despite the cost in money and crops lost, and discomforts suffered by the entire territory, the "Move South" was a huge success from the Mormon viewpoint. It focused the attention of the public on the plight of the Mormons and brought forth denunciation upon the policy of the White House. In fact, the entire debacle became known as "Buchanan's Blunder," and it would be a point of ridicule for the president by his critics for the remainder of his presidency. Most writers agree that it was a clever maneuver on the part of Brigham Young; an open clash was prevented, the Saints returned to their homes, and the army's triumphant march was through an empty city. Brigham Young, according to one contemporary non-Mormon, will be remembered as the man "who stood up to fight with the sword of the Lord, and with his few hundred guerillas, against the then mighty power of the United States, who has outwitted all diplomacy opposed to him; and finally who made a treaty of peace with the President of the great republic as though he wielded the combined power of France, Russia and England."[71]

Captain Winder returned from the front as somewhat of a hero. The "Utah War" experience had deeply shaped him in many ways. He had gained close friendships with President Brigham Young, Daniel H. Wells, Robert T. Burton, Joseph F. Smith, and others who would be influential in Utah affairs throughout the following decades. During the episode "he became a military man—not one of the carpet warriors, but a real fighter, and saw a great deal of hard active service against both palefaces and redskins."[72]

The hardships of 1857-58, however, would burn in his memory for the remainder of his days. In the October 1908 General Conference of the Church he would recall those times:

> This morning, when I awoke, my mind went back to the general conference of fifty years ago, and I was contrasting the many changes that have taken place, and the difference between our situation today and then. Just prior to that time the people had been in exile; they had moved away from their homes, and they were now returning. Within a few miles of this city a large army of the United States was stationed as a menace to the people here in the valleys of the mountains. As I compared conditions now and then I thought, what a change has come over us! At the time the foundation of our Temple was covered up; since then it has been uncovered and that beautiful edifice erected.[73]

John R. Winder would recite tales from the Utah War throughout his life. He would forever be in awe at the way the Lord protected the Saints and "fought our battles for us," without a single Mormon harmed in the process. "The Lord has preserved and protected His people," he later declared, "notwithstanding the fact that, at many times, they have been menaced by opposition, all things have been overruled for the good and benefit of the work of the Lord and for the advancement of His work upon the earth."[74] On another occasion he related the trials of the 'Utah War' while addressing a congregation in the Tabernacle on Temple Square. "I am referring to these things, my brethren and sisters, to verify the statement," he declared, "that this is the Lord's work, and that He overrules all these conditions for the good of His people, who will do His will and keep His commandments. If you look back and reflect, you will discover that every event I have mentioned led to one result—the Church took on new life, new energy, and advanced, increased and multiplied the more rapidly."[75]

Richard W. Young, a long-time friend of John R. Winder, would recite the many great deeds that Winder performed in the military years later at his beloved Captain's funeral. "He played no inconspicuous part as a soldier in the early history of our history," he said. After listing the principal points of Winder's distinguished military career, he added the following:

> [John Rex Winder]—a man who had strength, without harshness; a man who had gentleness, without weakness; who was a loyal man, without being a sycophant; a man who was pre-eminently just, a wise counselor and friend in need, willing to sacrifice for his friends.
>
> Now, may God grant that his example may be consecrated to the salvation both temporal and spiritual of his posterity.[76]

8

The Country Gentleman: Years at the B. K. Tannery and Establishing Poplar Farm, 1858-1864

"Pursuits which have always given me great pleasure"

The decade following the incident with Johnston's army was a good one economically for John R. Winder and the other Saints. "After the return of the people from the south," Winder reported, "we had a season of prosperity. Factories and all kinds of business were established, and the growth and increase was wonderful. . . . We had peace for a time."[1] Many Mormon families were quick to take advantage of the financial opportunity to supply meat, vegetables, hay and grain to the 5,500 troops stationed at Camp Floyd. Winder's father-in-law, John Parker, used knowledge gained in the bottling business in St. Louis to make lemon syrup, which he took to Camp Floyd and sold as soda water. His first barrel cost fifty dollars to make, but in going around the Point of the Mountain, the wagon tipped over and the head of the barrel came out, spilling all of the syrup. Parker returned home and made another barrel of syrup, took it safely to Camp Floyd and made a clear profit of $300 out of it.[2]

The army not only brought the goods that were needed, but money to buy other goods. The large army payroll was one of the few sources of actual money in the Rocky Mountain west and proved to be a godsend to Utah's early economy. When Johnston's army was called back at the outbreak of the Civil War, the camp was abandoned and the goods sacrificed. Hundreds of wagons valued at $150 to $175 were sold for $10 each. Flour, purchased by the government for $28.40 a sack, sold for fifty-two cents.[3] What the Mormons' enemies had intended for their destruction proved to be a blessing in disguise. As for Colonel Albert Sidney Johnston, he was killed by Union troops at the Battle of Shiloh.

The summer of 1858 found both Hannah and Elizabeth relieved to have returned to their home from "The Move." These two wives of John R. Winder's were both anxiously expecting the births of their firstborn and had just made the trek back from Provo while in this delicate condition. The women prepared their rooms in the Winder home on Third South west of Main Street, and just two days after the big Pioneer Day celebration Hannah's child was born. The entire household rejoiced over the beautiful baby boy, which John R. and Hannah named William Winder, a popular name at the time, and one that had peppered the Winder pedigree throughout the centuries.

Although the new mother was anxious to be up and about caring for the baby, in her weakened condition Hannah fell ill. "He was a large baby boy with broad shoulders and large in every way," Hannah recorded. "I had a very hard labor in the delivery, and had been careless in getting upon my feet too soon, and as a result took cold and had chills for eight days." She continues to describe her condition:

At the end of that time the cold settled in my bones of my left hip, and in the spine. They called it rheumatic pleuracy; I was pillowed-up in a chair for three months, as I felt better sitting than by lying down. I had to be lifted to and from bed. Both of my breasts gathered, and feeding did not agree with my baby's little stomach. I will not try to write the extent of my suffering. All my left side became helpless, and I cannot describe my suffering, nor do I like to dwell on the sorrow I had.

To make matters worse, little William caught the infection and continually grew weaker. "I had the misfortune of losing my baby," Hannah lamented, "and was left in a very bad state, caused from his birth." Hannah was crushed when her baby died after just nine weeks of life on September 29, 1858; "I should have been glad to have gone down in the grave with my baby," she declared of the time. The rest of the household shared her sorrow, especially Elizabeth. Nonetheless, the sorrowed mother looked forward with faith. "I was 23 years old and knew I had a mighty work to do on the earth," Hannah stated, "and took comfort from the comforting words spoken at the funeral. My Uncle Richard Ballantyne came and took lead and was so kind and sympathetic."

"It was while I was in my deepest sorrow and suffering," Hannah wrote, "that Elizabeth gave birth to her baby." In fact, it was the day after the tragic loss, September 30, 1858, that Elizabeth Parker Winder gave birth to her first child and her husband's tenth. John R. Winder named the boy William Charles Parker Winder, in honor of his infant half brother who had died the day before.

Ellen and Elizabeth soon nursed Hannah back to full recovery. She exhibited great faith to overcame her sorrow, and was pleased to be able to do her share of the house work again. "With careful nursing, and by perseverance, I began to get into action," she explained. "As soon as I could I would stand on one leg and wash the dishes, and sit down and wipe them. I was pleased when I could do that much to help." As the autumn days of October progressed ever colder, Hannah had to be moved to the store room downstairs. However, "the change was more cheerful," she declared, "and I had company and felt better."

At the time that William Charles was born, Elizabeth carried him to Hannah's room and laid him in her lap and said "I am going to give him to Hannah." Between them, in their sisterly loving and united way, Elizabeth and Hannah literally shared the new baby boy, little William C. Winder. "I took to Elizabeth's baby and loved and helped to raise him," Hannah later wrote. "He grew and done fine." He would continue to grow and do fine, marrying Rosalie Romney Taylor in 1883, fathering eight children, and living until the age of 78, passing away on June 19, 1937 in Granger (now West Valley City), Utah.

With an ever-growing household, Winder was always looking for ways to enlarge his income and provide comfortably for his family. As has been mentioned, Jennings bought out Winder's interests in their tannery upon the Saints' return from Provo in July of 1858. Winder "had hoped to resume his partnership business with William Jennings in the Butcher Business. It looked like business was going to be pretty lively, so Mr. Jennings thought that he would like to dissolve partnership and have it all his own way, which he did."[4]

Partnership with Brigham Young— the B. K. Tannery

However, ever the industrialist, John R. quickly applied his capital, brains, and managerial acumen to an even better business opportunity: "After 'the move' in 1858, I was a partner with President Brigham Young and Feramorz Little, and we built a tannery on Parley's canyon creek."[5] Winder had achieved a good deal of favorable publicity because of his valiant military service, and gained favor in the eyes of Brigham Young. He was elated that the Great Colonizer would ask him to be a partner, and his wives were proud of the fact that Brigham Young had "appointed our husband to be the manager of it."[6] It was indeed a prestigious appointment, and one that Brigham would not have given to just anyone. Winder and Young had first met just five years before, on the day that the Winder family entered the Valley, yet they seemed to have developed a relationship of mutual trust and admiration through their association in directing the "Utah War." By 1858, Winder had also established a solid reputation in the city as "a successful tradesman, tanner, shoemaker, a practical book-keeper."[7] The ex-Governor of Utah Territory was exactly two decades older than the 37-year-old John R. Winder, but saw in his new junior partner tremendous potential that he would put to use often over the remaining decades of his life.

Brigham Young was a great patron and promoter of home manufactures and home industries. In those days, Young was the largest employer of laborers, mechanics, business managers and clerks in the Territory, and all his establishments were for his own people and employees, and not for trade with the Gentile public.[8] The personality of Winder's new business partner was described in detail by the founder and editor of the *New York Tribune,* Horace Greeley. Greeley visited Salt Lake in 1859, the year after Winder began his business partnership with President Young, and wrote the following regarding the American Moses:

He spoke readily, not always with grammatical accuracy, but with no appearance of hesitation or reserve, and with no apparent desire to conceal anything; nor did he repel any of my questions as impertinent. He was very plainly dressed in thin, summer clothing, and with no air of sanctimony or fanaticism. In appearance, he is a portly, frank, good-natured, rather thick-set man of fifty-five, seeming to enjoy life, and to be in no particular hurry to get to heaven. His associates are plain men, evidently born and reared in a life of labor, and looking as little like crafty hypocrites or swindlers as any body of men I ever met. The absence of cant or snuffle from their manner was marked and general; yet I think I may fairly say, that their Mormonism has not impoverished them—that they were generally poor men when they embraced it, and are now in very comfortable circumstances.[9]

Feramorz Little, the other partner in the firm, was a brother-in-law of Brigham Young twice by marriage (his wife Fannie M. Decker was a sister of Lucy and Clara Decker, two of Brigham's wives.) Little, an ambitious industrialist like Winder's last business partner, was originally a New Yorker. However, while en route to California in 1850, he stopped in Salt Lake City, and "in finding ample scope for his ambition in Utah, he became a Latter-day Saint." Like his new colleague Winder, Little had worked previously in the leather business, giving them a common interest. And, also like John R. Winder, Feramorz Little would later be involved with the city government of Salt Lake. The two would later serve on the city council together, and in 1876 Little would begin his three consecutive terms as mayor of Salt Lake City.

Since his early days in Utah, Little had made his home at the mouth of Parley's Canyon where he had been conducting a flouring mill. It was at this place that he, along with Young and Winder, built their tannery.[10] The new facility, which they called the Big Kanyon (B. K.) Tannery, was on "Parley's Creek, about where the Country Club is now located."[11] At the tannery, Feramorz Little also carried on blacksmithing and shoemaking and established a school for his children and those of his workmen.[12]

As for John R. Winder, "he was required to fill a very responsible position, in the manipulating the boiler and vats, which required much of his presence and time. He had ten men at work digging a canal to take the water out of the creek and to do other construction work, and to arrange another home in which to move his two new families."[13]

Ellen Walters Winder was anxious for her husband to provide another location for the plural wives, and by early November, 1858 the tannery was built up to a point where Winder felt comfortable moving that part of his family there. "Neither of us was very able to attend to the shifting," Hannah said of herself and

Elizabeth making the move to the tannery, "but as obedience was again required, we put the best foot first and picked up our effects and was soon on the road in a lumber wagon on the way to the log house which had been hurriedly prepared for us. The plaster was still wet in the walls, but neither of us took cold. We took the spinning wheel with us."[14] They also took along their little Willie, who was then less than two months old.

One pioneer journal described the work that the men did at the B. K. Tannery:

> The hides were first salted to keep them soft, they were then put in a solution of lime to loosen the hair so it could be removed easily. The lime was rinsed off, the hides were then put in a solution made by pouring boiling water over hemlock or ground oak bark. Large vats were used to soak them in. They were hung up to dry.[15]

As manager, John R. was kept busy at the tannery, around town on business, and occasionally meeting with his partners regarding their prosperous enterprise. For example, one Tuesday afternoon in April, George A. Smith visited President Young "and found him in good spirits in his office conversing with the brethren on almost every variety of subjects." Winder had joined Brigham Young and some of the leading brethren that day, as they discussed "the subject of tanning leather," among many topics.[16] It must have been a tremendous education for John R. Winder to not only conduct business with the famed "Lion of the Lord," but to also be schooled at the feet of this prophet on numerous occasions and on myriad subject matters.

Hannah and Elizabeth kept busy making their barren accommodations more attractive. They spent their days preparing meals for the many laborers that were employed at the tannery. Hannah's autobiography is useful in illustrating their situation at the B. K. Tannery:

> We had a lot of men to cook for, and they would say their coffee would freeze as we poured it out, but the work was accomplished, and in a few months every thing was in running order. Industry, patience and perseverance overcomes many obsticles [sic].
>
> We did the best we could to make holesome [sic] meals for the men, with the material and conveniences then at our hands. We missed the Butcher shop, which was next door to the City home from which we had been moved.
>
> Our husband seemed very pleased to see his Celestial wives so united.

At the tannery, Elizabeth and Hannah also stayed busy spinning and straw braiding. Elizabeth's step-mother had taught her all the branches of home industry, even to the splitting of the straw. During the first summer at the tannery Elizabeth and Hannah made each of the twins and Ellen Winder a straw hat. "I did the coarse brading [sic] and she the fine," Hannah wrote. They were very contented at the tannery, but because of their distance from town, they were not able to go to their Sunday meetings. Instead of church, Elizabeth and Hannah spent their Sabbaths reading, resting, and occasionally taking a stroll down to the mill "where we had some No. 1 neighbors." Vilate Decker, (Brigham's daughter) and Fannie Little lived there and provided some good company for the women in their isolated circumstances. On the way home from their Sunday visits, the Winder women enjoyed picking flowers and would also begin their evening chore of bringing the cows up to ready them for milking. Together they raised a large vegetable garden which they took pride in: "we raised good mellons [sic], cantelopes [sic] &c." They also made butter and raised chickens and ducks to send to Ellen's family at the city home. Hannah remarked, "We enjoyed our country home amasingly [sic] as long as our husband had confidence in us."

Hannah recorded a humorous account of how little William C. Winder was weaned away from his mother's milk:

> Time sped on, the summer (of 1859) was advancing, and our boy between us, Willie was our all of joy. He was soon a year old. His mother was left in the City one night and couldn't get home, and the baby was left with me. His father had been trying to get his mother to wean him, so he was rather pleased she had been detained.
>
> The next morning when she returned, she found him sitting at the table rolling cakes with Aunt Hannah, and had eaten a good breakfast. He had only cried twice in the night, so that job was over with soon.

In the summers at the tannery, the women did most of their work in a shanty at the end of the house, where they had a large adobe bake oven. Despite being a large oven, sometimes it was filled twice per day when they had many workmen to feed. Hannah and Elizabeth also worked hard to keep the parlor clean, "for Brother Winder very often brought in his gentlemen friends, such as Doctor Bernhisel, who had at one time boarded with the Prophet Joseph Smith."

Hannah wrote that of all the lessons she and Elizabeth learned while at the B. K. Tannery, "the best one was that plurality of wives was from the Lord, and we were both converted to the principle." They counseled together about their work and made sure that they each did their fair share. "It was said in Salt Lake City, that Brother Winder had picked up two of the best girls on the main street; Lizzie Parker and Hannah Thompson. There was no first or second with us."

Despite the good times at the tannery, the Winder family also had their share of sorrows there. Just thirteen months after the birth of her first born, Hannah was ready to give birth to her second. "I was taken in labor very unexpectedly," she wrote. Hannah sent a note by one of the workmen to her husband "requesting him to hastily deliver it, but Brother Winder was so busy with business he could not leave, and sent the woman who was to wait on me." The delivery of little Henry Winder went alright, but shortly after the delivery, something at Hannah's bedside required the midwife's attention. She wrapped the baby in something and just laid him one side for a moment, and waited on Hannah. When she next turned her attention to the baby he was dead. "Some phlem [sic] had gathered in my darling's throat and he choked with it," Hannah lamented. "Oh my sorrow and disappointment!"

When John R. came and asked how everything was, and was told, he went out and sat down in a nearby tent and held his head in his hands in deep sorrow for some time. After he had composed himself, he returned to the house "with blessings and spoke all the kind words he could." Elizabeth at the time was waiting on eight men at the breakfast table, and by the time she reached Hannah's bedside, her darling had strangled. While in her depression, Hannah's beloved uncle Richard Ballantyne came again to comfort her. "My husband was truly kind" Hannah said of John R., "and I had Elizabeth's sympathy too, yet I had a hard struggle with myself in order to say: 'Father, Thy will be done.' The babies are sleeping side by side, in the Salt Lake City Cemetery . . . till that glorious resurrection. But as all things had to be borne, I had to bear up and endure. It is easy when you have a husband who is kind and considerate, and with you sharing the grief." Hannah struggled during this great trial; but there was still a greater one to come.

The coming winter was a little dreary for the saddened Winder family, "but the Lord gave me strength to work," Hannah acknowledged. "My mind was kept exorcised [sic] to see that every thing went on all right, and the men coming in to meals, it all was company for us. I soon regained strength and it was good to be around the house again."

Scandal Leads to Divorce

Hannah was a very compassionate person. During the holiday season of 1859 John R. was with Ellen and the city family and Elizabeth and little Willie were in town staying with the Parker's. "They were a jolly lot," it was said of the Parkers, "and she enjoyed the visit." As for Hannah, she stayed out at the tannery to cook for the few workers still out there. "It was a pleasing task for me to prepare the X-mas dinner for them," she said. Her relatives, being in Grantsville, 30 miles west of Salt Lake, would have to enjoy the holidays without her. "I became contented . . . and made things as comfortable as I could," she added.

When one of the chore boys, a teenage orphan named Joe, caught lice, Hannah was quick to examine his head. They had recently found some lice in Willie's head, and she didn't want it to spread to others. "It wasn't a pleasant task," she said, but having no child of her own, she felt like looking after someone's boy. She washed and cleaned his head, cut his hair, got him to take a bath, and gave him a fine comb with the instructions to comb his hair daily. "He seemed very thankful to me and expressed it in words," she said. Apparently, the chore boy Joe developed somewhat of a crush on Hannah during the experience, a problem which would blow up into a big scandal one year later.[17]

The year 1860 brought with it several new additions to the ever-growing Winder clan. Frederick William Winder was born on April 18, 1860, as John's twelfth and Ellen's ninth. He tragically died one month later in May 1860 and was buried in the Salt Lake City Cemetery.

Elizabeth's second child and first daughter, Alice Ellen Winder, was born on September 1, 1860. The mid-wife was late in getting there, as she lived six miles away in the city, and so Hannah and a neighbor delivered the lovely 11 pound baby girl. This child would grow to maturity, marry William Bradford in 1882, have nine children, and pass away at age 59 on the 27th of February 1920 in Salt Lake City.

Five weeks after Elizabeth gave birth, Hannah also gave birth. Anna Jane Winder was born on 6 Oct 1860 at the B. K. Tannery. Although Hannah's third born and John R.'s fourteenth, Anna Jane was the first of their union to live to maturity. She would marry Reuben G. Miller in 1884, become a mother of seven, and live until the age of 81, passing away on July 27, 1942 in Salt Lake City. "My darling baby girl," Hannah wrote, "she has been an everlasting blessing to both her father and mother."[18]

It was the holiday season of 1860 that a scandal erupted, "caused by mischief makers and misrepresentation." On Christmas Eve, Anna Jane, who was less than three months old, was restless and needed some attention. Hannah, still having much work to do, asked the chore boy Joe to rock the cradle for her. "It was Saturday night and I was left alone with the boy," Hannah explained. Elizabeth had gone to spend the holidays with her family, like the previous year, and in her absence Hannah occupied her room on the first floor since her upstairs room was less convenient and less comfortable. Joe had been sleeping out in the shed down at the mill, and when bed time came he said to Hannah, "I wish I didn't have to go down to the shed, mill to sleep." It was very dark outside, and because it had been raining, it was damp and cold. Feeling charitable on that Christmas Eve, Hannah told him to bring his bedding and she would make his bed upstairs in what was usually her room. "It was from that act of kindness all the trouble started," Hannah later declared.

The next morning, the young man Joe boasted to his fellow workmen: "I had a good place to sleep last night. I slept in Hannah's bed!" His stories of Christmas Eve with the boss's wife spread among the laborers at the tannery like a brush fire, probably being embellished with each retelling, as rumors tend to do. "It was from this remark the mischief maker started a gossip and caused the trouble which came between me and my husband," Hannah noted. As soon as the idle gossip reached John R. Winder, he evidently became enraged and immediately went to Hannah "in a cynical and accusing manner," and demanded "Where did Joe sleep last night?" Hannah was shocked: "I was dumfounded for a moment, before making reply." From that moment he ostracized her from his affection. "He never returned to my room from that time."

The saddened Hannah fasted and prayed much for her husband to converse with her, but he never would. However, she continued to make his clothes, knit his socks, spin yarn, cook for the men, milk the cows, and do the general work for several years after the incident, until she could bear it no longer. Several months after the Christmas Eve incident, Hannah suffered a nervous breakdown, which she felt was caused from having lost the confidence and affection of her husband. The attending physician concluded that her nervous trouble was due to hereditary factors, and advised John R. Winder that she should have no more children in order to prevent her from having an additional breakdown, and to prevent the danger of passing on physical or mental disorders to another generation of children. Winder agreed to the counsel for the sake of his wife, and determined that they would have no more offspring. In the process, he became aloof toward Hannah, and to her needs as his wife. The marriage further weakened to the point where there were continual incidents and misunderstandings between the once-happy couple.

Hannah felt depressed that she only had one daughter, and read her patriarchal blessing many times which promised her "sons and daughters" in the plural. "So, after Anna's fourth birth day, I began to think, and concluded to take a walk." She had never strayed far from her home, except when the family occasionally walked the six miles to meetings. In her wandering she had taken along her daughter Anna, and Hannah decided to go see what President Brigham Young would tell her. Hannah later recounted her thoughts from that long walk to the Beehive House:

> I prayed all the way, as I wanted children. I was a healthy woman and had committed no sin. I had only done a kindness to a poor orphan boy, and made him a comfortable bed up in my room with the hired man's bedding, in which he slept that night.
>
> However, it was here where Satan got a key and broke into our sacred affairs by circulating a scandalous story. I became heart-broken, worried night and day over the false-hood, fasted days and days, exorcising [sic] faith and hope as best I could, but to no avail. My husband would not relent and listen to me and know the truth.

She visited with President Young about the matter, who was sympathetic. After her visit with the prophet, she went to the home of John Taylor and her Aunt Jane Taylor. At the Taylor home, she "sat down and shed tears and cried bitterly." Her aunt comforted her with kind words and "Brother Taylor also was kind and considerate of my disappointment and sorrows." She remained there one week and sent a letter to her husband. Hannah's letter "planely [sic] informed him that it had been nearly 4 years since he had deprived me of a Husbands attention and affection, and that nothing short of him keeping the covenants that he had made with me in the House of the Lord would do, and that I would take steps to have a separation."

Her letter was not answered. Hannah consequently returned to President Young's office and signed her divorce, with the prophet's consent, and was granted a cancellation of their sealing. She left the paper there for Winder to sign, which he later did. He then mailed the signed document to her, along with a pair of shoes for little Anna. Hannah felt it would be better to leave Anna Jane in Elizabeth's care, feeling that the child would undoubtedly have better opportunities there. With that, Hannah sadly departed for Grantsville to live with her sister, Margaret. In January of 1865, she became the fifth wife of Margaret's husband, Ariah Brower. Hannah and Ariah became the parents of three beautiful daughters and a son, all perfectly healthy and normal. Their mother fared well too. Evidently, the doctor had made the wrong diagnosis. In her later years, Hannah spent much of her time in the Logan Temple doing work for the dead, until she passed away on September 8, 1919.[19]

Some may wonder how a man, who was so seemingly kind and generous to others in his later years, could have had such deep misunderstandings with his wife, even to the point of driving her to divorce. While it is important to realize that the primary document used to retell the sad story was Hannah's diary, and therefore her point of view, even John R. Winder eventually admitted that it was he who had made some grave mistakes. Nonetheless, it was not an unusual circumstance in early Utah, but even one that other leaders in the Church had experienced. There was apparently an enormous pressure on these pioneer women to provide their husbands with children. A biography of Joseph F. Smith, for example, related the following incident regarding "a serious problem in his family."

> It involved his first wife, Levira, to whom he had been married for almost a decade. During that period, this faithful woman had been unable to conceive. The feelings of frustration and unhappiness her barrenness had produced apparently were magnified when Julina, the second wife, conceived within a few months after being sealed to Joseph. And this, added to the ill health she had suffered periodically during most of the marriage, ultimately caused her to seek a legal separation from her husband and go to California where she hoped her health would mend.[20]

The incident with Hannah was certainly not the Winder family's finest hour, and John R. deeply regretted the divorce for the rest of his life. Even some of his final deathbed thoughts, as shall be told, were concerning Hannah and her well being. Years later, Hannah reflected on the cheerful times she had enjoyed with the Winder family and also the sad unraveling of her happiness and remarked: "It would seem that Satan concluded that we as a family had been too united."[21] One of John R.'s granddaughters, Mary Winder Johnson, added, "It is not for us to judge her, grandfather, or Pres. Young for this divorce or the cause. If mistakes were made, someone wiser that we, will make the logical conclusion."[22]

Establishing Poplar Farm—
Winder's Country Estate

Meanwhile, while in the early 1860's a storm was brewing at the Winder household that would lead to a separation, a greater conflict on the national scene was erupting, which would also cause a separation and even lead to the Civil War. The journal entry of 4 March 1861 for Wilford Woodruff noted that "J. R. Winder" was again elected as a director in the Deseret Agriculture and Manufacturing Society. At that meeting national politics also seemed to be a hot topic, and Elder Woodruff added in the day's entry, "This day Abe Lincoln is Inaugurated as the President of the United States, or that portion which is left."[23] The Civil War did not affect the Winder family or the other people of Utah as greatly as it did their countrymen back East, although they followed the events with great interest. The Mormon community viewed it as the realization of a famous prophecy made by Joseph Smith on Christmas Day, 1832: "The wars that will shortly come to pass, beginning at the rebellion of South Carolina ... will eventually terminate in the death and misery of many souls; And the time will come that war will be poured out upon all nations, beginning at this place."[24] President Lincoln would ask Brigham Young to muster a small force to guard the telegraph lines and mail routes in the west, but there is no record that Captain Winder was part of this, the only Civil War operation of the Nauvoo Legion.

On the home front, the Winder family saw a couple new additions during the Civil War. Fortunately, these two babies were healthy and lived long and fruitful lives. Susan Sophia Winder, John R. Winder's fifteenth child and Ellen's tenth, was born on November 10, 1861 in what was then known as "the John R. Winder cottage" at Third South and Main Streets. Named for both of her grandmothers, she would marry Thomas Allen Williams in 1883, be the mother of eight, and live to see 89 years, passing away on September 15, 1951.

Richard Henry Winder, John R. Winder's sixteenth child, and Elizabeth's third, was born on July 30, 1862. Named for his grandfather, he would marry Mary Emma Cahoon in 1887 and be the father of five. He died on May 6, 1936 at the age of 73.

Meanwhile, the partnership with Brigham Young and Feramorz Little had proven profitable for Winder. "While so engaged," he said regarding the tannery, "I purchased my present home, 'Poplar Farm.'"[25] It was not unusual for one talented, such as Winder, to make an admirable profit while working for Brigham Young. It was said in Utah that "hundreds of our citizens have obtained their lots, their houses and their supplies for years in the employment of President Young," who was generous in the compensation of his employees and partners.[26] The new Winder farm was built on a large tract of land on 2700 South that he had purchased in 1863. That year he moved his wives Hannah and Elizabeth, and children William C., Alice, Anna, and baby Richard into a two-room log house located on the corner of 2700 South and 300 East, which was to be their home until their grand farmhouse was built on the site two years later. Hannah did not reside long at the farm for, as has been mentioned, it was not long after they moved there that she left.

The original plan for Salt Lake City's blocks ended at 900 South, so Poplar Farm really was out in the country for its time. The area south of 900 South to present-day 2700 South was referred to as the "Big Field," and was a popular area for pioneers to cultivate crops. The land just south of the Big Field, which included Winder's new property, was called Millcreek, after the creek that runs through the area to the Jordan River. One Winder grandson described the setting of Poplar Farm:

> Mill Creek gushing out of the Wasatch Mountains to the east then flowing westward across the Salt Lake Valley to join the Jordan River before flowing into the Great Salt Lake provided the south boundary of our big pasture, an eighty acre tract of excellent pasture land. Near our west boundary the creek was wide and deep and here was the best swimming hole in Salt Lake County.[27]

Besides Poplar Farm, other improvements were made in the area at the time. Husler's Mill was built not far away in 1865 on the bank of Millcreek on Territory Road, which is today's State Street. Calder Park was also developed at that time and grew into the finest amusement park between the Missouri River and the Golden Gate. As the Winder children grew, they loved to go down to Calder Park where there was a small lake for boats, a merry-go-round, a dance pavilion, and a racetrack for horses.[28]

Pioneers took a great interest in building their homes. When Brigham Young built his Beehive House, "he wanted his roots down deep and firm in this valley . . . This house represents his ideals and feeling of permanence." The same could be said for John R. Winder's approach to building his beloved Poplar Farm. One poet has mused:

> What does a man think when he
> Builds a house?
> What are his plans?
> Does he reveal himself in its conception?
> Is it merely to house his growing family?
> Or is this effort his way of giving
> Birth to ideas—to ideals?

Can you know Washington
When you see Mt. Vernon?
Or Jefferson after Monticello?
Or Jackson, from the Hermitage?
(A house is a great man's)
Symbol of Faith and Work
And frugal care.[29]

In 1865, John R. Winder began the construction of his large, attractive farm-house for Elizabeth and her children. It would be, in essence, his country estate. "Ideally, the country estate possessed the virtues of country simplicity modified by the social and political structures of civil society, and this synthesis was rei-fied in the architectural entity of the house."[30] Such it was with Winder's Poplar Farmhouse. It was a two-story white mansard roofed structure with a flowing well in the basement and tanks of water for refrigeration purposes. The original

The Poplar Farmhouse, 1880. It was located at 300 East and 2700 South. This was Winder's "country estate" and the original site of Winder Dairy.

two log rooms were kept when the new farmhouse was built, one being used as a furnace room.[31]

Winder had loved the tree-lined lanes of his native England and intended to fashion his new farm after an English country manor. He obtained numerous hardy specimens of Canadian poplar (one grandson also recalls English and Lombardy poplars, too[32]) and literally surrounded his new farm with them. He planted a full grove on the south side of 2700 South running from 300 to 400 East. Evergreens were planted around the home and two flowing fountains were erected in the front for an ornamental effect.[33] Overall, six fountains graced the yard, and the grounds were maintained by a hired gardener, "who kept the place up very well." Poplar Farm eventually boasted huge barns, big vegetable pits, and lots of cows. There were three milk rooms that had running water all the time. Granddaughter Claire Bradford Kapple recalled, "It was like an English estate."[34] Winder had remembered the Biddenden Place of his childhood and the Henden Hall that was across the street that had also been occupied by his ancestors. Now, in the grand English tradition, John R. Winder had his own country estate, his beloved "Poplar Farm."

Elizabeth was thrilled with her new home and immediately busied herself weaving rag rugs for the public rooms, which added much warmth, color, and beauty.[35] Straw was put on the floor, as a padding under the carpets, and then they were tacked to the floors around the edges.[36] When it was completed, a huge entry hall opened into a lavishly furnished parlor and there were bedrooms on different levels. John R. had a gorgeous room with a black marble fireplace and magnificent furniture. The kitchen was very large and opened into a huge dining room. One granddaughter recalled that as a child she thought the kitchen "to be the size of a ward amusement hall." Off the kitchen was a laundry and a sunny sewing room.

A gorgeous ballroom with red carpeting and gold chairs took up one side of the house. It featured a music box and would be the site of many fancy dinner parties for the "who's who" in Salt Lake to attend. Winder, ever the classical English country gentleman, enjoyed dancing even very late in his life, and his grandchildren recalled the beautiful ballroom as the place "where the family did square dances." His wife Elizabeth was a gracious hostess and entertained many notable people in their home.[37] To assist Elizabeth, the family often employed a servant. For example, in the mid-1860's, Catherine Blake, or "Kate" as she was known, began work in the home as a hired girl. This young lady had recently arrived in the valley with her family from London.[38] Poplar Farm would later be a popular site for socials with the Church general authorities around the turn of the century. It soon became known in the town that the Winder family had "purchased and developed an excellent farm south of Salt Lake City."[39]

The B. K. Tannery proved to be a prosperous enterprise for several years, until 1863 when the native bark used in tanning had become too scarce and the cost of imported materials made it nearly impossible for the home product to compete with leather goods shipped into the territory.[40] Consequently, Winder reports that he "went to farming and stock-raising, pursuits which have always given me great pleasure."[41] Thereby occupied, he gradually withdrew from the tannery.[42] As for his partners, Feramorz Little was appointed in 1863 to be the emigration agent for the Church, and Brigham Young, already involved in a plethora of endeavors in the Territory, suffered no dearth of activity from no longer being involved with the tannery. In 1865, Young and Little would also reunite to purchase and operate the Salt Lake House on Main Street at 150 South, then the leading local hotel.[43]

In early Utah, virtually all pioneers had to become farmers to survive. Until the transcontinental railroad was completed in 1869, they had to raise enough food for themselves and for the immigrants who would arrive too late to grow anything.[44] However, for Winder farming became more of a passionate hobby than a bout for survival. He quickly developed a reputation as "a pains-taking and careful farmer and stock raiser, and was never satisfied unless he raised the best crops, and his fields were clear and tidy and free from weeds." It became well known among the citizens of Salt Lake that as a farmer "he succeeded admirably."[45]

Elizabeth remained at the farm full time and Ellen Winder maintained her home in the city. John R. Winder would divide his time between the two homes, but took a particular active interest in farming and the accumulation of a herd of purebred Jersey cattle.[46] There was something almost therapeutic for John R. in escaping the cares of the city for the simplicity of Poplar Farm. Even in later years when the business, civic, and ecclesiastical duties in the city would have seemed overwhelming, Winder could always find solace in working the land and tending his cattle. One scholar had this to say about English country gentlemen and their relationship to their manors in the country:

> In spite of the activity that was focused about the country estate, there is a sense in which country life was a retreat: as a minor eddy removed from the mainstream of society, the magistracy of the limited locality offered an excellent balm for pride wounded in the political arena and a valid justification for absence.[47]

The Beginning of the Dairy Herd

The cattle that the pioneers brought with them across the plains were varied specimens of Shorthorn, Devon and Hereford types. Winder's former partner, William Jennings, had even recently contracted for a herd of Texas Longhorns to be driven from Missouri to Utah. But the great milk-giving specimens of Holstein and Jersey cattle did not appear in Utah until Winder and others began importing them in. As population in the Great Basin grew, so did the need for dairy products. In 1858 there were 40,000 people, and by 1869 this number had doubled. In addition to the food demands for the Utah settlers, there was a strong demand from the California- and Oregon-bound emigrants, as well as those in the mine fields of Nevada and Colorado. Demand for beef was good, as John R. Winder had learned in his successful days at the tannery, but there was an even greater demand for butter, cheese, and flour.

Dairying flourished in the valleys, and became the main industry for many. Butter and cheese could be stored for long periods when properly cared for in the cool cellars, and the Winder family was in the forefront of bringing new methods to the dairy industry in Utah.[48] For instance, it was Winder, likely through his association with the D. A. & M., that first brought Jersey cattle to

Utah. "Many purebred Jersey cattle were brought from the Jersey Isles" one grandson recalled. "This foundation stock would later form the basis of the Winder Dairy herd for over one hundred years."[49] Jersey cattle were known as "a very special breed, the smallest of those of the Channel Islands, with some unusual features and a remarkable ability to adapt to extreme climates." Jersey cattle are also famous for their "extreme dairy conformation":

> It is a fine-boned animal, with small hoofs on slender but strong legs, and the very wide pelvis enables easy calving, even to large bulls. The total milk yield might seem small in comparison with that of a Holstein at an average of more than 4,000 kg per lactation, but the solids content is very high, with an average of 5.3 percent butterfat, so that the total yield of solids compares favourably. The fat globules are large and the cream therefore rises quickly when setting.

The whole style of the Jersey is "dainty, aristocratic and almost deerlike." This "island milch cow" decorated many of the great English estates, and was possibly one reason why John R. Winder, with his long memory of his Old World past, was initially interested in the breed.[50] In traditional English society, "The glorious uncertainty of animal breeding" was a prerogative of the wealthy, and to someone such as Winder, being able to indulge in this hobby was a social achievement.[51] The first registered Jerseys were not imported to the U.S. until 1850, and that year there were only nine. The fact that Winder was beginning his herd in the remote Great Basin a mere fifteen years after the first registered Jersey set hoof on American soil is truly remarkable. He was indeed a pioneer in stock-raising, as he was building his Jersey herd even before the American Jersey Cattle Club was organized in 1868.

Winder's involvement with the Deseret Agricultural and Manufacturing Society would have provided him with contacts from around the nation, which helped him acquire only the best of animals. Grandson George Winder recalled hearing that some of the first Jerseys

John R. Winder the stock raiser. The "Father of the Utah State Fair" was one of the first to import Jersey cattle to the American West. Utah's "pioneer dairyman," Winder kept an active interest in the family's prize-winning Jersey herd throughout the remainder of his life.

that the Winder's purchased were from a Mr. Richardson of Iowa, who had imported a large herd from the Isle of Jersey. George also said that much of the early herd was obtained from Hood Farms.[52] Hood Farm at Lowell, Massachusetts, was instrumental in developing a strain of Jerseys that held many production records. "The contribution of the Hood Farm herd and this strain to the income of Jersey breeders in America, is enormous and impossible to estimate . . . . On the death of the owner, Mr. C. I. Hood, the herd was dispersed."[53] However, despite the source, all of the Winder's cattle were registered, with pedigrees tracing them back to the Isle of Jersey.[54]

The majority of Utahns were involved in agriculture in the nineteenth century, and the state fair was generally the highlight of the year. The Winder family, as has been mentioned, was always a great contributor to the state fairs, and for nearly a century after the first fairs began, they were among the largest exhibitors. They always had a fine showing of purebred Jerseys in the various age groups. George Winder mentioned that the Winder family took first prize at the fairs with their fine Jersey cows for years, "until Joseph F. Smith's sons and some of the Cannon boys began to import cattle directly from the Island of Jersey."[55] The fair was also a time when they could purchase needed farming supplies from other farmers.[56]

In later years Winder also added some black-and-white Holstein cows, but the fawn-colored Jerseys remained his favorite. One historian noted that in his lifetime John R. Winder became famous for stock raising, "at which he has been one of the most successful men in the whole Western country, his beautiful residence, Poplar Farm, just south of the city, showing some fine specimens."[57] Another contemporary noted that Winder was impeccable regarding this passion, and that "he kept no inferior animals on his place."[58]

Not surprisingly, in the 1860's, Winder seemed to be involved more than ever with the Deseret Agricultural and Manufacturing Society. His good friend Wilford Woodruff was president of this group at the time, but for many meetings the apostle was absent and John R. Winder, as the next in seniority, would preside at the meetings of the board. Winder also served as the group's secretary, as needed, and often was called on by the board to prepare public announcements and other literature.

As Winder's personal wealth increased, he also became a generous benefactor of the fairs. For example, to help prepare for the fair of 1862, he paid $381.08, no small sum in those days, "for fencing Quarantine farm and for team work," to help prepare the fair grounds for the festivities. He also persuaded Brigham Young to donate the lumber for the new fence.[59] On another occasion, Winder and colleague Edward Hunter were appointed "to wait on President Young, and obtain the use of the Deseret Store, for our next exhibition in October."[60]

Often, the D. A. & M. board met in the Church historian's office, where they would plan the upcoming fairs and the various agricultural experiments that they were conducting. For example, at the September 19, 1863 meeting in the historian's office, it was "voted that Bros. Winder and Sheets arrange with the Bands about playing during the Fair." Other men who served as directors during this time were the former Salt Lake mayor A. O. Smoot, G. F. Sheets, Enoch Ruse, R. L. Campbell, F. A . Mitchell, L. W. Ellerbeck, A. P. Rockwood, George B. Wallace, and apostle George A. Smith. However, while many of these directors came and went, Woodruff and Winder were seemingly permanent fixtures with the fair board, always being elected as directors if not board president. Winder also stayed active with the Nauvoo Legion as evidenced by this entry in the minutes of the D. A. & M. Society from September 26, 1863: "In consequence of pressing military appointments Director Sheets and Winder requested to be excused."[61]

Travel Companion to President Young

As has been stated, John R. Winder had become a close friend and confidant of Brigham Young. Because of this friendship and because of Winder's courage and bravery as an officer of the Nauvoo Legion, he was often invited to accompany President Young as a sort of bodyguard-advisor on many of his travels throughout the territory. These trips were one key to Brigham's leadership and to the successful colonization of the Great Basin. As he visited with Saints throughout Deseret, the "American Moses" would listen, observe, renew friendships, counsel, scold, strengthen, bless, and teach.[62]

As early as July 1858, Winder had been asked to accompany Brigham to survey and camp in Big Cottonwood Canyon. The traveling party on the camping trip consisted of 15 wagons, 56 horses and mules, and 52 of the leading men of Salt Lake, including most of the First Presidency and Quorum of the Twelve.[63]

By 1864, Winder was asked to go with the Prophet on many of his travels, including one north to the Bear Lake area of Utah-Idaho. Winder was in elite company on this tour. Besides President Young, Church officials Heber C. Kimball, John Taylor, George A. Smith, Wilford Woodruff, and Joseph Young comprised the entourage, along with Jesse W. Fox, Professor Thomas Ellerbeck, a reporter, and their teamsters.

> On Monday morning, May 16, 1864, at 8:30 o'clock, this little company drove out of Salt Lake City on its journey. It consisted of six light vehicles and a baggage wagon. . . . They reached Franklin, Idaho on the afternoon of the third day. . . . There were no houses between Franklin and Paris, Idaho; consequently, the program was to drive directly through in one day if possible.

The fourth morning they got an early start and drove almost to Mink Creek without accident. Here Brother George A. Smith's carriage broke down, but as good luck would have it, the team had brought a light wagon along in case of such an emergency. The company was soon on their way again. When they reached the foot of the big mountains that divide Cache Valley from Bear Lake Valley they encountered some more troubles. "Here is where the tug of war began," it was said of the challenge. The mountain was so steep that everyone had to walk, "except Apostle Smith, who was so heavy that it would have been dangerous for him to undertake it, as he weighed nearly three hundred pounds." The mountain got increasingly steeper, and a creative solution was warranted. Winder and the other younger men in the group hitched some horses to large branches, "and President Young and others who were too heavy to help themselves, took hold of these singletrees with both hands and were helped up the mountain." The scene would have been a comical one as Brigham and a few other leading brethren were pulled up the mountain like a beginning skier on a rope tow!

Apostle Charles C. Rich and others, who had settled in the Bear Lake Valley the fall before, came to their assistance with some ox teams. Several yokes were attached to George A. Smith's wagon, but before he reached the summit his wagon was so badly broken that he was compelled to abandon it. "Everybody had a good laugh over the incident, it being the second vehicle broken down under his weight that day." With careful management under the supervision of President Young, John R. Winder and the other brethren managed to mount George A. on the largest saddle horse that could be found, and another start was made.

The company descended the mountain on the Bear Lake side and soon reached the head of Pioneer Canyon, "where they struck mud, mud, mud, and then some more mud. It had been raining all day, and everybody was wet through to the skin." Four horses were hitched to President Young's carriage and several yoked to the baggage wagon. Winder and the majority of those riding in vehicles had to walk "on account of the trail being in such a fearful condition; and to see that presidential procession waddling through the deep mud was enough to make every living thing smile. It was the muddiest outfit ever seen in that part of the country." It was a case of every man for himself, most taking the side hills. However, George A. Smith's horse soon gave out, and the party had to build a scaffold in order to lift him onto another one! "This amusing story caused the authorities to have another laughing spell at Brother Smith's expense."

The canyon was a mud hole throughout the entire four miles from beginning to end. The party finally reached the mouth of it at nine o'clock at night, taking an hour break to warm themselves with some bonfires and to dry their clothes somewhat. At ten, they continued on their journey. They drove down in the valley until they came to a small stream called Canal Creek. It was so narrow and so deep that they had to jump their horses across it and get the wagons over it as best they could.

Finally, at three o'clock the next morning, they reached their destination, the Bear Lake town of Paris, Idaho. The townspeople had eagerly anticipated the arrival of President Young and his party and had caught a wagon load of beautiful trout from the lake, which they fried for the brethren in "good, fresh butter." Despite the odd hour, the weary travelers rejoiced in a good warm meal, "and what a feast the brethren did have after living on hope and mud for twenty-four hours!"

The next day was spent recovering from the arduous journey, and the following two days were spent visiting with the local Saints. On Sunday morning, an outdoor meeting was held. The speakers were President Young, and Elders Heber C. Kimball, John Taylor, and George A. Smith. The prophet praised the locals for the fine houses, farms, orchards, and vineyards that they had established in the Bear Lake Valley.[64]

Later on in the summer of '64, Winder went with President Young and several of the apostles to visit the Saints in Tooele. The President's party was greeted with streets lined with children waving flags and banners, "on which were inscribed appropriate mottoes and elegant devices." On this trip, specific mention is made of John R. Winder's interest in inspecting the extensive orchard of E. B. Kelsey. He seemed impressed with the 500 apple trees, 1400 peach trees, 5000 currant bushes, and "grape vines sufficient for a vineyard of two acres." The group returned to Salt Lake City on Saturday, July 24, just in time for the Pioneer Day festivities.[65]

The following month, Winder, along with militia friend Robert T. Burton and Elders Wilford Woodruff, Franklin D. Richards, and Thomas McKean, visited the Heber area. They made a specific effort while they were there to visit Snake's Creek, four miles west of Heber. Here they saw the limestone rock that the locals called Snake's Den, on which two hundred snakes were killed in one day by two settlers.[66]

Another excursion that John R. Winder was privy to accompanying was Brigham Young's southern Utah trip that took place a few months after their Bear Lake adventure. During the 1860's the Saints of southern Utah had grown so prosperous that they urged President Young to bring along more people than usual in his visits as they would be in a condition to entertain them. In the summer of 1864, Young decided to heed their request and dispatched messengers on horseback to notify the Saints of southern Utah that his large excursion party was ready to start to "the land of cotton," and they were to govern themselves accordingly. The party consisted of thirteen light vehicles and two baggage wagons, and included Winder and many of his colleagues from the Bear Lake trip. Besides John R. Winder, Brigham Young, John Taylor, Wilford Woodruff, George A. Smith, Ezra T. Benson, Lorenzo Snow, Franklin D. Richards, Willard Richards and Robert T. Burton were among the leaders of the party that in total included 32 men and 15 women. Many in the party were wives or relatives of the leaders, such as Eliza R. Snow, Vilate M. Kimball, and Emily Partridge

Young, among others. Both Ellen and Elizabeth Winder apparently remained home to care for their respective households.

The large party started off at 9:45 am on a Monday morning, September 1, 1864. They were described as "one of the jolliest crowds that ever left Salt Lake City." The entourage drove to Pleasant Grove without a stop, but encountered "one of the severest hailstorms that ever visited that part of Utah" between Lehi and American Fork. In Provo they picked up William B. Pace and a first-class string band. The party reached Salt Creek, now Nephi, the morning of September 3. "The farther from home," it was said of the travelers, "the greater the enthusiasm became," and the more anxious the people became to reach the colorful country and warm weather of Utah's Dixie. This larger group went a good way towards making the prophet's long and often tedious journey south more pleasant. It was also an enjoyable time for all who went and "a blessing to all concerned."[67]

The presidential party was in St. George for a two-day conference with the Saints of Southern Utah, September 14-15. Besides faith-promoting sermons, those in attendance were treated to a feast consisting of "everything that could be desired in the shape of food." At sunrise, the day after the conference, some younger members of the party began their ascent of the Sugarloaf, a huge, square elevation on the hills outside of St. George. The men, with considerable difficulty, managed to scale the summit, "but the ladies required help." Winder and the other men lowered ropes some forty feet to the base, which were then securely fastened under the arms of the women. As they climbed up, one by one, the men above gently pulled up on the ropes, until they reached the summit. From here they used field glasses to survey the Virgin River Valley, and the vast wilderness. One observer noted, "It was plainly seen from this eminence that St. George is really and truly an oasis in the desert."

After a picnic on the summit, the hikers descended and joined President Young on a visit six miles west to see the little settlement of Santa Clara. That evening, after they had returned to St. George, a grand ball and banquet was given. Wednesday morning, the President's party bade farewell to the Saints of St. George and began the trek north home. The crew had experienced a very spiritual conference, amidst their fun, and President Young remarked several times that nothing like it had been experienced south of Salt Lake City. It has even been suggested that it was on this very trip to St. George that the prophet was inspired to construct a temple there.[68]

These trips were the first of many that President Young would invite John R. Winder to join him on. These excursions were important training grounds for Winder, as he had an opportunity to see much of the territory, see fellow Latter-day Saints in diverse circumstances, and continuously receive counsel from the Church's leading authorities. The friendships that Winder continued to cultivate on these trips with future Church presidents John Taylor, Wilford Woodruff, and

Lorenzo Snow would also be advantageous, as he would later work closely with each of them as a member of the Presiding Bishopric.

The years following the Utah War had been shaping years for John Rex Winder. It was at this time that he had begun to prosper financially through his partnership in the B. K. Tannery. It was a time when he was able to devote his resources towards furthering the cause of agriculture in the territory both through the fairs and on his own Poplar Farm. It was a time when his household experienced tremendous changes, including more children, and the tragic divorce of his second wife, Hannah. It was a time when he became a United States citizen (30 May 1862), paving the way for future government service.[69] It was a time when he traveled extensively with President Brigham Young and furthered his friendships with prophets and apostles. Through all of these experiences, the Englishman learned much about a variety of topics, from Utah geography and Jersey cattle to relationships and the bitterness of divorce. Through it all, he stayed busy helping to build the Great Basin Kingdom. Apostle John Henry Smith later said of him, "We count him among the strong and the capable that have assisted in the upbuilding and development of our great commonwealth."[70]

9
The Captain
Back in the Saddle:
The Black Hawk Indian
War, 1865-1868

"Naturally military"

Relations with the Native Americans

The relationship between Mormon settlers and Native Americans was usually friendly, yet often tense and hostile. Winder had heard of the Indian problems in the territory since the day he arrived in 1853, and had even participated in several military campaigns against them with the Nauvoo Legion. However, the greatest conflict with the Native Americans that would ever erupt with the Mormons had yet to occur.

The Indians saw the coming of the whites as a devastating clash of cultures, an encroachment upon their grazing, hunting, and gathering areas, and as the introduction of laws and customs that simply were not compatible with their traditions. Mormon settlement eventually followed a pattern well established in the rest of the United States, which was to require the Indians to abandon their ancestral homelands and move onto reservations. Conflict inevitably resulted.

In 1864 a reservation was created in Utah's Uintah Basin, and efforts were made to force the Utes to move. The animosity of the Native Americans led them to the brink of war with the settlers of central Utah.[1] One Ute chief named Black Hawk was especially incensed and riled his warriors and sub-chiefs. When one of his braves, known as "Jake," son of the late Chief Arapeen, was insulted in Manti in April 1865, raids and revenge followed. The incident in Manti began as a peace conference where white officials and Ute representatives had met to iron out charges of cattle rustling. One of the white men became involved in a personal controversy with Jake, the young Ute chief, whom he dragged from his horse and proceeded to thrash.

The anti-white message spread like wildfire from camp to camp, and Chief Black Hawk emerged as the leader. During the following two months in Sanpete and Sevier counties, Black Hawk's band began their raids. They first raided the

Lieutenant Colonel John R. Winder of the Nauvoo Legion, as he appeared during the Black Hawk Indian War. Colonel Winder was quickly promoted to adjutant general, assisting General Daniel H. Wells in conducting the operation.

cattle herds, killing the herdsmen, then attacked the local militia mustered to fight them, and finally began killing settlers, including women and children. His violent rampage terrorized central Utah for the next three years and became known as the Black Hawk War.[2]

During June 7-9, 1865, a delegation consisting of Indian Superintendent O. H. Irish, Brigham Young, and others met with the Utes at Spanish Fork for treaty negotiations. It was apparently quite a scene to witness Chiefs Saue-ett, Kanosh, Tabby, To-quo-ne, Sanpitch, and eleven other chiefs of lesser note, with a large crowd of Indians gently saunter down the hill to meet with the whites. They seemed to be trying to keep up an appearance of dignity, according to those in attendance. Then it was President Young's clout with the Indians that persuaded them to give up their lands and move to the reservation, and after several days discussion, the treaties were signed.[3] John R. Winder had accompanied the dignitaries in their meetings with the Indian chiefs, and upon their return home, a conference was held in Payson. Here, Winder was given an opportunity to preach to the congregation. Although he was not a general authority at the time, his remarks were given alongside the sermons of President Young, and Elders George A. Smith, George Q. Cannon, Orson Hyde, John Taylor, Wilford Woodruff, and other leading brethren.

Having Winder speak while traveling with Brigham Young and the apostles soon became commonplace. For example, during August 1865, while the entourage was visiting the Saints in Logan, Ogden, and Brigham City, Winder again spoke in conferences.[4] On that trip north, he was given the honor of presenting a banner to the Wellsville Brass Band, "which was received with three cheers."[5] While at the conference in Brigham City, "Elder J. R. Winder spoke very pertinently on the subject of self-preservation, pointing out the benefits to be derived from a strict attention to the principles which lead to it." The *Journal History* also noted that during the sermon, Winder referred "to past incidents in our history as illustrations."[6] Winder had a deep love of history, particularly the story of the Mormon people and their trials, and in his sermons he would frequently draw from Mormonism's rich heritage to illustrate gospel principles. The details about this sermon, the earliest recorded about the subject matter of any of Winder's public addresses, shows that even early in his ministry, he taught by recalling the heroic experiences from Church history.

In September 1865, Winder was again at the pulpit, this time in St. George.[7] During that conference, Elder Winder "encouraged the Saints to train up their children to have faith in God and in His servants."[8] Such grooming of the young Seventy by President Young would certainly have helped this future general authority focus on spiritual matters and learn to articulate the Gospel of Jesus Christ in public gatherings.

Meanwhile, despite the treaties with the main body of Ute Indians, Black Hawk and his band had refused to attend any of them, and they continued their raids on the whites.[9] General Pope of the U.S. Army refused to send out soldiers stationed at Fort Douglas and said that the Superintendent of Indian Affairs would have to depend upon the Nauvoo Legion.[10]

Mustering the Nauvoo Legion

In October 1865, General Daniel H. Wells, who had been in Europe, revived and reorganized Utah's militia, the Nauvoo Legion. John R. and other militia members quickly reported for duty. Major General George D. Grant, with whom Winder had previously tracked Indians in Tooele, had resigned, and Robert T. Burton was elected to fill his position as head of the Salt Lake Military District. General Burton, with whom Winder had begun a life-long friendship in Echo Canyon, mustered the troops at Camp Utah, southwest of the city near the Jordan River, for three days of drilling on November 1-3.[11]

Heber M. Wells, son of General Wells and Utah's first governor, recalled seeing Winder at just such a muster:

> I particularly recall the fine figure of a man, in full dress uniform, in the annual encampments of the militia which were then called 'musters,' and held just over the Jordan river, riding upon a dashing horse that danced when the band played. The boys called the horse 'Croppy' because his ears had been partially shot off, and the tradition among the boys at the time was that they were shot off in battle with the Indians.[12]

Winder loved his war-horse Croppy and would rely on this faithful animal throughout the war. On July 19, 1866, Winder showed his concern for Croppy when he lamented in his log, "My Mare very sick."[13]

By the time of the Black Hawk War, Winder had already distinguished himself in various Indian expeditions and received another advancement in rank.[14] "My commission as lieutenant-colonel of cavalry came,"[15] he said of the time. So Colonel Winder, his cavalry company, and others trained near the Jordan River while awaiting their time to go south to the battlefield.

Black Hawk's band in early 1865 had been small—twenty to thirty warriors—but a few successful raids brought him prestige and his force grew to over a hundred braves by winter, and to three hundred by spring 1866. Twenty-five whites were killed in the raids of 1865.[16] During the winter of 1865-66, Chief Black Hawk and his followers holed up south of Fish Lake with nearly 2,000 head of stolen cattle, but with the coming of the new year, they were back on the attack.[17]

Up to this point, the Saints in central and southern Utah had been on the defensive. Several towns and villages, including such major settlements as Richfield, Circleville, Panguitch, and Kanab, were abandoned as they gathered to larger settlements where protective forts were built.[18] However, when the first three attacks of 1866 took seven more settlers, General Wells mustered all the men of Piute, Sevier, and Sanpete counties into service as cavalry and infantry, and also called on units from neighboring counties to help.

With the conflict heating up, companies from the northern counties were called out. On April 28, 1866, a cavalry company under Heber P. Kimball became the first from Salt Lake to head south to the battlefield. This company was used to help the settlers in Piute and Sevier counties retreat to Sanpete.[19]

By the end of May, Major General Burton had passed on orders for Lieutenant-Colonel Winder "to organize a company of Cavalry in West Jordan and place a suitable guard to watch the movements of the Indians east and west of Jordan river." After organizing the ranks and holding elections for their captains, Winder provided "some excellent instructions" which were apparently of great motivation to the young volunteers. The excited militia "enjoyed a good time together" and "the West Jordan 'boys' manifested a full share of interest and energy in the proceedings."[20]

In June, General Wells entered the field of action, establishing headquarters at Gunnison, Sanpete County. Colonel Winder led his newly organized cavalry company south to accompany Wells, and an infantry company from Salt Lake followed.[21]

When John R. left to join in the Indian wars, he had to bid farewell to two households and wives, and eleven doting children, including infant Mary Ann, who was born April 28, 1865. This little one was Elizabeth's, and she would live to later marry James Steadman and be the mother of five. While the "City Winders" would miss their father and husband, the "Country Winders" at Poplar Farm would also miss his contributions on maintaining the farm.

Consequently, before Winder departed again for the battlefield, he had a "man to man" talk with eight year-old Willie at Poplar Farm. In this father-to-son chat, he placed a great deal of responsibility upon the boy's shoulders by instructing him to assist his mother in caring for the livestock and the pastures. Willie was an industrious and sober boy and took his responsibilities seriously, realizing at an early age his role as man of the house. After chores on Sunday, for example, he had to prepare the family carriage for church attendance at the Millcreek Ward at 3900 South and 600 East. Because of these duties at the farm, Willie never schooled beyond the fourth or fifth grade.[22]

Pursuing Black Hawk's Band

Upon Winder's cavalry regiment arriving at the field headquarters in Gunnison, General Wells gave the orders that the pursuit of Black Hawk should resume at once. The trail of the raiders was struck, and Colonel Winder and his troops found that they had been at the time within twelve miles of the enemy and the stolen cattle. "In his military career he was never autocratic," it was said of Colonel Winder. "He never sent others where he was not willing to go himself, hence all were ready and glad to follow when he called, 'Come on, boys!'"[23]

A wild march to pursue the Indians ensued, a difficult one as described by a member of Winder's cavalry company:

> The trail was followed over rocky ridges, up and down almost impassable gorges, across occasional streams of alkali water and into the most forbidding and desolate deserts. At the conclusion of the first day's march the men and animals were well-nigh exhausted from the trials of the journey, all having suffered intensely from thirst. During two days more and the larger part of two nights the toilsome march continued; and when the futility of further pursuit was recognized and the condition of the troops was seen perilous, a retreat was again ordered, and it was none too soon; the command was scarcely able to get out of the desert, owing to weakness of both horses and men; of the latter there were several whose mouths and tongues were so sore that they could scarcely speak.[24]

John R. Winder kept a simple log book while on expedition to Sanpete with Lieutenant-General Wells. He recorded on June 29, "Indians seen in various places," including Thistle Valley, and the pursuit continued. Winder also spent time with the other officers figuring out how best to fortify the settlements. At an assembly in the Council House at Manti, Generals Wells and Snow, and Colonel Winder each took turns encouraging the Saints to "secure themselves against Indian depredation [and] not to allow the Indians to get another animal." Other encouragement was given, and Winder wrote, "I am confident much good will result from this wise council given, and readily received by the people."[25]

Throughout the remainder of the summer, Indian attacks continued, but the battles between militia and Indians were indecisive.[26] Nonetheless, according to Anthon H. Lund, Colonel Winder tirelessly "spent month after month in that region and devoted himself to the great object of protecting the people there."[27] Richard W. Young remembered Winder as one who figured conspicuously in the battles against Black Hawk. "Brother Winder, then a lieutenant-colonel of the militia, was sent to the front with his body

This drawing appeared in Ruth Winder Robertson's "Family History for Children." Credited to "the Eugene Winders," it shows one youthful interpretation of the heroic tales of John R. Winder fighting Black Hawk and his band. Note the ears on Colonel Winder's horse, Croppy, which had been shot off in battle.

of troops to take part in defending the people against the Indians from the south. In this he was eminently successful."[28]

Colonel Winder developed a great love for the young men who served with him, and was proud of them like a father was of his own sons. In one letter to Brigham Young, Winder said of his cavalry company that they were "200 of the best Mounted, Armed & Equipped Men I have seen on any Expedition in these Mountains."[29] Even decades after the end of the war, Winder still loved to reminisce about their adventures together in central Utah. When he was invited as a guest of honor at a reunion of Indian war veterans in 1894, he offered the following recollection:

> Many of the scenes we passed through together in the years 1865-6-7 pass vividly before my mind. I can recall the patience, endurance and self sacrifice of the brave men who, as minute men, at the sound of the drum, supplied themselves with the necessary outfit for campaign services, year after year, in defense of the citizens in isolated parts of our Territory. The fight in Salina canyon in 1865, the conflict at Gravelly Ford in 1866, and the battle of Thistle valley in the same year, are all fresh in our memories.[30]

"Brother Winder was always a friend of the young man," it was said of him by a young soldier. "He seemed to love to listen to their stories of hope and ambition, and always lent an encouraging word." John R. Winder never disassociated himself with these young soldiers after the war, but rather, remained for them a mentor and father figure. Briant H. Wells, a son of the lieutenant general, went on to be a captain in the United States Army, later fighting in the Spanish-American War. Upon his return to Salt Lake City, after various tours of duty with his regiment in foreign lands, Briant never failed to call upon Colonel Winder to pay his respects. He frequently told his brother Heber that "he derived more inspiration and good wholesome advice from Brother Winder than any public man in his acquaintance."[31]

Although they often stole food and horses, Black Hawk and his band also stole five thousand head of cattle and killed perhaps ninety settlers and militiamen between 1865 and 1867. At the height of the raids, 2,500 men were enrolled in the Nauvoo Legion's fight against him.[32] In a letter to President Young during the height of the Black Hawk War, Winder remarked, "I can also see the force in the remark in your letter that this is a light chastisement from the Lord. I hope the People will <u>Hearken</u> and <u>obey</u> that this affliction may pass away."[33]

Adjutant General Winder

As the war progressed, the administrative talents of John R. Winder were required by Daniel H. Wells, the Nauvoo Legion's commander. "During the Blackhawk Indian war in Sanpete county," Winder recalls, "I acted part of the time as aid to Gen. Wells."[34] In fact, it was shortly after Colonel Winder's cavalry arrived at the new headquarters in Gunnison that General Wells asked him to

serve as the adjutant general, aiding him as an administrative assistant, of sorts.[35]
Heber M. Wells, later a close friend of Winder's, had his first memories of John
R. Winder while Winder served in that capacity: "I remember . . . that he was my
father's adjutant when my father was Commander of the Territorial Militia."[36]

The adjutant general was the most significant officer in terms of record keeping for the Legion. He was responsible for furnishing subordinates with blank
forms, keeping a rank roll of officers, keeping muster rolls from throughout,
keeping a record of property, and keeping the proceedings of all departments
with a full record of all expeditions and expenses incurred. The Legion supply
officers, such as the quartermaster and commissary generals, and the various
lower ranking commanders were obligated to keep up their records so that they
could report to the adjutant general.[37]

Among his many duties as an adjutant, Winder wrote and answered much of
the correspondence relating to the war effort. It was not uncommon for him to
record in his daily log: "I wrote long Letter to Pres Young," which only strengthened the relationship that these two friends shared. He also recorded the minutes
of important meetings and the results of voting that would sometimes take place.
He even helped keep track of the tithing coming from the area, which was prin-
cipally paid in bushels of wheat, oats, or corn. Colonel Winder also traveled
throughout the area with General Wells and frequently joined him and other officers in planning their pursuit and defense of the Indians.[38] Often, when General
Wells was away from the headquarters at Camp Indian Farm near Gunnison, he
would leave John R. Winder "in charge of Camp" until he returned.[39]

In this function as the adjutant, Winder was in a position to get needed supplies for the men on the front. However, occasionally requests of a more personal nature were made of him, such as when John R. Young, an officer, wrote
Winder, "requesting him to pick up some wine and shoes for him."[40] On
another occasion, an officer wrote a request "to get his boy an overcoat and a
pair of gloves."[41]

Winder was an excellent selection for the important adjutant general's office.
"His work was like clock work, precise and perfect," it was noted, "With a pen
he was swift and accurate—his accounts were well kept, clean, and methodical.
In all respects he was a perfect soldier and a perfect gentleman."[42]

The battles against Black Hawk and his band were seasonal, and during the
colder months, the soldiers were apparently dismissed until mustered again in
the spring. Winder recorded that the militia was fighting only three months in
1865, six months in 1866, and six months again the following year.[43] However,
while Colonel Winder was away from home, he had some of his friends check
on his household for him. For example, in July 1866, his family was visited by
H. W. Laurence, "who reports that all are well."[44] Although Winder still traveled
extensively in the off-season with the officers of the Legion, he was home
enough to sire his eighteenth child. Edwin Joseph, was born to Elizabeth at

Poplar Farm on June 8, 1867. Upon reaching manhood, Edwin would marry Ada Calder and move to Vernal, Utah, where they would rear seven children.

Because of his prominence with the Nauvoo Legion, Colonel Winder was often called upon to help in a variety of capacities, even when on leave back in Salt Lake. For example, in the spring of 1867, the Saints' beloved President Young returned to the city following a lengthy tour of the outlying settlements, and the citizens of Salt Lake thronged the streets to welcome him home. Colonel Winder, along with Majors A. Burt and W. Calder were "energetically employed acting as a Committee of Management" to maintain order and crowd control during the triumphant celebration. However, "their office was not by any means so laborious as such positions generally are, for everybody kept order and desired to see it preserved."[45]

On many occasions while back in Salt Lake City, Colonel Winder was called upon by his friend and former business partner, Brigham Young, to stay close to him as a sort of personal bodyguard. In this duty, Winder spent many nights stationed outside of the Great Colonizer's bedroom door, assuring the prophet's safety. Angus M. Cannon, a brother of George Q., recalled first getting to know Winder while he served in this security capacity:

> I became acquainted with Brother Winder intimately when he lay on his sheepskin in the President's Office, watching over the life and to preserve the liberty of the late President Brigham Young. I was associated with him there for a great length of time. In this humble position I learned to love him and esteem him for his valor, his integrity, and his persistence in maintaining the right.[46]

By the autumn of 1867, the hostilities with the Native Americans required other counties to prepare their volunteers to help finish the fight. In late October, Lieutenant General Wells, General Burton, Colonel Winder, and other officers visited the Cache, Weber, and Davis Military Districts and held a general muster and drill of the militia with each. The troops were inspected, as was the quality of the arms and their ability to handle them. In all ways they were prepared by Winder and his associates for "if they should be called upon to act in such a capacity, as some of the militia of other districts have had to do during the past summer in defending the settlement against Indian outrages."[47]

During the first part of November, the militia of Tooele County was mustered together at an encampment half way between Tooele and Grantsville, which they called Camp Stansbury. Lieutenant General Wells, General Burton, and Colonel Winder came out, escorted by a company of cavalry, to train and prepare the troops at Stansbury. "The first day was spent in company and battalion drill," and the following day there was a standing review, inspection, and addresses given by the visiting officers. "The Militia of the district consist of two battalions of infantry and one battalion of cavalry," it was reported, "most of them well armed and equipped."[48]

Observers were impressed with Winder's action and demeanor during the Black Hawk War. "John R. Winder was naturally military," declared Heber M. Wells, son of the lieutenant general and Utah's first governor. "His bearing was military," he added, "He was straight as an arrow. His movements were quick and his carriage alert and graceful."[49] Longtime acquaintance Richard W. Young had the following to say about his Lieutenant-Colonel:

> Colonel Winder had many of the attributes of a soldier. He had unflinching courage. He was tireless in energy; he was sleepless; he was always alert. His judgement was quick and almost unerring, and above all he had loyalty—uncapitulating loyalty. These are the qualities of which soldiers are made. I have often thought that these early experiences in Utah developed a number of men who would have been prominent even in our Civil war, had they had the opportunity of figuring there as soldiers. Among them was General Burton, who, in my humble judgement, had the ability to command not only army divisions and corps, but a full army. I believe the same with reference to Colonel Winder; he would have been distinguished in any staff, department commissary, adjutant-general's department, or in command of troops in the field.[50]

By the first of February, 1868, the Utah Territory was celebrating the virtual end of the hostilities with Black Hawk's band. The officers and associates of the Nauvoo Legion were the guests of honor that evening at a "military band party" where Captain Mark Croxall's Brass Band entertained President Young, General Wells, Colonel Winder, and the other guests. "The party was an elegant one—plenty of brave men and fair women," wrote the *Deseret Evening News*, "and all seemed to enjoy themselves exceedingly."[51]

Even after the hostilities abated, however, occasional raids continued for a few years. Ironically, by 1870, Black Hawk himself was touring several settlements, speaking to LDS congregations, asking for forgiveness, and trying to explain his motives. He claimed that it was the starvation of his people that had forced the raids. Eventually, the Utes gradually moved to the reservation, and the Black Hawk War proved to be the final outbreak of hostilities against the Mormon settlements in Utah.[52]

Accounting the War's Expenses

After the trouble subsided and most of the militia was released, Adjutant General Winder remained busy. Winder noted that throughout 1868 he "collected and made up the accounts of the expenses of the war, amounting to over a million dollars. This claim was duly submitted to Congress, but has never been paid."[53] Winder's financial acumen was put to the test as he sifted through the Legion's complex notes, receipts, and ledger entries to compile the

$1,121,037.38 claim, a very sizeable sum for the time.[54] Richard W. Young remarked that Winder's work was massive—"a voluminous account of the expenditures made in the prosecution of these Indian wars."[55] This report took Winder most of the year to compile, and was finally submitted to the Territorial Legislature for their review on Christmas Day, 1868. "I have the honor to hand you the above," he wrote in the cover letter to George A. Smith.[56]

Winder's report noted that the militia used to put down the Indian uprisings consisted of a cavalry of 2,525, an artillery of 179, an infantry of 9,207, and numerous officers, staff, and a topographical and ordinance department. The total manpower, according to Winder, totaled 12,024.[57] In addition to the enormous cost of the militia's service and supplies which totaled over a million dollars, he estimated that $170,000 worth of stock was lost. Winder also estimated a loss of $175,000 "by breaking up and vacating about 20 settlements in Sanpete, Sevier, Piute, Kane, Summit, Wasatch and other counties in Utah Territory."[58]

It was Delegate William H. Hooper of Utah who submitted the report to the U.S. Congress, which was largely ignored. This, despite being accompanied by a memorial endorsing it, which had been passed by the Legislature and approved by Utah's governor.[59] This document pointed out that the citizens had appealed repeatedly to General Connor for military aid in "putting down the renegades," but had been denied and was left with no choice but to summon the Nauvoo Legion. The least that Uncle Sam could do, they reasoned, was help compensate for a costly struggle that had caused 32 settlements in seven counties to be abandoned.[60]

The labor of assembling the report of the Black Hawk War was an important endeavor for Winder, one that he made reference to often throughout the remainder of his life. For example, while addressing a reunion of Indian war veterans in 1894, twenty-seven years after the conclusion of the three-year conflict with Black Hawk, the Colonel noted:

> All of this three years service was performed, and the entire expense, amounting in all to more than one million dollars, was borne by the citizens, and not one dollar has been received by them for it from the government.
>
> The accounts were promptly furnished and certified to by Governor Durkes. I saw him sign the certificate that the service had been performed by his order, and that the accounts were just. This certificate was sent to Washington with the accounts. The document was presented to Congress and ordered printed.

"Comrades," seventy-three-year-old Colonel Winder concluded, "I believe that, ere long, you will be paid for your services, so generously, and bravely performed."[61] It was later reported, ironically in the year of Winder's death, that "only recently, and after many efforts, has there been hope of recognition."[62]

Shortly thereafter, the federal government would finally reimburse the territory (now a state) for "costs incurred in fighting Indians."[63]

As for the Nauvoo Legion, it was rendered inactive in 1870 by Acting Governor J. Wilson Shaffer, who forbade gatherings of the militia except on his express orders. Colonel Winder's beloved Nauvoo Legion was ultimately disbanded by the Edmunds-Tucker Act of 1887, and in 1894 the National Guard of Utah was organized to serve as Utah's new militia.[64]

Nonetheless, the experiences that John R. Winder had with the Nauvoo Legion were formative for him. He expanded his knowledge of Utah geography as well as his ever-growing circle of friends and admirers. He increased his faith as the militia relied on God for assistance in waging their battles. As adjutant general, he honed important accounting and writing skills that would assist him in the subsequent stages of his professional life. But perhaps most importantly, John R. Winder had immersed himself in the service and protection of others, and for decades later it would be known among the Saints in the Utah Territory that he "was unselfish in his devotion to the people amongst whom his lot was cast."[65] Heber M. Wells would later make this appraisal of Winder's service:

> Although in rank as an officer in the Territorial Militia he was designated as Colonel, in reality in that greater service to which he devoted his life—the service of God—he was a General, and in my opinion there are few greater in all the armies of the Lord.[66]

10
The Able Administrator: Active Years in Business, Politics, and the Church, 1869-1886

"Of great executive ability"

During the Black Hawk War, John R. Winder was given opportunities to let his financial and organizational acumen shine, which would result in responsible civic positions after the war. As a captain, a colonel, and an adjutant general, Winder had for years acted as a knight in defending the kingdom to which his allegiance lay, not unlike many of his Winder, Henden, Toke, and Dyke ancestors. Now, in the grand tradition of his progenitors, John R. Winder would actively immerse himself in civic and community affairs. This call to duty would be one that would stir in the blood of his descendants, many of whom would also become active in the public arena, as well.

A hero of the recent military campaigns, Colonel Winder was asked to lead a detachment of cavalry to march alongside Beesley's Martial Band in the city's big Independence Day parade of 1869.[1] Winder's daughter Matilda recalled being very proud of her father, "especially one time when he was dressed in his captain's uniform and rode old Crop, the pony he had in the army. He sat so straight and rode so well."[2]

Assessor and Collector of Salt Lake City

Winder's prominence in the militia, which was such an integral part of early Utah society, made him an attractive candidate for government posts. "For fourteen consecutive years from 1870," Winder noted, "I was assessor and collector of Salt Lake City."[3] He had succeeded his friend from the Nauvoo Legion, Robert T. Burton, in this post, one at which he would excel.[4] "He has been placed in some of the most delicate situations or positions that usually fall to the lot of men," noted Elder John Henry Smith. "For many years he was our Assessor and Collector in this part of the Lord's vineyard, and a man must posses rare tact who is able to discharge that obligation without arousing antagonisms of a bitter sort in the breasts of many of his fellow men."[5]

In 1875, when Heber M. Wells was just sixteen years old, he went to work for John R. Winder in the Tax Collector's office, where he remained continuously in his service until 1883, when Wells was elected City Recorder. "During the time I was in his employ," recalled Wells, "I was very closely associated with Brother Winder, and had an opportunity to know him as a younger man may know his elder—as a subordinate—as a son may learn to know his father."[6] John R. knew the young Wells boy from serving as his father's adjutant during the recent war, and the two developed a life-long mutual admiration. "Among his great characteristics were his untiring energy and his perfectly wonderful industry," explained Winder's assistant about his boss. "Six o'clock in the morning never found him in bed, and he worked, worked, worked, cheerily, but incessantly, from morning till night, and until all his daily tasks were done."[7]

John R. Winder in the 1870's. During this and following decades, the business "rustler" proved to be a powerful and active citizen in Salt Lake City. Such energies did not escape notice of the Church authorities, who would later call him to be a general authority.

After achieving statehood, Heber M. Wells would become Utah's first governor. He always recalled what he had learned from Winder in the Tax Collector's office, however, and they were deep impressions that he was able to recall with ease even later in his life:

> Brother Winder was a man of great executive ability, a natural leader of men, yet careful in details, and bent upon attending to all the most important duties himself. In this respect he might be likened to the great Napoleon, who believed that if a thing needed to be well done he should do it himself.[8]

> He was a man of much wisdom, keen discernment, and great sense of justice. He was full of courage and optimism, and with it all had a keen sense of humor which enlivened his spirits and kept his soul sweet and his days full of love and sunshine. He was one of the most approachable men I ever knew,—kind to the poor—a friend to the widows and the fatherless—a counselor to all who sought his advice—and their name was legion.[9]

As the city assessor, Winder was required each year to complete an "Assessment Roll of Great Salt Lake City." This was a list, organized by ward and then alphabetically. It included the name of the "owners or possessors" of each property, the valuation of the land, the number of cattle, horses, donkeys, mules, sheep, goats, and swine. It also included the number of vehicles, clocks and watches, merchandise, value of stocks, gold dust or bullion, value of gold and silver plates or ornaments, money loaned and on hand, value of taxable property not enumerated, and a total value for each household.[10] Assessor Winder would also register the citizens to vote, and on occasion was interviewed by the newspapers regarding the number of eligible voters and other information relevant to forthcoming elections.[11]

Especially during his first few years as an assessor and collector of taxes, Winder would personally visit every house in the city. During this, he came to know almost everyone in Salt Lake City by name, as well as the financial circumstances of almost every taxpayer. These experiences gave him unsurpassed wisdom in knowing whether or not persons were able to pay their taxes. Such insight, combined with Winder's merciful heart, helped many.

One day, while he was busy at the city offices, a young woman who had recently lost her husband and was struggling to provide a scanty living for her and her small children, came in to see him. She told Winder that she had read in the city ordinances that it was within the power of the city to remit the taxes of the insane, idiotic, infirm, or indigent, but as she did not belong to any of these classes, she wondered what she could do. "Never you mind," said the genial collector, "just leave that to me. If anybody should attempt to collect taxes from you in your condition he would be entitled to a worse name than anything mentioned in the ordinance!"[12]

On another occasion, one poor but worthy widow saved up her money to pay her taxes, but to her surprise she did not receive her tax notice. After inquiring about the missing notice, she discovered that her taxes had been paid. "This was while Brother Winder was assessor and collector," it was remembered, "and instead of sending the poor widow her notice, he paid the taxes himself."[13]

As city assessor, Winder was the gate keeper of a tremendous trove of public information which he would occasionally share with others in the community's hierarchy. "Dear Sir," he wrote to his friend Brigham Young from City Hall, "I thought the following would perhaps be interesting to you." Winder then proceeds to report exactly "what proportion of the whole amount of property in this City was owned by the entire Gentile population including all the Apostate Mormons." After providing a breakdown of the figures, he concludes with this summary: "Thus showing that the entire Gentile and Apostate Mormon population Represent about one seventh of the whole amount of Real Estate, and about one third of the merchandise and other property, or about one fifth of the whole amount of all kinds."[14]

Perhaps because of his prominence with the city through his role as assessor and collector, Winder was often called on to assist with various civic functions. For example, in June 1871, the city council "decided upon an elaborate celebration of Independence Day, and appointed a committee to carry out the patriotic purpose." John R. Winder, along with seven other prominent men, were appointed to be the committee, which "represented different classes of citizens irrespective of religious affiliation."[15]

Years in the City Council

Winder was later drafted to further serve the city, even while still holding the post of assessor and collector. "During that period," Winder said, "[I] served three terms in the city council."[16] At the time in Utah's history, politics were organized along religious lines, and elections were contested between the Mormon People's Party and the Gentile Liberal Party. However, during the election year of 1872, an interesting turn of events occurred in Salt Lake City politics which landed Winder in the city council.

A group of non-Mormons seeking to take political control of the largely Mormon city sought to hold a mass meeting of their own to build opposition to the largely Mormon People's Party. As a political party of their own, targeting the middle of the political spectrum, they were hoping to promote their own agenda and candidates. In order to draw as large a crowd as possible to witness the launching of their new political vessel, the Independents, as they called themselves, placarded the town notifying the general public of the mass meeting. "Come one, come all," they invited.

The populous, including members of the People's Party, mischievously took their invitation literally, and "thronging the hall at an early hour, took full possession of the meeting, practically deposing Chairman Kelsey," and electing their own chairman. They proceeded to nominate their own slate of officers for the upcoming municipal contest, including the following: Daniel H. Wells, the Nauvoo Legion's lieutenant-general, as Mayor; and John R. Winder, Robert T. Burton, Theodore McKean, Thomas Jenkins, Heber P. Kimball, Henry Grow, John Clark, Thomas McLellan, and Lewis S. Hills as councilmen. Having dispatched this business, the meeting adjourned. This *coup d'etat* by the People's Party in accepting an invitation addressed to "the people," and capturing superior votes at the meeting, was regarded by the Independents as "a gross outrage," and of course was viewed as a scheme directed by "the Church officials," which it was not. "No outrage had been intended," wrote Elder Orson F. Whitney of the incident, "It was simply a practical joke." Nonetheless, it was a practical joke that propelled John R. Winder into the powerful chambers of the Salt Lake City Council.

Despite the unusual manner in which Winder first found his seat on the city council, he proved to be popular with the voters of Salt Lake, and was re-elected in both 1874 and 1876, finishing his third term in 1878. In one election, Winder had 2,003 votes out of 2,301 cast.[18] Joseph F. Smith improved his friendship with Winder during this period. "I have also been associated very closely with President Winder in the government of Salt Lake City," he later declared, "being a member of the City Council a number of terms while he, too, was a member; also associated with the City Council for a term of years while he held his office as Assessor and Collector of Salt Lake County."[19]

One story which illustrates the great love that Joseph F. Smith felt for John R. Winder was when the latter became stricken with a very serious illness. Heber M. Wells shared the experience to show Winder's great faith and the great friendship between the two:

> Brother Winder was lying on a bed of pain at his farm, south of the city, and in spite of all that was done or could be done for him he grew rapidly worse, until by many of his friends and relatives his life was despaired of. With a divine faith and reliance upon the Almighty, but with a humility and resignation and preparedness for death, if it be the will of the Father that he should go, he threw away the medicines, dismissed the physicians, and asked his friend and brother, Joseph F. Smith, then a member of the Twelve Apostles, to stay with him and pray with him and minister to him. Apostle Smith responded with cheerfulness to the call. I do not remember how long the two stayed together, but I remember calling at the farm many times and seeing Brother Winder upon an improvised bed, in the orchard, with Apostle Smith sitting by his side, fanning him and cheering him with words of comfort and consolation. Day and night he labored over the poor stricken friend, and at the end of a week or so, slowly but surely, Brother Winder began to improve. From that time on it was apparent the victory was won, the prayer of faith had been answered, and Brother Winder was saved to a long life of usefulness.

> When many years afterward President Smith, who had ascended to the Presidency of the Church, selected John R. Winder to be his first counselor it excited some wonder, perhaps, among those who did not know their abiding love for one another, but I remember to have thought to myself, how fitting it is that brethren who have been down into the valley of the shadow of death together, who may have seen the very face of God, should be associated together in unity and harmony as long as either one shall live.[20]

The Salt Lake City Council met in the City Hall each week and heard various petitions. Citizens would come before them and petition for a new road, or to alter a zoning ordinance, for example. Much of their time was spent in hearing reports from various city committees. There was a Committee of Improvements, a Committee on Markets, a Committee on Insane Asylum and Hospital, and a Committee on Claims, to name a few. One of the great concerns of the city council when John R. Winder was a member was providing systematic growth for the burgeoning city that had exploded in growth since the coming of the railroad.

Although a municipal entity, the city council was a very religious group and began and ended each meeting with prayer. Examples of some of the bills passed in Winder's day would be one in February 1873 that gave the city eight more policemen budgeted at $4 per day. Another bill authorized $15 per meal to be spent on feeding the 322 prisoners in the city.[21] The city council at this time set aside tracts of land to develop Liberty Park and Pioneer Park, two important open spaces which still grace the city today.[22]

One special duty that was performed by Councilman Winder came in 1875. Mayor Wells appointed him to be on a select committee that was to greet King Kalakaua of Hawaii at the train station in Ogden as His Majesty passed through Utah. "The Mayor and this delegation left this city, in a special train, at 3:40 pm," it was reported in the Salt Lake newspapers. "The delegation had to wait about fifty minutes at Ogden, at the expiration of which time the King arrived on the U. P. train." Mayor Wells was introduced to the King, and then the Mayor in turn presented John R. Winder and the other members of the delegation. The sovereign of the Sandwich Islands seemed pleased to meet the party from Salt Lake, and it was reported that the meeting was "of a very cordial character, and entirely free from affectation, stiffness and formality, which generally prevail on such occasions."[23] The year following King Kalakaua's stopover in Utah, a similar one was made by His Majesty Dom Pedro, the Emperor of Brazil. Councilman Winder was again asked by the Mayor to help represent the City at this welcome of royalty.[24]

Winder worked hard in all aspects of city business, and developed a good reputation for his work ethic, his sound advice, and his wealth of knowledge. "He was a great reader, especially of the daily newspapers," it was said of Councilman Winder, "and having a very retentive memory, he came to be regarded as a walking encyclopedia of information on current history."[25]

Winder's peers on the council were especially complimentary of his service and character. "During all these years I ever regarded President Winder as an example to me and to all mankind," stated fellow-councilman Smith. "Being a much older man than myself, in the days of my boyhood I came to regard him as a superior man, a man of intelligence, a man of unquestioned integrity, a man of meekness and humility, of gentleness of character, mildness of word and speech, always kind, always affable, always considerate of others, and in every way fitted for every position in which I have ever seen him called to act."[26]

Other Public Service Roles

In February 1880, the legislature passed an act providing for the creation of the Territorial Insane Asylum and appointed John R. Winder to the board of directors. Before this time, the Salt Lake City Insane Asylum and Hospital was the only institution which specifically cared for the mentally ill. The Board of Directors met for the first time on March 17, 1880 and elected Robert T. Burton as president, Warren H. Dusenberry as vice president, Winder as secretary, and Lewis S. Hills as treasurer. The legislature appropriated $25,000 and instructed the board to choose a site in Salt Lake, Utah, Davis, or Weber counties for the location of the institution, "upon the grounds of healthfulness, adaptability to the purposes of the institution, cost of material for construction and convenience of access from the different portions of the Territory." The building was to accommodate not more than 250 patients. Governor Eli H. Murray, who was very interested in the project, often accompanied the board in their searches for a suitable site.[27]

Eventually a 40-acre site for the asylum was chosen one mile east of downtown Provo, on the foothills of the Wasatch Mountains in Utah County. It was recorded that "the board took its responsibility seriously," and they were commended for their vision and foresight in anticipating future needs. Excavations began on August 13, 1881, and the facility was completed in 1886.[28]

Winder was a notable figure in not only city government, but in territorial politics, as well. "I was a member of one of the early constitutional conventions," he stated.[29] This convention, which was called in 1882 to frame a constitution for Utah, was chaired by Joseph F. Smith, who was president of the Territorial Senate at the time. It was thought by the Latter-day Saints that if they could prepare a constitution which would be acceptable to the federal government, that Utah might be admitted into the Union as a State. This privilege had been denied previously with proposals for a State of Deseret because of the bitterness which the nation as a whole felt towards the "peculiar people" of Mormondom.[30]

Members of the convention drafted the following provisions, which they hoped would help persuade Congress to grant Utah statehood: "There shall be no Union of Church and State; nor shall any Church dominate the State," also, "Bigamy and polygamy being considered incompatible with a republican form of government, each of them is hereby forbidden and declared a misdemeanor." John R. Winder was called upon to chair a committee of five delegates, which was assigned by the convention to wait upon the Utah Commission and request them to allow the Territory's citizens at the general election in August to be able to vote upon the Constitution, prior to its presentation to Congress. Because of the particular wording regarding polygamy, the Commission agreed that a popular vote would be a good idea.[31] Nonetheless, despite the convention's best efforts and even after receiving the approval of the people, their good intentions were for naught. Feelings against the Church and its members was too strong at that time and for many years thereafter to allow Utah to join the sisterhood of the states.[32] A convention and resulting constitution in 1887, which was also drafted with Winder's help, faced the same fate.[33]

His leadership on the territorial level was also felt when he was initiated into the Council of Fifty on 8 April 1881. The Council of Fifty, which was a sort of "shadow government" for the unofficial State of Deseret, included some of the most prominent men in the territory. Winder later was promoted to the executive "Committee of Seven" within that body.[34]

John R. Winder resigned his position as Assessor and Collector of Salt Lake City in 1884 to be appointed to another position.[35] William W. Taylor succeeded him as assessor and collector,[36] and, Winder states "From 1884 to 1887 I was city watermaster."[37]

Winder's career as a publican, however, did resume later with a different appointment. John R. recalled that he was "at one time United States gauger in the internal revenue department."[38] The Bureau of Internal Revenue had been created in 1862 to help finance the Civil War. However, the taxes levied during the Civil War were gradually abolished until only taxes on liquor and tobacco remained by 1883. Gauging and collecting this "sin tax" would have been Winder's chief duty while serving in the predecessor of the Internal Revenue Service (IRS).[39]

"As a public servant, he gave splendid satisfaction to the city, the county, the territory, and the state in the many offices held by him," declared Frank Y. Taylor about John R. Winder. "In all his public duties, his labors were for the people. He was the people's man—true to every trust, seeking not his own advancement or honor, but being satisfied if he performed his duty well and if the people received the benefit."[40]

When asked to list the many activities that he was involved with, Winder noted, "My extended official connection with the old political regime as chairman of the territorial and county committees of the People's party, may also be mentioned."[41] In 1872 Winder served as a delegate to the nominating convention of the party, and two years later was elected to the Territorial Central Committee.[42] He later served during the 1880's as the county chairman. He was elected chairman of the Territorial Central Committee of the party on June 16, 1887 "in the place of John Sharp who resigned today."[43] He would serve in this important political post until the dissolution of the People's Party in 1891.[44] Winder maintained a remarkably clean record while participating as one of Utah's chief politicians. "He has figured also in a political sense in our communities, and has been enabled to pass through that species of fire which few men succeed in doing without being singed," exclaimed Elder John Henry Smith of Chairman Winder. "In all the stations and conditions that President Winder has been called to act in, so far as I have any knowledge—and it has been my lot to have had part with him in the political way and in the official way. . . I feel that my own experience with President Winder is but the experience of the great mass of the Latter-day Saints, that they have ever found him to be capable, devoted, fearless, if necessary to display fearlessness, considerate and kind, and ready always with his views when necessary upon any question affecting the interest or well-being of the people."[45]

As a Captain of Industry

From early on in his Utah career, Winder had been active in seeking out productive ways to use his money. "John R. came across many financial opportunities through his prominence in the LDS Church," declared grandson George Winder, "When the brethren began businesses, John R. would make investments and acquire directorships."[46] This was a pattern that began with Brigham Young and the B. K. Tannery, and one that would be repeated over and over throughout the remainder of Winder's remarkable career as an industrialist. His ambition gained some notoriety in the West, and contemporary Orson F. Whitney quipped of Winder, "In business he is known as a 'rustler.'"[47]

John R. Winder possessed a strict code of ethics that tempered his ambitious business acuity. "If any business proposition was put up to him, it had only one solution: Is this right? Is this just? Is it equitable?" This, according to Elder William W. Riter, was his guiding code. "In all my life I never heard him figure over a business proposition with a view of 'How much am I to get out of this? How much profit is coming to me?',," Riter reported, "But the only consideration that he ever gave these questions was the justice and righteousness that might accrue to his fellow men, to his friends and his brethren."[48] Then, as Winder made money, he spent it frugally and always lived within his means. "From the day I came into the valley, I have proposed never to go into debt," said he, "I have always tried to live within my means. A person who has $100 a month salary is on the safe side if he lives on $90 a month, but if he spends $110 he is going down hill all the time."[49]

In light of his earlier successes in the tannery business, it was natural that Winder returned to the profession he knew best. In the spring of 1868 he and H. Milton Masser attempted to purchase another tannery that Brigham Young owned. "Bro. Winder will give it his personal attention," Masser promised Young. They also promised Brigham Young that the "Trustee in Trust" (a.k.a. whomever is president of the LDS Church), would always be able to "obtain all the hides and skins" that they would ever need.[50]

About this same time, John R. built and operated still another tannery, this one located in the Nineteenth Ward. His partners in this one included two previous business associates, William Jennings and Feramorz Little, Winder's close friend George Romney, and W. H. Hooper and Elias Morris. The tannery did so well that it was soon acquired by the new ZCMI in 1870.[51] The "Big Boot," as the shoe factory was often called, was soon manufacturing 83,000 pairs of boots and shoes yearly for ZCMI.[52] John R. Winder, Jr. for years had worked with his father in both farming and with tanneries, but in 1870 he stayed with the shoe and leather department at ZCMI.[53] As for the entrepreneurial founders, they all moved on to their next money making endeavor.

In May of 1875, John R. Winder, along with Wilford Woodruff, A. P. Rockwood, and H. Dinwoody bought one-half interest in the Rotery Harror for Utah Territory for the sum of $1,400 "which we Consider to be one of the best Harrors in the world for the Farmer," according to Woodruff.[54] A harrow was an implement for leveling or breaking up plowed land, and was apparently quite useful in pioneer agriculture. John R. Winder also wielded considerable stock in the Consolidated Wagon and Machine Company.[55]

"Winder was an example of economy, and his financial success in life is largely due to this most excellent trait in his character," it was said of him. "He could not bear to have anything go to waste. . . . He was a man of order in every phase of his life, never leaving anything half done. If he undertook any work, he completed it and then went at something else, and he believed in the principle of 'What is worth doing, is worth doing well.'"[56] Such a work ethic only increased Winder's attractiveness for having him involved with business enterprises.

Another venture for Winder was a cooperative tannery called the Deseret Tanning and Manufacturing Company. The tannery committee held its first meeting in June 1877, and John R. Winder, who had long developed a reputation as one of the great tanners in the territory, was elected to the board of directors. In November 1877, Winder, along with fellow board member and friend Robert T. Burton, boarded the train for Chicago, Illinois. Their mission was to tour the most modern tanneries in America and order equipment to be installed in a building the company was constructing in the Nineteenth Ward. This great train ride halfway across the continent would have been an exciting opportunity for Winder to see beyond Utah's borders. The last time he had seen the vast prairies of America's Great Plains or the mighty Mississippi would have been nearly 25 years prior, when he was a pioneer trekking with his family towards a new home. President John Taylor dedicated their new tannery on March 23, 1878.[57]

In May of 1880, Winder's skills were required for yet another business venture, the Utah Eastern Railroad, which would run between Salt Lake City and the now booming mines of Park City. The *Salt Lake Herald* explained "The Utah Eastern was not devised as a moneymaking scheme for a few individuals. . . . The Company was organized and the road is to be built for the purpose of breaking a monopoly that is sorely suppressing the people." The organizers of the Utah Eastern also acquired a number of important coal mines in Summit County under the auspices of the Home Coal Company, which guaranteed their railroad business.[58] John R. Winder was involved from the beginning with the railroad, and the *Deseret News* of November 11, 1880 quoted this "pioneer stockman and military leader" as stating that this railroad "had to be built so that thirty thousand people would not be dependent on one man or one company."[59]

Utah Eastern officials were concerned from the beginning that Union Pacific would try to take over the railroad by buying the controlling interest, so stockholders devised a plan to keep power in their hands, regardless if the stock was sold. Under the plan, three trustees were elected in whose hands was placed a majority, or $400,000, of the stock. For fifteen years, it was set up so that the stock could be sold but would still be subject to the control of the trustees for voting purposes. John R. Winder was elected to this important position of trustee, along with fellow Church member Leonard W. Hardy, and Fred H. Auerbach, a non-Mormon Salt Lake businessman.[60] In addition to the Utah Eastern Railroad, Winder was also a director of the Utah and California Railroad Company, the Cedar and Iron Railroad Company, the Emigration Canyon Railroad Company, the Salt Lake and Pacific Railroad Company, and the Utah Light and Railway Company.[61]

Winder acquired another directorship with the Utah Iron Manufacturing Company, along with George Q. Cannon, William Jennings, Feramorz Little, and several others. President John Taylor was the Trustee-in-Trust. Incorporated June 1, 1881, the Utah Iron Manufacturing Company listed its business as the "mining and production of coal & manufactury of coke, also mining and production of iron ores and the manufactury of iron in all its branches, qualities, and depts."[62] Abraham H. Cannon remembered one meeting of the Iron Company in 1883 in President Taylor's office. They discussed the feasibility of purchasing railroad cars and other supplies for the mining company, and appointed J. R. Winder to see on what terms they could borrow $15,000 for these purchases.[63]

Other businesses that Winder the Industrialist was involved in included the Alberta Colonization Company; Armstrong, Winder, and Company; Bar-Ka-Two Stock Company; Bear River Water Company; Beneficial Life Insurance Company; Blackfoot Stock Company; Daynes Jewelry Company; Deseret Meat and General Provision Store; Deseret Tanning and Manufacturing Company; Herald Company; Herald Publishing Company; Hydraulic Canal Company; Inland Crystal Salt Company; Knight Ranching Company; P. W. Madsen and Company; Provo Woolen Mills Company; Rexburg Milling Company; Salt Lake Knitting Works; Saltair Beach Company; Utah and Pacific Improvement Company; Utah Hotel Company; and Zion's Central Board of Trade. In addition to these many directorships, Winder was also a stockholder in the Alaska Ice and Storage Company; Consolidated Music Company; Heber J. Grant and Company; Home Fire Insurance Company; Portland Cement Securities Company; San Vincente Lumber Company; Union Fuel Company; and the Woolley Smokeless Furnace Company.[64]

It was of little surprise that Winder was in such great demand for these executive positions. He was "distinctively a business man, prompt, careful, economical, possessing in a marked degree the practical judgement necessary to the successful financier," according to Orson F. Whitney. "He was seldom if ever late to an appointment, and delighted in punctuality and industry. An early riser, his habits were temperate, and his manner and methods active and bustling."[65]

Zion's Cooperative Mercantile Institution, known as ZCMI, or the "People's Store," came into being in 1868 as America's first department store. Sales totaled over $1.25 million the first year as clothing, wagons, machinery, sewing machines, and carpets became available to Utahns at a reasonable price.[66] It is not surprising to learn that John R. Winder was involved with this enterprise, as well. Probably a large shareholder from its inception, Winder was elected a director for ZCMI on October 5, 1885, in order to fill a vacancy created by Septimus Wagstaff Sears. By the time ZCMI was reincorporated in 1895, Winder had acquired 28 shares of stock, which was considerably more than Wilford Woodruff's 17 shares or George Q. Cannon's 12 shares.[67] He would serve as a director until his death twenty-five years later.[68]

"I have been acquainted with him in a great many of our large corporations, in the banks . . . in Zion's Co-operative Mercantile Institution, in the Sugar Company, and in a great many others where I have been intimately associated with him," declared George Romney, a fellow industrialist and close friend. "I have never known him to try to do anything that was not for the benefit of the whole people. . . He never took into consideration his own interest, but it was for the good of the community."[69]

During these years of vigorous business activity, John R. still found time for one of his favorite organizations. During this time he spent many enjoyable hours continuing to serve as a director in the Deseret Agriculture and Manufacturing Society. The minutes of a meeting in 1874 showed Winder as the chairman of a committee to ornament the Agricultural Park, as well as in charge of all Class G exhibits that year at the fair, which included "poultry, fish and bees, etc."[70] Winder made sure that each fair ran smoothly. "The 'rush' was, if possible, greater than yesterday," it was reported on day two of a fair, "but the excellent precautions of the committee of arrangements, Messrs. J. R. Winder and F. A. Mitchel, prevented anything like a jam, and everything passed off with 'eclat.'"[71]

Frank Y. Taylor summarized Winder's financial success as follows: "He succeeded as a butcher, attained to prominence as a banker, and was interested in the leading industrial, manufacturing, and mercantile institutions of our state. He not only had his name identified with them, but was an active factor in their management." Taylor continues, explaining why Winder was often involved with important businesses: "His good judgement was such that people believed in and had confidence in him, and felt that their money was safely invested as long as he had a voice in the management of the business."[72]

John R. Winder never allowed his financial successes to corrupt him with greed, but rather, he allowed his resources to bless the less fortunate. "President Winder's charities were many," it was said, "but were best known among the poor, the widow, and the orphan." Only a handful of anecdotes survive to help illustrate the charitable nature of this spiritual giant, for Winder "gave on the principle of not letting his left hand know what his right hand did." However, his acts of kindness appear to be legion, and it was said that "those who most needed his sympathy and help, received it."

One tale is about a widow, who was sitting around the hearth with a large family on a cold Christmas Eve. Her anxious children were asking their poor mother what they were to receive for Christmas. "I was almost in despair," she said, "when in answer to a knock at the door, in walked Brother Winder loaded down with everything to make us happy—a veritable Santa Claus."[73]

On another occasion, an orphan boy, who was a neighbor of the Winders', was struggling for a new home. He was in debt and felt he must sell some of his land to pay the obligation, but remembering that he always had a friend in Brother Winder, he first went to him for advice. Winder put his arm around the young man and told him not to sacrifice his land, as it would increase in value, and he himself would furnish the necessary money. As a result of this help and advice, the young man later became several thousand dollars better off.[74]

"I have never known a father's love," proclaimed Heber J. Grant, who later became an apostle and seventh president of the LDS Church, "but John R. Winder, Daniel H. Wells, and many other men who were associated with my father have bestowed a world of affection upon me." Grant, who himself was an extraordinary businessman and financial genius, declared, "John R. Winder has done more for me in the hours of deep distress and financial difficulty than any other man that ever lived."[75]

It is indeed remarkable that one who had become so extremely well off financially would be so filled with compassion, charity, and kindness as was John Rex Winder. It seemed to be a gift with which he was blessed. Indeed, Winder had been told in his patriarchal blessing that "the spirit of influence of sympathy will oft affect thy heart."[76]

Founding of Winder Dairy

However, in addition to the fast-paced world of a "Captain of Industry," J. R. Winder relished wearing yet another of his many hats—that of the stock raiser. "Most of Brother Winder's friends knew him best in the financial circles of big undertakings," it was said of him, "but one of the best places to become acquainted with his many beautiful traits of character, was at the place where most great men come from—the farm."[77]

As was mentioned before, Poplar Farm was a peaceful eddy for Winder in the otherwise bustling stream of life. "There he practiced best the simple life where he came in actual touch with nature which seemed to be part of his very self." Indeed, farming seemed to provide a transcendental therapy that prepared him to face again the hectic business world. "He communed with nature in the cornfield, in his vegetable garden, under the shade of the orchard, among the stock, with his fat herd of jerseys, in the raising of which he excelled, in the midst of his sleek brand of horses, the best in the land. There were few weeds in his farm. The ditches were cleaned, in fact everything about the place was neat and tidy."[78]

By 1880, Winder's farm consisted of 65 acres, $2,500 worth of fine live-stock, three times as many "milch cows" as other farms in Millcreek, 200 apple trees, two acres of potatoes, two acres of Indian corn, and a barnyard of 100, which had produced 950 eggs the previous year.[79] Winder was a very competi-tive farmer, as illustrated by this clip from the *Deseret Evening News:*

> Brother John R. Winder says he is not to be outdone in the way of turnips, and to prove it showed us a specimen, which on measuring and weighing, we found to be twenty-seven inches in circumference; and nine pounds twelve ounces in weight. This turnip was raised on Brother Winder's farm, Mill Creek, and he says by the time the Fillmore man beats it he will probably be ready with another specimen still larger. We should judge that one such turnip as the one described above would be a decent meal for any cow with an ordinary appetite. The weight in proportion to the measurement shows the turnip was sound.[80]

"If our people farmed and raised stock in the same orderly line as he did," it was said of Winder, "our land would be a delight to look upon and profit those who engage in it."[81] His breeding of cattle was notorious throughout the Terri-tory. For example, Abraham H. Cannon recorded in his diary one Saturday, "I bought for $60 a fine Holstein bull calf from John R. Winder today."[82]

Like all of his financial records, precision and order reigned on the farm, as well. "At his farm, every wisp of hay or ear of corn was carefully picked up and stowed away. In the feeding of his stock at his farm, there was no tramping of feed under the feet of the animals or careless scattering of hay to the winds. Everything was saved and put into its proper place."[83]

Although John R. Winder is best remembered from his farming days as a pioneer dairyman, the great stock-raiser was also famous in his day for his sleek brand of horses—the best in the land. "He knew a good horse when he saw it and took great pleasure in driving one," it was said of the Colonel. Abraham H. Cannon reported that once in May, 1883 he "Went down to Bro. Winder's farm this forenoon to see his thoroughbred horse 'Octabus.'" The animal must have been an impressive sight, for he writes, "In the evening I took father to the farm, and then returned and stopped with Mina."[84] The 1880 Utah agriculture census noted that Poplar Farm had twenty "horses of all ages." Jean Winder Jones, a granddaughter, recalled, "There were beautiful horses and Shetland ponies" at her grandfather's farm, and that each family was given a pony.[85]

Winder's wife who resided at Poplar Farm, Elizabeth Parker Winder, enjoyed making butter, which she sold to her friends and relatives in the city. In 1879, 750 pounds of butter was produced at the farm, while neighboring farms were only making 150 pounds or less.[86] In 1880, however, Elizabeth quit selling just butter as the family began concentrating on milk delivery. On April 17 of that year, a retail trade was established with Winder milk being supplied to the Knutford Hotel, which was located on 200 South and Main Streets. After securing this account, there were several other hotels and lodging houses, such as the Valley House and the Continental Hotel, in addition to several neighbors who began to get Winder milk delivered.[87] From those humble beginnings grew what became the Winder Dairy.

Winder Dairy quickly became well known for their rich, pure Jersey milk, of which there was quite a demand at the time. It originated as a small business working out of the cattle barn east of the Poplar Farmhouse, and for the first two decades only required one horse, one milkwagon, and one delivery man. The cows would have their first milking at night, and the milk was collected in five-gallon cans and stored in the fifty-two-degree well water in the Poplar Farmhouse basement to keep it sweet overnight. The cows would have their second milking early in the morning and the morning milk would be quickly cooled by being hurriedly stirred into the cold night milk that had been stored in cans in the cold well water. The milk would then be taken for immediate delivery on the milkwagon, arriving to the customers within hours of leaving the cow. The milk at this time was delivered raw, without any sort of pasteurization or homogenization.[88]

"My earliest recollection is a log room which had shelves all around it to hold the milk pans," recalled one of Winder's daughters, Ella Winder Mackay. "Later when the flowing well was drilled, a milk house was built with a cement floor, which was higher in the center, leaving about one and one-half feet around the room two inches lower with a drain in it," she added. "A box was built in one end of the room which held ten five-gallon creamers with spouts in the bottom which could be turned to drain off the milk, leaving the cream. The water ran into the box at the top and out the bottom, then around the lower part of the floor to the drain. The cold water running all the time kept the milk house cool."[89]

When the milk was first delivered, it was done by horse-drawn carts. The horses were shod with hard rubber horseshoes.[90] However, since the same horse that was used to pull the milk wagon on weekdays was used to take the family to church on Sundays, it took a constant effort to keep the horse from stopping at every house that received milk during the week.[91] Winder milk was stored in milk cans, some as large as ten gallons. When the milk wagon stopped at a customer's house, the milkman would reach into the can with a one-quart dipper and scoop out the milk, pouring it into the customer's pan. The customer would later wait for the cream to settle on top, which they would skim off and turn into butter and whipping cream.[92] Often, especially for larger orders, the milk cans were left for the customer one day and collected the next. Three-gallon cans were left for the hotels, and one-gallon cans for the retail customers. Elizabeth's butter, made in churns, was also a popular item among the first Winder Dairy customers.[93]

Poplar Farm became well known throughout Salt Lake County, with its stately trees, kind hospitality, and famous dairy products. One contemporary noted, "Scores directed the course of their afternoon rides there to imbibe the delicious butter-milk from the ice cold tankard in the cellar."[94] An example of just such a visit was recorded in the journal of Wilford Woodruff on July 20, 1889. Although he was president of the LDS Church at the time, he still found time to visit the young Winder Dairy: "I spent the day at the farm," he cheerfully penned. "I visited J. R. Winder Creamery and 20 Jersey and Holstein Cows all of which were in lowing."[95] The famous Poplar Farm was even featured in the tourist booklet "Salt Lake City Illustrated," which included a beautiful engraving of the shaded farmhouse done by D. C. Dunbar of Omaha.[96]

John R. Winder managed the farm until he became too involved in Church and civic affairs to continue. Eventually he turned over all of the dairy business to his son William C. Winder, who, along with his sons, worked hard to see the business grow and prosper.[97] Nonetheless, whenever John R. would arrive for his stay at the farm, he would promptly call his son to provide a full accounting of the farm's activities. Winder, who was precise and exacting, would tour the farm carefully to see if everything was in order and if anything was amiss, he wanted to know why and would issue firm directives to his son.[98]

During the period of civic and business activity that followed the Black Hawk War, Winder also enjoyed a continuing growing family. For example, he and Elizabeth had five more children during this period. Florence Luella was born September 11, 1869, later married James Giles in 1911, and died July 7, 1944. Matilda Edna joined their home on December 9, 1871, married Reuben Hamilton in 1894, and passed away on June 12, 1953. Another daughter, Ella May, was born January 14, 1875, married Walter Mackay in 1897, and died January 23, 1949. Still another girl, Gertrude, was born August 23, 1877, married Mark Young Croxall in 1900, and died February 10, 1925 in Tacoma, Washington. The final child of John Rex Winder, by any wife, was Rex Parker Winder, who was born September 9, 1878, when his father was 56 years old. Rex married Reuhanna Fisher in 1906, and later had a second marriage to Thurza Malin in 1924. He outlived all of John R.'s children, passing away July 21, 1967.

The children of John and Elizabeth enjoyed a close and happy association and were successful in raising their own families. They loved to sit at the feet of their mother around the hearth and listen to stories or gather at the piano to sing. Daughter Matilda recalled her mother's long thick brown hair with no gray, which she loved to comb and brush while she listened to the stories her mother read to her.[99] Elizabeth encouraged her children to participate in plays and musicals and to develop their talents.[100] An industrious, yet warm and tender mother, she had taught her children to work by working with them.[101] She encouraged thrift and adherence to gospel principles. Even through service in the Church, Elizabeth was able to teach many of her children, as she served in the Primary Presidency in the Millcreek Ward in the early 1880's.

Elizabeth was an excellent homemaker who had a knack in making a home cozy and attractive. She was a good cook, and taught her many daughters the finer points of homemaking. The boys were encouraged to be of assistance to their father and brother, Willie, and Elizabeth made sure their practical education was complete—even teaching them to knit. John R. made sure Elizabeth had a sewing machine, a rarity in those days.[102] When Ed was about five years old he stood beside his mother in the sewing room at Poplar Farm and watched as her feet moved on the treadle to make the machine run. As he saw less and less spool on the thread, he exclaimed, "Sew faster, Mother, so the thread won't run out!"[103]

Elizabeth Winder was afflicted with muscular dystrophy, a crippling disease that causes the gradual wasting away of muscle tissue in the body. As the years wore on, her state of health diminished greatly. This illness, which can only be passed on genetically, was so prevalent in her own family that it became known as "Parker's disease" in Pioneer Utah. However, only one of Elizabeth's children ever picked it up, Alice Winder Bradford.

Because of her difficulty in walking in her later years, John R. bought his wife a low carriage, which was easy to get into to go riding. By late 1882, Elizabeth's condition worsened to the point that she was totally paralyzed, languishing in bed for over a year, unable to even turn her head. As the holidays of 1883 approached, her condition worsened further, and she passed away peacefully the morning of Christmas Day, at the age of forty-six. She had her husband and her ten children, ages four to twenty-five, at her bedside at the moment of her passing.[104] Several of these were still small children, who now looked to their father to raise them, he being their only living parent.

A lovely Christmas dinner was brought in, but no one seemed to be able to eat. There was always a sadness among John R. and his children at each Christmas thereafter. The days before the funeral were busy and people came to help with the sewing of the black clothing that was worn by all the family, as was the custom.[105] Funeral services were conducted two days later in the Poplar Farmhouse, with Bishop George Romney as the principal speaker. In the final moments before the closing of the casket, John R. Winder lifted little Rex to kiss his mother goodbye. A funeral cortege of fifty vehicles filled with mourners made its way to the Salt Lake Cemetery.[106] Her obituary stated that "she had the reputation for being as good a wife, mother and Latter-day Saint as could be found."[107]

In the late 1870's John R. built a stylish new home for Ellen located downtown at 62 South on 300 East. Ellen filled the yard with flowers, which proved to be an impressive sight every spring and summer.

John R. Winder still had his first wife, Ellen Walters Winder, but she resided in the city with her children, leaving the "country" Winders to be largely raised by their older siblings, with their father sharing his time between the two households. In the late 1870's, John built a stylish new home for Ellen located downtown at 62 South on Third East. Ellen filled the yard with flowers, which proved to be an impressive sight every spring and summer. She, too, was a remarkable lady, and was known as an exemplary wife and mother. Ellen was mild and supportive, considerate and deeply compassionate.[108]

John R. Winder was viewed by his children as a loving father, but one who retained many of his "old world" ways and was extremely difficult to please. It was said of William C. Winder, that he felt "a good deal of affection, respect, and trepidation for his dynamic father."[109] One daughter, Matilda, recalls crying when their strict father kept the children home from school on a day when the weather was so bad that the mile and a quarter walk to school had turned completely to mud.[110]

Nonetheless, as patriarch of his plural households, John R. Winder did well to provide for his children and see that they were taught both the Gospel of Jesus Christ and the ethics of industry, frugality, and hard work. "One of the highest testimonials of his nobility, was the purity and scrupulousness of his home life," it was said of him. "He loved his family and surrounded them with every opportunity for development of sturdy manhood and womanhood. He never lavished upon them superfluous expenditures which would lead their thoughts to the lighter things of life, but he always provided the necessities."[111] Another observer added, "Brother Winder was a firm believer in work. Everybody worked at his home."[112]

One notable event for the Winder family in the 1870's was a fire. On December 18, 1872 an arson apparently started a fire in the Winder's barn on East Temple Street and Third South. One of the daughters was the first to notice it and quickly called the attention of her father. John R. told the newspapers that the fire was confined to a small bundle of straw on which coal oil had been poured. Had he a couple of buckets of water, he said, the fire could have been put out right there. However, while trying to extinguish it with a board, Winder witnessed the flames spread to the hay loft overhead. Both the city fire brigade and the ZCMI fire company soon arrived at the scene, but the fire had consumed the barn and the partially completed new house before it was put out. The loss was estimated at $3,500.[113]

Service in the Church

While John R. Winder excelled in civic leadership, business responsibilities, the art of farming, and as a father and husband, he also provided valuable ecclesiastical leadership. The callings he was asked to perform during the 1870's and early 1880's did much to prepare him for still greater responsibilities in the Church that would come in subsequent decades.

On March 4, 1872, Thomas Taylor was called as Bishop of the Salt Lake Fourteenth Ward, and he chose as his counselors Lewis S. Hills as his first and George Crimson as his second. Hills had only acted as a counselor a few months when John R. Winder was called to serve as first counselor in his stead. This change took place in the fall of 1872.[114] Bishop Taylor was enjoying the prosperity of being the owner of a grocery store, a hotel, and considerable grasslands. He was recognized as a leading merchant in Salt Lake City, and increased his wealth through mining interests in Iron County and by promoting the rail service between Salt Lake and Los Angeles. The Taylors had attended church meetings for years with the "city" Winders and had developed a good friendship with them.[115] It was through this association that William C. Winder became introduced to his future wife, the Bishop's daughter, Rosalie Romney Taylor, whom he wedded in December of 1883.

As the president of his Quorum of Seventy, Winder had already been very involved with events in the Fourteenth Ward. For instance, in 1870, Winder, along with Joseph Horn, constituted the building committee that supervised the construction of "a new commodious brick building, about thirty-two feet long by twenty-two wide, two-stories high," that would serve as the new meetinghouse.[116]

The Fourteenth Ward had as its boundaries South Temple Street on the north, East Temple Street on the east, 300 South Street on the south, and 200 West Street on the west. About two-thirds of the population within the boundaries were LDS, but the non-Mormons owned about two-thirds of the real estate. While it was said "quite a number of the 'Mormon' families are poor," it was also noted that "President Wilford Woodruff and other prominent men in the Church reside in this Ward."[117]

Winder, who had held the office of a Seventy in the priesthood, was ordained a High Priest on March 4, 1872 by Presiding Bishop Edward Hunter. As first counselor in the ward bishopric, he was placed in charge of the Fourteenth Ward during the absence of Bishop Thomas Taylor when he was on missionary work in the east. One of his first acts as "bishop" was to invite his good friend, who happened to be the President of the Church, to attend any of the ward's meetings. Since he was now in charge, Winder also shifted the time of the evening meeting one half-hour earlier, which he apparently preferred.

> 14th Ward Salt Lake City
> November 9, 1872
> President B Young
>
> Dear Brother,
> Whenever convenient and agreeable to yourself we most respectfully Invite you to attend meeting in the 14th Ward. Meeting tomorrow as follows: Sunday school 10 a.m. Afternoon meeting 2 p.m. evening 7 p.m. after tomorrow our meetings will commence at 10 am 2 p.m. and 6 1/2 pm
>
> In behalf of the Ward
>
> Very Respectfully
> John R. Winder[118]

After Bishop Taylor returned, Brother Winder continued to act as his first counselor until his promotion to the stake level.[119] Angus M. Cannon remembered Winder's service: "I was familiar with him as a Bishop's Counselor in the Fourteenth Ward, where I live, and the manner in which he filled that calling and sustained the hands of the Bishop."[120]

Another calling soon came to the faithful bishop's counselor. Elder Wilford Woodruff recorded in his journal on May 4, 1873, "the Presidency & Twelve Met for Prayer & After Prayers We Appointed 13 Men to be ordained to the High Council in salt Lake City." Among the brethren appointed to the High Council of the Salt Lake Stake at that meeting was John R. Winder.[121] As for Bishop Taylor, whom Winder had served with for a season, he later stumbled into trouble. In 1886, while he was in his fifteenth year of service as Bishop of the Fourteenth Ward, various morality charges were brought against Thomas Taylor and he was promptly excommunicated. He would die in 1900 in Los Angeles.[122]

Winder would serve on the High Council for fourteen years (1873-1887).[123] For many of those years, until 1877, the Salt Lake Stake embraced not only all of Salt Lake County, but the counties of Tooele, Davis, Morgan, Summit, and Wasatch.[124] The High Council represented such a large number of the Saints that they were honored by sitting on the stand at general conferences in the Tabernacle. In this capacity, Winder's opinions became valued greatly. "I always appreciated his judgement," declared a fellow stake officer, "for I considered it always sound."[125]

President Angus M. Cannon said of Winder, "In speaking in behalf of the Presidency of the Salt Lake Stake of Zion, where Brother Winder has ministered, and we have been close observers of his course in life, I can testify that I never knew him to slip a cog in any position that he ever filled." Cannon continues, "I have loved him because of his integrity, his unswerving integrity in maintaining the right, and his anxiety to have everything go for the glory of the Lord and the salvation of His people, to promote union, fellowship and love in the lives of the Saints."[126]

In addition to service on the ward and stake levels, John R. Winder had also experienced some Church-wide prominence through his service to Brigham Young. Elder Francis M. Lyman of the Twelve noted, "He was a very remarkable fixture in the administration of President Brigham Young."[127] As has been mentioned, he was invited by the prophet to frequently accompany him on his travels among the Saints. One particularly long journey in 1870 occupied 53 days, as the party explored beyond St. George into southeast Nevada and northwest Arizona and up to the new settlements near Kanab. This was the longest trip south that Brigham ever took, and of course he requested Winder to accompany him on it. Robert T. Burton, a good friend from the Nauvoo Legion days, was Winder's traveling companion that trip. "Such journeys wearied human participants and taxed animals. Very often, spent horses were exchanged for fresh ones, and some died along the way."[128]

Three journeys that same year, in February, July, and November, took Brigham Young and his party, including Brother Winder, north again through the Ogden area. On one trip, Bishop Christopher Layton joined the party at Kaysville, which already included the First Presidency, five of the Twelve, and the Presiding Bishop.[129] A similar "preaching tour" was made in June 1870 to Brigham City and the Bear Lake region.[130] In 1873, Winder joined the Prophet's party on a preaching tour to Provo.[131]

On Wednesday, August 29, 1877, Feramorz Little, the Mayor of Salt Lake City called a special meeting of the city council. It was at this somber meeting that John R. Winder and his fellow councilmen learned that the great Lion of the Lord, Brigham Young, had died earlier that day. Winder would have deeply mourned the loss of his friend and spiritual mentor. His closeness to the prophet is evident in that he was asked, along with four others, to draft and present the resolutions honoring the founder of their city, Brigham Young.[132]

President Young's successor, John Taylor, had known John R. Winder since they first met in Liverpool in 1850. Winder had been with President Taylor on many occasions as a member of the same "prayer circle," a sacred association that they enjoyed from 1859 to 1882.[133] Shortly after he was sustained as president of the Church, John Taylor prophetically warned the Saints: "There are events in our future, and not very far ahead, that will require all our faith, all our energy, all our confidence, all our trust in God, to enable us to withstand the influences that will be brought to bear against us." It was not long after that the dark clouds of hatred and persecution which had haunted the Saints from the beginning gathered once again and burst a storm upon the heads of the Latter-day Saints.[134]

Intolerance concerning plural marriage had exploded, resulting in hundreds of families broken up as husbands and fathers were sent to prison. Leaders had to flee in many towns, and the Saints lost the right to vote. During this terrible time for the Mormon people, John R. Winder stepped in to do as much as he could, even little things, to help the brethren, and the Saints in general, weather the storm.

General Daniel H. Wells had been serving time in the Penitentiary for violating the federal statutes regarding polygamy. Just prior to his release in May of 1879, "the idea of giving him a grand popular reception on his emergence from prison was conceived." John R. Winder, Mayor Feramorz Little, William Jennings, and a few of their associates arranged for a grand pageant to meet and welcome General Wells and escort him back home as a hero. This they did, much to the chagrin of the federal marshals, who had hoped that the imprisonment of prominent polygamists like Wells would have discouraged the Mormons.[135]

When President George Q. Cannon was arrested by the federal marshals, he was quickly brought before U.S. Commissioner McKay who set his bail. His bonds were fixed at $2,500, which security was promptly furnished by Cannon's friends John R. Winder and Elias Morris.[136]

By October of 1884, the persecutions of the Church leaders became so intense that many who were still active polygamists, like Joseph F. Smith, dared not even attend the Church's general conference. A few days after the October conference, John R. Winder found out that federal marshals had been appointed to specifically hunt down, subpoena, and arrest President Smith and Daniel H. Wells again. However, Winder heroically beat the marshals to Smith's home and warned him of the imminent danger, helping him to escape. From the time of Winder's timely warning, Joseph F. Smith began his odyssey "on the underground," in attempting to avoid arrest.[137]

The judicial crusade against polygamists severely disrupted Church society as more and more men became fugitives in the Mormon "underground," frequently moving from place to place to escape federal marshals hunting "cohabs." Between 1884 and 1887, general conferences were held in Provo, Logan, and Coalville, rather than Salt Lake City, to help attendees avoid arrest. "I remember," said John R. Winder, when "conditions were such in this city that it was advisable to hold general conference in Provo."[138]

Whether assisting the LDS general authorities, his stake, or his ward; whether organizing tanneries, railroad companies, or other business enterprises; or whether busy as the patriarch of an ever-growing family or as a pioneer dairyman, John R. Winder excelled as a builder of the Great Basin kingdom. "There is no phase of the state's substantial development and improvement with which he was not in some way connected," it was said of him.[139]

One of his closest friends, from the militia, the city council, and the Church, was Joseph F. Smith, who praised the able administrator as follows:

> Speaking of his civil service and business connections, his associations in many of the enterprises which have been mentioned here, I have only to say this, that President John R. Winder never, to my knowledge, ever sought honors, or office, or business. He was so endowed, so talented and gifted that business, and office, and honors were ever in search of him; and if he could be multiplied by hundreds, I believe that the same honor, preferment, and distinctions would have followed a multitude of such men as he. True? Why, heaven itself could scarcely be truer to anything than President Winder was true to his convictions, to his friends, and to the discharge of the duty that was imposed upon him.[140]

*This drawing of Bishop John R. Winder appeared in **The Biographical Record**, a publication that featured brief biographical sketches on many Church leaders. Bishop Winder was known for his charitable heart and his keen financial insights.*

11
"The Raid" and "The Manifesto:" Early Years in the Presiding Bishopric, 1887-1891

"Faithful counselor"

The decades of the 1870's and '80's were years when John R. Winder was a tremendous "doer" in building up his city, territory, and church, and such energies did not escape the notice of the LDS general authorities. "I know the military part of the Church tried to make a soldier of him," said Bishop George H. Taylor, a fellow ward member. "He made a fine looking man on horseback; but the Church triumphant took hold of Brother Winder and made him a Bishop's Counselor."[1]

Call to the Presiding Bishopric

On April 8, 1887, 65-year-old John R. Winder was called to serve as the second counselor to Presiding Bishop William B. Preston. A native of Virginia, 57-year-old Bishop Preston had come west with the pioneers and had served as the presiding bishop since 1884. His first counselor, Robert T. Burton, had been in the Presiding Bishopric since 1874. Sixty-seven-year-old Bishop Burton had enjoyed a long association with Winder.[2] At Burton's funeral in 1907, Winder said that he and Robert "had been like twin brothers for sixty years, coming to the valley together, then serving in the Indian wars, the departments of national and city government, and finally in the Church Tithing Office as members of the Presiding Bishopric." Winder was not much younger than Burton, and these two kindred spirits enjoyed a close association during their years together.[3] "My connection with the Presiding Bishopric, which began in 1887, covered a period of fourteen years," reported Bishop Winder.[4]

The previous second counselor in the Presiding Bishopric had been John Q. Cannon, a son of President George Q. Cannon. Young Bishop Cannon had been called to the Presiding Bishopric in October of 1884 at the age of 27. However, he had not even served two full years when he was excommunicated on

September 5, 1886.[5] This vacancy created a void of a very important position that would need to be filled by someone with unquestionable loyalty and whom was also exceptionally responsible.

It is up to the Presiding Bishop to select his counselors, but they needed to be approved by both the First Presidency and the Quorum of the Twelve before they could be called. Brethren chosen for the Presiding Bishopric "have been recognized for their business and management skills as well as their religious commitment."[6] Consequently, Bishop Preston would have undoubtedly seen John R. Winder as particularly qualified for the position, and his counselor, Bishop Burton, would have enthusiastically agreed. When the name of Brother Winder was presented to the First Presidency, it would have also been pleasantly accepted by Winder's longtime friends, Presidents John Taylor, George Q. Cannon, and Joseph F. Smith. When the proposal came before the Quorum of the Twelve Apostles, they, too, would have known of Winder's good works and agreed. The Twelve at the time of that decision included Wilford Woodruff, Lorenzo Snow, Erastus Snow, Franklin D. Richards, Brigham Young, Jr., Moses Thatcher, Francis M. Lyman, John Henry Smith, George Teasdale, Heber J. Grant, and John W. Taylor.[7] And so it was that John R. Winder joined the ranks of the LDS General Authorities and began a sweet spiritual and working relationship with these Brethren that would last for the remainder of his days. He was set apart by President George Q. Cannon and Elder Franklin D. Richards of the Twelve.[8]

The Presiding Bishopric, one of the presiding councils of the Church, was responsible for many of the temporal affairs of the Church. Receiving, distributing, and accounting for member tithes, offerings, and contributions formed a large part of Bishops Preston, Burton, and Winder's duties. The administrating of programs to assist the poor and needy; designing, constructing, and maintaining places of worship; and the auditing and transferring of records of membership were also important responsibilities. The Presiding Bishopric would meet frequently with the First Presidency and the Twelve as a "Council on the Distribution of Tithes." This council would consider matters of financial importance and authorize budgets for Church organizations and departments.

An example of the Presiding Bishopric acting in regards to the acceptance of tithes is related by Abraham H. Cannon. In those days, much of the tithing consisted of crops and livestock. One day he went with partners James Sharp and LeGrand Young to see Bishops Preston, Burton, and Winder "about the settlement of our Sheep accts. The latter decided that as soon as I had turned over all contracts and accounts they would see that our notes were returned to us."[9]

The Presiding Bishopric in Winder's day also presided over the Aaronic Priesthood and the youth of the Church. These duties were clarified by Brigham Young in the years prior to his death, and he commissioned the Presiding Bishopric to organize full quorums of deacons, teachers, and priests throughout the Church. At that time, the Presiding Bishopric also directly supervised other bishops. They would travel frequently, visiting wards and stakes and conducting training sessions for the bishops.[10] Because Bishop William B. Preston was a decade younger than his counselors, he assumed the greater responsibility for travel to the outlying stakes. Winder and Burton would remain busy maintaining the duties at the Presiding Bishop's office in his absence.[11] In fact, during his first few weeks in the Bishopric, Winder constantly met at Bishop Burton's home to conduct Church business while Bishop Preston was in Virginia.[12] Nonetheless, Winder still did his share of the traveling, such as in 1887 when he went to Provo to report to the Saints there on the ramifications of the Edmunds-Tucker bill.[13]

Enduring "The Raid"

John R. Winder joined the ranks of the General Authorities at a time when the Church was facing some of its gravest trials. Various acts of Congress, such as the Edmunds-Tucker Act, had curtailed LDS political power and paved the way for an all-out assault on plural marriage. These dark days, which intensified during the late 1880's, became known by Latter-day Saints as "the Raid."

When the First Presidency went into hiding to evade arrest, the Presiding Bishopric assumed unparalleled autonomy in conducting Church finances. The jurisdiction of the Presiding Bishopric relative to the First Presidency became an issue of discussion among the General Authorities that took two decades to resolve. In the meantime, Bishops Preston, Burton, and Winder met often with the Twelve and the First Presidency, enjoying influence as few Presiding Bishoprics had before or have since. President John Taylor considered this "right and proper, as temporal and spiritual affairs were inseparable, and the representatives of both must act in unison and in concert."[14]

In the subsequent administration, however, "Prest Woodruff was not satisfied with this method & said there must be some change." Even the church president's secretary, L. John Nuttall complained, "The Bishopric seem to be drawing away all the business from the Presidents office." In 1889 first counselor George Q. Cannon said it was humiliating for the president to be required to apply to the Presiding Bishopric for even "a dollar to mend a desk." However, his comment was countered by second counselor Joseph F. Smith, who declared that "he did not believe in ignoring the Presiding Bishopric any more than he did in having the Presidency of the Church ignored." Besides, chimed in other apostles, it was no more humiliating to ask the Presiding Bishopric to arrange for money than it was to ask a First Presidency clerk to arrange for it. As a result of these differences in opinion, the status quo continued for another seven years, even though it irritated the Church president. However, despite an extremely powerful Presiding Bishopric, this quorum worked well with the other leading councils.[15]

When the Edmunds-Tucker Act was passed in 1887, it disincorporated the body known as The Church of Jesus Christ of Latter-day Saints. However, before it became law, President Taylor and the leading brethren scrambled to "sell" all of the Church property to various stake and temple associations, syndicates of Mormon capitalists, and other bodies which were organized as separate nonprofit organizations. At the April 1887 general conference, the LDS authorities nominated the Presiding Bishopric to hold trust for the unincorporated body of worshippers known as The Church of Jesus Christ of Latter-day Saints, the meetinghouses, burial grounds, and other properties belonging to that body. The legal papers were filled in the probate court, and on May 19, 1887, William B. Preston, Robert T. Burton, and John R. Winder became the legal trustees.[16]

This began a pattern of Bishop Winder stepping in to keep the property of the Church in Mormon hands. As a result of Edmunds-Tucker, the Utah Supreme Court decided to simply lease important Church property to the highest bidder. During subsequent years, vicious auctions ensued, with well-intentioned Mormon industrialists competing with bitter apostates and enemies of the Church for control of what was once undisputed Church property. On June 24, 1889, the court ordered the Church farm leased to John R. Winder for $401 per month. The Gardo House, which at the time served as the official residence of the president of the Church, was rented to Bishop Winder on March 10, 1890 for $450 per month. Two days later, the Tithing Office grounds and Historian's Office were rented to Bishop Winder for $500 per month, the court recognizing Winder as the highest bidder in each of these cases.[17]

Frank H. Dyer, United States marshal for Utah, was appointed by the Utah Supreme Court to be receiver of the remaining Church property for the federal government, and he made a diligent effort to identify all such property, which included Temple Square and the President's Office. In July of 1890, Dyer resigned as receiver and was replaced by Henry W. Lawrence. Being regarded as an "apostate Mormon," his appointment was obnoxious to the Latter-day Saints who still held an interest in the property to be turned over to the receiver.[18]

Bishop Burton had to work in secret with Bishops Preston and Winder, for he was being hunted by marshals for "unlawful cohabitation." The first counselor in the Presiding Bishopric could not conduct business in predictable places, or even be seen at Sunday meetings or funerals for friends or family. Nonetheless, the trio kept busy, although often in secret, conducting Church business.[19] Meeting clandestinely, Bishops Preston, Burton, and Winder worked to transfer the property which was not kept in their control and to maintain that which they held in trust. They worked at the General Tithing Office or president's office on occasion, but more often met at the homes of Charles Burton, Lewis Hill, or George Crimson.[20] During these years of "the Raid," it was not uncommon to see John R. Winder, who was now a monogamist, as the only Presiding Bishopric member on the stand at the Church's general conferences. At the October 1888 conference this was the case, and only five of the Twelve were in attendance, with no representation from the First Presidency.[21]

"The leading men of the Church knew him and loved him," it was said of Bishop Winder, "because he was capable in all the Church positions that he held, and was true to his place, to his brethren, and to his God. The authorities had confidence in him. His home was an asylum to all."[22] Poplar Farm, which was conveniently located several miles south of the city, was a frequent asylum for John Taylor, who used it as a temporary "Church headquarters" on numerous occasions. "During the dark days of persecution it was my pleasure to assist in shielding him when pursued by his enemies," Winder later wrote of President Taylor. "Many a night he spent at my home and transacted important Church business, the memories of which are always pleasant reflections."[23] Elder Francis M. Lyman of the Twelve later spoke of becoming especially close to John R. Winder "in the administration of President John Taylor. He was a man with a heart broad enough to embrace everybody," Lyman said of him at the time. "He was thus godlike." Elder Lyman also noted that during the Taylor administration, "at his home our councils of the greatest possible importance have been held."[24]

For two-and-a-half years, President John Taylor had presided over the Church in exile, and the strain of living on the "Underground" was taking a great toll on his health. While in hiding in Kaysville, President Taylor died on July 25, 1887, and

POPLAR FARM. THE COUNTRY RESIDENCE OF BISHOP JOHN R. WINDER.
Situated about three miles south of the Salt Lake Temple.

Salt Lake City, _____ 189___

This engraving done by D. C. Dunbar of Omaha first appeared in the 1888-89 edition of "Salt Lake City Illustrated." Showing the recently expanded Poplar Farmhouse, this print was used as Bishop Winder's letterhead in the 1890's.

Wilford Woodruff succeeded him as president, reorganizing the First Presidency in April 1889. The Latter-day Saints mourned the loss of their beloved prophet, as did John R. Winder particularly. "From the time President Taylor visited my home in Liverpool in the year 1850 until the day of his death, he was a friend to me," Winder later wrote, "and I always took pleasure in doing him honor."[25]

The Coming About of the Manifesto

Like other leaders of the time, President Woodruff had gone into seclusion to avoid imprisonment for polygamy. By the summer of 1890, federal legislation against polygamy had almost totally destroyed the effectiveness of the Church, and now even threatened their temples. On August 30, Bishop Winder secretly met with President Woodruff and shared with him some ominous news. "Bro. Winder stated that Ex-Receiver Dyer had told him confidentially that an attempt would soon be made on the part of the government to confiscate the Logan, Manti, and St. George temples on the grounds that they are not used for public worship." Winder suggested to the Prophet that a letter be sent to the Temple corporations instructing them to have their accounts and records in legal shape. President Woodruff was deeply concerned, and asked Winder to map out in writing the items to which the attention of the officers should be directed.[26]

The rumors that Winder had heard seemed to be true, for just two days later on September 1, an investigation began into Receiver Dyer's business in connection with Church property. It focused greatly on the issue of plural marriage, and, in the words of Abraham H. Cannon, "The questions put to John R. Winder show that the desire is to seize our Temples."[27] It would not be the first time that he had to testify before the courts, for in 1889 the enemies of the Church had Bishop Winder arrested for "conspiracy to misappropriate public funds." The ludicrous charges were dropped the following year, however.[28]

When he was asked to testify in the polygamy case, Winder strategically said as little as was actually required so as not to incriminate the leaders of the Church or any other polygamist. Keeping in mind that at one point Winder had been the husband of three wives, that he had served in the Presiding Bishopric for several years by this point, and that he had been a very close associate with many of the polygamists being hunted down, his stubborn responses are rather amusing. Consider the following exchange with federal lawyer C. S. Varian:

Q: How long have you been a member of the church?
A: About 40 years . . . .
Q: During all that time were you acquainted with the doctrine and its practice by the church and its people . . . . of plural or celestial marriage?
A: I have not been a very close observer of it; I know something about the doctrines.
Q: Do you know there was such a doctrine?
A: Yes sir.

Varian continued to press Winder for specific details concerning the practice of polygamy, including the places marriages were contracted, only to be served vague or monosyllabic answers. Finally, Varian asked:

Q: Don't you know from your general instruction and training, and the general knowledge of the times that [the performance of plural marriages] was so?

A: No, sir; I can't say that that was so; my understanding is that there are such things done, but I know nothing about it myself.

Next, Winder was questioned by Parley Williams, the attorney representing Frank Dyer, the Federal Receiver, where he again reiterated his lack of knowledge of the facts pertaining to plural marriage. This Winder did again for the Church counsel LeGrand Young, and then again faced Varian. By this point, Varian was obviously exasperated by what he believed was Winder's "stonewalling," and he asked:

Q: Do you wish to be understood having been a member of the church for forty years, and having also been one of the Seventies, and still holding some office, that you have no knowledge and are not familiar with the uses to which its buildings are to be put?

A: I don't understand.

Q: Do you wish to go upon record as saying, that you don't know as a fact, that the temples and endowment house were in part dedicated to the use of plural marriage—solemnizing plural marriage?

A: I can't say that I know it as a fact.

Q: Is there any doctrine or tenet of your faith that you know as a fact?

A: Well, I may know some things about it.

Q: Is there anything that you know as a fact, as being taught by the church?

A: Oh, yes, there is a good many things that I know have been taught by the church.

Q: Do you know whether or not plural marriage, or polygamy as it is called, was taught by the church.

A: Oh a great many years ago I have heard it taught, but it is a great many years since I heard anybody teach it.

Q: Do you know of its being taught in 1887?

A: I don't remember ever hearing it taught publicly by anybody.

The examinations soon became ridiculous:

Q: You are a member of the Mormon church—you have been married, I suppose.

A: Yes sir.

Q: To your wife?

A: Yes sir.[29]

With such pressure mounting to confiscate even the holy temples, President Woodruff spent much of September pleading with the Lord for a solution. For weeks President Woodruff "wrestled mightily with the Lord," and then, on September 24, 1890, after seeing in vision the consequences of inaction, he issued the now-famous Manifesto of 1890, which announced the end of the official practice of plural marriage.

But before such an earth-shaking document as the Manifesto could be pronounced to the world, much thought and prayer would be engaged in by the leaders of the Church. After "praying to the Lord and being inspired by his spirit," President Woodruff called in some of his most trusted advisors the morning of September 24 to consult with on how best to translate this pivotal vision into an official declaration. "One morning during the dark days of persecution," related John R. Winder, "I met Pres. Woodruff and asked him how he was feeling. 'Pretty well,' he said, 'only I did not get much rest during the past night. I was wrestling with the Lord all night.'" Winder continues his narrative, "Handing me some sheets of paper, he said, 'And this is the result of my wrestling.'"[30]

John R. Winder, Charles W. Penrose, and George Reynolds were then asked to review and edit the 510-word manuscript of the vision and "arrange it for publication."[31] "We transcribed the notes and changed the language slightly to adapt it for publication," said Reynolds.[32] "The Lord showed me by vision and revelation exactly what would take place if we did not stop this practice," Woodruff later said, "the confiscation and loss of all the Temples, and the stopping of the ordinances therein, both for the living and the dead, and the imprisonment of the First Presidency and Twelve and the heads of families in the Church."

After Winder, Penrose, and Reynolds reviewed and edited the declaration, the final draft was carefully reviewed and approved by the First Presidency and the Twelve, then publically announced by President Woodruff. The 356-word. final document included the powerful language: "I hereby declare my intention to submit to those laws, and to use my influence with the members of the Church over which I preside to have them do likewise." The published Manifesto burst like a bombshell on both the Church and the country as a whole. Disbelief and consternation were mingled with feelings of relief and elation, but in the end, the inspired and well-crafted Manifesto would be the instrument to lead to Utah statehood in 1896 and open the door for the twentieth-century progress and growth of the Church.[33]

Assisting Utah's Economy and the Finances of the Church

During the late 1880's and 1890's, the Church undertook a number of financial enterprises, hoping to recover from the debts incurred under the Edmunds-Tucker Act and to finance increased welfare and educational expenses.[34] Bishop Winder, respected as one of the leading financial minds of the Church, was often at the heart of these. In 1889, he collaborated with Abraham H. Cannon, P. L. Williams, James T. Little, and Lewis Hills to began streetcar service in Salt Lake.

Originally, these brethren "proposed to run lines on the State Road, to Brighton, the Warm and Hot Springs, the R. R. depots and to various parts of the city."[35] For decades after, the electric streetcar was the popular mode of transportation throughout the city. "He was for a long time identified in the management of our electric light and street railway systems," it was noted of Winder, "and was respected by the many employees of these institutions."[36]

Because of his many business contacts in the city, and having developed a reputation as a creative financier, Winder was always considered one to go to with new ideas. For example, when Frank J. Cannon came up with a new plan for public lighting, his father, President George Q. Cannon, sent him John R. Winder's way.[37] No stranger to public utilities, Winder served as the vice president of the Pioneer Electric Company, and later was president and a director of the Union Light and Power Company (1897), as well as a director of the Utah Power and Light Company.

Winder also became a director in the Deseret National Bank in 1891, a

This sketch was featured in the April 1906 publication of "Men of the Day in Caricature," a turn-of-the-century "Who's Who" printed in Denver. Winder was "for a long time identified in the management of our electric light and street railway systems." It was said that he was "respected by the many employees of these institutions."

director in the Deseret Savings Bank beginning in 1892, and later a director in Zion's Savings Bank and Trust Company in 1901. He would serve in each of these banking directorships until his death. His banking investments also included interests in the Bank of Garland, the Bank of Randolph, First National Bank of Murray, and Idaho State and Savings Bank.[38]

Winder also became a director in the Utah Sugar Company in 1895, and of the Ogden Sugar Company. He was a stock holder of the Amalgamated Sugar Company and a director in the Fremont County Sugar Company, the Idaho Sugar Company, the Knight Sugar Company, the Sanpete and Sevier Sugar Company, the Utah-Idaho Sugar Company (1907), the Western Idaho Sugar Company, and the Sugar City Townsite Company.[39]

Wilford Woodruff made mention in his journal of meeting with John R. Winder in 1892 "on some Mining Business."[40] Winder was involved in several mining interests, including Emigration Canyon Rock Company, Grass Creek Coal Company, Holladay Coal Company, Iron Manufacturing Company of Salt Lake, Silver Brothers Iron Works Company, Trapper Mining Company, and the Utah Iron Manufacturing Company.[41] By 1900, Bishop Winder was also a director of the Saltair Beach Company, a popular turn-of-the-century attraction at the Great Salt Lake.[42]

One important business that Winder was involved with was the Deseret Investment Company, founded on July 22, 1890. John R. Winder was a founding member, held more shares than anyone else, and was president of the organization. It was incorporated in his office with the object "to purchase and hold real estate, erect buildings and hold or lease them, to engage in mining, stock-raising or manufacturing." The capital for the firm was $200,000, and the first act of business was for J. R. Winder and Abraham H. Cannon "to negotiate for the purchase of a piece of real estate which lies between the [*Deseret*] *News* office and the Lion House."[43] Before the end of the year, the company had built warehouses and offices in the city, and had purchased the 300-acre Granite Rock Quarry.[44]

John R. Winder's business successes allowed him to support his large family. When his son Will needed money to enlarge his home in 1890, his father gave him an advance allowing the home to be doubled. When Will was called to serve in the Southern States Mission in late 1891, John R. promised to finance the mission in addition to supporting Will's wife Rose and the children. While this allowed William C. Winder to serve his mission, Rose dreaded having to implore her rather tight-fisted father-in-law for enough funding to get by from week to week.[45]

One associate, William W. Riter, had this to say regarding Winder's character as a businessman:

> I was thinking . . . whether I ever heard of any circumstance that would reflect on the character of John R. Winder as an honest, upright businessman and citizen. I know that in this fast and commercial age men of responsibility are subject to all kinds of temptations, and it is a rare character, indeed, that passes through this life without having yielded, here and there, to some seductive influence along the line of the acquirement of dollars and cents. But, I can truthfully say that under no conditions and under no circumstances whatever have I ever heard the faintest whisper of scandal in regard to Brother Winder."[46]

However, despite some aid that was contributed to the financially distressed Church as a result of these enterprises, overall the situation was grim. Winder's colleague in the Presiding Bishopric, Robert T. Burton, penned in his journal: "We are now having a very serious time financially."[47] Tithing receipts had been down drastically during the late 1880's and early 1890's because Church members hesitated paying tithing if they feared that the government was going to get it.

During one heated meeting of the General Authorities in the Gardo House in 1890, George Q. Cannon declared, "Our financial affairs merit our earnest attention. The calls upon the church are numerous and pressing, and we are constantly going deeper into debt." President Woodruff exclaimed that "There are $5 now required to carry on the work where $1 was sufficient." At the same meeting, John R. Winder spoke of the political pressure that plagued them, as well: "It will require a great and united effort on the part of our people to elect our Delegate to Congress." While the Mormons made up a majority of the voters, he explained, "the 'Liberals' are determined by fair means or foul to overcome this . . . Smart, intelligent men should be chosen to look after the political affairs," he exclaimed. President Cannon, obviously upset with some of the unfair practices of the anti-Mormons, declared: "I feel like saying 'Damn the law!' We can expect neither justice nor mercy in the administration of the law with the present corrupt administrators."[48]

Several months earlier, the leading brethren had even attempted to reduce the crushing debt by secretly selling much of the Church's non-essential real estate to eastern speculators. Abraham H. Cannon recorded the details of that secret meeting, of which Bishop Winder was an active participant:

> I went by invitation to the Gardo House. There, where we hold our usual prayer circle, the following brethren met: Presidents Woodruff, Cannon, and Smith. Bros. John R. Winder, BY Hampton, F Armstrong, JW Fox Jr, NV Jones, Geo Reynolds, Arthur Winter and myself. Before the business of the meeting commenced we were all placed under obligation to keep the matter entirely secret. . . . After thought and prayer on the subject he [Pres Woodruff] felt impressed that we should carefully begin to sell our surplus property at the exorbitant figures now being paid by outsiders for real estate . . . . All the brethren expressed their approval in general of the plan. . . . The necessity of perfect secrecy and the utmost care in this movement was apparent to all, for should it once be known among the Saints that it would not meet with disapproval to sell their property to speculators a great panic would immediately ensue. Bros. Winder, Armstrong, Hampton, Fox and Jones and I were appointed a committee to take this matter in hand and work it up. We accordingly met at 2:30 pm and after considerable discussion adopted the following recommendations: That two or more real estate agencies be organized . . . Also a loan agency be organized under the direction of Armstrong, Winder and Co. . . It was found that the brethren present could immediately list over one and one half million dollars worth of property. Our recommends were approved.[49]

However, even this grand scheme led to naught, and by October, 1890, the plan was abandoned. "Since the brethren were called together some months ago and it was decided to sell our real estate at high figures," reported Abraham Cannon, "the boom has declined and no business to speak of has been done. The result is we find ourselves in debt."[50]

A Leader in Politics, Agriculture, and Society

Despite the trials financially, some progress was made in the 1890's with respect to the political situation of the Church. As early as September 1888, President Woodruff had appointed a committee of Elders Franklin D. Richards and Moses Thatcher of the Twelve, along with John R. Winder to take into consideration "some of our political affairs."[51] Winder was a wise choice for such a committee, with his vast experience in public affairs and having occupied the position of territorial chairman of the People's Party at the time. The inevitable decision, which was reached the year following the Manifesto, was to end Utah's "unique" political arrangements and conform politically with the rest of the nation. They dissolved the local People's Party, of which Winder had led for years, and encouraged members to affiliate with the national Republican and Democratic parties.

As a participant in the Gardo House meeting which led to the dissolution of the People's Party, Winder doubtlessly shared the view expressed by George Q. Cannon at the meeting: "One thing certain," Cannon declared, "the old party fight as between Mormons and Non-Mormons must not be allowed to continue," if Utah was ever to achieve statehood or stability.[52]

Many assumed that the traditional ties of many Church leaders to the general Democratic party philosophy, along with the Republican party's hostility to polygamy, would make Utah a strong Democratic state. However, the Church made a conscious effort to help both national parties achieve legitimacy in Utah. Stories abound of Church leaders dividing congregations down the middle aisle into Republicans and Democrats, or of block teachers walking from door to door designating one house Democratic and the next Republican. Even the Church leaders aligned themselves with different parties; Joseph F. Smith and Anthon H. Lund declared their support for the Republicans, for example, while Heber J. Grant and Charles W. Penrose remained Democrats.[53] As for Winder, he was described as an "ardent Democrat."[54]

In February 1892, Apostle Abraham H. Cannon recorded, "I was surprised to see the warmth of feeling in John R. Winder when his Democratic principles were assailed, and he did not hesitate to oppose the expressions of Joseph F. Smith in favor of Republicanism."[55] Winder attended a mass meeting of the Democrats in 1891, and was a delegate to their 1892 convention.[56] In his later years, Winder would be less vocal in political affairs. He was regarded as "a good Democrat and fine man" by James Henry Moyle, who also noted that Winder was a "Democrat but a silent one."[57] As a result of his enthusiasm towards their politics, the party of Jefferson and Jackson officially honored John R. Winder posthumously by listing him among the "one hundred prominent Democrats" of Utah's history in 1942.[58]

Despite the unimaginable stress that Winder and the other General Authorities must have been experiencing during these years of persecution and financial distress, time was found for the enjoyable hobbies of life. In Bishop Winder's case this meant farming and working with his beloved Deseret Agricultural and Manufacturing Society. After having served as a faithful board member since the organization's inception in 1856, John R. Winder was elected president of the Society in 1888. He replaced Wilford Woodruff, who had been president for many years, and had Francis Armstrong as his vice president. His old friend Heber M. Wells served as secretary, and Elias A. Smith was the treasurer.

Although that term ended in 1890, Winder was reelected to the post in 1893 and served until 1901, for a total of eleven years. The fairs continued to grow each year under his leadership, particularly after statehood, and Winder consequently became known as the "Father of the Utah State Fair."[59] The *Deseret Evening News* published a column on this "Veteran Exhibitor" following the territorial fair of 1891:

> We were shown, yesterday, by Bishop John R. Winder, several beautiful gold and silver medals and diplomas he had just received from the D. A. & M. Society. They were awarded at the late Fair. He was also given the Studebaker special premium, "a steel self-binder valued at $175.00, for the best Utah bred team for all farm purposes." He claims his team has no superior in Utah. They are of the proper size, weight 1300 pounds each, have splendid action, kind disposition, and marked powers of endurance. They will draw 4000 pounds at a fast gait, plough, or haul a mowing machine without apparent fatigue, and, if desired, will take you 10 miles an hour in your carriage. These magnificent animals are of a bright bay color, six and seven years old, are full sisters and inherit many of the good qualities of their great grand dam, which was purchased by Col. Winder from California emigrants in 1859. In 1860 she had a colt—the grand dam of this team. This was bred to "Wagener," which is the dam of this Utah bred team for all farm purposes. She is still raising colts and was awarded $25.00 at the last Fair. The youngest mare in the team took the first prize as best carriage mare. The team, Lady Wagener first and second, have taken first prize four years in succession against all competitors. Bishop Winder has been breeding from this stock thirty-two years, occasionally infusing new strains of blood.

In answer to interrogations propounded by a *News* reporter, Bishop Winder imparted the following information with regard to his operations as a stock raiser:

> "Yes, I exhibited other stock at the Fair—Jerseys and Holsteins. In the Jersey class I got a gold medal and $25 for the best Jersey herd bull and four cows; first prize for two year old heifer, first prize for yearling heifer; first prize for heifer calf, and my prize Jersey cow "Bessie" took the gold medal and $25 for

the best cow of any age or breed for dairy purposes, quality considered. Her milk was tested on the fair grounds. Three Holsteins competed for this premium. I also got two first prizes in the Holstein class, for best bull one year old, and best heifer two years old."

Answering other questions, Bishop Winder said he had been amongst the largest exhibitors of manufactured articles, agricultural products and live stock at every fair since the organization of the society. In 1856 he was elected a director, and later was elected president. He does not now give these matters so much personal attention, but leaves it to his boys, who have been trained to it from infancy. We have no hesitation in saying that as a promoter of the arts, manufactures, agriculture and stock raising, Bishop Winder stands in the front rank in the interior west, and his long and active past connection with the fairs that have been held in this Territory has enabled him to be of great service to the public in the development of pursuits that have enhanced the material interests of the commonwealth.[60]

During this time, Winder was a director and supporter of the Salt Lake Dramatic Association, as well.[61] Another hobby was his membership in the Salt Lake Literary and Scientific Association, which held regular meetings in the Gardo House.[62] In 1897, Winder became one of the charter members of the Utah State Historical Society, as well.[63] It was important that John R. had the outlets of stock-raising and these other associations, for it provided him with refreshing diversions from the cares of his many other responsibilities. One contemporary recorded of him: "With all of this weight of business and ecclesiastical cares he yet was genial, pleasant, and hospitable, in fact a living embodiment of all the virtues."[64]

As a counselor to Presiding Bishop William B. Preston, John R. Winder proved time and again that he was a "workhorse," not a "show horse." It was said of the Bishop's Counselor that he "was first and foremost a supporter of other men rather than a leader himself. He possessed those qualities essential for such a role. He was loyal, prudent, punctual, frugal, well-informed and well-read and dependable. He was also by nature self-effacing but at the same time was not a sycophant or a yes-man to the leaders he served." One scholar, John R. Sillito, observed that Winder "spoke his mind freely and forcefully in church counsels, but once a decision on a particular matter had been reached he supported it wholeheartedly, and without reservation."[65] It was by proving himself to be such a faithful Church administrator that caused him to be chosen to execute perhaps the most important work of his career—overseeing the completion of the Salt Lake Temple.

12
A Herculean Task: Completing the Temple, 1892-1900

"It can be done and it must be done."

By removing the great burden of sustaining plural marriage with the Manifesto of 1890, the Church was free to move forth unencumbered on their greatest project of the latter half of the Nineteenth Century—completing the Salt Lake Temple. Since April 6, 1853, encompassing the entire time that John R. Winder had been in Utah, the Saints had labored on a great temple in the heart of Salt Lake City. The previous decades had been filled with challenge after challenge, interruption after interruption: the Utah War with Johnston's army, the Raid on the Church following the Edmunds-Tucker Act, a poor foundation that had to be completely removed and replaced with granite hauled from 40 miles away in Little Cottonwood Canyon, and the financial debt and burdens which often slowed or halted the work. Nonetheless, exactly 39 years from the beginning of the work on that sacred edifice, the capstone was placed and the exterior of the magnificent House of the Lord was declared complete. This was a joyous occasion that the Winder family and all the Saints rejoiced in, but it also marked the beginning of some of the greatest responsibilities that John R. Winder would ever know.

Appointed General Superintendent of Completing the Temple

Over forty thousand people gathered within Temple Square on April 6, 1892 for the capstone ceremony, including the Winders. Thousands of others stood in nearby streets, for the square was literally filled with people. Bands played and choirs sang. President Wilford Woodruff at the appropriate time declared from the stand:

> Attention all ye house of Israel, and all ye nations of the earth! We will now lay the top-stone of the Temple of our God, the foundation of which was laid and dedicated by the Prophet, Seer, and Revelator, Brigham Young.

At that point the Prophet closed an electric circuit near the pulpit, and the granite hemisphere, forming the highest block of the great Temple, slowly descended into position. The crowd cheered and was led in the Hosanna shout by Lorenzo Snow, after which they erupted in singing "The Spirit of God like a fire is burning!" However, despite the completion of the exterior, the Temple was far from complete on the inside, prompting Elder Francis M. Lyman of the Twelve to present to the large crowd the following resolution:

> Believing that the instruction of President Woodruff, respecting the early completion of the Salt Lake Temple, is the word of the Lord unto us, I propose that this assemblage pledge themselves, collectively and individually, to furnish, as fast as it may be needed, all the money that may be required to complete the Temple at the earliest time possible, so that the dedication may take place on April 6th, 1893.

On April 6, 1892, tens of thousands gathered to witness the laying of the capstone on the Salt Lake Temple. Shortly thereafter, the herculean task of completing the interior within a year was placed on the shoulders of John R. Winder. (C. R. Savage photograph, Church Archives)

The resolution was adopted by a deafening shout from the crowd and the raising of their hands. James E. Talmage, who was a prominent educator in the city at the time, and who was later called to serve in the Council of the Twelve Apostles, recorded the following regarding the challenge that the Saints had taken upon themselves:

The adoption of a plan or the formal passing of a resolution by vote is an easy matter, compared with which the working out of that plan, the achieving of what was provided for by the vote, may be a gigantic task. Such was the contrast between the action of the assembled multitude on the 6th of April, 1892, and the work accomplished in the year that followed.

When the capstone of the Temple was laid, the scene inside the walls was that of chaos and confusion. To finish the interior within a year appeared a practical impossibility. The task the people had taken upon themselves was almost superhuman. Nevertheless, they considered the instruction to complete the building within the specified time to be verily the word of the Lord unto them, and they remembered the utterance of the ancient prophet, "I know that the Lord giveth no commandments unto the children of men, save he shall prepare a way for them that they may accomplish the thing which he commanded them." The Saints regarded their act of voting to be equivalent to the affixing of their individual signatures on a note of promise. As to how well they met their obligation and kept their promise, let the achievements of the year speak. . . .

In the work of finishing the Temple, it was all-important that there be a competent, responsible man in charge, who should be invested with executive authority in every department of the labor. While the First Presidency and the Council of the Twelve retained in their hands the directing power, they needed an agent who could be trusted to act with promptness, decision, and authority on every question that should arise. The choice of the presiding authorities for a man to fill this responsible position fell upon John R. Winder, who was at that time Second Counselor in the Presiding Bishopric, and who afterward became First Counselor in the First Presidency of the Church. At the time of his appointment to the responsible position of General Superintendent of Temple Work, April 16, 1892, President Winder was in his seventy-second year, yet he possessed the energy and activity of youth, combined with the wisdom and discretion that age alone can give. Under his efficient supervision, work on the interior of the Temple progressed at a rate that surprised even the workers. Laborers of all classes, mechanics, masons, plasterers, carpenters, glaziers, plumbers, painters, decorators, artisans and artificers of every kind, were put to work. The people verily believed that a power above that of man was operating to assist them in their great undertaking. Material, much of which was of special manufacture, came in from the east and the west, with few of the usual delays of transit. Heating and lighting systems were installed; and this installation necessitated the erection of a boiler house, with all accessories of equipment.[1]

Abraham H. Cannon recorded in his journal about the day that Bishop Winder was appointed superintendent of completing the Temple. "Friday, April 15, 1892 - At one o'clock I was at the temple with Pres. Woodruff, Father [George Q. Cannon], Lorenzo Snow, John H. Smith, H. J. Grant and two of the

Presiding Bishopric, where we spoke to the workmen about our desires that the building should be finished by the 6th of April next. We requested all to use their best endeavors to crowd the work ahead, and to refrain from evil conversation, discussion of politics, etc., as well as to cease the use of intoxicants, while at work on this sacred edifice. J. R. Winder was then appointed to assist in the superintendency of the work yet to be done."[2]

Bishop Winder was no stranger to the work that needed to take place in the Temple. As early as 1885, during the dark days of the "Raid," and even before Winder was a general authority, he had been involved with planning the interior of the Salt Lake Temple. In July of that year, George Q. Cannon wrote in his journal of being bundled and disguised from federal marshals as he took a carriage to the home of John R. Winder for a meeting about "the internal arrangement of the temple at Salt Lake City."[3]

Overcoming All Obstacles

The most serious problem in completing the Temple was raising money to pay for the construction. During a meeting of the April General Conference of 1892, President Woodruff spoke of the heavy expenses under which the church was laboring, and that they hoped to get relief soon. Bishop Winder then came to the pulpit with some grim figures from the Tithing Office. The tithing received in 1891 was $134,500 less than in 1890. There were 6,750 persons who should have paid tithing who did not, he said, and the amount paid per capita dropped from $30.13 in 1890 to only $26 in 1891. Bishop Winder also lamented that the temple offerings for 1891 amounted to only $18,262, which he said was only about enough to pay for one month's work on the structure.[4]

At the October 1892 conference, which woodcarvers worked right on through, Bishop Winder gave a report of the work being done on the Temple and outlined what still needed to transpire in the remaining months.[5] Pleas from the pulpit were made for more contributions to the Temple fund, and the Saints soon discovered that J. R. Winder was not afraid to put his money where his mouth was. It became known that "he contributed liberally to the fund to defray the heavy expenses entailed."[6] Bishop Winder, Moses Thatcher, George Romney, Heber J. Grant, and John R. Murdock each generously donated $1,500, each sponsoring the completion of one of five large windows.[7] Winder paid for the beautiful stained glass window depicting the visit of the Father and the Son to the boy Joseph Smith. A photograph of this window was taken, and John R. gave it to his friend Joseph F. Smith, "with compliments of John R. Winder."[8] Within ten days of the General Conference, John R. Winder also met with several of the leading brethren "in apportioning to the various stakes the amount each should raise for the Salt Lake Temple."[9]

Elder Seymour B. Young, of the first seven presidents of seventies, provides this report of Bishop Winder's efforts on the Temple:

John Rex Winder—was appointed by the Presidency of the Church and by the united wish of the entire Latter-day Saints, to be the superintendent of this great work. And it was a work of great magnitude, let me tell you; for it was said by the architects and by men of experience in building great edifices that the work required to finish this structure could not possibly be done in the time set; but John R. Winder said, It can be accomplished, and it shall be accomplished. Many times I visited the temple during the completion of this great work, and I have always found President Winder echoing that statement again and again.[10]

John R. Winder declared to posses faith that the structure would be completed on time from the beginning. "I remember . . . when I was called to assist my brethren in completing this house," he recalled, "I never had a doubt in my mind but it would be accomplished. It never entered my mind that it could not be accomplished."[11]

One of the first steps towards completing the interior was a day of solemn fasting and prayer, which was declared for Sunday, the first of May. "To this call the people responded faithfully," it was said. "Mingled with their thanksgiving for the manifold blessings of the past, were fervent supplications for success in the work of completing the Lord's House within the time prescribed."[12]

Bishop Winder was given the responsibility and the credit for seeing that the 250-man crew met this deadline.[13] This was no small task, according to one contemporary, but one that Winder was determined to see through:

> Sometimes when the work would hitch through some mistake of the workmen, or through the lack of seasoned lumber, or some other material, and someone would say that that would detain the work so that it would be impossible to finish it in time, President Winder would always say, This must not occur again; there must be no lack of material or labor.[14]

Such an undertaking was not without its tense moments. Winder recalled that on one occasion he overheard some of the brethren at work on the Temple say that it could not be completed on schedule. Upon hearing such nay-saying, Bishop Winder promptly gathered all 250 workmen to one room. "I was standing in there talking to them and telling them that if there was a man among them that felt this work could not be accomplished, let him please get his pay and go to work somewhere else. I did not know that President Woodruff was in the house, but it appears that he stood right behind a curtain that was up there, and heard what I said, and throwing aside the curtain he said, 'That's right; the work has got to be done, and if there is anybody here that thinks it can't be done, let him leave.'"[15] The workers pressed on from there, never again publically doubting. Even on holidays, such as Thanksgiving Day 1892, "nearly all the men were at work as usual."[16] Their superintendent expected the sacrifice and "discharged that duty with characteristic energy and zeal."[17]

Several times in his famous journal, Wilford Woodruff makes mention of meeting with J. R. Winder "about Temple Affairs." On September 8, 1892, for instance, Bishop Winder and the architect, Don Carlos Young, took the First Presidency on a tour of the unfinished Temple "from top to Bottom," where the Prophet "found the work in a good State of Progression." A month later, Bishop Winder, the architect, and Loras Pratt met with President Woodruff "on the Deckaration of the Temple."[18]

As the April deadline loomed nearer, however, the deadline seemed all the more impossible. James E. Talmage noted that "Even as late as one month prior to the date set for the dedication, there was so much yet to be done, as to make many feel that for once at least, the people had been mistaken in their belief that the Lord had spoken, and the completion of the work by the time set, was a physical impossibility."[19]

On the 18th of March, 1893, the First Presidency issued a lengthy epistle to the Saints promising that as the people cleansed their hearts, buried their enmity, ceased their bickering, adjusted their differences, and continued at top speed, then the great Temple would indeed be completed on time and be "momentous in the highest degree." The communication also declared another day of fasting and prayer for March 25. It was imperative that all the Church shared Bishop Winder's faith and enthusiasm that the great work could be completed on time.[20]

The final stretch of this great work was "pushed through with his usual energy and dispatch."[21] It was said throughout the Church that Bishop Winder "fully justified the confidence reposed in him."[22] Elder Anthon H. Lund of the Twelve recalled, "It seemed a herculean task." Yet he noted of Brother Winder, "he did it well, but it took every day of the year, and he had to work hard both in raising means and in having the things done to get all the work finished in time. He was proud of that labor."[23]

John R. Winder had his crews literally working up to the last minute, the finishing touches of the building being made the very day before the dedication. "At noon on April 5th 1893 the work was completed" Winder noted, "and I reported to Wilford Woodruff that the Temple was ready for dedication."[24] In the evening of that day, the Temple was open to general inspection. Both members of the Church and non-members were invited to tour the new crown jewel of the Church. The following day the Temple would be dedicated, exactly forty years to the day from when Brigham Young laid the cornerstone.

Dedication and Service in the Temple Presidency

On the morning of the 6th of April, Wilford Woodruff, President of the Church, led the way through the south-west doors into the completed Temple for the dedicatory service. The general authorities of the Church, including Bishop Winder, followed him in, as well as other members specifically chosen to attend the first dedication service. More than 2,250 people crowded the large Assembly Room on the fourth floor for the service, which included the dedicatory prayer given by President Woodruff. "All who attended the dedicatory services on the morning of the 6th of April, 1893, remember the impressiveness of the day," it was said. "The sky was overcast and lowering . . . but the peace and serenity of the assembly was rendered the more impressive by contrast with the turmoil and storm without."[25]

The glorious day of dedication would be especially memorable for John R. Winder, for members of the First Presidency expressed deep gratitude to him during the ceremonies. During the dedication, Joseph F. Smith highly commended "the faithful, persistent and efficient labors of Bishop Winder, in his superintendency of the sacred edifice."[26] One authority in the audience remembered:

> I heard President Joseph F. Smith say with pleasure at the dedication of this house, that to no other person could there be more praise and credit attached than to John R. Winder, for his faith and indomitable will in pressing forward this work, and always maintaining that it should be accomplished in the time set.[27]

When publicly complimented for his "faithful and efficient labors," Winder modestly put aside all praise, giving all the credit to the First Presidency. On that occasion President Smith also pronounced a fervent blessing upon him for time and all eternity.[28] These two friends had grown still closer during the great year of completing the Temple. "I have been closely associated with him in his capacity as a counselor to the bishop, likewise in his appointment to take charge of the completion of the temple," President Smith recalled.[29] At that glorious dedication, "John R. Winder was truly in his element. He had a great love for Temple work, and spent nearly every day of his life involved in the business of Salvation of the Dead."[30]

After the dedication of the Temple, in May 1893, he was appointed First Assistant to President Lorenzo Snow, in charge of the edifice.[31] When President Woodruff informed Bishop Winder of his new calling he said, "I do not know how many brethren I may call to fill a mission on this earth [before I die], but I have a mission for you to fill and that is to be President Assistant to Brother Lorenzo Snow in the Salt Lake Temple."[32] Bishop Winder humbly replied that he did not feel qualified for such a place. "Never mind," said the president, "I will appoint you and the Lord will qualify you."[33] The Prophet explained to John R. that he "had labored hard in the completion of the temple and he wished him to fill that position."[34] He was set apart to this task by President George Q. Cannon, and Adolph Madsen was set apart as Second Assistant.[35] After seven years as First Assistant, Winder would be called to be President of the Salt Lake Temple.[36]

While serving in the presidency of the Temple, which he did for the remainder of his days, John R. Winder had many opportunities to conduct temple work, both for the living, and vicariously for the dead. In this capacity he was able to officiate for many temple sealings, including many of his own children.[37] He "virtually had full charge of the sacred edifice until the day of his death."[38]

The happy years that followed proved to fulfill a promise made to Winder in his patriarchal blessing given nearly forty years prior. In that blessing he was told that he would be blessed "to officiate by proxy for the redemption of thy Father's household that they may with thee enjoy the blessings and receive the opportunity of the everlasting gospel through thy faithfulness for their welfare." He was also promised that "their redemption will produce in a time to come a star in thy crown."[39] One joy would have been to see his children come to the temple to assist in the work of redeeming the dead. His son Ed Winder recorded in his journal on September 5, 1894: "Get up and prepare to go to the Temple. Go through for Grandfather Richard Winder and take endowments and am sealed for him to his wife, with Maria Winder."[40]

How the boy from Biddenden must have thrilled to see one of his sons act as proxy for his father in the Temple! Further family history work was attempted by his son Ed while on his mission in England. In February of 1895, Ed spent some time in Kent "in search of some of Father's relatives." He was joined by John R. Winder, Jr. in July.[41]

By the time of his death in 1910, John R. Winder had become an icon in the Temple that he loved so dearly. "From the day it opened until the day

This life-size bronze bust of President Winder, cast by Mahonri Young, sat for many years in the Celestial Room of the Salt Lake Temple. In 1968 it was generously donated to the Winder family by President David O. McKay.

he left it and was taken sick he never missed but one day, and that was on account of sickness," according to Anthon Lund. "So punctual was he that when they would look at the clock and it would lack about a minute or two of the appointed time, President Winder would take his place on the stand and open the meeting. He was never late, and he was always there; and how the people who attend the labors in the temple loved him and looked upon him as a father!" It indeed was no secret in the Church that "Brother Winder loved the work that he was engaged in. He loved the temple work."[42]

His significant contribution to the completion of that sacred edifice and his work therein was marked by a beautiful bronze bust of him, cast by Mahonri Young, that sat for many years in the Celestial Room of the Salt Lake Temple. "There isn't a soul that ever worked in that building but what loved Brother Winder from the bottom of his heart," declared George Romney at Winder's funeral. "I can truthfully say this for each one of them."[43] Bertha A. Kleinman related her thoughts about Bishop Winder: "President Winder I had learned to love and revere, as one of my employers, for he was one of the Presiding Bishopric, and I was the first girl to ever work in that office. He was counselor to the President of the Temple and left me every day to perform his marriages and sealings. He it was who married me, and kissed me. Well do I remember his radiant countenance, his sparkling eyes, his quick step."[44]

The Widower Takes a New Bride—Maria Burnham

During the hectic months of completing the Temple, John R. suffered the tragic loss of his beloved first wife. Ellen Walters Winder passed away quite unexpectedly of heart trouble on November 7, 1892 at the age of seventy. She was known as an exemplary wife and mother, mild and supportive, considerate and deeply compassionate. "Her testimony of the Gospel of Jesus Christ was unfailing," it was said, "and her love for her husband and family was immense." This is not surprising to learn when one considers all that she and her husband went through together in the forty-seven years that transpired since their wedding at St. Clements Church, London. Ellen had served valiantly for many years in the Salt Lake 12th Ward Relief Society, and had been serving as their secretary at the time of her death.[45] Bathsheba Smith, a friend, later recalled, "I was acquainted with Sister Winder, and enjoyed her society. She was a noble, blessed woman."[46] Rex Williams noted, "Truly her life was a sermon, so effectually preached by example as well as precept, that all her posterity have become the beneficiaries of the wonderful Gospel."[47]

The death of Ellen Winder left the one-time husband of three women a lonely widower. Despite his seventy-one years, John R. Winder was still very vital and energetic and clearly preferred marriage to the single life.[48] Fortunately for him, "a blessing came to him from the Lord after he began his faithful labors in this holy house." In the words of one friend, "A wife was provided for him, by the direct inspiration of the Spirit of the Lord to him to choose one of the faithful workers, a fair daughter of Zion."[49] In the months that followed the dedication, Winder became acquainted with a dark-eyed girl by the name of Maria Burnham.

Maria Burnham was born September 30, 1869 in Hyde Park, Utah to Clinton and Matilda Barnett Burnham. She had grown up throughout the Southwest, as her father was called to help colonize Savoia, New Mexico, St. Johns, Arizona, and Fruitland, New Mexico. When she was only thirteen her mother died but her father quickly remarried. Maria, who exhibited an ability to freely love and accept others, grew to love her step-mother as much as her own.

She had traveled with her father and step-mother to the dedicatory services of the Salt Lake Temple, where to her surprise she was called as an ordinance worker. She bid her parents farewell and made her home with relatives in Salt

Lake City so that she could attend to her new duties in the Temple. Maria, who was commonly known as "Rye," had a number of suitors over the years, but was greatly impressed with John R. Winder, despite his being forty-eight years her senior. They were married on October 27, 1893 in the new Salt Lake Temple, and Winder was a widow no longer.[50] As those who knew of Winder's hard work saw his new beautiful bride, they exclaimed that "this was one of the rewards of his faithful ministration."[51]

Bishop Winder was very proud of his attractive young wife and was in a position to lavish elegant gifts of jewelry and clothing on her. However, Maria, as was her modest nature, would rarely don her exquisite finery in public, embarrassed that she might put some of her less fortunate friends to shame.[52] One of

Maria Burnham Winder (1869-1948), was the fourth and final wife of John R. Winder. Beloved "Aunt Rye" proved to be an amicable companion for President Winder during his twilight years. She was also a favorite among the Winder grandchildren. (C. R. Savage photograph)

her friends shared an experience demonstrating this humility and thoughtfulness:

> I remember so well the night you invited me to share your theater box at a rendition of Shakespeare's *Mid Summer Night's Dream* . . . That night I borrowed long gloves for the occasion, but you didn't wear long gloves—you could have worn them to your shoulders, you could have trailed your silks and your velvets and flashed your jewels. No, you came in your usual attire to make the rest of us feel at home. And you sat back in the shadow of the drapes, while we—your guests—sat out in front against the velvet rails.[53]

"Aunt Rye" was younger than all but four of John R.'s sixteen living children, but received a gracious welcome at Poplar Farm, nonetheless. William C. Winder was a bit surprised, however, upon returning home from his mission to see that his elderly father had married a light-hearted, twenty-three-year-old girl! The grandchildren adored her, and with her darker features and New Mexican background whispered among themselves the mistaken impression that "Aunt Rye is an Indian!" She in turn was endlessly amused with their antics, and allowed them to play freely about the home, getting away with behavior that their own mothers would not have tolerated had they known.

As witty and willing to give love as easily as she was, Aunt Rye soon became the major attraction at Poplar Farm. She was usually the instigator of fun and diversion, as if the lighthearted Winder family needed any encouragement. John R. Winder, like many of his contemporaries in the leadership of the Church, loathed card playing.[54] "Card playing is an excessive pleasure," declared Joseph F. Smith.[55] Nonetheless, some of Winder's offspring were hopelessly addicted and fast paced, hilarious card games became the regular entertainment in the evenings. Aunt Rye would post a lookout for her husband. If he approached, the signal would be given and all of the cards would be dumped into a pocket of Rye's apron. The card players would quickly kneel and pretend to be in the middle of a fervent family prayer. John R. would peer into the room, and delighted with his family's piety, would immediately withdraw so as to not disturb them.

Maria Burnham Winder was a rare, good-hearted woman who supplied her husband with a great deal of support and diversion in his later years. She brought a joy and a light into his life and the life of all the Winder family as the hostess of Poplar Farm. She was an amicable travel companion for John R. during his Church-related travels, and shared with him a deep love and commitment for temple work. She was particularly successful in tracing her own genealogy back through many generations, and performed the ordinance work for many of them.[56]

Maria carried the perfect blend of class and benevolence. She possessed the noble ability to lift and inspire others, and was the perfect lady to accompany John R. Winder, the gentleman of gentlemen. Admired by the Saints throughout the Church, one wrote to her: "You, who have been first lady in the greatest Temple, who have moved in the highest circles in the Church and State; who has the bearing of a Duchess—you are just as much at home in the humblest abode, and made the obscurest people feel your equal."[57]

Poplar Farm continued to be a favorite among the prominent citizens of Salt Lake. Apostle Rudger Clawson recorded the following in his journal: "The First Presidency and the Twelve Apostles and their wives were invited to take dinner with Brother John R. Winder at 'Poplar Farm,' a few miles south of Salt Lake City. All were present. A sumptuous repast was provided and the afternoon passed swiftly and pleasantly away."[58] Another gathering at Poplar Farm that was reported was a celebration of Winder's 76th birthday. Many family members attended, as did the First Presidency and their wives and many of the prominent citizens of Salt Lake.[59]

Receiver of All Church Property

Service in the Temple presidency yielded some interesting experiences for John R. Winder, such as when Lorenzo Snow planned a four-day excursion to Brigham City for the First Presidency, the Temple presidency, and many of the temple workers. They took the train north to Box Elder County for what President Snow called "a sacred excursion."[60]

Another time, on a morning in 1894, Prince Galatzin of the Russian Imperial Council and Lieutenant of the Russian Army visited Salt Lake City. Accompanied by a local Catholic priest, the Prince called on President Woodruff where "to my astonishment," wrote Abraham H. Cannon, "he was given permission by pres woodruff to visit the temple." Elder Cannon, along with Bishop Winder, gave these visitors a tour of the already dedicated Holy Temple. "They were much struck with the elegance of the place," it was noted.[61] Such visits were strictly forbidden in later years, and it was John R. Winder who announced the policy in a 1901 priesthood meeting that "No person who has married out of the Church can be admitted to the Temple under any circumstances. No one can be admitted to the Temple without a recommend."[62]

Winder's contributions during this time were not confined to the Temple, however. A victory for the Latter-day Saints was achieved on August 31, 1894, when the obnoxious Henry W. Lawrence was replaced as Receiver of all Church property. In looking for a compromise candidate, the Utah Supreme Court sought someone who was deeply respected by the "Gentile" community of the territory, yet who would also be acceptable to the Latter-day Saints. John R. Winder had developed an excellent reputation with the non-Mormon businessmen of Salt Lake, and it was known that "His promise is a gilt-edged bond, his word a pledge of honor which is never forfeited to friend or foe."[63] As a result of such trust, the Saints were thrilled to learn that Bishop Winder was the one appointed to the important post. Winder acted as the third and final receiver of

Church property, with the responsibility to hold and report on "all its real property and debts pertaining to said real property, and the money . . . arising from the rents, issues and profits of such real estate."[64] Unlike his predecessor who drew a large salary for his services, John R. vowed to serve as receiver without pay.[65] Shortly after statehood, on June 8, 1896, Winder ended his duties as U. S. Receiver by returning all of the Church's property back to them.[66]

The respect that was given to Winder by the "Gentile" businessmen in town is illustrated by an incident that took place in April 1895. One of the Twelve Apostles had tried to borrow some money for the First Presidency through a local bank, but was met with refusal. He wrote, "i got john r winder to work on the matter, however, with some prospect of success."[67]

The relative jurisdictions of the First Presidency and the Presiding Bishopric were discussed again in 1896, just as they had been in 1889. With so much financial control being exercised by the dynamic Presiding Bishopric, the brethren felt that there needed to be a change. Apostle Heber J. Grant commented about "the greater prestige acquired by the Presiding Bishopric than by the First Presidency in financial circles through the working of the present system." The apostles agreed to support changing the Church's financial system, and by the end of 1897 meetings between Presiding Bishop William B. Preston and the First Presidency

John R. Winder was a leader in the community who was respected by both the Latter-day Saints and the non-Mormon "Gentile" population. This helped him fulfill delicate assignments, such as serving as the Federal Receiver of all Church property during "The Raid."

resulted in returning ultimate financial control to the First Presidency.[68] John R. Winder, well known as a brilliant financier, was not the root of such disagreements; but it was perhaps because of the respect he helped bring to the Bishopric that the previously existing set-up was taken into review.

Statehood and a Time of Transition

An historic occasion occurred on January 4, 1896. On that day, President Grover Cleveland proclaimed Utah the forty-fifth state. The new government went into effect two days later. The previous year, Republican nominee Heber M. Wells was elected to serve as the first governor of the state. Governor Wells had been a friend of John R. Winder's since the former's boyhood, and would be re-elected in 1900.

With the intense persecution of the Saints by many non-Mormons, statehood had been delayed time and again. In December of 1893, those hostile to the Saints and Utah statehood almost obtained what could have proved to be a detrimental weapon. A letter book of President Brigham Young's was obtained by a dealer who said that "the liberals desired to use it against statehood this winter." It had been written during the Utah War and was "very strong in some places." The Church authorities sent Abraham H. Cannon and John R. Winder to negotiate obtaining the book before it fell into hostile hands. The Apostle and the Bishop were successful, and secured it with $200 cash and the verbal promise of an additional $200 after Utah became a state, providing that none of the contents of the book were brought to the attention of the public in the meantime.[69]

As Utah became a state, the Winder Dairy, which was sixteen years old at the time, continued to grow. Towards the turn of the century, the Dairy began selling milk to Parkin Dairy, who had customers of their own but would also deliver the Winder milk to the Winder customers. The raw Winder milk was delivered to Parkin Dairy, who began using quart-size bottles made of heavy glass. These first bottles had "plug" caps made of baseboard, which were labeled with a stamp that read "Winder Dairy: Pure Jersey Milk." By the turn of the century, the Dairy was still a small business working out of the cattle barn located just east of the Poplar Farmhouse. They used one horse, one milkwagon, and one delivery man.[70]

John R. Winder continued to turn more and more of the farming duties over to his sons Will and Rex, and to Will's sons. There even came the day when he became so busy with his duties in the temple presidency and the Presiding Bishopric that he had to resign as head of his much-beloved State Fair. On December 11, 1900, the headlines of the papers cried, "Resignation of Col. J. R. Winder." The article that followed noted that Winder had "been president of the Deseret Agricultural and Manufacturing Society for the past forty-four years," and that when word of his resignation got out, "there was a chorus of protests from the people, who have recognized Col. Winder's special fitness and qualifications, both by his ability and experience for the place." His resignation letter noted that it was his 79th birthday, and that he had important ecclesiastical duties to perform "which always take precedence." As the "Father of the Utah State Fair" stepped down, he did express his vision that "the time had arrived for the placing of the State fairs at a permanent location." He even suggested a forty-six acre plot of land "on North Temple street, on the banks of the Jordan River." The organization shortly thereafter heeded the advice of their founder, and the Utah State Fair has been held on that very site ever since.[71]

The closing years of Wilford Woodruff's administration were marked with continued financial stress for the Church. As the opening speaker in the April conference of 1894, John R. Winder lamented that tithing had decreased about 25% over the last year and that more and more of the funds were being used up.[72]

"I Borrowed $2,000 this morning of J R Winder & George Romney to pay upon our Notes that were Crouding upon us," wrote President Woodruff in September, 1896. "We are in a terrible financial Condition."[73] Deteriorating health also plagued the Church president, but his friend John R. Winder called on him often during his illness.[74] Wilford Woodruff died on September 2, 1898 while in San Francisco seeking relief for his health. John R. Winder would later be the one to offer the prayer at his monument in the city cemetery.[75]

Shortly after Lorenzo Snow became president of the Church in the fall of 1898, the Presiding Bishopric began meeting with the First Presidency to discuss the financial problems of the Church. Some of the greatest burdens being faced by the Church were discussed in these intense meetings consisting of Presidents Lorenzo Snow, George Q. Cannon, Joseph F. Smith, and Bishops William B. Preston, Robert T. Burton, and John R. Winder. As a result, President Snow directed the issuance of $1.5 million in 6-percent bonds to replace many short-term loans. The first issue of $500,000 was offered on January 1, 1899; the second on January 4, 1899; the third was not needed. Nearly all the bonds were purchased by Mormons and Mormon financial institutions. Next, President Snow moved to get the Church out of some business enterprises by closing or selling mining, milling, and railroad ventures. Finally, he told the Saints that the Church would get out of debt and Zion be redeemed if they would observe the Lord's law of tithing. All three of these monumental decisions were reached during important council meetings in the winter of 1898-99, of which Bishop Winder had a shaping influence. Winder's role in formulating the Church's fiscal policies is shown by the following excerpt from the *Journal History*:

> The First Presidency met with Bishop John R. Winder at their office this morning and spent considerable time in the investigation of the financial condition of the Church, with a view of taking steps to introduce a better system, to cut down expenses, so as to come within its income, and of devising means to meet demands and contingencies.[76]

In May 1899, Bishop Preston accompanied President Snow to the now-famous conference in St. George where the prophet promised that the Lord would open the "windows of heaven" if the Saints would pay their tithes.[77]

The Presiding Bishops rejoiced at the renewal of the doctrine of tithing and welcomed the increase in activity at the General Tithing Office. In just one year—1900—tithes increased from $800,000 to $1.3 million.[78] At a fast meeting in the temple in July, 1901, President Snow spoke on tithing. "There is a sister in this meeting, who has contributed to the church for educational purposes something like $23,000," the Prophet announced. "And such things may be said of the man at my right (Heber J. Grant) and of the man at my left (J. R. Winder). There is a great improvement among the Latter-day Saints in tithe-paying, and I rejoice in it."[79]

The new century consequently dawned with a brighter hope of better times for the Church financially. Politically, much progress had been made with the achievement of statehood for Utah, as well. The Church was now poised for a new era of moving forward in its mission of proclaiming the gospel of Jesus Christ in a manner that was less encumbered than ever before. At the dawn of a new century, President Snow encouraged Saints in foreign lands to remain and build Zion there, essentially closing the pioneer era and opening an era of developing a worldwide church.

The twentieth-century, however, also quickly brought an end to the service of two of Mormondom's greatest leaders. George Q. Cannon, who had served in the First Presidency for many years, passed away on April 12, 1901. Charismatic Cannon had been a friend of John R. Winder's, and had actually been the one to set Winder apart to both the Presiding Bishopric and the temple presidency. Bishop Winder mourned the loss of President Cannon with the rest of the Church, and even served as the "marshal of the day" at his funeral, in charge of all seating and arrangements.[80] Elder Rudger Clawson would be called to fill the vacancy in the First Presidency, but before he could be set apart to that office, death took another Church leader.

A mere six months after George Q. Cannon died, on October 10, 1901, President Lorenzo Snow died of pneumonia in the Beehive House, the residence of the President. Since President Snow had called John R. Winder to serve as his first counselor in the Salt Lake Temple presidency nearly nine years prior, the two had worked side by side on a daily basis. Bishop Winder had even been the one to host birthday celebrations for President Snow the previous two years.[81] As a result of such friendship and camaraderie within the temple, Bishop Winder especially mourned the passing of his close associate. At the funeral of Lorenzo Snow, it was John R. Winder who pronounced the benediction.[82]

The death of the fifth president of the Church and of his first counselor left the Saints looking to new men to lead them. At this time, the good works of Bishop Winder were well known throughout the Church. It was said that "His great service to the Church in his superintendence of the Temple, won him the marked recognition of all the leaders of the Church."[83] One leader who had developed a particularly strong admiration for John Rex Winder was the senior member of the Quorum of the Twelve Apostles. "Bishop Winder was brought favorably to President Smith's attention in 1892 when he was placed in charge of preparing the Salt Lake Temple for dedication."[84] It was while experiencing such positive impressions of John R. Winder that Joseph F. Smith began to receive inspiration regarding the composition of a new First Presidency.

13
At the Prophet's Right Hand: Call to the First Presidency, 1901-1905

"To occupy this exalted position."

In October of 1898, several of the brethren were gathered at the home of President Lorenzo Snow. In the course of the get together, he predicted that Brother John R. Winder "would do a greater work in the future than he had ever done before and would be more greatly honored by his brethren and sisters." Now that the great Prophet was gone, it was time for this particular prophecy to come to pass.[1]

Call to the First Presidency

Before he passed away, President Snow made another prophecy, this one to Joseph F. Smith: "You will live to be the President of the Church of Jesus Christ of Latter-day Saints, and when the time comes you should proceed at once to reorganize the Presidency of the Church."[2] Now that President Snow was gone, it was time to do just that. Joseph F. Smith shared the following about how he determined who were to be his counselors:

> Now, regarding the selection of my counselors, I have this to say, I thought about it and prayed over it. Had I consulted my personal feelings, the present arrangement is not exactly as it would have been. I had thought of others but whenever I came to the point of making a selection, these brethren who were chosen came into my mind, and I could not get away from them. I felt very warmly towards Brother Rudger Clawson, whom Pres. Lorenzo Snow chose as his second counselor, and would like to have taken him, but these my counselors were ever before me, and I feel that they were chosen of the Lord and that time will show it.[3]

On another occasion, he again recalled the heaven-directed process. "In the selection of my counselors I thought over the matter night and day and prayed earnestly to the Lord. I asked him who his choice was, and over and over again the names of John R. Winder and Anthon H. Lund came to my mind. I had thought of other brethren . . . but the Spirit of the Lord whispered that it should be otherwise."[4] Hugh Nibley shared the anecdote that it was one morning while shaving that the name of John R. Winder came to President Smith, and from that moment on he could not get it out of his head. He knew that God wanted Brother Winder to serve as his first counselor.[5]

John Henry Smith of the Twelve was very close to his cousin, Joseph F., and they confided much in one another. On Wednesday, October 16, 1901, he recorded in his diary: "President Joseph F. Smith and me had a talk over his Councillors. He will choose John R. Winder and Anthon H. Lund." John Henry Smith therefore became the first to know of the new First Presidency.

Another apostle to first learn of John R. Winder's selection was Anthon H. Lund. The morning of the meeting to reorganize the Presidency, Elder Lund walked with President Smith from his home at the Beehive House to the Temple. He wrote that President Smith "told me that he felt impressed to have the Church organized fully. He asked me what I thought of Bro. Winder as his First Counselor? I thought he was a conservative man and being known as such he would help to continue the confidence of the people in money matters."[6]

Later that morning, Thursday, October 17, 1901, the apostles of the Church met in the Salt Lake Temple. Present at that 11:00 am meeting were Joseph F. Smith, Brigham Young, Jr., John Henry Smith, George Teasdale, John W. Taylor, Marriner W. Merrill, Anthon H. Lund, Matthias F. Cowley, Abraham O. Woodruff, Rudger Clawson and Reed Smoot. Francis M. Lyman was presiding over the mission in England at the time, and Heber J. Grant was laboring in Japan. John Smith, the Church Patriarch, was also present, as was George F. Gibbs, who acted as clerk. John Henry Smith offered the opening prayer.

After they had transacted some business, he moved that they proceed at once to organize the First Presidency. The motion was carried unanimously. Brigham Young, Jr. then moved that Joseph F. Smith be sustained as the president of The Church of Jesus Christ of Latter-day Saints. This action was approved unanimously, as well. President Smith then announced that he would have John Rex Winder, then age 79, serve as his First Councilor, Anthon Henrik Lund serve as his Second Counselor, and Brigham Young, Jr. serve as President of the Quorum of the Twelve Apostles. Elder Lund, a native of Denmark, had been an apostle since 1889 and was already well known and respected by both the Saints and their leaders. All three were unanimously sustained.

Patriarch John Smith was mouth in setting apart Joseph F. Smith as President of the Church. John R. Winder, who labored daily in the Temple, was then called in and notified by President Smith of his appointment. It was clear to those in attendance that it was a humbling surprise, and that he "was much affected." Winder related to the group that his feelings at that moment were similar to the time President Woodruff called him to serve in the Temple. He did not feel worthy, he said, but President Woodruff assured him that the Lord would qualify him. "That is how I feel," said he, "in regard to the present appointment."[7]

The new President Winder was then set apart under the hands of them all, with President Smith acting as voice, to be the first counselor. Although John Henry Smith's diary mentions that Winder was "ordained an Apostle" in that blessing, President Smith, himself, later stated emphatically that John R. Winder was never ordained an apostle. Anthon H. Lund and Brigham Young were then each set apart to their respective callings. "The spirit of the Lord was with us in power," it was said of that meeting, "good feeling prevailed."[8] The humbled newest member of the distinguished group was asked to give the benediction. President John R. Winder was probably very emotional as he did so.[9]

The whole process did not take very long. George Romney, who was working in the Temple with President Winder that day, said this: "When he was sent for, to come into the room with the Presidency of the Church, he went up, and in about a half hour he came back, having been ordained and set apart as the first counselor."[10] Romney described President Winder's shock of the call, which lingered even as he returned to his temple duties: "When the word came that afternoon, Brother Riter and I were sitting in the sealing room, and I never saw a man so taken back and surprised; but I never saw a man occupy a position like this that he now occupies and be as humble."[11]

The following morning the *Salt Lake Tribune* flashed the headline: "PRESIDENCY IS FORMED;" with one of the subheadings being: "Surprise Expressed Because President Smith Chose a Counselor Who Is Not One of the Apos-

tles." Part of the accompanying article states that the action of choosing a counselor outside of the Quorum

*The front page of **The Salt Lake Tribune** on October 18, 1901, the day after the new First Presidency was organized, with John R. Winder as first counselor.*

of the Twelve "created surprise." The newspaper said that this had not been done since 1856, when Brigham Young called Daniel H. Wells to be a counselor. "Some surprise was manifested in some quarters over the action of President Smith in displacing Rudger Clawson, who was elevated by President Snow" to the First Presidency, and was only privileged to serve five days. "Apostle Clawson said yesterday, however, that he had no complaint to make."[12]

"President Joseph F. Smith sprung upon this people one of the greatest surprises they ever had," said George Taylor, "when he mentioned Brother Winder as his first counselor; but," he continues, "it was met with the heartiest response of anything, I think, that was ever presented to this people. The people felt it was the voice of God. *Vox Dei, Vox Populi*—the voice of God was the voice of the people; and the Spirit of God bore testimony to everyone with whom I spoke that it was indeed the voice of God."[13]

The Saints were greatly impressed with President Winder's humility, despite his new call to serve as the Prophet's right-hand man. From the day of his new calling, to the day of his death, George Romney reported, "I have never seen one particle of change, but he has been the same John R. Winder, filled with humility, treating his brethren and sisters with all the kindness that it was possible for a man to do."[14] Other contemporaries made similar observations. "I do not think any amount of honor bestowed upon Brother Winder would ever have caused him to deviate from the purest principles of brotherhood and good citizenship," reported William Riter. "He was totally without guile, totally without that spirit of superiority which so many of us assume over our fellow men when we are clothed upon with a little brief authority. Those things never occurred to him." President Winder was never viewed as being extravagant, or superfluous. "He was plain in his deportment," it was said, "plain in his dress, plain in his thoughts, plain in all his expressions."[15]

President Winder shared his feelings about his new call in a letter written from Poplar Farm on Christmas Day, 1903. Sent to Elders Heber J. Grant in Japan, and Francis M. Lyman in London, he writes of his call to the Presidency. "When I think of that event, and it is constantly uppermost in my mind, I am led to wonder how it is possible that a person, uneducated, and, in my own estimation, so unfitted for the position, could have been chosen. . . . Notwithstanding," he continues, "I have the assurance that it was the will of the Lord that I should occupy this position, consequently I am fully reconciled and am determined with His aid and assistance to discharge my full duty."[16] When Elder Lyman first received word of the change in the Presidency via cablegram, he wrote, "I announced to the household the news I had received, and we agreed it was the will of the Lord." He also observed how well suited the two new counselors were for the places they had been called to fill, and "how faithful and conservative they were."[17]

A week after the organization of the First Presidency, the brethren met again in the Temple, this time to fill the vacancy that still remained in the Twelve.

President Smith nominated his son, Hyrum Mack Smith, to fill the spot. Also at that meeting, Orin P. Miller, president of the Jordan Stake, was approved to fill the vacancy in the Presiding Bishopric created by John R. Winder's departure.[18] Bishop Preston had noted that he "felt the loss of Bp. Winder."[19] The other counselor in the Presiding Bishopric, Robert T. Burton, wrote about Winder's new call, "This removes from our Quorum our very dear friend and fellow laborer."[20] President Winder remained friends with his former associates in the Bishopric for the remainder of their lives. Once he saw a young elder give Bishop Preston a tongue-lashing for some trivial matter. Afterwards, Winder remarked to his old friend that he was impressed that he took it in silence. Besides, Winder pointed out, it humorously reminded him "of a little fritz barking at a Newfoundland dog!"[21]

One of his first duties in the First Presidency was to speak at the Granite Stake conference. Winder noted that "my call to the Presidency was a great shock to me." He said that "when people congratulate me upon my connection with the First Presidency, I say to them: 'Pray for me.'" President Winder expressed his pleasure with the conditions in the new stake and concluded by declaring "it is my determination to stand by and sustain President Smith to the last."[22]

Although they had just recently held the October session of conference, a special conference was called to ratify the new leadership changes, which was held November 10, 1901. In that solemn assembly, the new First Presidency and the Twelve were sustained as "prophets, seers, and revelators." In his sermon, Joseph F. Smith reminded the congregation that "The Lord never did intend that one man should have all the power. . . I propose that my counselors and fellow presidents in the First Presidency shall share with me in the responsibility of every act which I shall perform in this capacity. I do not propose to take the reins in my own hands to do as I please, but I propose to do as my brethren and I agree upon, and as the Spirit of the Lord manifests unto us. I have always held, and do hold, and trust I always shall hold, that it is wrong for one man to exercise all the authority and power of the presidency of the Church of Jesus Christ of Latter-day Saints. I dare not assume such a responsibility, and I will not, so long as I can have men like these (pointing to Presidents Winder and Lund) to stand by and counsel with me in the labors we have to perform, and in doing all those things that shall tend to the peace, advancement and happiness of the people of God and the building up of Zion."[23]

In the *Improvement Era* in May 1902, President Smith squelched any speculation that not being ordained an apostle somehow disqualified a worthy high priest of serving in the First Presidency: "We do know positively that John R. Winder, Sidney Rigdon, William Law and Hyrum Smith, all of whom were members in the First Presidency of the Church, were never ordained apostles . . . The main point we wish to make is this, that it was not necessary that they should be ordained apostles in order to hold the position of counselor in the First Presidency." Regarding such a high priest who is called to officiate in the First Presidency, President Smith notes that "he is 'accounted equal' with the President of the Church in holding the keys of the Presidency (section 90:6) as long as the President remains. When he dies, the calling of his counselors ends, and the responsibility of Presidency falls upon the quorum of Twelve Apostles."[24]

Two years after President Winder's death, Smith reminded the Saints again that "it does not follow and never has followed that the members of the First Presidency of the Church are necessarily to be ordained apostles. They hold by virtue of their rights as Presidents of the Church all the keys and all the authority that pertains to the Melchizedek Priesthood."[25] President Winder would not be the last member of the First Presidency to never be an apostle. In 1925, President Heber J. Grant called Charles W. Nibley from the position of Presiding Bishop to that of his second counselor; and in 1965, Thorpe B. Isaacson would become a counselor to President David O. McKay, after having served in the Presiding Bishopric and as an Assistant to the Twelve. Nonetheless, such moves continue to be rare.

A Sage Among the People

At the turn of the century, the average life expectancy was 44 years old. Consequently, the elderly President Winder was viewed by his fellow brethren and by the Saints in general as a venerable sage. His birthday each year was met with congratulations by the members of the Church, and by celebrations. December 11, 1901, for example, saw a grand gathering of general authorities and temple workers in the Celestial Room of the Temple to commemorate Winder's eightieth birthday. It was a fitting place. As Winder noted, "in the house of the Lord we are nearer heaven than in any other place." At that gathering, the 80 year-old spoke about obedience, noting, "in the kingdom of heaven we would be willing to answer every call." In his 50 years as a member of the Church, he did not remember a single instance where he failed to respond to the voice of the priesthood.[26]

The following year it was said of him, "His mind is an encyclopedia of general information on Utah affairs, much of which pertains to times fast passing beyond the memory of the oldest inhabitant. . . At the advanced age of eighty-one years the veteran is still in good health, brisk, lively, active in the performance of his many duties, and seems to enjoy life as much as in the days of his youth and prime."[27] President Lund marveled at his counterpart's ability of recollection, "He was able to recollect business affairs; it was not with him as with so many who lose some of their mental powers when they climb the rounds of life's ladder to old age." Lund also noted that, "There are not many who, when they reach their eighties, can remember so well the early events of their lives. . . Brother Winder was a remarkable man in this respect. He could remember the details in our office, which are of so multitudinous a variety and character."[28]

When John R. Winder reached his eighty-second birthday, the general authorities and his fellow temple workers again held a "Birthday Reception" in his honor in the temple. William W. Riter, who acted as chairman for the event, said in his remarks, "Brother Winder, allow me to say it for myself, for all those who are present here, and for all of Israel, you have a warm place in our hearts. We love you." President Smith commented that the leaders of the Church have never been "more united and more harmonious in their feelings and sentiments than they are today." In behalf of the temple workers, Bishop George H. Taylor said, "They honor him in his position; they venerate him for his age, and they love him for himself. He is always kind and considerate of our feelings." President Lund said of him, "he is indeed like a cheering

Birthday Reception

You are cordially invited to attend a Reception in the Salt Lake Temple in honor of

President John R. Winder

on his eighty-second birthday, December the eleventh, nineteen hundred and three.

Please come not later than 2:30 p.m.

Committee

Wm. W. Riter   *John Nicholson*
Bathsheba W. B. Smith   *Emma S. Woodruff*
Edna L. Smith

This is an invitation to President Winder's 82nd birthday celebration, held in the Salt Lake Temple. President Winder celebrated his natal day on several occasions with such gatherings, and there was no better place to host them than in the Temple he so dearly loved. The button dates from a similar gathering celebrating his 83rd birthday.

ray of sunshine when he comes into the office," and Elder John Henry Smith noted on behalf of the Twelve that "his selection was a pleasure to us." On behalf of the seventies, Elder Seymour B. Young prayed that "Brother Winder may be spared for many, many years to come."

George Romney then presented President Winder with an autograph album, so that his posterity "in perusing this book, may find it an incentive to them, that in seeing the love and good feelings manifested. . . may be stimulated to follow in your footsteps." Romney noted that his friend "certainly has followed his prototype, Jesus Christ, who was filled with humility from the day of His birth to the day of His death." A deeply moved and humbled John R. Winder then gave his remarks of gratitude. He thanked everyone for their presence and kind thoughts on his birthday and asked, "Why should I be singled out for this distinction?" President Smith then quipped, "We are not all as 'young' as you, Brother Winder." The assembly chuckled, and President Winder continued with his famous smile and sparkling eyes, "Well, my being the 'youngest' may be the reason for it." He then expressed his gratitude for all of his blessings. "I woke up about three o'clock this morning," he said, "as I most always do, and I generally lay awake till I get up, and I have time to think of many things." This morning he counted his blessings, reaching as far back in his memory as he could. President Winder then related to this group of friends the story of him praying and feeling peace as a little boy in the grain fields in Biddenden. He shared his conversion experience in Liverpool and some of the challenges faced while completing the temple. He then admonished all in attendance to "prove faithful unto the end."

Presiding Bishop William B. Preston then spoke, as did Angus M. Cannon on behalf of the Salt Lake Stake Presidency. "I never knew him to slip a cog in any position that he ever filled," reported President Cannon. The concluding remarks were made by Bathsheba Smith, in behalf of the sisters of the temple. Then Brother Orson F. Whitney read the following original poem, composed for the occasion:

> There's a name writ oft—a name writ large
> In the book of human life.
> What name, than this, more in glory's charge,
> Or more with merit rife?
>
> John the Beloved—'twas the name he bore
> Who wrote as the Spirit spake;
> And John, that other, who went before
> And bled for the Master's sake.
>
> The name of Wycliffe, "the morning star;"
> Of Calvin, and Knox, and Huss;
> Of Milton divine, whose fame from afar
> Has descended unto us.

The name of many a sapient sage
In science, letters and art;
Warriors and statesmen in every age—
Giants in mind and in heart.

Till chosen of God and honored of man,
That radiant name appears,
Now shining down from that snowy van
Of two and eighty years,

Silvering the brow of a son of God—
A man of war and of peace,
Who fought for the right; then plowed and sowed,
And hath reaped the rich increase.

A pillar he in God's temple now,
No more to go out for aye;
And to him the gathered hundreds bow
On this glad natal day.

Next to the Prophet, our chief in charge,
Victor in peace as in strife;
John Rex Winder—a name writ large
In the Lamb's great Book of Life.[29]

The following summer, the venerable President greatly impressed his associate, President Lund, at the annual Pioneer Day Parade celebrating the 24th of July. While Presidents Winder and Lund and General Burton were forming their places in line with the veterans of the Nauvoo Legion, "Pres. Winder jumped out and helped to arrange the procession." Despite being 82 years of age, the old Colonel was whipping the Days of '47 Parade into shape just like the many public functions he used to administer. "He did as much work at this as five of the aids," Lund remarked. Once the parade began, the Colonel was not to be found back in his comfortable carriage, but rather, "He walked in the parade the whole distance."[30]

Later that same year, when President Winder reached eighty-three, the *Millennial Star* declared that he is the "youngest old man" in the Church. The *Deseret News* declared that he was still "strong physically and mentally. . . In fact, President Winder appears stronger today than he was ten years ago."[31] In 1907, Winder celebrated his eighty-sixth birthday. On that occasion, the *Young Women's Journal* extended their congratulations: "He has certainly acquired the art of growing old gracefully, if we can say he has grown old, for he is mentally as bright and active as a young man."[32] When he turned 88, the *Deseret Evening News* noted, "President Winder today looks about as young as he did twenty years ago, and he is in full enjoyment of mental and physical vigor. . . The Church has had a number of such 'grand, old men,' and President Winder is one of them."[33]

The venerable president's notoriety extended throughout the Mountain West. In April 1906, for example, he was featured in "Men of the Day in Caricature," a Denver publication that was a sort of turn-of-the-century "Who's Who." They printed the following prose alongside his biographical sketch:

> Old? Yes, full of years is he;
> Probity and dignity,
> And his native industry
> Have rewarded him with wealth,
> Long in happiness and health,
> May he see the seed he's sown
> Into richest harvests grown.

The sketch concluded with "But, best of all, when he can get away from the city he likes to retire to the quiet ease of his beautiful country home and contemplate his cattle and his crops with the luxurious sense of one whose days are at peace."[34]

Working with the Brethren

In those days, the president of the Church lived in the Beehive House on South Temple Street, and the Presidency worked in a small office building between the Beehive House and the Lion House to the west. There, the First Presidency was burdened with decisions ranging from the trivial to the complex. There was an overwhelming volume of routine work, and, since this was in the days without large staffs to assist them, even the most routine expenditures required the approval of the First Presidency. From early in the morning until late

Presidents Smith, Lund, and Winder spent many long days in the First Presidency office, located between the Lion House and the Beehive House. Here they answered countless amounts of correspondence, counseled with other leaders, and planned for the needs of an ever-changing and growing church.

at night, the three men would pour over correspondence, meet with visitors on personal and ecclesiastical problems, and consult with members of the Twelve and the Presiding Bishopric.[35]

It was because of these long hours spent working closely together that Presidents Smith, Winder and Lund became a very unified team. "He was a wise counselor," noted Anthon Lund, "a man of clear judgement, and a man whose integrity never wavered." The second counselor became close to his associate, and looked forward to working with him each day. "I was pleased when I saw him come into the office;" Lund recalled, "there was always a pleasant smile on his face. I have often watched him coming along in the street, walking as if he were a young man—active, energetic, and he did not seem to feel the heavy weight of the years he carried." President Lund said that "day after day, he came to work cheerfully, and he never shirked it, though often it would take till late in the evening. Brother Winder seemed to be the youngest of the three." He also noted that Winder "works hard and sits with us till late at night. We often wish that we could let him go a little earlier, for he ought to have more rest; but questions come up, and he is as interested in them as any of us, and desires to do his share of the work." These two counselors often went home a similar way, and enjoyed their talks after work. "I was always pleased to hear his opinions, to hear what he had to say," noted Lund, "He was a man whose word could be relied on."[36]

Anthon H. Lund also described the special bond between Presidents Winder and Smith. "He loved President Smith with a deep affection, and President Smith loved him. There was a bond of tender affection between the two, and I loved to see them meet one another."[37] Joseph F. Smith hoped that his first counselor would be his right-hand man throughout his administration, saying, "I think we could get along nicely, congenially, happily and unitedly together."[38] By none was Winder more appreciated and esteemed than by the leader whose right hand man he was.

President Winder continued to work daily as the presiding authority in the Salt Lake Temple. In 1902 he drew up "the rules now used in the Salt Lake Temple." The brethren immediately felt to adopt these rules for all the temples. Some, however, were provisions that made sense in pioneer Mormondom, where the temples were spread out across great distances, which no longer apply today. For example, it was approved "that where couples, who have never had their endowments, are sealed under proper authority in distant places they should be instructed to come to the temple when opportunity offered, have their endowments, and be resealed over the altar, but if the opportunity never came the first sealing would stand."[39] Another rule said that "a woman who lives and cohabits with a gentile husband cannot be received into the temple." Winder also declared that "people who come to the house of the Lord should be cleanly in their persons."[40] In 1902, President Winder also oversaw the completion of the temple annex building.[41]

For a while, the First Presidency and the Council of the Twelve had been having their weekly meetings on Wednesday. However, President Winder often had to leave early because "his temple duties were heavier on Wednesday than on the other two days on which endowments were given." Finally, he meekly asked the Council if the meeting date could be changed to Thursdays. "If the change could be made consistently," Winder explained, he would "feel very much accommodated." So, out of deference to their elder associate, the brethren voted to change their meeting day. The First Presidency and the Twelve have had their weekly meeting in the Temple, for the most part, on Thursdays ever since.[42]

President Winder was a spiritual giant, as one would expect from a First Presidency member and president of the Salt Lake Temple. One anecdote regarding his inspiration is particularly interesting. Sometime in the early part of 1910, Agnes Sloan Nibley, daughter-in-law of Winder's friend Charles W. Nibley, the Presiding Bishop, attended the Salt Lake Temple. She was in the midst of a difficult pregnancy and most likely went to the temple seeking peace and comfort. While she was there, President John R. Winder approached her and asked to give her a blessing. In that blessing, President Winder spoke about the son Sister Nibley would soon deliver, stating that he would accomplish an important work. According to the Nibley family story, some of Winder's final words as he lay dying on March 27 of that year were inquiring whether Sister Nibley had yet given birth to her son. Significantly, the Nibley's son was born that very day, and, in honor of President Winder, the baby boy was named Hugh Winder Nibley. Hugh Nibley would grow to become one of the greatest LDS philosophers of the twentieth-century. He achieved distinction as a scholar, a writer, a professor, a linguist, a researcher, a theologian, and a scriptorian. Nibley has noted that "John R. Winder was a very inspired and prophetic man." The details of the blessing given to his mother that day in the temple are "sacred," he says, "and I have not shared them with anyone, including my siblings." He did note that the things that President Winder prophesied have all come to pass. "I was told by my mother that President Winder was unlike any of the other Church leaders of his day. He was in a class all by himself," Nibley exclaimed, "He was a singular man, not like everyone else, not by a long shot."[43]

Strengthening the Auxiliaries and the Missions of the Church

The First Presidency of Smith, Winder, and Lund worked hard to strengthen the auxiliary organizations of the Church. For example, many conferences were held for such groups; "Pres. Winder attended fast meeting at temple a week ago, Primary conference at assembly hall on Saturday last, and young people's conference on the day following," it was reported. Within the week, President Winder also presided at a Relief Society conference of the Salt Lake Stake, and the Granite Stake Sunday School conference.[44] After attending one Sunday School conference in the tabernacle, Winder exclaimed, "It was a splendid occasion. The multitude of children assembled attracted the attention of strangers, who expressed great surprise at what they saw."[45] President Winder remained heavily involved with many of these auxiliaries, for he served on the Sunday School General Board (1901-1910),[46] the Church Board of Education (1901-1910), and the Young Men's Mutual Improvement Association (YMMIA) General Board (1909-1910). One decision by the Church Board of Education was, on October 15, 1903, to change the name of Brigham Young Academy to Brigham Young University. However, President Smith emphasized that they would not receive any more money because of it, and "this was also the view of Bro. J. Winder."[47]

In 1906, the Sunday School was instructed to organize classes for adults. The first ones were a parents' class to emphasize the importance of the home and of the parents' role in teaching their children the gospel. Other changes for the auxiliaries followed in April 1908, when the First Presidency created a General Priesthood Committee on Outlines, which served until 1922. The committee was charged with creating definite age groupings for Aaronic Priesthood offices, providing systematic programs for year-round priesthood meetings, and in other ways to reform, reactivate, and systematize priesthood work.

In January 1902, the first edition of the *Children's Friend* was published. The magazine, which was originally intended for the Primary Association teachers, later widened its audience to include children, and finally was devoted exclusively to them. It was published until 1970 when it was replaced by the *Friend* magazine. One of the Church magazines, *The Improvement Era*, once desired to print a character sketch of John R. Winder's life, and obtained a near friend to prepare it. When the paper was presented to him, he modestly objected: "It will not do," he said, "to write that way of me. There are so many good, faithful men who have done as much or more for the cause than I have, that it is not wise, in my position, to hold me up as a special example. In my feelings I am always opposed to distinctions among the Latter-day Saints. Not that I do not appreciate the kind sentiments expressed, but it will not do. Why should I be singled out?" So out of deference to his wishes, the article was never printed.[48]

The Smith administration worked diligently to promote missionary work both at home and abroad. A mission in Japan had been opened in 1901, and Mexico, which had been closed since 1889, was reopened that year, as well. In 1903, the First Presidency also authorized the reopening of a mission in South Africa, which had been closed since 1865. "The work of the Lord has spread abroad in the world," declared President Winder in the October, 1908 general conference, "The foreign missions have been multiplied in many nations of the earth."[49]

Seeing a need to educate tourists about the Latter-day Saints, their beliefs and history, a Bureau of Information and Church Literature was set up in a small octagonal booth on Temple Square in August 1902. This first visitors center was later replaced by a larger building in March 1904 where President Winder, a great supporter of the project, gave the dedicatory prayer.[50] This building was later replaced by the present visitors centers in 1966 and 1978.

LDS First Presidency, 1903.
John R. Winder, Joseph F. Smith, Anthon H. Lund.

The Smoot Case, Teddy in the Tabernacle, and other Political Situations

Politically, the LDS Church was thrown back into the national spotlight again when on January 29, 1903, Elder Reed Smoot of the Quorum of the Twelve Apostles was elected to the United States Senate. Immediately controversy arose over his ties to the Church, and the Senate refused to seat him until they investigated charges that he and the Church still promoted plural marriages and that the Church controlled Utah politics. While many blamed President Smith for allowing Smoot to run, many of the leaders were supportive of the decision. There are even reports that John R. Winder, "a Democrat, was reported as 'eager' to have Smoot in the Senate."[51]

Shortly after the controversy began, Winder met a former Senator and apostate son of George Q. Cannon Frank J. Cannon, on the street in Salt Lake. President Winder expressed hope that when Cannon went "to Washington on the Smoot case" he would not "betray" his "brethren." Cannon replied that he would not be going to Washington as a witness in the Smoot case, but that Winder should warn the men at Church headquarters that it might be them on the witness stand. President Winder replied with indignant alarm, "I don't see what the brethren have to do with this!"[52] But sure enough, many Church officials, including President Smith, would be called to testify before the Senate's investigative committee.

Finally, after several years of official investigations and Church officials testifying in regards to the Church's involvement in politics and stance on polygamy, the Senate voted to allow Reed Smoot to retain his Senate seat. This joyous day occurred February 20, 1907. At the following April conference, the members voted to approve the First Presidency's 16-page summary of the Church position in the Smoot hearings.

Politics continued to involve the Church on a local level, as well. When the non-Mormon community in Salt Lake began to seek office under a new American Party label, Heber J. Grant and John R. Winder attempted to bring about a Republican-Democratic fusion in Salt Lake County. This soon seemed impossible, and many Latter-day Saints resorted to voting for the Republican ticket, at least on a local level, in order to keep the "Gentile" American Party from winning control in the elections of 1908. Louis Kelch declared "Mormon Democrats who do not vote the Republican ticket this year have not the spirit of God in them," and conveyed the impression that he spoke by authority of President Winder. Of course, when Winder heard his name was being invoked as the authority of such controversial statements he was furious. "NO LIVING SOUL IS AUTHORIZED TO USE MY NAME IN CONNECTION WITH ANY POLITICAL MATTER WHATEVER." This emphatic statement was reported by the *Salt Lake Herald* in an article entitled "Whispers Repudiated by President John R. Winder."[53]

Nonetheless, when the election came in January even stalwart Democrats voted for the GOP in order to maintain some voice in politics. John R. Winder, however, "was somewhat embarrassed when, because of a malfunction of a voting machine, it became public knowledge that he had voted for the Republicans."[54]

One bright spot for the Church politically in that decade was that they had a friend in the White House. President Theodore Roosevelt was the first chief executive to openly embrace Utah and its citizenry, and even made a visit to the Beehive State on May 29, 1903. The "Rough Rider's" train rolled into Salt Lake City at 8:35 in the morning. After a short speech to school children on the lawn of the City and County Building and a parade through the streets, the youngest president arrived at the Tabernacle at 10:05. Just moments before his arrival, "a ripple of excitement spread through the overflowing crowd" as Presidents Smith, Winder, and Lund took their seats on the stand. The band in the loft soon struck up the chords of "Hail to the Chief," and President Roosevelt entered the building. As they immediately recognized the familiar face, "the vast audience rose, cheered, stamped, clapped and made every manner of noise." Teddy Roosevelt acknowledged the applause with a bow and turned to meet some of the occupants of the platform who were awaiting introductions. He warmly greeted Joseph F. Smith, as well as John R. Winder before meeting the other Church authorities. President Winder had met the Emperor of Brazil, the King of Hawaii, the Prince of Russia, and even, as a young boy, the Archbishop of Canterbury, but this was the first time that this British immigrant had ever met the President of the United States. "He received me with open arms as an old friend," remarked one of the Church authorities, when describing Roosevelt's warm greeting. The President gave a stirring speech, praising the pioneers and the people of the West, and reminding them of their duty to protect the environment. After a breakfast at the mansion of Senator Kearns on South Temple, he left Salt Lake via the railway. Several years later, during the heat of the Smoot hearings, Roosevelt would publish a bold article refuting the anti-Mormon falsehoods.[55]

Celebrating Church History
and Reemphasizing the Manifesto

The Church was active in historical matters during the opening decade of the century, which is not surprising considering Joseph F. Smith's ancestry and historical roots. The other members of the First Presidency were avid history buffs, as well. John R. Winder displayed a keen interest in the past through the many recollections that he shared during his public addresses, and Anthon Lund had worked for years in the Church historian's office. Consequently, the brethren were delighted to facilitate the publication of B. H. Roberts' multi-volume *Documentary History of the Church*. Volume one came out in 1902, volume two in 1904, volume three in 1905, volume four in 1908, and volume five in 1909.

Many historic properties were acquired under the direction of this First Presidency. In April 1902, John R. Winder declared over the pulpit in general conference that he "was anxious to see the time when we would have means to purchase lands in Jackson County."[56] Carthage Jail was purchased in Illinois in 1903, and 25 acres of land in Independence, Missouri were acquired in 1904 on the site of land originally owned by the Church in 1831. Joseph Smith's birthplace in Vermont was purchased in 1905, and the 100-acre Smith family farm near Palmyra, New York, including the Sacred Grove, was purchased in 1907. Property at Far West, Missouri was acquired in 1909.

To mark the one-hundredth anniversary of Joseph Smith's birth, a party consisting of many of the Twelve, and led by Joseph F. Smith and Anthon Lund made a pilgrimage to his birthplace in Sharon, Vermont. There, on December 23, 1905, the Joseph Smith Monument was dedicated, along with the Joseph Smith Memorial Cottage. The monument was a thirty-eight-and-one-half-feet-high central spire, a foot marking each year of the Prophet's life. The Saints were pleased to honor the memory of the Prophet Joseph this way. President Winder presided during the weeks while this party was away from Salt Lake City.

Despite the Manifesto which declared that the Church would no longer sanction plural marriage, the first decade of the twentieth century still held some confusion for many. In 1902, President Winder said that a young woman called upon him and desired to know if the privilege of taking plural wives was now extended to the brethren of the Church. "He informed her that she was misinformed and Pres. Smith confirmed what Pres. Winder had said by stating that the Presidency had given no such authority."[57] On April 5, 1904 President Smith issued an official statement upholding provisions of the 1890 Manifesto and invoking excommunication against members violating the "law of the land" by contracting plural marriages. This declaration became known as the "Second Manifesto" and helped to quiet critics of the Church, local and national, who still doubted the sincerity of the Church as to that matter.

Although a former polygamist himself, President Winder was a fierce defender of the new direction of the Church. When he met Frank Cannon in the street towards the end of 1905, he chastised him saying, "Frank, you need not continue your fight against plural marriage. President Smith has stopped it."[58] In 1902, President Winder penned the eight-page article "Mormonism Not A Menace," which was printed in *The National Magazine*. This publication had a large circulation, for it was published both in Boston and London, and it shared the message to many that polygamy is dead among the Mormon people and that plural marriages are not sanctioned by the LDS Church. President Winder gives "a vigorous reply to the falsehood so industriously circulated by ministers of different denominations that 'Mormonism is a menace to this nation.'" He also "succinctly set forth in plain yet forcible language" a sketch of the doctrines, purposes, and achievements of Mormonism.[59]

As a result of such courage, President John R. Winder proved to be a stalwart example of obedience and faith. In all of the many tasks that he performed as first counselor in the First Presidency, his example was sterling. Consequently, the Lord was proven correct in calling John Rex Winder to be President Joseph F. Smith's right-hand man.

One of the final photographs taken of the venerable President Winder. Notably, his exceptional memory and intellect remained with him until the end.

14

The Venerable President Winder: His Ministry Comes to a Close, 1906-1910

"It is better to wear out than to rust out."

Strengthening the Stakes of Zion

Prior to the turn of the century, the mammoth Salt Lake Stake, in which John R. Winder had previously served on the high council, covered the entire Salt Lake Valley and consisted of 51 wards. In 1900, the First Presidency began carving up the stake by organizing the Jordan and Granite stakes. President Smith, along with Presidents Winder and Lund, felt it wise to continue this pattern, and in 1904 they created the Ensign, Liberty, and Pioneer stakes. John R. Winder was especially vocal in their meetings that "the time had come for the division." [1] These smaller administrative units allowed stakes to move in new directions to meet the needs of Church members. The Granite Stake, for example, soon piloted the family home evening program, which was later adopted by the entire Church. In 1908, President Winder rejoiced to note in general conference that, while recently "there were only a few stakes of Zion," now "they have been multiplied until there are between fifty and sixty stakes of Zion." [2]

The members of the Presidency and the Twelve frequently toured these stakes, as well as the more outlying ones. For instance, President Winder accompanied the Prophet down to the Emery Stake in 1902, and presided over a group that visited the Box Elder Stake that same year. He also visited the Cache Stake and presided at the Davis Stake Conference where he reported, "The bishops complained a little as to the slothfulness of some of their members who are market gardeners." [3] Organizing and visiting wards was also a major duty, and each week found John R. Winder visiting a different ward or stake. For example, one week he is found speaking at a meeting of the East Mill Creek Ward, and the next week he is reorganizing the bishopric of the East Jordan Ward. [4] One special assignment for President Winder was organizing the Winder Ward in 1904. He set apart Joseph A. Cornwall as the first bishop of this ward, which President Smith insisted be named in honor of his first counselor. [5]

At the time of this publication, the Winder Ward has grown into two stakes, the Salt Lake Winder Stake and the Salt Lake Winder West Stake.

The Saints loved to hear his wise counsel, both over the pulpit and in conversation. Edward Anderson, for example, declared that he "treasures many crisp counsels, wise sayings, and pointed expressions, heard at various times, in various places, under different circumstances, and uttered by the lips of President John R. Winder." Anderson noted, "His personal advice and counsel were not always agreeable at first, for he had a very terse way of saying things, but in the end they generally proved pleasant, best, and a blessing to him who followed them." [6]

"As he was somewhat advanced in years," remarked one contemporary of President Winder, "he did not travel very extensively in the Stakes of Zion, but he was seen nearly every day at his desk in the office of the First Presidency and in the Salt Lake Temple, of which he was president." [7] For instance, Winder did not accompany the party that traveled to Vermont to dedicate the monument at Joseph

President and Sister Winder while accompanying the Prophet on a visit to the Pacific Northwest. The traveling party included President Joseph F. Smith, Sarah E. Smith, President John R. Winder, Maria B. Winder, Elder George Albert Smith, Lucy E. W. Smith, Patriarch John Smith, Emily J. Smith, Lucy M. Smith, Rachel Smith, Jeannetta Smith, Frank Smith, Calvin S. Smith, Joseph F. Nibley, Presiding Bishop Charles W. Nibley, and Julia Nibley.

(Manuscripts Division, J. Willard Marriott Library, University of Utah)

*President Winder worked very closely with many of the "giants of the king-
dom," several of whom later became presidents of the Church. In his life he was
personally acquainted with every Church president between Joseph Smith and
Harold B. Lee.*

Smith's birthplace; and he likewise stayed home when Joseph F. Smith became
the first Church president to visit Europe in 1906. Although the venerable President Winder was usually the one to "mind the store" while President Smith was
away, he did on occasion accompany him on his travels among the Saints. One
such visit took place during the first three weeks of July, 1908. The party was led
by Presidents Smith and Winder, Elder George Albert Smith of the Twelve, and
Patriarch John Smith. They traveled primarily by train and toured Oregon and
California, returning on July 18.[8] In July of 1909, President Winder again traveled to the Northwest. In Oregon he stayed with Bishop Nibley and his family,
who had an interest in a lumber mill there along with David Eccles. In a letter to
President Smith, Winder notes that they have been to visit the Saints in Perry, La
Grande, and Portland. In that letter he also mentions his indigestion and says his
handwriting is poor because "that same old finger is still troubling me."[9]

The Work Moves Forth

While John R. Winder served in the First Presidency there were several
changes in the membership of the Quorum of the Twelve Apostles. Brigham
Young, Jr. died in 1903 and was succeeded by Francis M. Lyman as president of
the Quorum. George Albert Smith, son of John Henry Smith and later to serve as
the eighth Church president (1945-1951), filled Young's vacancy in the Twelve.

Abraham Owen Woodruff, son of the late prophet, tragically died in El Paso, Texas at the young age of 31. He was succeeded in the Quorum in 1904 by Charles W. Penrose. Marriner W. Merrill passed away in 1906 and was succeeded by George F. Richards. On October 28, 1905, Elders John W. Taylor and Matthias F. Cowley, finding themselves out of harmony with Church policy on plural marriage, submitted resignations from the Council of the Twelve that were announced to the Church April 6, 1906. They were succeeded by Orson F. Whitney and David O. McKay, who later served as the Church's ninth president (1951-1970). When George Teasdale died in 1907, his vacancy was filled by Anthony W. Ivins.

The increase in tithes since President Snow's vigorous admonishments allowed the first issue of bonds to be paid off in 1903. In 1907, the second issue was redeemed, and the Church was finally out of debt. At the April conference of that year, President Smith was able to announce that the Church "owes not a dollar that it cannot pay at once. At last we are in a position that we can pay as we go."[10] That year, Charles W. Nibley was called to succeed William B. Preston, who was released due to ill health, as the Presiding Bishop. Nibley, who was a shrewd businessman and friend of John R. Winder, and especially close to Joseph F. Smith, worked with these brethren to implement a number of changes in the way the Church was operated financially. An immediate change was made in 1908 when the Church closed the Bishop's tithing storehouse and moved to an all-cash basis, no longer issuing tithing scrip.

John R. Winder understood the fiscal details of operating the Church as well as any other man alive at the time. With his brilliant financial mind he had been deeply involved with helping to get the Church out of debt. Always a student, Winder payed very close attention to all of the Church's financial reports, both during his years in the Presiding Bishopric, and even after he was put in the First Presidency. As the director of many businesses which held large amounts of Church capital, Winder helped make some bold moves to free up the Church's financial obligations. One such was the difficult decision to sell the Church's interest in the Utah Light and Power Company.[11]

Frequently, in general conferences it was Businessman Winder that would congratulate stake presidents for their frugality in using Church funds, thank the members for their tithes, admonish the payment of fast offerings, counsel the Saints to free themselves from debt, and report cheerfully that the "financial condition of the church favorable; never better for years past."[12] He also explained to the members that the Presidency of the Church was engaged in various business enterprises not for personal profit, "but for the benefit of the church" and to provide employment for the Saints.[13]

John R. Winder was a strong advocate of building what became known as the "Hotel Utah." Rumors of this proposal leaked out in 1902, and President Winder declared in general conference that the report of "erecting a million-dollar hotel" was untrue. At that time, however, he said, "a memorial building in honor of the Prophet Joseph and Patriarch Hyrum Smith is under contemplation for the future."[14] President Winder was the one to present the resolution before the brethren about building such a memorial building and was appointed chairman of the planning commission.[15] However, during the following years, the brethren reluctantly tabled the idea for a Joseph Smith Memorial Building, feeling that the monument placed at his birthplace would suffice, and leaned towards erecting the hotel. In a meeting with the general authorities on October 5, 1909, the veteran leader led the effort in approving the building of Hotel Utah. After Winder's speech on the matter, the project was unanimously approved.[16] After serving as Hotel Utah for many decades, this beautiful building was renovated and renamed the Joseph Smith Memorial Building. John R. Winder's original intent reached fruition after all.

Church Doctrine and "The Origin of Man"

The First Presidency of Smith, Winder, and Lund was primarily occupied with administrative duties. However, they did find time to study doctrinal matters, as well. One Friday in 1904, for example, Presidents Smith, Winder, and Lund, along with Elders Francis M. Lyman, John Henry Smith, Hyrum Mack Smith and George Albert Smith, and theologians B. H. Roberts, James E. Talmage, and Charles W. Penrose, "spent the day reading and studying the Doctrines of the Church."[17] One can only imagine the interesting discussions had by this elite study group!

As the Church came into the new century, the once isolated Great Basin became more and more "Americanized." This led the Presidency to issue bold statements on morals and the behavior of the Saints. Joseph F. Smith made his famous statements about the "evils of face cards" at this time, primarily because of his abhorrence of gambling and because many women in the Church had become so addicted with the games that they would skip Church meetings and turn down Church callings![18] President Smith also warned "of the great evil of placing mortgages on the homes of the saints. It weakens the very bulwarks of Zion and we feel to proclaim against it."[19] As for President Winder, he too frequently preached on "the evil of indebtedness and placing mortgages on our homes."[20] He also declared that "he felt there is too much familiarity between the sexes at the Latter-day Saints University."[21]

During the first decade of the twentieth-century, the theories of Charles Darwin regarding organic evolution had taken a great hold on the beliefs of academia and the public in general. Many members of the Church were confused by what seemed to contradict the stories of creation as put forth by the scriptures. In November, 1909 the First Presidency responded by issuing a formal pronouncement under the title, "The Origin of Man." In this official proclamation, the Presidency intended to set forth "the position held by the Church" upon the subject of evolution. Much thought and prayer had gone into preparing this document, and Presidents Smith, Winder, and Lund had even met with some of their fellow brethren at times to better develop it. One such meeting occurred as early as September of that year when the Presidency shared their inspiration, which began as an "Article on the Godhead," with a few of the Twelve along with Professors John

A. Widtsoe and James E. Talmage. The eventual outcome, announced to the world as an official proclamation on "The Origin of Man," was moderate in tone while emphasizing the Church's teachings regarding the special creation of humans.[22]

This document explains the scriptural passages relative to the creation and preexistence, and notes: "All men existed in the spirit before any man existed in the flesh, and all who have inhabited the earth since Adam have taken bodies and become souls in like manner." They boldly assert that ideas of the original human having been developed from lower orders of animal creations are simply "the theories of men." Furthermore, the Presidency asserts that "Man began life as a human being, in the likeness of our heavenly Father." They also explained that Adam's race differs from the tadpole, the ape, the lion and the elephant because God "did not make them in his own image, nor endow them with God-like reason and intelligence." They conclude by affirming that "Man is the child of God, formed in the divine image and endowed with divine attributes, and even as the infant son of an earthly father and mother is capable of in due time of becoming a man, so the undeveloped offspring of celestial parentage is capable, by experience through ages and aeons, of evolving into a God."[23]

Doctrinally, "The Origin of Man" was significant, but it was historically important, as well. It established a precedent on how the First Presidency might effectively influence others and provide "an anchor in a rapidly changing world society." For example, in 1916 the Presidency issued "The Father and the Son," a statement defining the relationship of God the Father and Jesus Christ, and in 1939 an official message on world peace was issued. In 1980 a Proclamation to the World was issued, reaffirming the restoration of the Gospel and the truthfulness of the Book of Mormon, and in 1995 a proclamation on the family was issued to encourage strengthening of the family unit and recognizing the sacredness of the family. As a result of the long-term effects of "The Origin of Man" and other doctrinal declarations, "Statements of the First Presidency and Quorum of the Twelve on important doctrinal matters" was ranked as number three in the "Top 10 Stories of the Twentieth Century" published in the *Deseret News 1999-2000 Church Almanac*.

The Social Side of President Winder

Poplar Farm continued to be a popular place for entertaining the general authorities during Winder's presidency years. In 1906 John R. bought the W. B. Dougall home on West Temple, directly across the street from Temple Square, and that became his principal residence.[24] It became a tradition among the First Presidency, the Twelve, the Patriarch and their wives to retreat to President Winder's residence at the conclusion of general conference. On April 7, 1908, for example, John Henry Smith recounts such an evening. "We had an excellent dinner," he reported, "and lots of singing largely by Horace Ensign."[25] After the April conference of 1908, a story in the *Deseret Evening News* reported "President Winder Host: Reunion of First Presidency and Quorum of the Apostles at His Home Last Night." The article reads as follows:

For a period of 10 years the close of conference, annual and semi-annual, has witnessed an interesting reunion of the first presidency and twelve apostles at the home of President John R. Winder. In line with that custom, the venerable first counselor and his wife entertained last evening at the family residence. The three members of the first presidency and as many of the apostles as were in the state were in attendance, and their wives and a few other guests were also present.

The company assembled some time previous to the hour announced for supper and did not retire until long after the function was over. Music, speeches and reminiscent stories preceded and followed the repast, and all present rejoiced at the privilege of meeting under the roof of President Winder in a capacity that has come to be considered as an aftermath of conference.[26]

Once, at a New Year's party in the Lion House, "after supper they had a contest to see who could discern the most scents." Ironically, the oldest in attendance showed the keenest sense. "Bro. Winder was the winner," and this despite being 85 at the time![27] Elder Abraham O. Woodruff reported on a "splendid dinner party" given by Reed Smoot, where Winder was in attendance.[28] At a similar social gathering, Elder Woodruff noted, "Prest. John R. Winder in his 80th year gave a lively dance assisted by my Helen. We returned home quite late."[29] And on still another occasion, Woodruff records, "We had a delightful time. Prests. Jos. F. Smith and John R. Winder were present. We danced in the same set with them. Had a grand feast & good time."[30] It seems that the old Englishman had loved socials and dances since his young days in Biddenden, and that he was as at home at them as his progenitors of English peerage would have been.

Although he loved to entertain and be among Salt Lake's social circuit, his health was sometimes prohibitive. For example, he turned down an invitation to a birthday celebration in memory of John Taylor in 1902 for health reasons. "I have to forego many pleasant social enjoyments on account of my health," he wrote, "which I am trying to guard with care so that when duty calls I may be ready and able to respond."[31]

John R. Winder always enjoyed music and the arts. In fact, President Winder arranged to have the general priesthood meeting at the April 1902 conference moved to Friday night so that Professor Evan Stephens and his choir could perform a concert on Saturday night in the Tabernacle![32] Winder was also an advocate of sending the 250-member choir to perform at the 1904 World's Fair in St. Louis.[33]

Another artistic indulgence of the day was the Salt Lake Theater. As a member of the First Presidency, the Winder family enjoyed access to the Church-owned box. These, the best seats in the house, were on the third tier, immediately to the left wing of the stage. Many major productions from the east coast would tour the country, playing in various cities on their way to San Francisco, and would often stop in Salt Lake City.[34]

John R. Winder was not as excited about journal writing, however, and never kept a journal himself. In a meeting with the Presidency and the Twelve in October, 1909, President Winder expressed concern about the private journals of the brethren of the Council, and that many things were written in them which, if they were to fall into the hands of the enemy, might bring trouble on the Church. He declared, "It was very unsafe and risky for the brethren to write down that which occurred in these meetings. This duty belonged to the clerk of the council and to nobody else." President Winder then made a motion that the brethren should no longer write in their journals about what occurred in the council meetings. Obedience prevailed. For example, that entry proved to be the final one in Rudger Clawson's journal of 777 pages.[35]

The final decade of Winder's life, the first decade of the twentieth century, saw many additions to modern society. John R. Winder, always a voracious reader of newspapers, would have been interested to learn of Orville and Wilbur Wright and their historic flight at Kitty Hawk in 1903. By 1907, the U.S. Army had even began their aeronautical division, the forerunner of the U.S. Air Force. Transportation modernized in other ways during this decade, as the Boy from Biddenden, who had spent much of his life with horses and buggies, began to witness an increasing number of "horseless carriages" on Salt Lake City streets. The automobile became especially prevalent following Henry Ford's introduction of the Model-T in 1908.

The first Olympic Games held in the United States took place as part of the St. Louis Exposition of 1904, forty-eight years after Winder had passed through that city via steamboat. The San Francisco earthquake of 1906, which leveled 490 city blocks, would have been of great concern to President Winder and the other Church leaders. Many missionaries were stationed in San Francisco, and many passed through en route to the Pacific or Asia, and the brethren were concerned for their well being as well as that of the Saints who lived in that area. Other newsworthy events of the day included Robert E. Peary's discovery of the North Pole in 1909, and the founding of the Boy Scouts of America just a month prior to Winder's death.

As Remembered by His Grandchildren

John R. Winder's grandchildren had some strong memories of their grandfather. He was often the recipient of gifts of candy or fruit from acquaintances and admirers and occasionally received a box of oranges from California. The grandchildren would generally contrive an excuse to visit Aunt Rye when Grandfather was not home to see if they could get a handout. It was always a temptation to snitch a bit if an offer was not extended. They were sometimes a bit apprehensive of their famous yet somewhat severe grandfather. They held a great deal of respect and deference to him and recognized his role in the community. John R. would leave his city house two or three times a week and come riding through the fields immaculately dressed in a black suit, riding in a stylish trim phaeton pulled by a polished driving horse named "John." (Every horse John R. drove was named John.) He would have an early dinner and then proceed to ride down 300 East between his farm and son Will's to inspect. If any of Will's boys were within striking distance, he would administer a short flick of his horsewhip as he passed. If the boys happened to be in an apple tree as he approached, they would freeze until he passed by, hoping he wouldn't notice them.

Once Will sent two of his boys, Ed and Shirl, over to Poplar Farm to get a sack of wheat from the granary for feed for the chickens. The two boys, seven and ten respectively, were hauling the wheat back in their little red wagon. As they were attempting to get through the barbed wire fence, the sack tore open, spilling a pile of grain on the ground. Will came by and saw their predicament. He didn't want his stern father to see it for fear he would think they were wasteful, so he ordered, "You two boys pick up every last kernel!" They scooped up what they could, but were unable to get it all. Shirl, in his desperation to please Grandfather, had the idea of bringing over several chickens to eat the remaining kernels. As soon as they turned them loose, however, the chickens refused to eat and immediately flew back home.[36]

Jack Winder, another of Will's sons, shared several experiences about how his Uncle Rex (President Winder's youngest son), helped the boys seek some fun times, despite their stern grandfather. "Grandfather was very strict and ruled with an iron hand," said Jack, "but Rex could figure out more ways of doing what we all wanted to do." For instance, they would hide Rex's buggy next door at their own place, so he could sneak out on Friday nights to take them down to the bicycle races at the Old Salt Palace, a place Grandfather always considered "a den of vice." On Sunday afternoons, while President Winder attended church meetings, Rex would entertain the boys by arranging rooster fights, pony fights, and even cow fights. Always, however, when Grandfather returned home at 4:30, "everything around the farm would be as calm and serene as it should be."[37]

Claire Bradford Kapple, a granddaughter of John R.'s through his daughter Alice, remembered her grandfather having a gorgeous room with a black marble fireplace and magnificent furniture. "One day," she said, "Phyllis (Will's daughter) and I went into Grandpa's room. He was reading. He asked me whose little girl I was. He had so many grandchildren he couldn't always keep track. He knew we were his grandchildren, but he wasn't exact on all of us—whose children we were."

Some stories illustrate just how firm Winder became in his later years as his "Old World" ways came through. For example, when his daughter Alice's home burned down, he only gave them $20. "He was so rich," she said, "but he believed that children should make their own way."[38] Another time, Will's son Shirl was walking with one of his friends along the street downtown when they happened upon President Winder. While he was as warm as he could be with Shirl's friend, Shirl felt as if he were all but ignored. When asked why the stoic reception by his grandfather, Shirl replied, "I guess I hadn't proven myself yet."[39]

Mary Ann Winder Steadman, John R.'s daughter who was nicknamed Min, used to write poetry. One poem was called "Annie's and Willie's Prayer." It tells the story of two motherless children whose father, concerned over the stock

market, sent the children to bed early on Christmas Eve. He had made no preparation for a visit from Santa Claus. Later, he went upstairs and arrived at the door
to hear both their prayers. Annie said, "Bless Papa, dear Jesus, and cause him to
see that Santa Claus loves us far better than he." Of course the father relented
and went out in the cold to bring them presents before morning. After John R.
Winder had heard his daughter recite this poem, the family claimed that they
received nicer presents after that. There was a large family dinner on Christmas
Eve each year at the Poplar Farmhouse, involving all the children and grandchildren. They used to delight in hearing Grandpa's sleigh bells coming home on
Christmas Eve.[40]

John R. Winder had an interesting business arrangement with his son Will,
who managed the farm for him. Besides being allowed to use what foodstuffs
and dairy products his family needed, Will kept an earthen jar on the second shelf
in his pantry. This "bank" often held a five dollar gold piece, but when it was
empty, he would take the jar to his formidable father and ask meekly for a refill.
Eventually, Will's wife Rose insisted that her husband talk to his father about
establishing a dependable salary. Will didn't like to tangle with his father, and
was reluctant to face him. He viewed him as a fairly severe man with many of
his old-world ways intact. However, when approached with the concern, John R.
Winder was quick to rectify the situation. At this point he had a vast private
income from various sources, and decided he could easily do without the dairy
and turned the entire operation over to Will, with a few stipulations: Will was to
receive no real estate at that time, and John R.'s youngest son, Rex, was to
receive six of the cows that were his pets. All seem pleased with the arrangement, which occurred in about 1904, and the young Winder Dairy passed on
from the first generation to the second.[41]

In his final years, John R. Winder continued to take a great interest in what
his son was doing with the dairy, and often traveled over to observe the ongoing
construction as Will built modern barns and the first silos in Salt Lake County.
John R. was very proud of his son's accomplishments.[42] One technological
advancement came in 1907, when the dairy's management began their own bottling process. The heavy glass bottles were put into cases that held twelve quart-
size bottles. The case would be placed on a platform where a lever was pulled
that raised the case up to the fillers. After they were filled with milk, the bottles
were capped with "plug caps" made of baseboard. When the empty bottles were
returned to the dairy, they were soaked in a 40-gallon tank of wash water, held
up to a single brush that was driven by a steam turbine which caused the brush
to rotate at high speeds, and then placed in a 40-gallon tank of rinse water. In
1907, the dairy herd was also moved from the "Old Place" on 300 East and 2700
South to William C. Winder's farm, just one block east.[43]

George Winder, who grew up to be the dairy's manager for fifty years, had
one memory of his Grandfather visiting the farm. In 1908 John R. came out to
see what Jerseys were going to be shown at the State Fair that year. George

remembered him being a bit taller than his own 5' 8" father, William C. Winder. George also seemed impressed that the family patriarch stood as straight and upright as he was for his age. He was "quite erect for an 87 year-old man," George recalled. Grandfather wore a black overcoat and patted six-year-old George on the head when he saw him and spoke to him some. Little George led the cows out in front of the barn to show Grandfather, and he took great pride in being able to report on the names and pedigrees of a good part of the herd. He remembers his Grandfather being impressed with the quality of the animals and with the young lad's report.[44]

One granddaughter, Mary Winder Johnson, had two memories of John R. Winder:

> Only twice do I remember seeing Grandfather. My home was in Vernal and when I was about six years old, I came to Salt Lake City with my parents to visit relatives and friends. I remember standing near the back door of the home at Poplar Farm, watching for Grandfather to come from the temple. He drove into the yard and climbed from the surrey. I still vividly recall him as he turned and saw me. Although he was almost eighty-five years old, he stood there so very straight. He looked so spotlessly clean; his white hair and beard seemed a shining contrast to his dark clothes. His eyes twinkled and he gave a merry smile as he said, "Well, who is this?"
>
> The other short visit with Grandfather was in the summer before his death. He was living with Aunt Maria in the home across the street west from the tabernacle. He seemed very tired that day. Most of the time that we were there, he was lying on a hammock.[45]

John R. Winder in the 1900's. Many of his grandchildren recall how straight and tall he stood, despite his advanced age. George Winder remembered him as somewhat taller than his own 5'8" father.

The Final Weeks—Battling Pneumonia

All of the Church was concerned about their veteran leader's deteriorating health, and updates on his condition were provided daily in the *Deseret Evening*

News. "President John R. Winder is very poorly indeed," wrote John Henry Smith on March 18, 1910, "President Jos. F. Smith and I called upon him and blest him."[46] Tuesday, March 22, John Henry Smith noted, "President John R. Winder is still alive and getting a little better."[47] President Anthon Lund visited him almost daily. After one visit he wrote, "Bro. Winder was better I thought; though he had been bothered during the night with a hacking cough." After another visit in his final days, Lund reported, "He is suffering with an itching in his lower limbs."[48] During a visit by his son-in-law Rueben Miller, the dying John R. Winder established a fund whereby his former wife, Hannah Brower, might be taken care of.

The final days of John Rex Winder are best described by Benjamin F. Grant, a young man who looked to President Winder as a mentor. Fred Grant, as he was known, was a son of Jedediah M. Grant and brother of Heber J. He was with Winder in his final hours:

> President Winder had said to his wife, "Mamma, there is one man in Salt Lake that I would like to come and see me." She said, "Papa, if you will tell me who it is, we will try and get him here." He said, "I would like to have B. F. Grant come to me." They telephoned the message to me, and in less than ten minutes I was by his bedside. President Lund and Brother John Henry Smith came into the room and we surrounded his bed. While standing there he said to the brethren: "I do not want any special ceremony performed, or anything of that kind; but," he said, "you brethren have blest me; now I have sent for Brother Grant, and I want you all to place your hands upon my head; I want Brother Grant to give me the blessing."
>
> I had the privilege of attending John R. Winder for five weeks. I was by his bedside almost night and day. . . Brother Williams, his son-in-law, sat there every other night. . . I had the opportunity during those hours, those nights and days, to read the inmost soul of President John R. Winder in the last hours of his life. I want to say to you that I believe if there was a man on earth that had learned to know God, that had in his heart the desire to only do that which was in accord with the mind and will of the Lord, that man was John R. Winder.
>
> In regard to his wife, I never saw a person in my life more devoted, who could stand by the bedside, night and day, and administer to his wants. Many and many nights we would plead with her, time and time again, saying that she could not stand this stress, but she felt in her heart that she should be there as long as he wanted her. He often said, "Mamma, I can't bear to have you out of my sight," and she was true and steadfast to the last.
>
> Whenever we would administer to him, that wonderful character of his always came to the front. You never could give him a glass of water, you never could do one thing to relieve that suffering but what he would always turn around, even in the midst of pain, and say: "Thank you, my brother; thank you, my sister; God bless you for what you are doing for me. What have I done in

life that I should have such kind friends to administer to me in my last hours." To show you the modesty of the character of this man, he told his wife, "Mamma, if anything happens to me, I do not want you to attend the funeral in black." She told him that she would look, perhaps, rather strange to appear there alone in white, and the request was made that the whole family should wear white as far as possible, the sisters to wear white waists and dark skirts, also that the temple workers should be arrayed in white. (This request was carried out.)

The oldest son, John R. Winder, Jr., was so touched with the pain of his father that it seemed it was almost impossible for him to come into the room and visit him, and for that reason he never was by his bedside but a short time.

Night after night I have heard that man lying there on his bed dedicating himself to the Lord, and in these words he has ofttimes said: "O Lord, here I am—poor, weak mortal man that I am. Father, I am Thine; do with me as Thou wilt. If it be Thy will, O Lord, I am willing to stop my labor in this life; but, Lord, if it please Thee to take me unto Thyself, Father, I am ready. There is nothing in my heart, Father, but to say Thy will be done, not mine." Many and many a night has he said this, and many and many is the night that he has repeated this to me, and said: "Fred, remember in all your life, as long as you live in this world, that the Lord has the last say in everything. Remember that no matter what men may do, no matter what men may say, Fred, this is the Church and kingdom of God; this is God's work upon the earth."

During the last Sunday, or Easter Sunday, that President Winder was alive there seemed to be a marked improvement; in fact there never was a day during his sickness that there was more feeling of encouragement in the hearts of his family, and in the hearts of the doctors and the nurse, than there was on that day. On that Sunday afternoon, I told him that I was going to meeting and I would see him again. He took my hand in his and shook it. He said "God bless you; I know you will be back." He felt well and insisted on our going out, so the nurse and the rest of us went to meeting. . . His wife telephoned to his oldest son, John R. Winder, and asked him if he would be kind enough to come down and sit by his bedside until we returned. Of course he was more than glad to do this, as he had been on several occasions. When the closing hours came, John R. Winder, Jr., and Sister Winder were both sitting by his bedside.[49]

It was on Easter Sunday, March 27, 1910, that the 88-year-old President John Rex Winder passed away after battling pneumonia for nine weeks.[50] The old Colonel had been promised in his patriarchal blessing nearly 45 years prior that "It is thy privilege to tarry upon the earth until thou art satisfied with life."[51] John R. Winder, older than any of the general authorities that were serving with him, was finally satisfied with life and anxious to move on to his next field of labor.

Funeral and Burial

The following day, which was a Monday, saw Presidents Smith and Lund, along with all of the Twelve who were in the city, and a few of John R.'s close friends, meeting to talk over funeral matters. A committee consisting of Elder John Henry Smith, Richard W. Young, B. F. Grant, Charles W. Nibley, and Elias Smith were "appointed to arrange the funeral matters of Prest. John R. Winder." These brethren met and talked over the matter with the family that evening.[52] In the meantime, Presidents Smith and Lund sent the following message out to the officers and members of the Church:

> It is with feelings of sadness and regret that we are called upon to announce to you the death of President John R. Winder, our fellow servant and associate in the Quorum of the First Presidency of the Church of Jesus Christ of Latter-day Saints, which took place at his residence, No. 49 North West Temple Street, this city, at seven twenty o'clock last evening.[53]

In the days that followed Winder's death, tributes poured in from far and wide. Even the non-Mormon *Salt Lake Tribune* praised President Smith's right-hand man. "He may be said to have been better known than any other of the leaders of the sect," they reported, "and was the least dictatorial of any of them." The "Gentiles" of Salt Lake respected Winder for being "a shrewd business man, a wise financier, an active industrialist, and a maker of friends among all classes."[54] Elders Heber J. Grant and B. H. Roberts composed a tribute on behalf of the general board of the Young Men's Mutual Improvement Association which began, "In the life and character of the late President John R. Winder the young men of the Church of Jesus Christ of Latter-day Saints may see at once the triumphs of the gospel when applied to human life, and the value of human life when consecrated to the service of God and fellowmen."[55]

On Thursday, March 31, the day of the funeral, the committee met at 9 am at his home across the street from Temple Square. It was noted that "the undertaker removed the remains to the Tabernacle," with "Twelve of his grandsons acting as Paul bearers and guard of honor."[56] Winder's optimistic spirit prevailed to the last, for he requested that there be no "moaning at the bar when he put off to sea," and that his family should wear white instead of black at his funeral.[57]

A lover of music, President Winder's favorite hymns were sung at his funeral: "O my Father," "Who are these arrayed in white?" "'Mid scenes of confusion," "Rest for the weary soul," and "Zion stands with hills surrounded," the last being sung at the cemetery. The service in the Salt Lake Tabernacle began at 11 am on March 31, 1910. That thousands attended, including leading authorities from all parts of the Church, the governor and officers of the state, the mayor and officers of the city, judges and leading businessmen and citizens, was a testimony of the love and esteem in which he was held by all classes of people.[58]

Each of the speakers gave very emotional and heartfelt tributes to the Giant in the Kingdom whose passing they mourned:

W. W. Riter: "He was totally without guile; plain in deportment, and had only one standard—right and justice."

Bishop George Romney: "I feel I have lost one of my very best friends on earth. I know that Brother Winder was one of the best men that ever lived. He was satisfied that Jesus was the Redeemer of the world and that Joseph Smith was a prophet of the Most High God. He felt this truth through his entire system, and he believed it from the bottom of his heart."

B.F. Grant: "He has been true to every trust that has been given him in this life."

President Anthon H. Lund: "He was a wise counselor—a just man. He ever had a smile on his face. I learned to love him—I was proud of his confidence. His opinion was sought; his word was to be relied on and he spoke what he meant, and meant what he said."

Richard W. Young: "Colonel Winder had many of the qualities of a soldier—bravery, foresight and keen judgement. He was a man of strength, without harshness, a man pre-eminently just and considerate."

Former Governor Heber M. Wells: "Among his eminent characteristics were his perfectly wonderful industry and his untiring energy. He was good to the poor and ever kept his life sweet. He was a friend and an inspiration to the young man."

Nephi L. Morris: "I shall cherish his memory as long as I shall live."

President Francis M. Lyman: "He sought the Lord early, and was never forsaken. No man ever came more worthily into the First Presidency than he."

Elder Heber J. Grant: "John R. Winder has done more for me in the hours of trouble and financial stress than any other man that ever lived. I wrote him a letter the night before I left for Japan, pouring out my love for him, a letter such as I would not have dared to write to him after he became one of the first presidency, because it might have been misconstrued."

President Joseph F. Smith: "If any man loved him more than I do, I say God bless that man. In his military career and all other phases of his life, he never sought office nor honors; they were always in search of him. Heaven itself could scarcely be more true than President Winder was true."[59]

Seventy carriages loaded with people went to the cemetery, where more than two thousand gathered. The grave was dedicated by Bishop Franklin S. Tingey, and a large monument to "WINDER" was placed at the head of the family plot. The grand funeral, a fitting memorial service to a live well lived, cost $2,022.45.[60]

"It has been a most satisfactory funeral service," wrote Elder John Henry Smith in his journal that day. The following week in general conference, this friend of Winder's would be called to be the second counselor in the First Presidency, replacing Anthon H. Lund who was at that time promoted to first counselor. The vacancy thus created in the Twelve was filled by Joseph Fielding

The remains of John R. Winder rest in the Salt Lake City Cemetery next to three of his wives, his son John R. Winder, Jr., and daughter Florence Luella Winder Giles.

Smith, the son of the current Prophet, who would someday himself become the tenth president of the Church (1970-1972). One of the first acts of the new presidency was to clean out "President J. R. Winder's desk and sent his family the papers belonging to him," a melancholy reminder of the leader they so dearly loved.[61]

Aunt Rye and the family were well taken care of financially. John R. Winder's estate was valued at $146,710.17, a gigantic sum in 1910. By way of illustration, Winder's estate was seven times the size of Lorenzo Snow's when he died, and over three times the value of Apostle-Senator Reed Smoot's when he died in 1941. Of the leading brethren at that time, only Joseph F. Smith and George Q. Cannon left behind a larger inheritance.[62]

Once widowed, Aunt Rye continued to work in the temple for a time while serving on the General Primary Board (June 27, 1906 to March 24, 1911). Poplar Farm was sold to the Church where they built the Central Park Meetinghouse, and Rye moved into the bungalow on West Temple. One of her sisters and her husband moved in with her, and George Winder recalled delivering milk to her for several years. Aunt Rye was still a favorite of the Winder family, and she would faithfully attend the family reunions held at the Granite Stake House on 3300 South and State Street. When the Mesa Temple was dedicated in Arizona in 1927, Maria, who had moved there to be closer to her family, became an ordinance worker there. Later she became ill and moved to San Bernardino, California to live with a sister. After a long illness, Maria Burnham Winder, "Aunt Rye," the last of John R. Winder's four wives, left this earth to join her husband. It was May 14, 1948.[63]

15

The Legacy Left by President John R. Winder

"God bless his memory."

When President John R. Winder passed from mortality he left his old, pain-racked body and entered Paradise. The hosts on the other side would have welcomed this great man in a most triumphant manner. "Oh, the welcome that he will meet!" remarked his old friend George Romney at his funeral. "There are thousands that are in the spirit world who will bless his name, for he has been the instrument in redeeming them, taking them out of their prison house, opening unto them the door to eternal life. They will meet him on the other side; and such a meeting it will be! I sometimes almost envy him."[1] However, even in death Winder would not have ceased laboring to build the kingdom of God. "Many of our Prophets and Apostles have gone there [to preach in Spirit Prison]," he taught while in mortality. "There is an organization there, so that as soon as the ordinances are performed here, the parties are informed of it."[2] Can there be any doubt that John R. Winder immediately "rolled up his sleeves" and went to work in that heavenly organization? Edward Anderson summarized it best: "In the death of President John R. Winder, a strong man and remarkable pillar of the Church passed from the activities of this existence to new achievements in the world of spirits."[3]

Regarding those who have passed on, President Brigham Young taught that "They can see us, but we cannot see them unless our eyes were opened."[4] Is there any doubt, then, that President Winder gazes down from the heavens on occasion to observe how his posterity and the causes he fought for are faring?

On his death bed, John R. Winder told his friend B. F. Grant, "I desire above all other things in this world that my posterity, down to the last generation, may prove faithful and true to the work of God in the earth."[5] Similarly, in the invocation at President Winder's funeral, Joseph E. Taylor prayed, "We have heard him speak many times, our Father, manifesting great anxiety concerning the future of his family, and we pray Thee that Thy Holy Spirit may rest upon them and permeate their bosoms and influence them in thought and in feeling and desire, and prompt them in action, that they may be as faithful, as honorable, as pure as their ancestor, their father, their head, their patriarch." Elder Taylor continued, "We pray Thee, O Lord, that Thy servant may realize an answer to the anxiety that he has manifested and the many prayers he has offered in behalf of his offspring that they may prove themselves worthy of exaltation in Thy presence . . . that they may receive Thy recognition and have the honor of dwelling and associating with their father in the other world."[6]

In his patriarchal blessing, John R. Winder was promised that he would be placed "at the head of thy family, placed as a Father at the head of a numerous posterity which will be given thee."[7] Through his four wives he had 23 children, who in turn gave their father 107 grandchildren. At the time of this publication the seventh generation of the John R. Winder family is beginning to appear and his descendants literally number in the thousands. Indeed, he has been blessed with a numerous posterity. "I pray that the Lord may bless his children, his grandchildren, and his posterity, and grant that his name may never be lost from the face of the earth," said Bishop George Romney. "If they will be faithful they will meet with their good father again. I am as satisfied of that as I am that I am standing before you today."[8]

The posterity of President Winder has included scores of missionaries for the Church he so fervently believed in. They have produced dozens of bishops, members of stake presidencies, members of temple presidencies, patriarchs, mission presidents and regional representatives. Several descendants have labored in the temples, as sealers, just as their grandfather did before. Barbara Woodhead Winder, who married into the family, even served as the General Relief Society President from 1984 to 1990. President Winder surely smiles down on those furthering the cause of Mormonism, just as he did, despite their calling or position. Seeing The Church of Jesus Christ of Latter-day Saints with membership numbering ten million, and seeing that Church with over one hundred temples dotting the globe, certainly brings him great satisfaction.

He would surely be pleased to know that his descendants are organized as the Winder Family Organization and have diligently extended their ancestral line.

Thousands of names have been added to the family tree, some as far back as 200 B.C.

Grandfather Winder would have delighted in the many family reunions that have kept his family close.

President Winder had a great love for agriculture, and as "Father of the State Fair" would possibly be curious to see how that organization has fared. His son, William C. Winder, continued in his father's footsteps as a director on the Utah State Fair Board, and beginning in 1920 as its president. Under his able administration, the Fair expanded in size, number of exhibitors, and in prize money awarded. Many of the buildings that are presently standing were constructed while he was President. At his death in 1937, the Governor appointed William C. Winder's son George to the fair board. Other descendants of John R. Winder have also been involved in various committees of the State Fair, including Ned Winder who serves as Vice President of the Utah State Fair Foundation. President Winder was an active participant in the Pioneer Day Parade in Salt Lake

City, and Ned has also been heavily involved as the parade's head dispatcher and in other Days of '47 capacities.

In keeping with his love of dairying, Utah's pioneer dairyman would also be interested to see the Winder Dairy, which he began in 1880, still in the hands of his family. The dairy now delivers milk and nearly 100 other items to over 20,000 Utah homes, from Brigham City to St. George. The ownership is primarily held by a coalition of several descendants of John R. Winder. Gordon Liddle, the current company president, is his eldest great-great-grandson. His executive vice president, Kent Winder, is a direct descendant as well. Several sixth-generation members of the family also make up some of today's management.

John R. Winder loved Salt Lake City and loved the state of Utah. Typically involved in every festivity, Winder would certainly be pleased to see Salt Lake City hosting the world at the Winter Olympic Games in 2002. The quality of life in the city and state would also be impressive, although he would abhor any type of wastefulness, vandalism, or gangster activity. He would be pleased to see many of his descendants through the generations contribute through public service, just as he often did. Several of his posterity have served terms in the state legislature, on city councils, in leadership posts with chambers of commerce, on various civic committees, school boards, improvement district boards, and planning commissions, and in numerous volunteer capacities to improve their communities. One great-grandson, David K. Winder, has achieved distinction as a federal judge, and another Winder by the same first name presides over Utah's Office of Economic Development. Duty has stirred in the blood of many Winders, just as it did for many centuries prior in England, and just as it did with John R. Winder, himself.

William Riter said of President Winder, "His life and his character and his virtues are such that every person, whether of the Church to which he was devotedly attached, or of the state to which he has given so much of his time and talents, every citizen can find a standard of purity in his life and character which it would be well to adopt and follow. May God bless his memory. May it live in the affections of his friends and fellow citizens. May it live, as I know it will, in the hearts of his numerous posterity; and may his memory ever be held sacred and green by all who admire justice and righteousness."[9]

The LDS *Biographical Record* said that Winder was "a good citizen, devoted to his religion, and to the general interests of the people of his Church, and to the development of the State." Of Winder's place in history, they note, "His uprightness and integrity have won for him the respect and esteem of all the people of the West, and the career that he has made may well be an object of pride, alike to the Church and to his posterity."[10] Similarly, the Daughters of Utah Pioneers remember Winder as "a humble, kindly man; a man of faith and good works. He lived a complete life," they note, "devoted to the Church and to the interests of the State of Utah."[11]

Sadly, however, the memory of John R. Winder has dimmed with the passage of time. Periodically the local newspapers reminisced about President

Winder in the years following his death, and the *Deseret News' Church News* has featured an article about him on a couple of occasions, as well. Some excellent family histories have been done by Mary Winder Johnson, Ruth Winder Robertson, and Harlan Bangerter, among other members of the Winder Family Organization, but little academic work has been done on the man to put him in his rightful place in history. At a conference of the Mormon History Association entitled "Prophets' Right Hand Men," John R. Sillito gave a presentation entitled: *John R. Winder: Faithful Counselor, Builder of the Kingdom*. This presentation, given from a 14-page paper on the subject at Brigham Young University on May 11, 1984, was perhaps the first academic treatment of the life and character of John Rex Winder. These previous works all helped lay the groundwork for this project, the first published book on the man.

George Romney hoped "that [his] name may never be forgotten amongst the Saints of God,"[12] and it is the hope of the author that this work will help further that prayer. Winder's life was indeed significant, and he stands as a legitimate symbol of a time of important change and growth for the Church and the state of Utah. During Winder's time, the Mormon goal of building a social, economic, and political empire was gradually replaced by efforts toward doctrinal clarity and ecclesiastical reinvigoration. John R. Winder was a key figure in the Church's efforts to retain as many of their nineteenth-century goals as possible, a period where they met the challenges with what Leonard Arrington and Davis Bitton have aptly called "creative adjustment."[13] This adjustment, in which Winder played important roles, helped the Church maintain much of its uniqueness and prevented it from being dissolved into theological and cultural anonymity. The name of President John R. Winder should, and will, live on. His patriarchal blessing promised him: "Thy name and memory will be revered and handed down to the rising generation who will hear thy name down to the latest ages of posterity."[14]

As a teenager, Winder's son Ed was told by his father of his noble English heritage, of being a descendant of knights and ladies, of William the Conqueror and other royalty. "I got quite puffed up with pride when my father told me this," Ed said. "But that humble, sweet man said to me, 'I would not trade what I have for all of the kingdom of Great Britain. I know where my royalty comes from. It comes from God.'"[15] This is perhaps, the greatest distinction of President John Rex Winder, that despite being born with a noble pedigree, achieving the highest honors in business, political, and ecclesiastical life, he maintained his humility and his fervent testimony that God lives and attributed all of the glory to Him.

16
Wise Counsels
and Crisp Sayings

The Quotable John R. Winder

AMERICA

"The Latter Day Saints hold that America, the entire Western Hemisphere, is the land of Zion, 'a land choice above all other lands,' held in reserve for ages by the God of heaven for the accomplishment of the most glorious purposes, the climax of which is the advent of the millennial reign of peace and brotherly love."

— "Mormonism Not a Menace," *The National Magazine,*
(Boston and London) August 1902.

"We are taught to view the setting up of this nation as an act of divine providence, and as one of the steps preparatory to the ushering in of the millennium. The Constitution of the United States we believe to have been inspired of God, and the union of these states we look upon as a necessary condition in the carrying out of the divine program."

— "Mormonism Not a Menace," *The National Magazine*,
(Boston and London) August 1902.

"[I] regard Christopher Columbus, George Washington and Joseph Smith as heaven directed instruments, and the discovery of this land, the founding of this nation, and the establishment of the Church of Jesus Christ of Latter Day Saints as the greatest events in American history."

— "Mormonism Not a Menace," *The National Magazine*,
(Boston and London) August 1902.

COVENANTS

"Remember the covenants you have made — in the waters of baptism, and in the House of the Lord. Remember, O remember, to keep all your covenants — with yourself, with your families, with your brethren and with God! So will God remember you and yours, in the day when he makes up his jewels."

— *Improvement Era*, Volume 13, pp. 623-624.

"May the Lord bless you all and help us to be true and faithful to our covenants that we make in the house of the Lord, and everywhere else."

— Final words to the Saints in his final general conference, *Conference Report*, October, 1909.

DEBT

"Live within your means. Keep out of debt and you will keep out of trouble."

— Quoted in Mary Winder Johnson's sketch on JRW

"I have proposed never to go into debt. . . A person who has $100 a month salary is on the safe side if he lives on $90 a month, but if he spends $110 he is going down hill all the time. . . We may not always have sunshine, we may not always have prosperous times, and now is the time for us to trim our sails and keep as close to the shore as possible."

— *Conference Report*, October 6, 1903.

"It is said by some that we are going to have an era of prosperity. All right; let prosperity come, and if during that time we can get out of debt, we will rejoice that we are out of debt. But if, on the other hand, a time of adversity should come, and we are in the bondage of debt, what will be the result?"

— *Conference Report*, April 1903.

FAITHFULNESS

"It is a glorious work that we are engaged in; may we never tire of it, but always be willing and faithful in the discharge of every duty that is required of us."

— *Conference Report*, April 1904.

"Help me O Lord, I pray Thee, to be faithful and true the remainder of my days, that when I have finished my work, I may receive salvation in Thy kingdom."

— *Conference Report*, April 1907.

FASTING

"Don't you know that a blessing comes from fasting? It is not so much the dollars and cents as it is the blessing we are after, and unless we observe this we cannot expect the blessing."

— *Conference Report*, October 4, 1902.

GOD, OMNIPOTENCE OF

"Remember in all your life, as long as you live in this world, that the Lord has the last say in everything. Remember that no matter what men may do, no matter what men may say, this is the Church and kingdom of God; this is God's work upon the earth."

— Related at the Funeral Service of John R. Winder, page 9.

"This is His work, and His hand is stretched forth, and He will control all these matters to bring about the best results."

— *Conference Report*, April 1905.

GLORY TO GOD

"All that I am I owe to 'Mormonism.' The blessings of the Lord have followed me all the days of my life, and to Him I give the glory for what may have been accomplished through my humble endeavors."

— *Messages of the First Presidency*, volume 4, page 27.

HONESTY

"Be honest in your dealings with your own people, and with all the world beside."

— *Improvement Era*, Volume 13, page 624.

INDUSTRY

"My life has been a very busy one, a fact to which I believe I owe much of my longevity and present good health, and spirits. It is far better to wear out than to rust out, and my experiences and observation teach me that those who work, if they avoid excesses and live temperately, will outlive those who shirk."

— *Messages of the First Presidency*, Volume 4, page 27.

MAN'S DIVINE ORIGIN & DESTINY

"Man is the child of God, formed in the divine image and endowed with divine attributes, and even as the infant son of an earthly father and mother is capable in due time of becoming a man, so the undeveloped offspring of celestial parentage is capable, by experience through ages and aeons, of evolving into a God."

— Quoted along with Joseph F. Smith and Anthon H. Lund in
The Origin of Man

"Mormonism teaches, as Moses, Jesus and Paul taught, that man is in the image of God, and it therefore holds as a logical sequence that God is in the image of man, and that is, in the form of man; and that as a man, the child of God, is endowed with divine attributes, there is no reason why he should not by development, by progress unto perfection, become divine, like his Father in heaven. This is the meaning of celestial glory. They who attain to it are heirs of God and joint heirs with Jesus Christ, and in heaven they reign, while others serve."

— "Mormonism Not a Menace," *The National Magazine*,
(Boston and London) August 1902.

MORMONISM

Mormonism is to its adherents the ancient Christian religion, restored after centuries of absence, to prepare the way before the personal coming of the Son of God to reign as King of Kings over a sanctified earth. There is but one true religion, says Mormonism, though it has been upon the earth at different times and places, and from it have sprung all the truths contained in the many creeds and systems professed by men the world over."

— "Mormonism Not a Menace," *The National Magazine*,
(Boston and London) August 1902.

OBEDIENCE

"In the kingdom of heaven we will be willing to answer every call."

— Quoted in *A Ministry of Meetings: The Apostolic Diaries of Rudger Clawson*, p 364.

"Let us do it as well as say we will do it. If we will do so, the Lord will continue to bless and prosper us, no matter what transpires."

— *Conference Report*, April 1905.

PLAN OF SALVATION

"He proposes to save, as He has saved other worlds and their inhabitants, this world and its inhabitants, exalting to His own glorious presence all who will render themselves worthy of that ineffable reward."

— "Mormonism Not a Menace," *The National Magazine*, (Boston and London) August 1902.

PRAYER

"I have many times been compelled to seek the Lord in the hour of need, and I want to say today that I never failed to find Him. . . My dependence is on the Lord, and I propose to seek after His Spirit to guide and direct me."

— *Conference Report*, November 10, 1901

PRIDE

"Never seek for place or power, for fame or honor, lest you embitter another life with jealousy, or canker another heart with envy."

— *Improvement Era*, Volume 13, page 623.

SACRAMENT

"In relation to the administration of the Lord's supper, when visiting wards and stakes I have thought there is not that solemnity surrounding this ordinance that ought to be. It is a matter the presiding officers should look after."

— Conference Report, October 4, 1902.

"I believe we are too careless in relation to this ordinance. When the bread and the water are passed around, we are too apt to partake of it in a mechanical kind of way, without thinking of what we are doing."

— Conference Report, October 4, 1902.

SUSTAINING THE PROPHET

"The aim and object of my life from this time on will be to stand up and sustain my President as the Lord will give me strength and ability."

— Conference Report, April 4, 1902.

TEMPLE WORSHIP

"In the house of the Lord we are nearer heaven than in any other place."

— Quoted in *A Ministry of Meetings: The Apostolic Diaries of Rudger Clawson*, p 364.

"While the world is ridiculing and scoffing at what we are doing in the temples, I wish to say to you all, that every ordinance, every ceremony that is performed therein is of a sacred and holy character. Every ordinance performed there, makes better fathers, better mothers, better children, better citizens. Nothing occurs in that house that we need be ashamed of; but everything that takes place there is for the betterment of all who attend."

— Conference Report, April 6, 1903.

"How many of you in this congregation have relatives and friends on the other side waiting for you to do your work for them? Take this matter into consideration, and try to make an effort to carry on the work and release those who are waiting for you."

— Conference Report, April 4, 1902.

"Many of our Prophets and Apostles have gone there [to preach in Spirit Prison]. There is an organization there, so that as soon as the ordinances are performed here, the parties are informed of it."

— Conference Report, April 4, 1902.

"We ought to avail ourselves of the opportunity to obtain blessings in [the temples]. Remember the words of the Prophet Joseph, that it is the duty of every person to seek out their dead."

— Conference Report, October 4, 1902.

TESTIMONY

"I am thankful to the Lord that He has given me a testimony of the truth of this Gospel. I know that Joseph Smith was a prophet of God, and that he laid the foundation for this great work. This work will increase and multiply upon the earth."

— Conference Report, October 6, 1904.

"I was convinced of the truth when I heard it, and I knew that Joseph Smith was a prophet of God. I am thankful to say, this morning, that faith has grown and increased with me as the years have passed along; and every day I live I see new evidences of the truth of this work. I testify to you, my brethren and sisters, that I know that Joseph Smith is a prophet of God. I am thankful that this testimony has never left me since I first heard the Gospel more than sixty years ago."

— Conference Report, October 1909.

"Every day that I live I have renewed assurances that this is the work of the Lord, and that Joseph Smith is a Prophet of the Most High God. This testimony gives me joy, and strength, and satisfaction."

— Conference Report, October 1908.

"If we live near to the Lord, this testimony will continue to abide with us. This is the Lord's work that we are engaged in. The nearer I live to the Lord the more strength He gives me, and my faith in his promises is increased."

— Conference Report, October 1906.

TITHING

"This is a principle that I believe in with all my heart. I believe it is the duty of all faithful Latter-day Saints to pay their honest tithing and donations. . . We do receive blessings from the Lord by paying tithing; I know I have been blest by so doing; I can testify to that."

— *Conference Report,* October 1908.

TRUST IN THE LORD

"I realize that if we live near the Lord, this testimony will continue to abide with us. This is the Lord's work we are engaged in. The nearer I live to the Lord, the more strength He gives me, and my faith in His promises is increased. We may be feeble in our efforts, yet we know that when we are sustained by Him the work will progress."

— *Conference Report,* October 1906.

WHAT HE EXPECTS OF HIS POSTERITY

"This is the last dispensation of the gospel of Jesus Christ, which was revealed from Heaven through the prophet Joseph Smith for the salvation of all who would obey it. Therefore, remain true to the covenants which you have made or may make hereafter. Be steadfast in the truth, whether in adversity or prosperity, enduring faithful unto the end, is the most earnest admonition and desire of your father. — John Rex Winder."

— Penned in his daughter Lizzy's autograph book
shortly before his death.

Pedigree Chart
of John Rex Winder

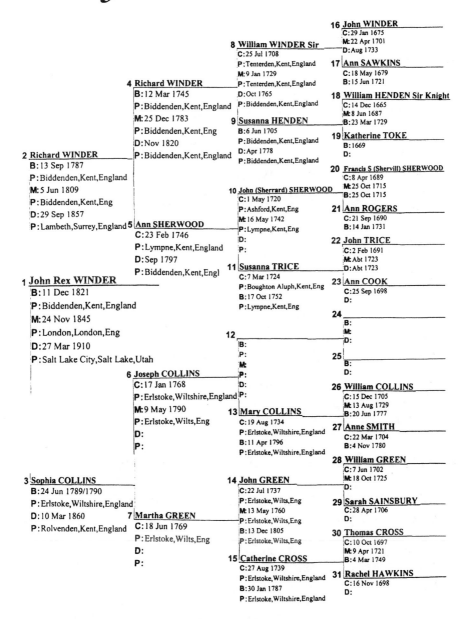

1 John Rex WINDER
B: 11 Dec 1821
P: Biddenden, Kent, England
M: 24 Nov 1845
P: London, London, Eng
D: 27 Mar 1910
P: Salt Lake City, Salt Lake, Utah

2 Richard WINDER
B: 13 Sep 1787
P: Biddenden, Kent, England
M: 5 Jun 1809
P: Biddenden, Kent, Eng
D: 29 Sep 1857
P: Lambeth, Surrey, England

3 Sophia COLLINS
B: 24 Jun 1789/1790
P: Erlstoke, Wiltshire, England
D: 10 Mar 1860
P: Rolvenden, Kent, England

4 Richard WINDER
B: 12 Mar 1745
P: Biddenden, Kent, England
M: 25 Dec 1783
P: Biddenden, Kent, Eng
D: Nov 1820
P: Biddenden, Kent, England

5 Ann SHERWOOD
C: 23 Feb 1746
P: Lympne, Kent, England
D: Sep 1797
P: Biddenden, Kent, Engl

6 Joseph COLLINS
C: 17 Jan 1768
P: Erlstoke, Wiltshire, England
M: 9 May 1790
P: Erlstoke, Wilts, Eng
D:
P:

7 Martha GREEN
C: 18 Jun 1769
P: Erlstoke, Wilts, Eng
D:
P:

8 William WINDER Sir
C: 25 Jul 1708
P: Tenterden, Kent, England
M: 9 Jan 1729
P: Tenterden, Kent, England
D: Oct 1765
P: Biddenden, Kent, England

9 Susanna HENDEN
B: 6 Jun 1705
P: Biddenden, Kent, England
D: Apr 1778
P: Biddenden, Kent, England

10 John (Sherrard) SHERWOOD
C: 1 May 1720
P: Ashford, Kent, Eng
M: 16 May 1742
P: Lympne, Kent, Eng
D:
P:

11 Susanna TRICE
C: 7 Mar 1724
P: Boughton Aluph, Kent, Eng
B: 17 Oct 1752
P: Lympne, Kent, Eng

12
B:
P:
M:
P:
D:
P:

13 Mary COLLINS
C: 19 Aug 1734
P: Erlstoke, Wiltshire, England
B: 11 Apr 1796
P: Erlstoke, Wiltshire, England

14 John GREEN
C: 22 Jul 1737
P: Erlstoke, Wilts, Eng
M: 13 May 1760
P: Erlstoke, Wilts, Eng
B: 13 Dec 1805
P: Erlstoke, Wilts, Eng

15 Catherine CROSS
C: 27 Aug 1739
P: Erlstoke, Wiltshire, England
B: 30 Jan 1787
P: Erlstoke, Wiltshire, England

16 John WINDER
C: 29 Jan 1675
M: 22 Apr 1701
D: Aug 1733

17 Ann SAWKINS
C: 18 May 1679
B: 15 Jun 1721

18 William HENDEN Sir Knight
C: 14 Dec 1665
M: 8 Jun 1687
B: 23 Mar 1729

19 Katherine TOKE
B: 1669
D:

20 Francis S (Shervill) SHERWOOD
C: 8 Apr 1689
M: 25 Oct 1715
B: 25 Oct 1715

21 Ann ROGERS
C: 21 Sep 1690
B: 14 Jan 1731

22 John TRICE
C: 2 Feb 1691
M: Abt 1723
D: Abt 1723

23 Ann COOK
C: 25 Sep 1698
D:

24
B:
M:
D:

25
B:
D:

26 William COLLINS
C: 15 Dec 1705
M: 13 Aug 1729
B: 20 Jun 1777

27 Anne SMITH
C: 22 Mar 1704
B: 4 Nov 1780

28 William GREEN
C: 7 Jun 1702
M: 18 Oct 1725
D:

29 Sarah SAINSBURY
C: 28 Apr 1706
D:

30 Thomas CROSS
C: 10 Oct 1697
M: 9 Apr 1721
B: 4 Mar 1749

31 Rachel HAWKINS
C: 16 Nov 1698
D:

The Families
of John Rex Winder

John Rex Winder as a Son

Father:	Richard Winder (1787-1857)
Mother:	Sophia Collins (1789-1860)
Brother:	Richard Winder (1809-1890)
	married Louisa Pooley (1848)
Sister:	Sophia Winder (1812-1835)
Brother:	John Rex Winder (1814-1819)
Sister:	Matilda Winder (1817-1850)
	married William Parten Betsworth (1850)
Sister:	Elizabeth Winder (1819-?)
	married Stephen Ward (1847)
Self:	John Rex Winder (1821-1910)
	married Ellen Walters (1845),
	Hannah Ballantyne Thompson (1855),
	Elizabeth Parker (1857),
	and Maria Burnham (1893)
Brother:	William Henden Winder (1824-1855)
	married Caroline Smith (1847)
Sister:	Ann Winder (1827-?)
Sister:	Eliza Winder (1829-1863)
Brother:	Frederick Winder (1833)

John Rex Winder's First Wife and Their Family

Husband:	John Rex Winder (1821-1910)
Wife:	Eleanor or Ellen Walters (1822-1892)
Daughter:	Ellen Sophia Winder (1847-1848)
Son:	John Rex Winder, Jr. (1848-1923)
Son:	Alma Winder (1850-1852)
Daughter:	Mary Ann Winder [Twin] (1852-1936)
	married Charles Carrington (1872)

Daughter:	Martha Walters Winder [Twin] (1852-1930)
	married Newell Whitney Kimball (1870)
Daughter:	Emily Winder (1854-1855)
Daughter:	Lizzie Walters Winder (1856-1874)
Daughter:	Eliza Ann Winder (1858-1946)
	married John George Midgley (1879)
Son:	Frederick William Winder (1860)
Daughter:	Susan Sophia Winder (1861-1951)
	married Thomas Allan Williams (1883)

John Rex Winder's Second Wife and Their Family

Husband:	John Rex Winder (1821-1910)
Wife:	Hannah Ballantyne Thompson (1835-1919)
Son:	William Winder (1858)
Son:	Henry Winder (1859)
Daughter:	Anna Jane Winder (1860-1942)
	married Reuben G. Miller (1884)

John Rex Winder's Third Wife and Their Family

Husband:	John Rex Winder (1821-1910)
Wife:	Elizabeth Parker (1837-1883)
Son:	William Charles Winder (1858-1937)
	married Rosalie Romney Taylor (1883)
Daughter:	Alice Ellen Winder (1860-1920)
	married William Bradford (1882)
Son:	Richard Henry Winder (1862-1936)
	married Mary Emma Cahoon (1887)
Daughter:	Mary Ann Winder (1865-1943)
Son:	Edwin Joseph Winder (1867-1949)
	married Ada Calder (1898)
Daughter:	Florence Luella Winder (1869-1944)
	married James Joseph Giles (1911)
Daughter:	Matilda Edna Winder (1871-1953)
	married Reuben Seaburn Hamilton (1894)
Daughter:	Ella May Winder (1875-1949)
	married Walter Scott Mackay (1897)

Daughter: Gertrude Winder (1877-1925)
                               married Mark Young Croxall (1900)
Son: Rex Parker Winder (1878-1967)
                               married Thurza Malisea Malin (1924)

John Rex Winder's Fourth Wife

Husband: John Rex Winder (1821-1910)
Wife: Maria Burnham (1869-1948)

Endnotes

Chapter 1

1. Isaac Marley, *Patriarchal Blessing of John Rex Winder*, 31 December 1858, no. 107. In possession of LDS Historical Department, Salt Lake City.
2. Patrick Hanks & Flavia Hodges, *A Dictionary of Surnames* (Oxford: Oxford University Press, 1988), 578.
3. Basil Cottle, *The Penguin Dictionary of Surnames* (New York: Penguin Books, 1984), 426.
4. Richard McKinley, *The Surnames of Sussex* (London: Leopard's Head Press, 1988), 171.
5. Cottle, *op. cit.*, 426.
6. Arch Fredric Blakey, *General John H. Winder, C.S.A.* (Gainesville: University of Florida Press, 1990), 145.
7. Letter to the author from Carol Winder Tidy of Erith, Kent, England; 23 April 1999.
8. Michael Wood, *Domesday, a Search for the Roots of England* (New York: Facts on File Publications, 1986), 159.
9. Christopher Daniell, *A Traveler's History of England* (New York: Interlink Books, 1993), 45.
10. McKinley, *op. cit.*, 171-172.
11. *Sussex Archaeological Collections,* (Lewes: The Sussex Archaeological Society, 1991), vol. 129, p. 252.
12. See J. Cornwall, *Lay Subsidy Rolls for the County of Sussex,* 1524-25 (Lewes: Sussex Record Society, 1956), vol. 1-vi, pp. 5, 212, 324.; E. J. Courthope and B. E. R. Fermoy, *Lathe Court Rolls and Views of Frankpledge in the Rape of Hastings* (Lewes: Sussex Record Society, 1934), vol. xxxvii, 123.; *Sussex Archaeological Collections,* vol. 1-xxiv., 71.; M.T. Loefvenberg, *Studies on Middle English Local Surnames* (1942), 232.
13. *Sussex Archaeological Collections, op. cit.*, vol. 129, p. 252.
14. A. Mower and F. M. Stenton, *The Place-Names of Sussex,* (Cambridge: University Press, 1930), 501.
15. Sussex Public Record Office, 179/235/2 and p. 9.
16. A. Mower and F. M. Stenton, *op. cit.*, 533.
17. Ronald and Frank Jessup, *The Cinque Ports* (London: B . T. Batsford, Ltd., 1952), 19.
18. *Ibid.*
19. F. Hull, *Calendar of the White and Black Books of the Cinque Ports* (1966), p. xxx.

20. J. Manwaring Baines, *Historic Hastings* (St. Leonards-on-Sea, East Sussex: Cinque Port Press Ltd., 1986), 25-26.
21. Hull, *ibid.*
22. Jessup, *op. cit.*, 21.
23. Baines, *ibid.*
24. Hull, *op. cit.*, pp. 55, 60, 68, 74, 75, 87.
25. *Sussex Archaeological Collections,* vol. 95, p. 57.
26. Hull, *op. cit.*, pp. 55, 60, 68, 74, 75, 87.
27. *Sussex Notes and Queries,* vol. 8, p. 320.
28. Genealogical information regarding Richard Wynder and his descendants has been derived from records of the John R. Winder Family Organization, Jeanne M. Jensen, researcher, Murray, Utah. See also www.familysearch.org.
29. Gordon J. Copley, ed., *Surrey & Sussex* (London: Hutchinson, 1977), 65.
30. Ronald F. Jessup, *Sussex* (London: Methuen & Co., Ltd., 1949), 92.
31. Esther Meynell, *Sussex* (London: Robert Hale, Ltd., 1947), 133.
32. Meynell, *ibid.*
33. Jonathan B. Tourtellot, ed., *Discovering Britain and Ireland* (Washington, D.C., National Geographic Society, 1985), 128.
34. Richard Church, *Kent* (London: Robert Hale, Ltd., 1948), 270.
35. Walter Jerrold, *Highways and Byways in Kent* (London: Macmillan and Co., 1926), 210.
36. Church, *ibid.*
37. G. E. Mingay, *The Gentry: The Rise and Fall of a Ruling Class* (London: Longman, 1976), 6.
38. J. V. Beckett, *The Aristocracy in England* 1660-1911 (Oxford: Basil Blackwell Ltd., 1986), 103.
39. Mingay, *op. cit.,* 110.
40. *Ibid.,* 109.
41. Beckett, *op. cit.*, 104.
42. *Ibid.*
43. Beckett, *op. cit.*, 103.
44. Edward Hasted, *History of the County of Kent* (1822), 132.
45. Alan Everitt, *The Community of Kent and the Great Rebellion 1640-60* (Leicester: Leicester University Press, 1966), 32.
46. John R. Winder Family Organization, *ibid.*
47. Mingay, *op. cit.*, 108.
48. Ruth Winder Robertson, *Family History for Children* (Salt Lake City, 1985), Foreword.
49. Beckett, *op. cit.*, 104.

50. *Ibid.*, 103.
51. Conversation with the author during the week of July 4, 1992, Kent, England.
52. Everitt, *op. cit.*, 42.
53. Mingay, *op. cit.*, 188.
54. *Ibid.*, 58.
55. *Ibid.*, 2.
56. Virginia C. Kenny, *The Country-House Ethos in English Literature 1688-1750. Themes of Personal Retreat and National Expansion* (New York: St. Martin's Press, 1984), 6.
57. *Ibid.*
58. Report of Funeral Services in Honor of President John R. Winder, 31 March 1910, copy in author's possession.

Chapter 2

1. Biddenden Local History Society, *The Story of Biddenden* (Maidstone, England: Young & Cooper Ltd., 1989), 1.
2. Robertson, *op. cit.*, 9, 10, 12.
3. *Ibid.*
4. *Ibid.*
5. Everitt, *op. cit.*, 33.
6. Canterbury marriage register, mentioned in Parley H. Liddle, ed., Minutes of the Winder Family Genealogical Organization, 1993. Minutes of May 13, 1973 meeting.
7. Mingay, *op. cit.*, 111.
8. Will of William Winder of Biddenden, Kent, dated 17 Oct. 1765, Proved at Canterbury 30 May 1766.
9. Harlan L. Bangerter, *William C. Winder Family History* (Salt Lake City: Winder Family Association, 1981), i.
10. Robertson, *op. cit.*, 12. Emphasis added.
11. *Improvement Era* 13 (May, 1910): 617, 619; Winder Family Association, *op. cit.*, ii.
12. Peter Grieg, "A House With A Story" (Article in English newspaper clipping in possession of the author, newspaper unknown, 1971).
13. *Improvement Era, ibid.*
14. Hasted, *op. cit.*, 132-33.
15. "Home Buyer," 24 April 1992, a supplement to the *Courier Chronicle*, Kent, England.
16. Biddenden Place histories are found in Grieg, *ibid.*; Hasted, *ibid.*; *The Story of Biddenden* (1953), 12, 16.; "Home Buyer," *ibid.*; Biddenden Local History Society, *op. cit.*, 17-19.; John D. Wood & Co., Biddenden Place (London: a real estate brochure, 1992).

17. Grieg, *ibid.*
18. Mingay, *op. cit.*, 108.
19. Kenny, *op. cit.*, 3.
20. *Ibid.*, 206.
21. Will of Richard Winder of Biddenden, Kent, dated 25 April 1820, Proved at Canterbury 20 Feb. 1821.
22. Latter-day Saints' *Millennial Star* 71:811.
23. Bangerter, William, *ibid.*
24. James R. Clark, ed., *Messages of the First Presidency of The Church of Jesus Christ of Latter-day Saints,* volume four, 1901-1915 (Salt Lake City: Bookcraft, 1970), 24.
25. Report of Funeral Services in Honor of President John R. Winder, *op. cit.*, 11.
26. Stephen Neill, *Anglicanism* (New York: Oxford University Press, 1977), 231.
27. Biddenden Parochial Church Council, *Biddenden: A Newcomer's Guide* (Biddenden: Biddenden Parochial Church Council, 1991), 1.
28. Everitt, *op. cit.*, 27-28.
29. Barry Reay, *Microhistories, demography, society and culture in rural England,* 1800-1930 (Cambridge: Cambridge University Press, 1996), 228.
30. Robertson, *op. cit.*, 13.
31. W. W. Riter, et. al., *Birthday Reception In Honor of President John R. Winder on the Eighty-second Anniversary of His Birth* (Salt Lake City, 1903), 32-33.
32. *Improvement Era* 13, *op. cit.*, 618.
33. Reay, *op. cit.*, 73.
34. Clark, *ibid.*
35. S. L. Ollard, ed., *A Dictionary of English Church History* (London: A. R. Mowbray and Co., Ltd., 1912), 91.
36. *Ibid.*, 288-89.
37. *Ibid.*
38. Richard H. Wood, *A Cyclopedic Dictionary of Ecclesiastical Terms According to the Use of the Episcopal Church* (New York: Carlton Press, 1984), 136-38.
39. Ollard, *op. cit.*
40. *Ibid.*
41. Mary Winder Johnson, *John Rex Winder* (Salt Lake City, unpublished manuscript), 1.
42. Bangerter, William, *op. cit.*, ii.
43. Ollard, *op. cit.*, 288.
44. *Biographical Record*, 18.
45. Mingay, *op. cit.*, 105.
46. "Home Buyer," *op. cit.*
47. *Young Woman's Journal* 21 (1910), 271.

48. Riter, *op. cit.*, 32.

49. "Home Buyer," *op. cit.*

50. *Improvement Era* 13, *op. cit.*, 618.

51. Clark, *op. cit.*, 24.

52. *Conference Report,* October 1908.

53. Everitt, *op. cit.*, 28.

54. Reay, *op. cit.*, 228.

55. Clark, *Ibid.*

56. Nigel Yates, et. al., *Religion and Society in Kent, 1640-1914* (Woodbridge, England: The Boydell Press, 1994), 91.

57. *Biographical Record, Ibid.*

58. Report of Funeral Services in Honor of President John R. Winder, *op. cit.*, 15.

59. *Ibid.*, 10, 15.

60. *Ibid.*

61. Interview with the author, 26 September 1993, Salt Lake City.

62. Reay, *op. cit.*, 215, 218.

63. S. A. Kenner, *Utah As It Is* (Salt Lake City: Deseret News, 1904), 365.

64. Bangerter, William, *op. cit.*, 49-50.

65. Clark, *op. cit.*, 24.

66. Kenner, *op. cit.*, 365.

Chapter 3

1. G. M. Trevelyan, quoted in Mingay, *op. cit.*, xii.

2. Mingay, *op. cit.*, 80.

3. *Ibid.*, 165.

4. *Ibid.*, 168.

5. Christening records of Matilda, Elizabeth, William Henden, & John Rex Winder.

6. Robertson, *op. cit.*, 12-13.

7. John D. Wood & Co., *Ibid.*

8. Biddenden Parochial Church Council, *op. cit.*, 6.

9. Bangerter, William, *op. cit.*, ii.

10. Mingay, *op. cit.*, 165.

11. Neill, *op. cit.*, 230.

12. Dan Levine, *London '94-'95 on $45 a Day* (New York: Prentice Hall Travel, 1993), 8.

13. *Ibid.*

14. Bangerter, William, *Ibid.*

15. Tourtellot, *op. cit.*, 16.

16. *Ibid.*, 30.

17. Levine, *Ibid.*

18. *Young Woman's Journal* 21, p. 271.
19. James T. White & Company, *The National Cyclopaedia of American Biography,* Vol. 16 (Ann Arbor: University Microfilms, 1967), 14.
20. *Utah. The Inland Empire* (Salt Lake City: Deseret News, 1902), 16.
21. Christening records of Matilda, Elizabeth, & William Henden Winder.
22. June Swann, *Shoes* (New York: Drama Book Publishers, 1984), 43.
23. quoted in *Ibid.*
24. *Ibid.*, 42.
25. Robertson, *op. cit.*, 14.
26. Clark, *op. cit.*, 24.
27. *Young Woman's Journal* 21, *op. cit.*, 271.
28. Adelaide Eldredge Hardy, quoted in Mary Winder Johnson, *Wives of John R. Winder,* unpublished manuscript.
29. *Ibid.*
30. Harlan L. Bangerter, *John R. Winder Family History, part 2* (Salt Lake City: Winder Family Association, 198?), EWW 1.
31. Robertson, *op. cit.*, 13.
32. Hardy, *Ibid.*
33. Bangerter, John, *op. cit.*
34. Robertson, *Ibid.*
35. Hardy, *Ibid.*
36. Bangerter, William, *op. cit.*, ii.
37. Bangerter, John, *Ibid.*
38. Bangerter, William, *Ibid.*
39. Levine, *Ibid.*
40. *Ibid.*
41. Bangerter, John, *op. cit.*
42. Hardy, *Ibid.*
43. B. H. Roberts, *A Comprehensive History of the Church of Jesus Christ of Latter-day Saints,* vol. 3 (Provo, Utah: Brigham Young University Press, 1965), 396.
44. Johnson, *John Rex Winder*, *op. cit.*, 1.
45. Hardy, *Ibid.*
46. White, *op. cit.*
47. see *Utah: The Inland Empire, Ibid.*; and Orson F. Whitney, "President John R. Winder" in *The Juvenile Instructor* 45 (1910): 215.
48. Bangerter, John, *op. cit.*
49. Bangerter, William, *Ibid.*
50. Johnson, *Wives of John R. Winder, op. cit.*
51. Johnson, *John Rex Winder*, *op. cit.*
52. Tourtellot, *op. cit.*, 263.

Chapter 4

1. Tourtellot, *op. cit.*, 264.
2. *Ibid.*
3. V. Ben Bloxham, et. al., ed. *Truth Will Prevail. The Rise of The Church of Jesus Christ of Latter-day Saints in the British Isles 1837-1987* (Cambridge: University Press, 1987), 444.
4. *Ibid.*, 213.
5. Daniel H. Ludlow, ed., *Encyclopedia of Mormonism* (New York: Macmillan Publishing Co., 1990), 228.
6. *Ibid.*, 213.
7. Roberts, *op. cit.*, 396.
8. *Biographical Record, op. cit.*, 18.
9. Johnson, Wives, *op. cit.*
10. Johnson, *John Rex Winder, op. cit.*, 2.
11. The Juvenile Instructor 45, *op. cit.*, 215.
12. Clark, *op. cit.*, 25.
13. Bangerter, John, *op. cit.*, EWM 1.
14. Riter, *op. cit.*, 33.
15. Clark, *Ibid.*
16. Riter, *Ibid.*
17. Richard Wallace Sadler, *The Life of Orson Spencer* (Salt Lake City: Master's Thesis at the University of Utah, 1965), 53-54.
18. Clark, *op. cit.*, 25.
19. Quoted in Johnson, *Wives, Ibid.*
20. Bangerter, John, *Ibid.*
21. Clark, *Ibid.*
22. "From Shoe Clerk to Presidency—John R. Winder," *Deseret News,* March 10, 1962, *Church News,* p. 16.
23. Bangerter, John, *Ibid.*
24. Clark, *Ibid.*
25. Sadler, *op. cit.*, 52.
26. Clark, *Ibid.*
27. Sadler, *op. cit.*, 54-55.
28. Clark, *Ibid.*
29. Bangerter, John, *Ibid.*
30. *Millennial Star* 71, p. 811.
31. *Deseret News, Ibid.*
32. The Eightieth Semi-Annual Conference of the Church of Jesus Christ of Latter-day Saints (Salt Lake City: *Deseret News,* 1909), 9.
33. quoted in Johnson, *Wives, Ibid.*

34. Bangerter, John, *Ibid.*
35. Robertson, *op. cit.*, 14.
36. *The Young Woman's Journal,* 21, *Ibid.*
37. Sadler, *Ibid.*
38. Kenner, *op. cit.*, 365.
39. Robertson, *op. cit.*, 14.
40. Bangerter, John, *Ibid.*
41. *The Juvenile Instructor* 45, *Ibid.*
42. Clark, *op. cit.*, 24.
43. quoted in Johnson, *Wives, Ibid.*
44. *The Young Woman's Journal,* 21, *Ibid.*
45. Seventy-Eighth Annual Conference of The Church of Jesus Christ of Latter-day Saints (Salt Lake City: *Deseret News,* 1908), 8.
46. Clark, *op. cit.*, 24.
47. Bangerter, John, *Ibid.*
48. Bloxham, *op. cit.*, 204-205, 214, 442.
49. Robertson, *Ibid.*
50. *Millennial Star* 38, p. 448.
51. Hardy, *Ibid.*
52. Bangerter, John, *Ibid.*
53. William E. Berrett, *The Restored Church. A Brief History of the Growth and Doctrines of the Church of Jesus Christ of Latter-day Saints,* (Salt Lake City: Deseret Book, 1961), 303-304.
54. Roberts, *op. cit.*, 396.
55. John R. Winder, Letter, Oct 31, 1902, Salt Lake City, Utah, to Annie T. Hyde, Salt Lake City. Located at LDS Church Archives, Salt Lake City.
56. C. H. Wallace, et. al., Testimonial Presented to Elder John Rex Winder Secretary of the Liverpool Conference of the Church of Jesus Christ of Latter-day Saints by the Saints of the Said Conference on His Departure for Great Salt Lake City N. A. (Liverpool, 1853). Print of original in author's possession.
57. S. George Ellsworth, *Samuel Claridge: Pioneering the Outposts of Zion,* (Logan, Utah: S. George Ellsworth, 1987), 35.
58. Richard L. Jensen and Malcolm R. Thorp, ed., *Mormons in Early Victorian Britain,* (Salt Lake City: University of Utah Press, 1989), 206.
59. Bloxham, *op. cit.*, 442, 444.
60. *Ibid.*, 205.
61. *Ibid.*, 209.
62. Taylor, *op. cit.*, 271.
63. Bloxham, *op. cit.*, 165.
64. Latter-day Saints' *Millennial Star,* xxiii. 141 (2 Mar. 1861).

Chapter 5

1. Bloxham, *op. cit.*, 165.
2. Ludlow, *op. cit.*, 229.
3. Bloxham, *op. cit.*, 213-14.
4. Ludlow, *op. cit.*, 673.
5. Bloxham, *op. cit.*, 192.
6. Wallace, *Ibid.*
7. Johnson, *Wives, Ibid.*
8. Bangerter, John, *Ibid.*
9. Riter, *op. cit.*, 34.
10. Johnson, *Wives, Ibid.*
11. Riter, *Ibid.*
12. Bangerter, William, *op. cit.*, iii.
13. Bangerter, John, *op. cit.*, EWM 1.
14. Bangerter, William, *Ibid.*
15. Photo of original document in author's possession.
16. Kenner, *op. cit.*, 365.
17. *Biographical Record, op. cit.*, 18.
18. Bloxham, *op. cit.*, 178.
19. *Ibid.*, 214.
20. Bangerter, William, *op. cit.*, iv.
21. Sonne, *Ibid.*
22. James B. Allen and Glen M. Leonard, *The Story of the Latter-day Saints,* (Salt Lake City: Deseret Book, 1992), 291.
23. Dickens quoted in Ludlow, *op. cit.*, 229.
24. Conway B. Sonne, *Ships, Saints, and Mariners: A Maritime Encyclopedia of Mormon Migration 1830-1890,* (Salt Lake City: University of Utah Press, 1987), 66.
25. Frederick Hawkins Piercy, *Route from Liverpool to Great Salt Lake Valley,* (Cambridge, Mass.: Harvard University Press, 1962), 63-64.
26. Sonne, *Ibid.*
27. Robertson, *op. cit.*, 15.
28. Clark, *Ibid.*
29. Bangerter, John, *op. cit.*, EWM 1.
30. Riter, *op. cit.*, 34.
31. Bangerter, William, *op. cit.*, iv.
32. Robertson, *Ibid.*
33. Bangerter, John, *op. cit.*, EWW 2.
34. Bangerter, William, *Ibid.*
35. Taylor, *Ibid.*

36. Bangerter, John, *Ibid.*

37. Ludlow, *op. cit.*, 675.

38. Jensen, *op. cit.*, 245.

39. *Ibid.*, 247.

40. Ludlow, *Ibid.*

41. P.A.M. Taylor, *Expectations Westward: The Mormons and the Emigration of their British Converts in the Nineteenth Century* (Edinburgh: Oliver & Boyd, 1965), 178.

42. Kate B. Carter, ed., *Our Pioneer Heritage* (Salt Lake City: Daughters of the Utah Pioneers, 1968), vol. XI, 164.

43. Sonne, *Ibid.*

44. Piercy, *op. cit.*, 67.

45. *Ibid.*, 65, 68.

46. *Ibid.*

47. Sonne, *Ibid.*

48. Kate B. Carter, ed., *Our Pioneer Heritage* (Salt Lake City: Daughters of the Utah Pioneers, 1967), vol. X, 125.

49. Taylor, *op. cit.*, 209.

50. Piercy, *op. cit.*, 69.

51. Taylor, *Ibid.*

52. Clark, *op. cit.*, 24.

53. Frank Freidel, Our Country's Presidents (Washington D.C.: National Geographic Society, 1981), 89-90.

54. Sonne, *Ibid.*

55. Jensen, *op. cit.*, 247.

56. Anastasia Redmond Mills, ed., *Fodor's New Orleans* (New York: Fodor's Travel Publications, Inc., 1997), 170, 174.

57. Taylor, *op. cit.*, 209-210.

58. Piercy, *op. cit.*, 71.

59. Taylor, *op. cit.*, 209-210.

60. Carter, vol. XI, *op. cit.*, 164.

61. Mark Twain, *Life on the Mississippi,* (New York: Penguin Books, 1986), 65.

62. S. George Ellsworth, *Samuel Claridge: Pioneering the Outposts of Zion,* (Logan: 1987), 30.

63. Taylor, *op. cit.*, 210-211.

64. Ellsworth, *Ibid.*

65. Bangerter, John, *op. cit.*, EWW 2.

66. Kenner, *op. cit.*, 365.

67. Carter, vol. xi, *op. cit.*, 164.

68. William R. Sanford & Carl R. Green, *Missouri,* (Chicago: Childrens Press, 1993), 94, 124.
69. Carter, vol. X, *Ibid.*
70. Taylor, *op. cit.*, 211.
71. Ellsworth, *Ibid.*
72. Carter, vol. X, *Ibid.*
73. Ellsworth, *op. cit.*, 30.
74. Allan Carpenter, *Iowa* (Chicago: Children's Press, 1979), 84.
75. Ellsworth, *op. cit.*, 30.
76. *Ibid.*
77. quoted in Ellsworth, *op. cit.*, 31.
78. Ludlow, *op. cit.*, 675.
79. Bloxham, *op. cit.*, 179.
80. *Journal History,* 22 September 1853, 7.
81. Carter, vol. Xl, *op. cit.*, 164.
82. Piercy, *op. cit.*, 91.
83. Ellsworth, *Ibid.*
84. James A. Bennett, *Hereford History in Utah: With Brief Reviews of Cattle Industry History in Utah and the United States* (Logan: Utah Hereford Association, 1976), 14-15.
85. *Journal History,* 22 September 1853, 7.
86. Piercy, *op. cit.*, 94.
87. quoted in Ellsworth, *op. cit.*, 33.
88. *Ibid.*
89. *Doctrine and Covenants of the Church of Jesus Christ of Latter-day Saints,* (Salt Lake City: The Church of Jesus Christ of Latter-day Saints, 1988), 136: 2-5.
90. *Journal History,* 10 October 1853, 1.
91. Ellsworth, *op. cit.*, 33-34.
92. *Journal History,* 10 October 1853, 1.
93. Ellsworth, *op. cit.*, 34.
94. *Journal History,* 10 October 1853, 1.
95. Ellsworth, *op. cit.*, 35-37.
96. Carter, vol. III, *op. cit.*, 38.
97. *Ibid.*, 39.
98. Ellsworth, *op. cit.*, 40.
99. *Ibid.*, 39.
100. Carter, vol. III, *op. cit.*, 39.
101. Ellsworth, *op. cit.*, 40.
102. *Ibid.*, 38.
103. Carter, vol. III, *op. cit.*, 39.

104. Bangerter, John, *op. cit.*, EWM 1.

105. Ellsworth, *op. cit.*, 41.

106. *Ibid.*, 42.

107. *Ibid.*

108. *Ibid.*

109. Ellsworth, *op. cit.*, 44.

110. Carter, vol. III, *op. cit.*, 40-41.

111. *Journal History,* 10 October 1853, 27-28.

112. *Ibid.*

113. Bangerter, William, *op. cit.*, iv.

Chapter 6

1. Clark, *op. cit.*, 26.

2. Ellsworth, *op. cit.*, 50.

3. Ludlow, *op. cit.*, 675.

4. Bangerter, John, *op. cit.*, EWM 1.

5. *Ibid.*

6. Ellsworth, *op. cit.*, 50-51.

7. Bangerter, William, *op. cit.*, iv-v.

8. Robertson, *op. cit.*, 15.

9. Bangerter, William, *Ibid.*

10. Frank Taylor, *Young Woman's Journal* 21 (Salt Lake City: Deseret News, 1910), 271.

11. Bangerter, John, *op. cit.*, EWM 1.

12. *Ibid.*, EWW 2.

13. Report of Funeral Services in Honor of President John R. Winder, 31 March 1910, 5, copy in author's possession.

14. Johnson, *Wives, op. cit.*, 2.

15. Ellsworth, *op. cit.*, 47.

16. W. W. Riter, et. al., Birthday Reception In Honor of President John R. Winder on the Eighty-second Anniversary of His Birth (Salt Lake City, 1903), 27-28.

17. Report of Funeral Services in Honor of President John R. Winder, 31 March 1910, 7, copy in author's possession.

18. Clark, *op. cit.*, 26.

19. *Ibid.*

20. Leonard J. Arrington, "Economic Development in Early Utah"; S. Kent Brown, et. al., eds., *Historical Atlas of Mormonism* (New York: Simon & Schuster, 1994).

21. Clark, *op. cit.*, 26.

22. *Ibid.*

23. Kate B. Carter, *Heart Throbs of the West: A Unique Volume Treating Definite Subjects of Western History,* Vol. 3 (Salt Lake city: Daughters of Utah Pioneers, 1948), 78.

24. Preston Nibley, "John R. Winder Was Prominent Church Worker and Official," *Deseret News,* 22 Jan. 1955.

25. Carter, *Heart Throbs, op. cit.,* 217.

26. Kenner, *op. cit.,* 365.

27. Carter, *Heart Throbs, op. cit.,* 201.

28. George Winder, *Ibid.*

29. Bangerter, William, *op. cit.,* v.

30. Bangerter, John, *op. cit.,* EWM 1.

31. Ellsworth, *op. cit.,* 51.

32. Robertson, *op. cit.,* 16.

33. Bangerter, John, *op. cit.,* EWW 2.

34. Johnson, Wives, *op. cit.,* 2.

35. Andrew Jenson, *Latter-Day Saint Biographical Encyclopedia,* vol. I (Salt Lake City: Andrew Jenson History Company, 1901), 244-245.

36. *Ibid.*

37. *Biographical Record, op. cit.,* 18.

38. Clark, *Ibid.*

39. "In Old Salt Lake," unknown publication (*Deseret News*?), 1902, 13.

40. Andrew Jenson, *Latter-Day Saint Biographical Encyclopedia,* vol. 11 (Salt Lake City: Andrew Jenson History Company, 1914), 501.

41. *Ibid.*

42. Carter, *Heart Throbs, op. cit.,* 217.

43. "In Old Salt Lake," *Ibid.*

44. Jenson, II, *op. cit.,* 502.

45. "In Old Salt Lake," *Ibid.*

46. Leonard J. Arrington, *Great Basin Kingdom: An Economic History of the Latter-day Saints, 1830-1900,* (Cambridge: Harvard University Press, 1958), 162, 167.

47. Hannah Thompson Brower, Record of the Life of Hannah Thompson, (ca. 1911), 20.

48. *Ibid.,* 22.

49. Annie Clark Tanner, *A Mormon Mother,* (Salt Lake City: Tanner Trust Fund, 1976), 62.

50. Bangerter, .John *op. cit.,* EWM 1.

51. Tanner, *Ibid.*

52. *Ibid.*

53. Bangerter, William, *op. cit.,* v.; Bangerter, John, *op. cit.,* EWW 2.

54. Brower, *op. cit.,* 19-20.

55. Johnson, Wives, *op. cit.*, 2-3.
56. Brower, *op. cit.*, 19-20.
57. Johnson, *Wives, op. cit.*, 2-3.
58. Brower, *op. cit.*, 19-20.
59. Johnson, *Wives, op. cit.*, 2-3.
60. Brower, *op. cit.*, 21.
61. Council House records F 25163, pt 4, page 46; Church of Jesus Christ of Latter-day Saints.
62. Brower, *op. cit.*, 21.
63. Photocopy of selling document in authors possession; dated May 28, 1855, recorded with the Great Salt Lake County Recorder.
64. Brower, *op. cit.*, 21-22.
65. Bangerter, William, *op. cit.*, vi.
66. Brower, *op. cit.*, 21-22.
67. Endowment House Record of sealings F25165, pt. 14, page 46.
68. Endowment House Record of sealings F25165, pt. 14, page 82.
69. Clark, *op. cit.*, 26.
70. Utah State Archives, Series Inventories, Vol. 16, Series 59925.
71. *Utah Since Statehood: Historical and Biographical, IV* (Chicago: S. J. Clarke Publishing, 1920), 448.
72. Kate B. Carter, ed., *Treasures of Pioneer History,* Vl (Salt Lake City: Daughters of Utah Pioneers, 1957), 24.
73. Scott G. Kenney, ed. *Wilford Woodruff's Journal: 1833-1898 Typescript,* (Midvale, Utah: Signature Books), vol. iv, 436; vol. v, 302, 557; vol. vi, 67.
74. James B. Allen and Glen M. Leonard, *The Story of the Latter-day Saints,* 2nd ed., (Salt Lake City: Deseret Book, 1992), 285.
75. Utah State Archives & Records Service, Agency #367, Division of Expositions, History.
76. Quoted in Carter, *Treasures, op. cit.*, 24-25.
77. Utah State Archives & Records Service, Agency #367, Division of Expositions, History.
78. Brower, *op. cit.*, 22.
79. *Journal History,* 3 Oct. 1857, 1.
80. *Ibid.*, 6 Jul. 1857, 8 Sep. 1857.
81. Brower, *op. cit.*, 22.
82. Marley, *op. cit.*
83. Brower, *op. cit.*, 22-23.
84. Johnson, *Wives, op. cit.*, 5.
85. Bangerter, John, *op. cit.*, EPW 1-2.

86. Marriage recorded in the Council House records F25163, pt 4, pg. 91. The sealing is recorded on F21565, pt. 15 of the Endowment House records.

87. Bangerter, William, *op. cit.*, vii.

88. Bangerter, John, *op. cit.*, HTW 1.

89. Robertson, *op. cit.*, 26.

90. Ludlow, *op. cit.*, 675.

91. Bloxham, et. al., *op. cit.*, 193.

92. Alan Kent Powell, ed., *Utah History Encyclopedia,* (Salt Lake City: University of Utah Press, 1994), 55.

93. Bangerter, John, *op. cit.*, EWM 1.

94. *Biographical Record*, 17.

95. *Utah Since Statehood, op. cit.*, 448.

Chapter 7

1. Funeral services, *op. cit.*, 12.

2. Clark, *op. cit.*, 26.

3. Taylor, *op. cit.*, 271-272.

4. Kate B. Carter, *Our Pioneer Heritage*, 1, (Salt Lake City: Daughters of Utah Pioneers, 1958), 63.

5. Robertson, *op. cit.*, 16.

6. Taylor, *Ibid.*

7. Audrey M. Godfrey, "Relations with the U.S. Military," *Historical Atlas of Mormonism, op. cit.*

8. Ludlow, *op. cit.*, 619, 1500.

9. Robertson, *op. cit.*, 75.

10. Conference Report of The Church of Jesus Christ of Latter-day Saints, April 1905, (Salt Lake City: *Deseret News,* 1905), 7.

11. Robertson. *Ibid.*

12. Everett L. Cooley, *The Utah War,* (Salt Lake City: University of Utah, 1947), 34-35.

13. Carter, 1, *op. cit.*, 63.

14. *Conference Report,* April 1905, *op. cit.*, 7-8.

15. Bryant S. Hinckley, *Daniel Hanmer Wells and Events of His Time,* (Salt Lake City: Deseret News Press, 1942), 107.

16. Paul Bailey, *Holy Smoke. A Dissertation on the Utah War,* (Los Angeles: Westernlore Books, 1978), 123.

17. Johnson, *John Rex Winder, op. cit.*, 2.

18. Gustave O. Larson, *Outline History of Utah and the Mormons,* (Salt Lake City: Deseret Book, 1958), 88.

19. Funeral, *op. cit.*, 13.

20. *Conference Report,* April 1905, *op. cit.*, 8.

21. Bangerter, William, *op. cit.* 1.
22. *Biographical Encyclopedia, op. cit.*, 244-245.
23. Clark, *op. cit.*, 26-27.
24. Orson F. Whitney, *History of Utah,* (Salt Lake City: George Q. Cannon & Sons, 1892), 660-662.
25. Roberts, *Comprehensive History,* 6, *op. cit.*, 302.
26. Johnson, *John Rex Winder, op. cit.*, 3.
27. *Ibid.*
28. Ludlow, *op. cit.*, 1500.
29. Robertson, *op. cit.*, 79.
30. George Winder, *Ibid.*
31. carter, vol. xii, *op. cit.*, 105.
32. Birthday Reception, *op. cit.*, 6-7.
33. *Ibid.*, 26.
34. Andrew Jenson, *Church Chronology: A Record of Important Events,* (Salt Lake City: *Deseret News,* 1914), 60. Edward W. Tullidge, *History of Salt Lake City and its Founders,* (Salt Lake City: Edward W. Tullidge, c. 1875), 199.
35. Roberts, *Comprehensive History,* 6, *op. cit.*, 302.
36. *Millennial Star,* vol. 67, 38.
37. Tullidge, *op. cit.*, 199.
38. Robertson, *op. cit.*, 79.
39. *Ibid.*
40. *Biographical Record, op. cit.*, 18.
41. *Biographical Encyclopedia, op. cit.*, 245 & Whitney, *op. cit.*, 662.
42. Whitney, *op. cit.*, 662.
43. Funeral, *op. cit.*, 13.
44. *Biographical Encyclopedia, op. cit.*, 245.
45. Clark, *op. cit.*, 27.
46. *Biographical Encyclopedia, Ibid.*
47. State Archives & Records Service, Territorial Militia Records, 1849-1877, Reel 2, Personal Name Index.
48. Funeral, *op. cit.*, 3-4.
49. Funeral, *op. cit.*, 17.
50. Cooley, *op. cit.*, 82-85.
51. *Conference Report,* April 1905, *op. cit.*, 8.
52. Brower, *op. cit.*, 23.
53. Robertson, *op. cit.*, 31, 82.
54. Brower, *Ibid.*
55. Conference Report of The Church of Jesus Christ of Latter-day Saints, April 1905, (Salt Lake City: *Deseret News,* 1905), 8.

56. Kenner, *op. cit.*, 365.
57. In Old Salt Lake, *op. cit.*, 13.
58. Cooley, *op. cit.*, 89-91.
59. Funeral, *op. cit.*, 13.
60. Clark, *op. cit.*, 27.
61. Funeral, *op. cit.*, 18.
62. Francis M. Gibbons, *Joseph F. Smith: Patriarch and Preacher, Prophet of God* (Salt Lake City: Deseret Book, 1984), 45.
63. Birthday Reception, *op. cit.*, 7-8.
64. Bailey, *op. cit.*, 123.
65. *Journal History,* May 29, 1858.
66. *Conference Report,* April 1905, 8.
67. Cooley, *op. cit.*, 92.
68. Orson F. Whitney, "Lives of our Leaders—the Presiding Bishopric," *Juvenile Instructor,* 36 (Salt Lake City, 15 October 1901).
69. Brower, *Ibid.*
70. *Ibid.*
71. Richard F. Burton quoted in Susan Evans McCloud, *Brigham Young— An Inspiring Personal Biography,* (American Fork, Utah: Covenant Communications, 1998), 220.
72. Kenner, *Ibid.*
73. Conference Report of The Church of Jesus Christ of Latter-day Saints, October 1908, (Salt Lake City: *Deseret News,* 1908), 9- 10.
74. *Conference Report,* October 1908, 10.
75. *Conference Report,* April 1905, 8.
76. Funeral, *op. cit.*, 12- 14.

Chapter 8

1. *Conference Report,* April 1905, *op. cit.*, 8.
2. Robertson, *op. cit.*, 84.
3. McCloud, *op. cit.*, 217.
4. Bangerter, William, *op. cit.*, 1-2 & Brower, *op. cit.*, 23-24.
5. Clark, *Ibid.*
6. Brower, *op. cit.*, 23.
7. Taylor, *op. cit.*, 272-273.
8. Tullidge, *op. cit.*, 677.
9. Greeley, quoted in McCloud, *op. cit.*, 221.
10. Jenson, Volume 2, *op. cit.*, 486.
11. Quinn, *op. cit.*, 716; & Carter, Volume 3, *op. cit.*, 217.
12. Jenson, Volume 2, *op. cit.*, 486.
13. Brower, *op. cit.*, 23.

14. *Ibid.*
15. Carter, Volume 3, *op. cit.*, 217.
16. *Journal History,* 26 April 1859, 1.
17. Brower, *op. cit.*, 23-28.
18. *Ibid.*, 28.
19. *Ibid.*, 28-31. Also, Bangerter, William, *op. cit.*, 2-4.
20. Gibbons, *op. cit.*, 88.
21. Brower, *op. cit.*, 28.
22. Wives, *Ibid.*
23. Kenney, Volume 5, *op. cit.*, 557.
24. *Doctrine and Covenants* 87:1-2.
25. Clark, *Ibid.*
26. Tullidge, *Ibid.*
27. Bangerter, William, *op. cit.*, MSW 1.
28. Greg W. Sessions, City of South Salt Lake, 12/3/97, http://www.media.utah.edu/medsol/UCME/s/SOUTHSALTLAKE.html
29. S. Dilworth Young, *The Beehive House,* (Salt Lake City: The Church of Jesus Christ of Latter-day Saints, 1981), 1-3.
30. Kenny, *op. cit.*, Chapter 8.
31. Bangerter, John, *op. cit.*, RHW 1.
32. Bangerter, William, *op. cit.*, MSW 4.
33. *Ibid.* 4-5.
34. Robertson, *op. cit.*, 33 and Bangerter, John, *op. cit.*, AWB 1.
35. Bangerter, John, *op. cit.*, EPW 2.
36. Wives *Ibid.*
37. Robertson, *Ibid.* and Bangerter, John, *op. cit.*, AWB 1.
38. Carter, *Our Pioneer Heritage, op. cit.*, vol.viii, 46-47.
39. Nibley, *Ibid.*
40. Bangerter, William, *op. cit.*, 4.
41. Clark. *Ibid.*
42. *From Shoe Clerk. . ., Ibid.*
43. Jenson, *op. cit.*, 486.
44. Ludlow, *op. cit.*, 27-28.
45. Anderson, *op. cit.*, 620.
46. Bangerter, William, *op. cit.*, 4.
47. Kenny, *op. cit.*, 26.
48. Bennett, *op. cit.*, 15-16, 18.
49. Bangerter, William, *op. cit.*, MSW 4.
50. Valerie Porter, *Cattle: A Handbook to the Breeds of the World,* (New York: Facts On File, 1991), 82-83.

51. M. H. French, *European Breeds of Cattle,* (Rome: Food and Agriculture Organization of the United Nations, 1966), 1.

52. George Winder, *Ibid.*

53. E. Parmalee Prentice, *American Dairy Cattle: Their Past and Future,* (New York: Harper & Brothers, 1942), 384, 392-393.

54. George Winder, *Ibid.*

55. *ibid*

56. Bangerter, William, *op. cit.*, MSW 5.

57. Kenner, *op. cit.*, 365.

58. Taylor, *op. cit.*, 273.

59. Deseret Agricultural & Manufacturing Society, *Biennial Report 1863.*

60. *Journal History,* 5 Sept. 1860.

61. Utah State Archives, Series 59925, Reel 1, Deseret Agricultural & Manufacturing Society Minute Books.

62. Brown, *op. cit.*

63. *Journal History,* 26 July 1858.

64. Lesson Committee, ed., *Chronicles of Courage,* vol. vi, (Salt lake City: Daughters of Utah Pioneers, 1995), 111-113.

65. *Journal History,* 24 July 1864.

66. *Ibid.*, 22 Aug. 1864.

67. *Chronicles of Courage, op. cit.*, 94-95.

68. Kimball, Solomon F. "President Brigham Young's Excursion Party," *Improvement Era,* vol. xiv, (Salt Lake City: General Board YMMIA, 1911), 311-313.

69. Quinn, *op. cit.*, 717.

70. Birthday Reception, *op. cit.*, 19.

Chapter 9

1. Allen, *op. cit.*, 335-336.

2. Janet Burton Seegmiller, *The Life Story of Robert Taylor Burton* (Utah: Robert Taylor Burton Family Organization, 1988), 236 & Robertson, *op. cit.*, 17.

3. Peter Gottfredson, *Indian Depredations in Utah,* (Salt Lake City: Private Printing, 1969), 154-155.

4. Kenney, *op. cit.*, 226-227, 238-239.

5. *Journal History,* 7 Aug 1865.

6. *Ibid.*, 8 Aug 1865.

7. Kenney, *op. cit.*, 244-245.

8. *Journal History,* 17 Sept 1865.

9. Allen, *op. cit.*, 336.

10. Robertson, *op. cit.*, 17.

11. L.Seegmiller, *op. cit.*, 236.

12. Funeral Services, *op. cit.*, 14.

13. John R. Winder, *John R. Winder's Journal Kept While On Expedition to Sanpete with Lieutenant General Daniel Wells in the Year 1866,* State Archives & Records Service, Territorial Militia Records, series 02210, reel 28, box 1, folder 87, page 3.
14. Lawrence R. Flake, *Mighty Men of Zion: General Authorities of the Last Dispensation,* (Salt Lake City: Karl D. Butler, 1974), 94.
15. Clark, *op. cit.,* 27.
16. Seegmiller, *op. cit.,* 236.
17. Robertson, *op. cit.,* 17.
18. Allen, *op. cit.,* 336.
19. Seegmiller, *op. cit.,* 237.
20. *Journal History,* 31 May 1866.
21. Seegmiller, *op. cit.,* 237.
22. Bangerter, William, *op. cit.,* 5.
23. *The Young Women's Journal, op. cit.,* vol. xix, 37.
24. Gottfredson, *op. cit.,* 206-207. Also, Carter, Heart Throbs, *op. cit.,* vol. xi, 484.
25. John R. Winder, *op. cit.,* 1.
26. Seegmiller, *op. cit.,* 237.
27. Funeral Services, *op. cit.,* 10.
28. *Ibid.,* 13.
29. John R. Winder, Letter to Brigham Young, dated 8 July 1866, LDS Church Archives, MS 1234.
30. *Deseret Evening News,* 24 Aug 1894.
31. Funeral Services, *op. cit.,* 15.
32. Allen, *op. cit.,* 336.
33. John R. Winder, Letter to Brigham, *Ibid.*
34. Clark, *op. cit.,* 27.
35. Gottfredson, *op. cit.,* 206.
36. Funeral Services, *op. cit.,* 14.
37. Utah State Archives, Series Inventories, Vol. 6, Series 2210, Territorial Militia Records, 1849-1877 1905 undated, Description, 1.
38. John R. Winder's Journal, *op. cit.* 1-7.
39. John R. Winder, Letter to Brigham Young, *Ibid.*
40. State Archives & Records Service, Territorial Militia Records, 1849-1877, Reel 2, Personal Name Index, #1, 114.
41. *Ibid.,* #1, 135.
42. Funeral Services, *op. cit.,* 15.
43. *Journal History,* 25 Dec 1868.
44. State Archives & Records Service, Territorial Militia Records, 1849-1877, Reel 2, Personal Name Index, #909.

45. *Journal History,* 15 May 1867.
46. Birthday Reception, *op. cit.*, 38.
47. *Journal History,* 4 Nov 1867.
48. *Ibid.*, 16 Nov 1867.
49. Funeral Services, *op. cit.*, 15.
50. *Ibid.*, 13.
51. *Journal History,* 1 Feb 1868.
52. Allen, *op. cit.*, 336-337.
53. Clark, *op. cit.*, 27.
54. *Biographical Record*, *op. cit.*, 19.
55. Funeral Services, *op. cit.*, 13.
56. *Journal History,* 25 Dec 1868.
57. Gottfredson, *op. cit.*, 276-277.
58. *Journal History,* 25 Dec 1868.
59. *Biographical Record*, *op. cit.*, 19.
60. Gottfredson, *op. cit.*, 278.
61. *Deseret Evening News,* 24 Aug 1894.
62. Anderson, *op. cit.*, 620.
63. Utah State Archives, Series Inventories, Vol. 6, Series 2210, Territorial Militia Records, 1849-1877 1905 undated, Description, 3.
64. Ludlow, *op. cit.*, 999.
65. Funeral Services, *op. cit.*, 10.
66. *Ibid.*, 15.

Chapter 10

1. *Journal History,* 5 Jul 1869.
2. Bangerter, John, *op. cit.*, MWH 1.
3. Clark, *op. cit.*, 27.
4. Utah State Archives, Salt Lake City Assessment Rolls.
5. Birthday Reception, *op. cit.*, 19.
6. Funeral, *op. cit.*, 14.
7. *Ibid.*
8. Funeral, *op. cit.*, 14- 15.
9. *Ibid.*
10. Utah State Archives, Salt Lake City Assessment Rolls.
11. *Journal History,* 25 Dec 1879.
12. Funeral, *op. cit.*, 15.
13. *The Young Women's Journal,* vol. xxi, *op. cit.*, 274.
14. John R. Winder to Brigham Young, 24 Jan 1872, LDS Church Archives, MS 1234.
15. Whitney, *op. cit.*, vol. ii, 530.

16. Clark, *op. cit.*, 27.
17. Whitney, *op. cit.*, vol. ii, 385.
18. *Journal History,* 14 Feb 1870.
19. Birthday Reception, *op. cit.*, 8.
20. Funeral, *op. cit.*, 16.
21. Utah State Archives, Salt Lake City Council Minutes.
22. Smith, *op. cit.*, 230.
23. Carter, *Our Pioneer Heritage, op. cit.*, vol. xix, 21.
24. David L. Wood, "Emperor Dom Pedro's Visit to Salt Lake City," *Utah Historical Quarterly,* (Salt Lake City: Utah State Historical Society, 1969), vol. xxxvii, no. 3, 340.
25. Funeral, *op. cit.*, 15.
26. Birthday Reception, *op. cit.*, 8.
27. Seegmiller, *op. cit.*, 345.
28. Charles R. McKell, "The Utah State Hospital: A Study in the Care of the Mentally Ill," *Utah Historical Quarterly,* (Salt Lake City: Utah State Historical Society, 1955), vol. xxiii, no. 4, 305-307.
29. Clark, *op. cit.*, 27.
30. Joseph Fielding Smith, *Life of Joseph F. Smith: Sixth President of The Church of Jesus Christ of Latter-day Saints,* (Salt Lake City: Deseret News Press, 1938), 229-230.
31. Whitney, *op. cit.*, vol. iii, 584.
32. Smith, *op. cit.*, 230.
33. Quinn, *op. cit.*, 286.
34. *Ibid.*, 717.
35. *Biographical Record, op. cit.*, 19.
36. Tullidge, *op. cit.*, 882.
37. Clark, *op. cit.*, 27.
38. *Ibid.*
39. Eric Bittner, et. al., eds., *Guide to Records in the National Archives—Rocky Mountain Region,* (Washington, DC: National Archives and Records Administration, 1996), 11.
40. *The Young Women's Journal,* vol. xxi, *op. cit.*, 273.
41. Clark, *op. cit.*, 27.
42. Quinn, *op. cit.*, 323, 717.
43. Abraham H. Cannon, *op. cit.*, vol. viii, 16 June 1887.
44. Tullidge, *op. cit.*, 847.
45. Birthday Reception, *op. cit.*, 19-20.
46. George Winder, *Ibid.*
47. *Juvenile Instructor, op. cit.*, vol. xxxvi, 612.

48. Funeral, *op. cit.*, 4.

49. *Conference Report,* October 6, 1903.

50. H. Milton Masser to Brigham Young, 13 May 1868, LDS Church Archives, MS 1234.

51. Carter, *Heart Throbs, op. cit.*, vol. iii, 217.

52. Powell, *op. cit.*, 652.

53. *Deseret News,* 13 Feb 1923.

54. Kenney, *op. cit.*, vol. vii., 227-228.

55. George Winder, *Ibid.*

56. *The Young Women's Journal,* vol. xxi, *op. cit.*, 274.

57. Seegmiller, *op. cit.*, 334.

58. *Ibid.*, 336.

59. Leonard Arrington, "Utah's Coal Road in the Age of Unregulated Competition," *Utah Historical Quarterly* (Salt Lake City: Utah State Historical Society, 1955), vol. xxiii, no. l, 47.

60. Seegmiller, *op, cit.*, 337.

61. Quinn, *op. cit.*, 716.

62. Utah State Archives, Salt Lake County (Utah) Incorporation Case Files, Series 03888, Reel 11 - 293.

63. *Journal of Abraham H. Cannon,* vol. iv, 4 Dec 1883.

64. Quinn, *op. cit.*, 716.

65. *Juvenile Instructor, op. cit.*, vol . xlv, 217-218.

66. Powell, *op. cit.*, 652.

67. *Salt Lake Tribune,* 2 Oct 1895.

68. Martha Sonntag Bradley, *ZCMI. America 's First Department Store,* (Salt Lake City: ZCMI, 1991), 178.

69. Funeral, *op. cit.*, 5.

70. Utah State Archives, Series 59925, Reel 1, Deseret Agriculture & Manufacturing Society Minute Books.

71. *Journal History,* 5 Oct 1869.

72. *The Young Women's Journal,* vol. xxi, *op. cit.*, 273.

73. *Ibid.*

74. *Ibid.*

75. Funeral, *op. cit.*, 18.

76. Marley, *Ibid.*

77. *The Young Women's Journal,* vol. xxi, *op. cit.*, 274.

78. *Ibid.*

79. 1880 Utah Agriculture Census.

80. *Journal History,* 2 Sep 1872.

81. *The Young Women's Journal,* vol. xxi, *op. cit.*, 274

82. *Journal of Abraham H. Cannon,* vol. iv, 12 May 1888.

83. *The Young Women's Journal,* vol. xxi, *op. cit.*, 274.

84. *Journal of Abraham H. Cannon,* vol. iv, 14 May 1883.

85. Bangerter, John, *op. cit.*, RHW 1.

86. 1880 Utah Agriculture Census.

87. Bangerter, William, *op. cit.*, 9. Also Nancy Gwen Winder, *Winder Dairy,* (Salt Lake City: Unpublished manuscript in author's possession, 1973), 1.

88. Michael K. Winder, ed. *Winder Dairy, Quality Since 1880: The George Winder Interviews,* (Unpublished manuscript in author's possession, 1992-1995). Also, Bangerter, William, *op. cit.*, 21-22.

89. Kate B. Carter, ed., Historical Pamphlet. *First Hotels, Laundries and Dairies in the West,* (Salt Lake City: Daughters of Utah Pioneers, 1943).

90. Nancy Winder, *Ibid.*

91. Wynn, *Ibid.*

92. Michael Winder, *Ibid.*

93. Jeff Richards, "Pioneer dairy grows with west side," *Eagle Newspapers,* 18 Jul 1996, 9.

94. *The Young Women's Journal,* vol. xxi, *op. cit.*, 274.

95. Kenney, *op. cit.*, vol. ix, 44.

96. D. C. Dunbar, *Salt Lake City Illustrated,* (Omaha: D. C. Dunbar Co., 1888), 56.

97. Marion Winder Wynn, *Winder Dairy,* (Salt Lake City: Unpublished manuscript in author's possession, 1974), 1.

98. Bangerter, William, *op. cit.*, 5.

99. Bangerter, John, *op. cit.*, MWH 1.

100. Robertson, *op. cit.*, 33.

101. Bangerter, John, *op. cit.*, EJW 1.

102. Bangerter, William, *op. cit.*, 8-9.

103. Robertson, *op. cit.*, 107.

104. Bangerter, John, *op. cit.*, EJW 1 & EPW 2-3.

105. *Ibid.*

106. Bangerter, William, *op. cit.*, 9.

107. Bangerter, John, *op. cit.*, EJW 1.

108. *Ibid.*, EWW2.

109. *Ibid.*, WCW 2.

110. *Ibid.*, MWH 1.

111. *The Young Women's Journal,* vol. xxi, *op. cit.*, 273.

112. *Ibid.*

113. *Journal History,* 1 9 Dec 1872.

114. Jenson, *Historical, op. cit.*, 321.

115. Bangerter, William, *op. cit.*, 12.

116. *Journal History,* 25 Nov 1870.

117. Jenson, *Historical, op. cit.*, 320-321.

118. John R. Winder letter to Brigham Young, 9 Nov 1872, LDS Church Archives, MS 1234.

119. Jenson, *Historical, op. cit.*, 321.

120. Birthday Reception, *op. cit.*, 38.

121. Kenney, *op. cit.*, vol. vii, 133.

122. Bangerter, William, *op. cit.*, 12.

123. Lynn M. Hilton, *The Story of the Salt Lake Stake of the Church of Jesus Christ of Latter-day Saints: 125 Year History 1847-1972,* (Salt Lake City: Salt Lake Stake, 1972), 299.

124. Andrew Jenson, ed., *The Historical Record: Church Encyclopedia,* (Salt Lake City: Andrew Jenson, 1889) 281.

125. Birthday Reception, *op. cit.*, 38.

126. *Ibid.*, 39.

127. Funeral, *op. cit.*, 17.

128. Seegmiller, *op. cit.*, 267-268. Also Esplin, *Ibid.*

129. *Journal History,* 13 Nov 1870, 7 Feb 1870 & 10 July 1870.

130. *Ibid.*, 2 Jun 1870.

131. *Journal History,* 28 Aug 1873.

132. Tullidge, *op. cit.*, 881.

133. Quinn, *op. cit.*, 717.

134. Smith, *op. cit.*, 253.

135. Whitney, *op. cit.*, vol. iii, 68.

136. *Ibid.*, 335.

137. Gibbons, *op. cit.*, 133.

138. *Conference Report,* April 1905, 8.

139. *Utah Since Statehood, op. cit.*, 448.

140. Funeral, *op. cit.*, 19.

Chapter 11

1. Birthday Reception, *op. cit.*, 15.

2. 1997-98 Church Almanac, (Salt Lake City: *Deseret News,* 1996), 43-44, 76-77.

3. Seegmiller, *op. cit.*, 418.

4. Clark, *Ibid.*

5. Almanac, *op. cit.*, 78.

6. Ludlow, *op. cit.*, 1128.

7. Emerson Roy West, *Profiles of the Presidents,* (Salt Lake City: Deseret Book, 1974), 118.

8. Bangerter, William, *op. cit.*, ix.

9. Abraham H. Cannon, *op. cit.*, vol. x, 24 Nov 1888.

10. Ludlow, *op. cit.*, 1127- 1128.

11. Seegmiller, *op. cit.*, 412.

12. Robert Taylor Burton Diaries, 1856-1907, April 1887.

13. Abraham H. Cannon, *op. cit.*, vol. viii, 7 April 1887.

14. D. Michael Quinn, *The Mormon Hierarchy: Extensions of Power,* (Salt Lake City: Signature Books, 1997), 134.

15. *Ibid.*, 134-135.

16. Seegmiller, *op. cit.*, 387.

17. Jenson, *Chronology, op. cit.*, 175, 182-183.

18. Roberts, *op. cit.*, vol. vi, 196, 198.

19. Seegmiller, *op. cit.*, 381.

20. *Ibid.*, 387.

21. *Deseret Evening News,* 5 October 1888.

22. Taylor, *op. cit.*, 275.

23. John R. Winder, Letter to the family of John Taylor, *Ibid.*

24. Funeral, *op. cit.*, 17.

25. John R. Winder, Letter to the family of John Taylor, *Ibid.*

26. Abraham Cannon, *op. cit.*, vol. xiii, 30 Aug 1890.

27. *Ibid.*, 1 Sep 1890.

28. Quinn, *op. cit.*, 717.

29. The Supreme Court of the Territory of Utah, The United States of America vs. The Corporation of the Church of Jesus Christ of Latter-day Saints, 1 September 1890, Ms d 1144, LDS Church Historical Department.

30. Larson, ed., *op. cit.*, 461.

31. Bitton, *op. cit.*, 312.

32. Taylor, *op. cit.*, 35.

33. Ludlow, *op. cit.*, 853, 1583; Gibbons, *op. cit.*, 177; *Doctrine & Covenants,* Official Declaration 1.

34. Seegmiller, *op. cit.*, 412.

35. Abraham H. Cannon, *op. cit.*, vol. x, 23 Apr 1889.

36. *The Young Women's Journal,* vol. xxi, *op. cit.*, 273.

37. Bitton, *Ibid.*

38. Quinn, *op. cit.*, 716.

39. *Ibid.*

40. Kenney, *op. cit.*, vol. ix, 213.

41. Quinn, *op. cit.*, 716.

42. *Deseret Evening News,* 8 Mar 1900.

43. Abraham H. Cannon, *op. cit.*, vol. xiii, 22 July 1890.

44. *Ibid.*, 30 Aug 1890, 21 Nov, 1890.

45. Bangerter, John, *op. cit.*, WCW 3.

46. Funeral, *op. cit.*, 4.

47. Seegmiller, *op. cit.*, 412.

48. Abraham H. Cannon, *op. cit.*, vol. xiii, 7 Oct 1890.

49. *Ibid.*, vol. xii, 28 Feb 1890.

50. *Ibid.*, 9 Oct 1890.

51. Kenney, *op. cit.*, vol. viii, 514.

52. Gene A. Sessions, ed. *Mormon Democrat. The Religious and Political Memoirs of James Henry Moyle,* (Salt Lake City: LDS Church Historical Department, 1975), 179-181.

53. Alexander, *op. cit.*, 202.

54. Quinn, *op. cit.*, 332.

55. Quoted in Quinn, *op. cit.*, 338.

56. *Ibid.*, 717.

57. Sessions, *op. cit.*, 207, 424.

58. Quinn, *op. cit.*, 717.

59. Winder Family Directs State Fair Since '56, *Ibid.* Also, Utah State Archives & Records Service, Agency #367—Division of Expositions, History.

60. *Deseret Evening News,* 1 Dec 1891.

61. Quinn, *op. cit.*, 717.

62. Abraham H. Cannon, *op. cit.*, vol. xii, 25 Apr 1890.

63. A. R. Mortensen, ed., *Utah Historical Quarterly,* (Salt Lake City: Utah State Historical Society, 1958), vol. xxvi, number 4, 374.

64. The *Young Woman's Journal, op. cit.*, vol. xxviii, 78.

65. John R. Sillito, *John R. Winder—Faithful Counselor, Builder of the Kingdom,* Unpublished manuscript presented to the Mormon History Association, Brigham Young University, 11 May 1984, p. 9.

Chapter 12

1. James E. Talmage, *The House of the Lord: A Study of Holy Sanctuaries, Ancient and Modern,* (Salt Lake City: Bookcraft, 1962), 149-154.

2. Abraham H. Cannon, *op. cit.*, 15 Apr 1892.

3. Davis Bitton, *George Q. Cannon: A Biography,* (Salt Lake City: Deseret Book, 1999), 272.

4. *Ibid.*, 7 Apr 1892.

5. *Ibid.*, 8 Oct 1892.

6. *Biographical Record, op. cit.,* 19.

7. Harlan L. Bangerter, "Temple leader's faith: 'It can, must be done,'" *Church News, Deseret News,* 1996.

8. Art window in the interior of the Salt Lake Temple 1893, photograph at LDS Historical Department, call # PH 2387.

9. Abraham H. Cannon, *op. cit.*, 18 Oct 1892.

10. Birthday, *op. cit.*, 24.

11. *Ibid.*, 34.

12. Talmage, *op. cit.*, 153.

13. Lawrence R. Flake, *Mighty Men of Zion: General Authorities of the Last Dispensation,* (Salt Lake City: Karl D. Butler, 1974), 95.

14. Birthday, *op. cit.*, 24-25.

15. *Ibid.*, 34-35.

16. *Samuel Richards Journal.* 24 Nov 1892, LDS Church Archives.

17. *National Cyclopaedia, op. cit.*, 14.

18. Kenney, Wilford, *op. cit.*, vol. ix, 210, 218, 223.

19. Talmage, *op. cit.*, 155.

20. *Ibid.*, 155-158.

21. *Utah the Inland Empire, op. cit.*, 17.

22. *Juvenile Instructor,* vol. xlv, *op. cit.*, 217.

23. Funeral, *op. cit.*, 10-11.

24. John R. Winder, "Temples and Temple Work," *Young Women's Journal,* vol. xiv, no. 2, February 1903, pp. 50-53.

25. Talmage, *op. cit.*, 158-160, 171.

26. Gibbons, *op. cit.*, 214, & *Juvenile Instructor,* vol. xxxvi, *op. cit.*, 611.

27. Birthday, *op. cit.*, 25.

28. *Juvenile Instructor,* vol. xlv, *op. cit.*, 217.

29. Funeral, *op. cit.*, 18-19.

30. Bangerter, John, *op. cit.*, MBW 1.

31. *Biographical Record, op. cit.*, 19.

32. Richard Neitzel Holzapfel, *Every Stone A Sermon. The Magnificent Story of the Construction and Dedication of the Salt Lake Temple,* (Salt Lake City: Bookcraft, 1992), 88.

33. Larson, *op. cit.*, 339.

34. Holzapfel, *Ibid.*

35. Kenney, Wilford, *op. cit.*, vol. ix, 248-249.

36. Johnson, *Wives, op. cit.*, 7.

37. Bangerter, John, *op. cit.*, EJW 2.

38. *Juvenile Instructor,* vol. xlv, *op. cit.*, 217.

39. Marley, *Ibid.*

40. Bangerter, John, *op. cit.*, EJW 10.

41. *Ibid.*, EJW 12.

42. Funeral, *op. cit.*, 11.

43. *Ibid.*, 6.

44. Johnson, *Wives, op. cit.*, 7.

45. Bangerter, John, *op. cit.*, EWW 2.

46. Birthday, *op. cit.*, 41.

47. Johnson, *Wives, op. cit.*, 2.

48. Bangerter, John, *op. cit.*, MBW 1.

49. Birthday, *op. cit.*, 25.

50. Bangerter, John, *op. cit.*, MBW 1.

51. Birthday, *Ibid.*

52. Bangerter, John, *Ibid.*

53. Johnson, *Wives, op. cit.*, 7.

54. Bangerter, John, *op. cit.*, MBW 2.

55. Bruce R. McConkie, *Mormon Doctrine,* 2nd ed., (Salt Lake City: Bookcraft, 1979), 112.

56. Bangerter, John, *op. cit.*, MBW 2.

57. Johnson, Wives, *op. cit.*, 7.

58. Stan Larson, ed., *A Ministry of Meetings: The Apostolic Diaries of Rudger Clawson,* (Salt Lake City: Signature Books, 1993), 8-9.

59. *Journal History,* 13 Dec 1897.

60. Thomas C. Romney, *The Life of Lorenzo Snow: Fifth President of the Church of Jesus Christ of Latter-day Saints,* (Salt Lake City: Sons of the Utah Pioneers Memorial Foundation, 1955), 427-429.

61. Abraham H. Cannon, *op. cit.*, 22 Oct 1894.

62. Ivins, *op. cit.*, 153.

63. Kenner, *op. cit.*, 366.

64. Utah Territory Supreme Court, Appointment of John R. Winder 1894 Aug 31.

65. Roberts, *op. cit.*, vol. vi, 198. Also Abraham H. Cannon, *op. cit.*, 31 Aug 1894.

66. *Journal History,* 8 Jun 1896.

67. Abraham H. Cannon, *op. cit.*, 23 Apr 1895.

68. Quinn, *op. cit.*, 135.

69. Abraham H. Cannon, *op. cit.*, 7 & 12 Dec 1893.

70. Michael Winder, *George, op. cit.*, 1-2.

71. *Deseret Evening News,* 11 Dec 1900.

72. Abraham H. Cannon, *op. cit.*, 6 Apr 1894.

73. Kenney, Wilford, *op. cit.*, vol. ix, 426.

74. *Ibid.*. 453, 454, 552.

75. *Deseret Evening News,* 10 Nov 1900.

76. *Journal History,* 14 Dec 1897.

77. Seegmiller, *op. cit.*, 412-413.

78. *Ibid.*. 413.

79. Larson, *op. cit.*, 293.

80. Anthony Woodward Ivins Diary, 146. Also *Deseret Evening News,* 17 Apr 1901.

81. Larson, *op. cit.*, 143, 262.

82. *Ibid.*, 334.
83. *Biographical Record, op. cit.*, 19.
84. Gibbons, *op. cit.*, 214.

Chapter 13

1. Larsen, ed., *op. cit.*, 364.
2. Joseph F. Smith, *Gospel Doctrine,* (Salt Lake City: Bookcraft 1998), 172-173.
3. Larson, ed., *op. cit.*, 344.
4. Larson, ed., *op. cit.*, 364-365.
5. Conversation with the author, April 12, 1999.
6. The Diary of Anthon H. Lund, 17 Oct. 1901. LDS Historical Department, MS 5375.
7. Larson, ed., *op. cit.*, 339.
8. White, *op. cit.*, 496. Also, *Brigham Young, Jr. Diary* 1900 Oct-1902 July, Church Archives, MS 8575.
9. Larson, ed., *Ibid.*
10. Funeral, *op. cit.*, 6.
11. Birthday, *op. cit.*, 28.
12. *The Salt Lake Tribune,* 18 Oct 1901.
13. Birthday, *op. cit.*, 14-15.
14. Funeral, *op. cit.*, 6.
15. Funeral, *op. cit.*, 4.
16. *Journal History,* 25 Dec 1903, 5.
17. Albert R. Lyman, *Francis Marion Lyman,* (Delta, Utah: Melvin A. Lyman, 1958), 153-154.
18. White, *op. cit.*, 496.
19. Larson, ed., *op. cit.*, 340.
20. Seegmiller, *op. cit.*, 414.
21. Lund, *op. cit.*, 26 Nov 1901.
22. Larson, ed., *op. cit.*, 345.
23. Joseph F. Smith, *op. cit.*, 176-177.
24. *Ibid.*, 174-175.
25. *Ibid.*, 173.
26. Larson, ed., *op. cit.*, 364.
27. Whitney, *History of Utah, op. cit.*, vol. iv, 242.
28. Funeral, *op. cit.*, 10.
29. Birthday, *op. cit.*, 1-46.
30. Lund, *op. cit.*, 25 July 1904.
31. *Millennial Star, op. cit.*, vol. lxvii, 38.
32. *Young Women's Journal, op. cit.*, vol. xix, 36.
33. *Journal History,* 11 Dec 1909.

34. *Men of the Day in Caricature,* (Denver: April 1906).
35. Alexander, *op. cit.*, 99.
36. Birthday, *op. cit.*, 17. Also, Funeral, *op. cit.*, 10-11.
37. Funeral, *op. cit.*, 11.
38. Birthday, *op. cit.*, 9.
39. Larson, ed., *op. cit.*, 430.
40. Larson, ed., *op. cit.*, 578.
41. *Ibid.*, 435.
42. *Journal History,* 22 Dec 1909, 5.
43. Boyd Peterson, ed., *Oral History of Hugh Nibley,* 7. Also, conversation of Hugh W. Nibley with the author, April 12, 1999.
44. Larson, ed., *op. cit.*, 442, 444, 445.
45. Larson, ed., *op. cit.*, 478.
46. Quinn, *op. cit.*, 717.
47. *Lund Journal, op. cit.*, 30 Sep 1903.
48. Anderson, *op. cit.*, 622.
49. *Conference Report,* October 1908.
50. Larson, ed., *op. cit.*, 723.
51. Thomas G. Alexander, *Mormonism in Transition: A History of the Latter-day Saints, 1890-1930,* (Urbana: University of Illinois Press, 1986), 18-19.
52. Frank J. Cannon and Harvey J. O'Higgins, *Under the Prophet in Utah: The National Menace of a Political Priestcraft,* (Boston: C. M. Clark Publishing, 1911), 267.
53. *Journal History,* 24 Oct 1907.
54. Alexander, *op. cit.*, 32.
55. William W. Slaughter, "Teddy in the Tabernacle," *Pioneer* (Salt Lake City: Sons of Utah Pioneers, Fall 1995), 21-24.
56. Larson, ed., *op. cit.*, 421.
57. Larson, ed., *op. cit.*, 425.
58. Frank J. Cannon, *op. cit.*, 350.
59. *Journal History,* 19 Aug 1902. Also, John R. Winder, "Mormonism Not A Menace," *The National Magazine,* Aug 1902, 553-561.

Chapter 14

1. Larson, ed., *op. cit.*, 516.
2. *Conference Report,* October 1908.
3. Larson, *op. cit.*, 423, 446, 483, 503.
4. *Ibid.*, 427, 429.
5. Larson, ed., *op. cit.*, 702.
6. Anderson, *op. cit.*, 623.
7. Jenson, *Biographical, op. cit.*, vol. iii, 795.

8. White, *op. cit.*, 604-605.
9. John R. Winder, Letter to Joseph F. Smith, 22 July 1909, Church Archives, Access No. 138527-ARCH-88, Joseph F. Smith Papers.
10. *Conference Report,* Apr. 1907, 7.
11. Larson, ed., *op. cit.*, 349, 360, 363.
12. Larson, *op. cit.*, 420-421.
13. *Ibid.*, 661.
14. Larson, *op. cit.*, 421.
15. *Ibid.*, 725. Also Gibbons, *op. cit.*, 224.
16. White, *op. cit.*, 633.
17. *Ibid.*, 539.
18. Smith, *Gospel Doctrine, Ibid.*
19. Larson, *op. cit.*, 344.
20. *Ibid.*, 420.
21. *Ibid.*, 411.
22. White, *op. cit.*, 632.
23. McConkie, *op. cit.*, 249-250.
24. *Journal History,* 17 Jan 1906.
25. White, *op. cit.*, 598.
26. *Journal History,* 7 April 1908, 2.
27. Lund, *op. cit.*, 1 Jan 1907.
28. *Journal of Abraham O. Woodruff,* Abraham Owen Woodruff Collection, BYU Library, Vault MSS 777, Bx 1, Fld 3. 7 Oct 1901.
29. *Ibid.*, 25 Oct 1901.
30. *Ibid.*, 12 Feb 1902.
31. Winder, Letter to Annie Hyde, *Ibid.*
32. Larson, ed., *op. cit.*, 405.
33. *Ibid.*, 713.
34. Bangerter, William, *op. cit.*, 30-31.
35. Larson, ed., *op. cit.*, 777.
36. Bangerter, William, *op. cit.*, 29-30.
37. Bangerter, John, *op. cit.*, RPW 2.
38. *Ibid.*, AWB 1-2.
39. As told to Phillip C. Winder, related in conversation with the author, September 1999.
40. Bangerter, John, *op. cit.*, MWS 1.
41. Bangerter, William, *op. cit.*, 23-24.
42. *Ibid.*, 25.
43. Michael Winder, George, *op. cit.*, 3-4.
44. *Ibid.*

45. Johnson, John, *op. cit.*, 1.

46. White, *op. cit.*, 643.

47. *Ibid.*

48. Lund, *op. cit.*, 9 Mar 1910, 11 Mar 1910.

49. Funeral, *op. cit.*, 7-9.

50. White, *Ibid.*

51. Marley, *Ibid.*

52. White, *op. cit.*, 644.

53. Clark, ed., *op. cit.*, 214.

54. *Journal History,* 29 Mar 1910, 30 Mar 1910.

55. *Improvement Era, op. cit.*, vol. xiii, 628.

56. White, *op. cit.*, 644.

57. Anderson, *op. cit.*, 624.

58. *Ibid.*, 625.

59. *Ibid.*, 624, 626; also Funeral Services, *Ibid.*

60. White, *op. cit.*, 649; also Anderson, *op. cit.*, 624.

61. White, *op. cit.*, 644-646.

62. Quinn, *op. cit.*, 717.

63. Johnson, Wives, *op. cit.*, 7. Also, Winder, Visit with George, *op. cit.*, 1.

Chapter 15

1. Funeral, *op. cit.*, 6.

2. *Conference Report,* April 4, 1902.

3. Anderson, *op. cit.*, 617.

4. Brigham Young, *Discourses of Brigham Young,* (Selected by John A. Widtsoe, 1941), 378.

5. Funeral, *op. cit.*, 9.

6. *Ibid.*, 1-2.

7. Marley, *Ibid.*

8. Funeral, *op. cit.*, 6.

9. *Ibid.*, 4-5.

10. *Biographical Record,* p. 20.

11. Carter, *Heart Throbs, op. cit.*, vol. iii, 78.

12. Birthday, *op. cit.*, 31.

13. Arrington and Bitton, *The Mormon Experience,* 243-261.

14. Marley, *Ibid.*

15. Robertson, *Ibid.*

Bibliography

1880 Utah Agriculture Census. LDS Family History Library.

Alexander, Thomas G., *Mormonism in Transition: A History of the Latter-day Saints*, 1890-1930, (Urbana: University of Illinois Press, 1986).

Allen, James B. and Leonard, Glen M., *The Story of the Latter-day Saints*, (Salt Lake City: Deseret Book, 1992).

Arrington, Leonard J., *Great Basin Kingdom: An Economic History of the Latter-day Saints*, 1830-1900, (Cambridge: Harvard University Press, 1958).

Arrington, Leonard J., and Bitton, Davis, *The Mormon Experience: A History of the Latter-day Saints*, (New York: 1979).

Bailey, Paul, *Holy Smoke: A Dissertation on the Utah War*, (Los Angeles: Westernlore Books, 1978).

Baines, J. Manwaring, *Historic Hastings*, (St. Leonards-on-Sea, East Sussex: Cinque Ports Press Ltd., 1986).

Bangerter, Harlan L., ed., *John R. Winder Family History, part 2*, (Salt Lake City: Winder Family Association, 1984).

Bangerter, William C. *Winder Family History*, (Salt Lake City: Winder Family Association, 1981).

Beckett, J. V., *The Aristocracy in England 1660-1914*, (Oxford: Basil Blackwell, Ltd., 1986).

Bennett, James A., *Hereford History in Utah: With Brief Reviews of Cattle Industry History in Utah and the United States*, (Logan: Utah Hereford Association, 1976).

Berrett, William E., *The Restored Church: A Brief History of the Growth and Doctrines of the Church of Jesus Christ of Latter-day Saints*, (Salt Lake City: Deseret Book, 1961).

Biddenden Local History Society, *The Story of Biddenden*, (Maidstone, Kent: Young & Cooper, Ltd., 1989).

Biddenden Parochial Church Council, *Biddenden: A Newcomer's Guide*, (Biddenden, Kent: Biddenden Parochial Church Council, 1991).

Bittner, Eric, et. al., eds., *Guide to Records in the National Archives—Rocky Mountain Region*, (Washington, D. C.: National Archives and Records Administration, 1996).

Bitton, Davis, *George Q. Cannon: A Biography*, (Salt Lake City: Deseret Book, 1999).

____. *Guide to Mormon Diaries and Autobiographies*, (Provo, Utah: Brigham Young University Press, 1977).

Blakey, Arch Fredric, *General John H. Winder, C.S.A.*, (Gainesville: University of Florida Press, 1990).

Bloxham, V. Ben, et. al., *Truth Will Prevail: The Rise of The Church of Jesus Christ of Latter-day Saints in the British Isles 1837-1987,* (Cambridge: University Press, 1987).

Bradley, Martha Sonntag, *ZCMI: America's First Department Store,* (Salt Lake City: ZCMI, 1991).

Brower, Hannah Thompson, *Record of the Life of Hannah Thompson,* (ca. 1911). LDS Church Archives.

Brown, S. Kent, et. al., eds., *Historical Atlas of Mormonism,* (New York: Simon & Schuster, 1994).

Burton, Robert T., *Robert Taylor Burton Diaries,* 1856-1907. LDS Church Archives.

Cannon, Abraham H., Journal of Abraham H. Cannon. LDS Church Archives.

Cannon, Frank J., and O'Higgins, Harvey J., *Under the Prophet in Utah: The National Menace of a Political Priestcraft,* (Boston: C. M. Clark Publishing, 1911).

Carpenter, Allan, *Iowa,* (Chicago: Children's Press, 1979).

Carter, Kate B., ed., *Heart Throbs of the West,* 12 vols., (Salt Lake City: Daughters of the Utah Pioneers, 1936-1951).

____. *Historical Pamphlet: First Hotels, Laundries and Dairies in the West,* (Salt Lake City: Daughters of the Utah Pioneers, 1943).

____. *Our Pioneer Heritage,* 20 vols., (Salt Lake City: Daughters of the Utah Pioneers, 1958- 1977).

____. *Treasures of Pioneer History,* 6 vols., (Salt Lake City: Daughters of the Utah Pioneers, 1952-1957).

Church News (Salt Lake City). 1943- .

Church, Richard, *Kent,* (London: Robert Hale, Ltd., 1948).

Clark, James R., ed., *Messages of the First Presidency of the Church of Jesus Christ of Latter-day Saints.* 6 vols., (Salt Lake City: Bookcraft, 1965-75).

Conference Reports of The Church Of Jesus Christ of Latter-day Saints, (Salt Lake City: The Church of Jesus Christ of Latter-day Saints, 1885-).

Cooley, Everett L., *The Utah War,* (Salt Lake City: University of Utah, 1947).

Copley, Gordon J., ed., *Surrey & Sussex,* (London: Hutchinson, 1977).

Cornwall, J., *Lay Subsidy Rolls for the County of Sussex, 1524-25,* (Lewes: Sussex Record Society, 1956).

Cottle, Basil, *The Penguin Dictionary of Surnames,* (New York: Penguin Books, 1984).

Council House Records. LDS Church Archives.

Courthope, E. J. and Fermoy, B. E. R., *Lathe Court Rolls and Views of Frankpledge in the Rape of Hastings,* (Lewes: Sussex Record Society, 1934).

Daniell, Christopher, *A Traveller's History of England,* (New York: Interlink Books, 1993).

The Deseret News (Salt Lake City). 1867- .

Deseret News 1997-98 Church Almanac, (Salt Lake City: Deseret News, 1996).

Doctrine and Covenants of The Church of Jesus Christ of Latter-day Saints, (Salt Lake City: The Church of Jesus Christ of Latter-day Saints, 1988).

Dunbar, D. C., *Salt Lake City Illustrated,* (Omaha: D. C. Dunbar Co., 1888).

Eagle Newspapers (West Valley City, Utah) 1995-1998.

Ellsworth, S. George, *Samuel Claridge: Pioneering the Outposts of Zion,* (Logan, Utah: S. George Ellsworth, 1987).

Endowment House Records. LDS Church Archives.

Esshom, Frank W., *Pioneers and Prominent Men of Utah,* (Salt Lake City: 1913).

Everitt, Alan, *The Community of Kent and the Great Rebellion 1640-60,* (Leicester: Leicester University Press, 1966).

Flake, Lawrence R., *Mighty Men of Zion: General Authorities of the Last Dispensation,* (Salt Lake City: Karl D. Butler, 1974).

Freidel, Frank, *Our Country's Presidents,* (Washington D. C.: National Geographic Society, 1981).

French, M. H., *European Breeds of Cattle,* (Rome: Food and Agriculture Organization of the United Nations, 1966).

Funeral Services in Honor of President John R. Winder, Report of, 31 March 1910, copy in author's possession.

Gibbons, Francis M., *Joseph F. Smith: Patriarch and Preacher, Prophet of God,* (Salt Lake City: Deseret Book, 1984).

Gottfredson, Peter, *Indian Depredations in Utah,* (Salt Lake City: Private Printing, 1969).

Grieg, Peter, "A House With A Story," (Article in English newspaper clipping in possession of author, newspaper unknown, 1971).

Hanks, Patrick and Hodges, Flavia, *A Dictionary of Surnames,* (Oxford: Oxford University Press, 1988).

Hasted, Edward, *History of the County of Kent,* (1822).

Hilton, Lynn M., *The Story of the Salt Lake Stake of the Church of Jesus Christ of Latter-day Saints: 125 Year History 1847-1972,* (Salt Lake City: Salt Lake Stake, 1972).

Hinckley, Bryant S., *Daniel Hanmer Wells and Events of His Time,* (Salt Lake City: Deseret News Press, 1942).

Holzapfel, Richard Neitzel, *Every Stone A Sermon: The Magnificent Story of the Construction and Dedication of the Salt Lake Temple,* (Salt Lake City: Bookcraft, 1992).

"Home Buyer," 24 April 1992, a supplement to the *Courier Chronicle,* Kent, England.

Hull, F., *Calendar of the White and Black Books of the Cinque Ports,* (1966).

Improvement Era (Salt Lake City). 1897-1970.

Jensen, Richard L. and Thorp, Malcolm R., ed., *Mormons in Early Victorian Britain,* (Salt Lake City: University of Utah Press, 1989).

Jenson, Andrew, "Church Chronology: A Record of Important Events," (Salt Lake City: *Deseret News,* 1914).

____. *The Historical Record: Church Encyclopedia,* (Salt Lake City: Andrew Jenson, 1889).

____. *Latter-day Saint Biographical Encyclopedia,* 4 vols., (Salt Lake City: Andrew Jenson History Company, 1901-1936).

Jerrold, Walter, *Highways and Byways in Kent,* (London: Macmillan and Co., 1926).

Jessup, Ronald F., *Sussex,* (London: Methuen & Co., Ltd., 1949).

Jessup, Ronald and Frank, *The Cinque Ports,* (London: B. T. Batsford, Ltd., 1952).

Johnson, Mary Winder, *John Rex Winder,* (Salt Lake City, unpublished manuscript). Copy in author's possession.

____. *Wives of John R. Winder,* unpublished manuscript in author's possession.

Journal History of The Church of Jesus Christ of Latter-day Saints. Church Archives.

Juvenile Instructor (Salt Lake City) 1866-1930.

Kenner, S. A., *Utah As It Is,* (Salt Lake City: Deseret News, 1904).

Kenney, Scott G., ed., *Wilford Woodruff's Journal: 1833-1898 Typescript,* (Midvale, Utah: Signature Books).

Kenny, Virginia C., *The Country-House Ethos in English Literature 1688-1750: Themes of Personal Retreat and National Expansion,* (New York: St. Martin's Press, 1984).

Larson, Gustave O., *Outline History of Utah and the Mormons,* (Salt Lake City: Deseret Book, 1958).

Larson, Stan, ed., *A Ministry of Meetings: The Apostolic Diaries of Rudger Clawson,* (Salt Lake City: Signature Books, 1993).

Latter-day Saints' Millennial Star (Liverpool and London), 1840-1970.

Levine, Dan, *London '94-'95 on $45 a Day,* (New York: Prentice Hall Travel, 1993).

Lesson Committee, ed., *Chronicles of Courage,* 6 vols., (Salt Lake City: Daughters of Utah Pioneers, 1982-1995).

Liddle, Parley H., ed., *Minutes of the Winder Family Genealogical Organization,* (1973). Copy in author's possession.

Loefvenberg, M. T., *Studies on Middle English Local Studies,* (1942).

Ludlow, Daniel H., ed., *Encyclopedia of Mormonism,* 6 vols., (New York: Macmillan Publishing Co., 1990).

Lund, Anthon H., *The Diary of Anthon H. Lund.* LDS Church Archives.

Lyman, Albert R., *Francis Marion Lyman*, (Delta, Utah: Melvin A. Lyman, 1958).

Marley, Isaac, Patriarchal Blessing of John Rex Winder, 31 December 1858, no. 107. In possession of LDS Historical Department, Salt Lake City.

Masser, H. Milton. Letter to Brigham Young, 13 May 1868. LDS Church Archives.

McCloud, Susan Evans, *Brigham Young: An Inspiring Personal Biography*, (American Fork, Utah: Covenant Communications, 1998).

McConkie, Bruce R., *Mormon Doctrine*, 2nd ed., (Salt Lake City: Bookcraft, 1979).

McKinley, Richard, *The Surnames of Sussex*, (London: Leopard Head Press, 1988).

Men of the Day in Caricature, (Denver: April 1906).

Mills, Anastasia Redmond, ed., *Fodor's New Orleans*, (New York: Fodor's Travel Publications, Inc., 1997).

Mingay, G. E., *The Gentry: The Rise and Fall of a Ruling Class*, (London: Longman, 1976).

Meynell, Esther, *Sussex*, (London: Robert Hale, Ltd., 1947).

Mower, A. and Stenton, F. M., *The Place-Names of Sussex*, (Cambridge: University Press, 1930).

The National Magazine (Boston and London) 1902.

Neill, Stephen, *Anglicanism*, (New York: Oxford University Press, 1977).

Ollard, S. L., ed., *A Dictionary of English Church History*, (London; A. R. Mowbray and Co., Ltd., 1912).

Peterson, Boyd, ed., *Oral History of Hugh Nibley.*

Piercy, Frederick Hawkins, *Route from Liverpool to Great Salt Lake Valley*, (Cambridge, Mass: Harvard University Press, 1962).

Pioneer (Salt Lake City: Sons of Utah Pioneers, 1995).

Porter, Valerie, *Cattle: A Handbook to the Breeds of the World*, (New York: Facts on File, 1991).

Powell, Alan Kent, ed., *Utah History Encyclopedia*, (Salt Lake City: University of Utah Press, 1994).

Prentice, E. Parmalee, *American Dairy Cattle: Their Past and Future*, (New York: Harper & Brothers, 1942).

Quinn, D. Michael, *The Mormon Hierarchy: Extensions of Power*, (Salt Lake City: Signature Books, 1997).

Reay, Barry, *Microhistories: demography, society and culture in rural England*, 1800-1930, (Cambridge: Cambridge University Press, 1996).

Richards, Samuel, *Samuel Richards Journal.* LDS Church Archives.

Riter, W. W., et. al., Birthday Reception In Honor of President John R. Winder on the Eighty-second Anniversary of His Birth, (Salt Lake City, 1903). Copy in author's possession.

Roberts, B. H., *A Comprehensive History of The Church of Jesus Christ of Latter-day Saints.* 6 vols., (Provo, Utah: Brigham Young University Press, 1965).

Robertson, Ruth Winder, *Family History for Children,* (Salt Lake City, 1985). LDS Church Archives.

Romney, Thomas C., *The Life of Lorenzo Snow: Fifth President of the Church of Jesus Christ of Latter-day Saints,* (Salt Lake City: Sons of the Utah Pioneers Memorial Foundation, 1955).

Sadler, Richard Wallace, *The Life of Orson Spencer,* (Salt Lake City: Master's Thesis at the University of Utah, 1965).

The Salt Lake Tribune (Salt Lake City) 1871- .

Sanford, William R., and Green, Carl R., *Missouri,* (Chicago: Children's Press, 1993).

Seegmiller, Janet Burton, *The Life Story of Robert Taylor Burton,* (Utah: Robert Taylor Burton Family Organization, 1988).

Sessions, Gene A., ed., *Mormon Democrat: The Religious and Political Memoirs of James Henry Moyle,* (Salt Lake City: LDS Church Historical Department, 1975).

Sillito, John R., *John R. Winder: Faithful Counselor, Builder of the Kingdom.* Unpublished manuscript presented to the Mormon History Association, Brigham Young University, 11 May 1984.

Smith, Joseph F., *Gospel Doctrine,* (Salt Lake City: Bookcraft, 1998).

Smith, Joseph Fielding, *Life of Joseph F. Smith: Sixth President of The Church of Jesus Christ of Latter-day Saints,* (Salt Lake City: Deseret News Press, 1938).

Sonne, Conway B., *Ships, Saints, and Mariners: A Maritime Encyclopedia of Mormon Migration* 1830-1890, (Salt Lake City: University of Utah Press, 1987).

State Archives & Records Service, Territorial Militia Records, 1849-1877.

The Supreme Court of the Territory of Utah, The United States of America vs. The Corporation of the Church of Jesus Christ of Latter-day Saints, 1 Sep 1890, MS d 1144. LDS Church Archives.

Sussex Archaeological Collections, (Lewes: The Sussex Archaeological Society, 1991).

Talmage, James E., *The House of the Lord: A Study of Holy Sanctuaries, Ancient and Modern,* (Salt Lake City: Bookcraft, 1962).

Tanner, Annie Clark, *A Mormon Mother,* (Salt Lake City: Tanner Trust Fund, 1976).

Taylor, P. A. M., *Expectations Westward: The Mormons and the Emigration of their British Converts in the Nineteenth Century,* (Edinburgh: Oliver & Boyd, 1965).

Tourtellot, Jonathan B., ed., *Discovering Britain and Ireland,* (Washington D. C., National Geographic Society, 1985).

Tullidge, Edward W., *History of Salt Lake City and its Founders,* (Salt Lake City: Edward W. Tullidge, c. 1875).

Twain, Mark, *Life on the Mississippi,* (New York: Penguin Books, 1986).

Utah Historical Quarterly (Salt Lake City) 1932- .

Utah: The Inland Empire, (Salt Lake City: Deseret News, 1902).

Utah Since Statehood: Historical and Biographical, 4 vols., (Chicago: S. J. Clarke Publishing, 1920).

Utah State Archives, Agency #367, Division of Expositions, History.

____. Deseret Agricultural & Manufacturing Society, Biennial Report 1863.

____. Salt Lake City Assessment Rolls.

____. Salt Lake City Council Minutes.

____. Salt Lake County (Utah) Incorporation Case Files.

____. Series 59925, Reel 1, Deseret Agricultural & Manufacturing Society Minute Books.

____. Series Inventories.

____. Territorial Militia Records, 1849-1877.

Utah Territory Supreme Court, Appointment of John R. Winder, 31 Aug 1894.

Wallace, C. H., et. al., Testimonial Presented to Elder John Rex Winder Secretary of the Liverpool Conference of the Church of Jesus Christ of Latter-day Saints by the Saints of the Said Conference on His Departure for Great Salt Lake City, N. A., (Liverpool, 1853). Print of original in author's possession.

West, Emerson Roy, *Profiles of the Presidents,* (Salt Lake City: Deseret Book, 1974).

White, James T. & Company, *The National Cyclopaedia of American Biography,* (Ann Arbor: University Microfilms, 1967).

Whitney, Orson F., *History of Utah,* 4 vols. (Salt Lake City: George Q. Cannon & Sons, 1892).

Will of John Rex Winder, dated 17 Jan 1910, filed at Salt Lake County, 4 Apr 1910.

Will of Richard Winder of Biddenden, Kent, dated 25 Apr 1820, proved at Canterbury, 20 Feb 1821.

Will of William Winder of Biddenden, Kent, dated 17 Oct 1765, proved at Canterbury, 30 May 1766.

Winder, John R., John R Winders Journal Kept While On Expedition to Sanpete with Lieutenant General Daniel H. Wells in the Year 1866, State Archives & Records Service, Territorial Militia records, series 02210, reel 28, box 1, folder 87, page 3.

____. Letter, to Annie T. Hyde, 31 Oct 1902. LDS Church Archives.

____. Letter to Brigham Young, 8 Jul 1866. LDS Church Archives.

____. Letter to Brigham Young, 24 Jan 1872. LDS Church Archives.

____. Letter to Brigham Young, 9 Nov 1872. LDS Church Archives.

____. Letter to Joseph F. Smith, 22 Jul 1909. LDS Church Archives.

Winder, Michael K., ed., *Winder Dairy, Quality Since 1880: The George Winder Interviews,* (Salt Lake City: Unpublished manuscript in author's possession, 1992-1995).

Winder, Nancy Gwen, *Winder Dairy,* (Salt Lake City: Unpublished manuscript in author's possession, 1973).

Wood, John D. and Co., *Biddenden Place,* (London: a real estate brochure, 1992).

Wood, Michael, *Domesday, a Search for the Roots of England,* (New York: Facts on File Publications, 1986).

Wood, Richard H., *A Cyclopedic Dictionary of Ecclesiastical Terms According to the Use of the Episcopal Church,* (New York: Carlton Press, 1984).

Woodruff, Abraham O., *Journal of Abraham O. Woodruff.* BYU Library.

Wynn, Marion Winder, *Winder Dairy,* (Salt Lake City: Unpublished manuscript in author's possession, 1974).

Yates, Nigel, et. al., *Religion and Society in Kent,* 1640-1914, (Woodbridge, England: The Boydell Press, 1994).

Young, Brigham, *Discourses of Brigham Young,* (Selected by John A. Widtsoe, 1941).

Young, Brigham, Jr., *Brigham Young Jr. Diary* 1900 Oct - July 1902. LDS Church Archives.

Young, S. Dilworth, *The Beehive House,* (Salt Lake City: The Church of Jesus Christ of Latter-day Saints, 1981).

Young Woman's Journal (Salt Lake City). 1889-1929.

Index

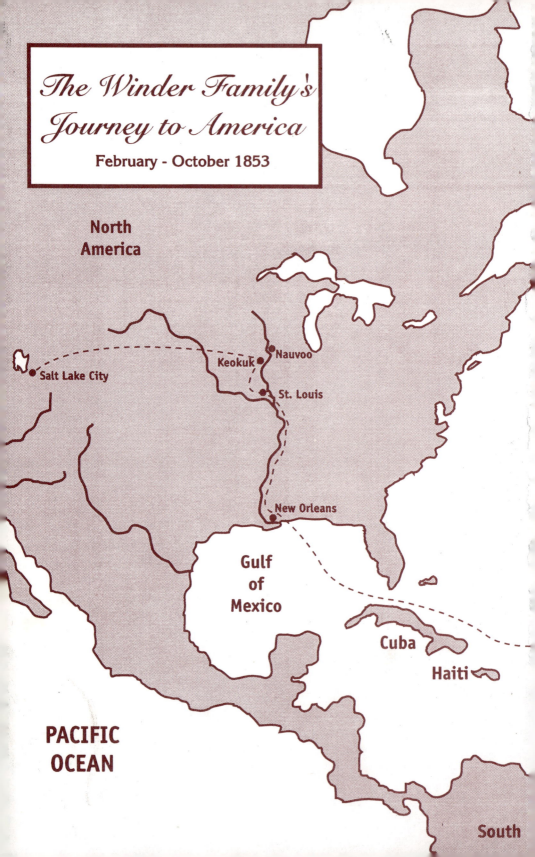